THE

SCIENCE OF

JURISPRUDENCE

CHIEFLY INTENDED

FOR

INDIAN STUDENTS

THE

SCIENCE OF

JURISPRUDENCE

CHIEFLY INTENDED

FOR

INDIAN STUDENTS

W. H. RATTIGAN

GYAN

Published by

GYAN

Gyan Publishing House
5, Ansari Road
Daryaganj, New Delhi-110002
Phone: 011-47034999, 9811692060
E-mail: books@gyanbooks.com

Distribution Network
gyanbooks.com
India, USA, Canada, UK, Australia

ISBN: 978-93-7097-086-1 (PB)

First Published, 1888

2nd Impression 2025

Printed at: Gyan Press, Delhi.

THE SCIENCE OF JURISPRUDENCE CHIEFLY INTENDED FOR INDIAN STUDENTS

Arthur W. H. RATTIGAN

THE

Science of Jurisprudence

CHIEFLY INTENDED

FOR INDIAN STUDENTS.

BY

SIR W. H. RATTIGAN, Q.C.,

DOCTOR OF LAWS OF THE UNIVERSITY OF GÖTTINGEN; HONOR. LL.D. OF THE UNIVERSITY OF THE PUNJAB; SOMETIME ADDITIONAL MEMBER OF THE COUNCIL OF THE GOVERNOR-GENERAL FOR MAKING LAWS AND REGULATIONS, AND OF THE PUNJAB LEGISLATIVE COUNCIL.

Indocti discant, et ament meminisse periti.

Chaque droit et chaque rapport de droit se fonde sur une raison de droit.
—Henri Ahrens.

THIRD EDITION.

LONDON:

WILDY AND SONS,

LINCOLN'S INN ARCHWAY, CAREY STREET, W.C.,

Law Publishers.

1899.

HARDINGE STANLEY GIFFARD,

HALSBURII COMITI,

TER MAGNI REGNI CANCELLARIO,

VIRO OMNI LEGUM DOCTRINA ERUDITISSIMO,

REIPUBLICAE GERENDAE PERITISSIMO,

Hunc Libellum

STUDIO ET OBSERVANTIA SUMMA,

D. D. D.

AUCTOR.

PREFACE

TO THE THIRD EDITION.

In revising this Edition for the press I have spared no labour to improve its usefulness, and have to the utmost of my power endeavoured to act up to the injunction which Cicero conveys to us through the mouthpiece of Cato, *Quicquid agas, agere pro viribus.* (De Senectute, ix. 27.)

I have felt this to be all the more a duty seeing that the book has been honored by several Indian Universities, which have made it a text-book for Law Students, and that I am permitted to have the great privilege of inscribing this Edition to the very distinguished lawyer who now adorns the Woolsack. In many parts I have entirely re-written or re-cast the old matter, and have brought the Case Law down to date. I have retained the old numbering of the paragraphs for facility of reference—adding letters (a), (b), (c) to distinguish the new paragraphs.

I trust, therefore, it will be found to be free from any serious errors.

W. H. RATTIGAN.

11, Old Square,
Lincoln's Inn,
7th December, 1898.

PREFACE

TO THE FIRST EDITION.

THE following pages have been written chiefly with the view of supplying a want felt by Indian Students, for whom no work on Jurisprudence at present exists in the English language which fully meets their requirements. Austin is above their comprehension, and his style is so heavy and unattractive that it wearies even the patient English student. Dr. Markby's *Elements of Law*, an admirable book, and one which is usefully read in all Law Classes in this country, is nevertheless written from a special point of view which does not completely satisfy the requirements I have referred to, while the arrangement of the work is not as simple as is desirable in a book meant for the class of students for whom this treatise is mainly intended. Professor Holland's *Elements of Jurisprudence*, again, has been found by those who have had to do with the practical teaching of Law in this country to be unsuited. It is not simple enough: in some respects it is too concise and assumes the existence of a knowledge which few Indian Students possess, while in others it is too diffuse and too full of foreign quotations, untranslated, to be readily comprehended by such Students. Besides, it does not take notice of the actual state of the Law in this country, which cannot, of course, be ignored by any teacher who desires to instruct Indian pupils in the principles of General Jurisprudence. It was therefore suggested to me, as one intimately connected with one of our Indian Universities, that this important subject might be treated with more direct attention to the wants of Indian Students, and I have endeavoured in the following pages to do so to the best of my ability. At the same time I have consulted all the standard English and Foreign works on Jurisprudence, and I have not hesitated to make free use of them in stating principles and in the general classification of Chapters. But wherever I have done so I have acknowledged my obligation in a foot note, and I need do no more here than to disclaim any intention of posing before my readers as an original writer. My sole object has been to compile a book which will be useful to Students in a branch of their legal studies which is too frequently neglected, and the importance of which cannot be exaggerated. To Professor Holland's well-known work on Jurisprudence I owe a special acknowledgment, and the frequent references to it in the text will prove that it has been constantly before me. But I would only wish to add that if at times, when I have not cited his work, it is found that what is stated in my own text agrees with what Professor Holland has also written on the same subject, the reason is probably due to the circumstance that we have both consulted the same authorities, and my foot notes will indicate the exact sources of my own information.

For the rest, my hope is that these pages may afford some substantial aid in the course of their studies to the class of Students for whom they are chiefly written, and in whom I take a special interest. What I wish particularly to impress upon them is, that without a knowledge of the general principles on which the Science of Law is constructed, and which it is my object to teach them at the outset of their legal education, their reading of the Codified Laws of India will lose half its value, and they will find themselves in constant difficulties in the application of those Laws to the recurring events of everyday life. But once they have mastered those elementary principles, which more or less underlie the Jurisprudence of all Nations, they will have laid a foundation of legal knowledge which will be of incalculable benefit to them hereafter, when as Advocates or Pleaders they have to practise the Profession of the Law. This is, after all, to quote the words of the Emperor Justinian, "the easier path by which the Student, without great labour and without any distrust of his own powers, may be led to the study of Law."—(*Institutes*, 1, 1, 2.)

W. H. R.

LAHORE,
The 25th January, 1888.

CONTENTS.

LIST OF PRINCIPAL AUTHORITIES CONSULTED.

AHREN'S *Philosophie des Rechts und des Staates*, Wien, 1870.
ANSON'S *Law of Contract*, Oxford, 1886.
ARNDT'S *Lehrbuch der Pandekten*, München, 1868.
BAGEHOT'S *Postulates of English Political Economy*.
BARON, *Pandekten*, Zweite Auflage, Leipzig, 1876.
BATES'S *Law of Limited Partnership*, Boston, 1886.
BEACH'S *Contributory Negligence*, New York, 1885.
BLUNTSCHLI'S *Das moderne Völkerrecht*, Nördlingen, 1878.
Gesammelte Kleine Schriften, 2 vols., Nördlingen, 1881.
BRINZ, *Lehrbuch der Pandekten*, 2 B., Erlangen, 1879.
BURGESS, *Political Science and Constitutional Law*, Boston, 1896.
COGLIOLO'S (PIETRO) *Filosofia del Diritto Privato*, Firenze, 1888.
CORPUS JURIS CIVILIS, *ediderunt Fratres Kriegelii*, 16 Auflage, Leipzig.
DANZ'S *Der Sacrale Schutz*, Jena, 1857.
DERNBERG, *Pandekten*, Berlin, 1897.
DICEY, *Conflict of Laws*, London, 1896.
HALL'S *International Law*, Oxford, 1884.
HARE'S *Law of Contracts*, Boston, 1887.
HEFFTER'S *Das Europäische Völkerrecht der Gegenwart*, 1844, Berlin, and the French edition par Jules Bergson, Paris, 1873.
HOLLAND'S *Elements of Jurisprudence*, Oxford, 1888.
HOLME'S *Common Law*, London, 1882.
HOLTZENDORFF'S *Encyklopädie der Rechtswissenschaft*, Leipzig, 1882.
HOSACK'S *Law of Nations*, London, 1882.
JANET'S (PAUL) *Theory of Morals*, Edinburgh, 1884.
KANT'S *Philosophy of Law*, by Hastie, Edinburgh, 1887.
LAGHI (FERDINANDO), *Diritto Internazionale Privato*, Bologna, 1888.
LIGHTWOOD'S *Nature of Positive Law*, London, 1883.
LIOY'S (DIODATO) *Philosophy of Law:* Italian, German, and English (Hastie's) Editions.
LONGO (ABATE), *Filosofia del Diritto*, Catania, 1885.
LORIMER'S *Institutes of the Law of Nations*, 1883.

MACKELDEY'S *Roman Law*, by Dropsie, Philadelphia, 1883.
MAINE'S *Early Law and Custom*, London, 1883.
MOMMSEN'S *Handbüch der Römischen Alterthümer*, Leipzig, 1876.
MUIRHEAD'S *Law of Rome*, Edinburgh, 1886.
PLOSZ'S *Beiträge zur Theorie des Klagerechts*, Leipzig, 1880.
POLLOCK'S *Essays in Jurisprudence*, London, 1882.
Law of Contracts, 5th Edition, 1885.
Law of Torts, London, 1887.
Science of Politics, 1890.
POTHIER, *On the Law of Obligations*, translated by W. D. Evans, 2 vols., London, 1806.
PUCHTA'S *Cursus der Institutionen*, Leipzig, 1865.
REVILLOUT'S *Les Obligations en Droit Égyptien*, Paris, 1886.
RIVIER, *Principes du Droit des Gens*, 2 vols., Paris, 1896.
RUGGIERI, *Il Possesso e gl' Instituti di Diritto Prossimi ad esso, &c.*, Firenze, 1880.
SALKOWSKI'S *Roman Private Law*, by Whitfield, London, 1886.
SAMTER'S *Das Eigenthum*, Jena, 1879.
SANDARS'S *Institutes of Justinian*, 2nd Edition, London, 1859.
SAVIGNY'S *System des heutigen römischen Rechts*, Berlin, 1840.
Das Recht des Besitzes, Sechste Auflage, Giessen, 1847.
SERAFINI'S *Instituzioni di Diritto Romano*, Firenze, 1888.
SPENCER'S (HERBERT) *Political Institutions*, Williams and Norgate, 1885.
STAHL'S *Die Philosophie des Rechts*, 2 Auflage, Heidelberg, 1837.
TOSCANO (FELICE), *Filosofia del Diritto*, Napoli, 1860.
TRENDELENBURG'S *Naturrecht*, 2 Auflage, Leipzig, 1868.
VAREILLES SOMMERIES (LE COMTE), *Les Principes Fondamentaux du Droit*, Paris, 1889.
VATTEL'S *Law of Nations*, by Joseph Chitty, London, 1834.
VON BAR'S *International Law*, by Gillespie, Edinburgh, 1883.
VON IHERING'S *Der Geist des römischen Rechts*, Leipzig, 1878.
Der Kampf ums Recht, Wien, 1877.
Der Zweck im Recht, Leipzig, 1884.
WEEKS'S *Doctrine of Damnum absque Injuria*, San Francisco, 1879.
WINDSCHEID'S *Lehrbuch des Pandektenrechts*, Frankfurt, 1882.
WOOLSEY'S *International Law*, New York, 1874.

THE

SCIENCE OF JURISPRUDENCE.

PART I.

CHAPTER I.

JURISPRUDENCE.

Chap. I.

1. As the following pages are intended to address a body of students who are just on the threshold of their legal education, I shall endeavour to eliminate everything which is calculated to confuse their minds, or to prevent them from grasping those general principles in their true light which it is my object to make clear to them, and which constitute the foundation of the Science of Law in its simplest and truest conception.

Importance of subject of Jurisprudence.

2. Precisely as it is essential for a medical student to understand the mechanism of the human frame, that is to say, not only the general structure of its parts, but the intimate relation of those parts to one another, before he attempts to minister to its ailments, or proceeds to the study of the other branches of his profession, so must the student of Law, if he wishes to comprehend the Rules which will be taught to him in the course of his legal studies, begin with the general ideas and principles which lie at the root of those

CHAP. I.

Rules. These ideas and principles will serve to train his mind into legal ways of thought, and will afford him a key to the solution of many provisions of the Positive Law, which would otherwise appear to him, as they appear to ordinary lay-men, singular and unaccountable—giving the lie to the celebrated dictum of the Roman Jurists, *jus est ars boni et aequi*,[1] and suggesting the thought, whether, if that which seems so strange, so contradictory, and so liable to such a perpetual state of change, can really be, as Montesquieu represented it, the embodiment of "human reason, in so far as it governs all the people of the earth?" It cannot, therefore, be too strongly insisted upon that the early mastery of principles should form an essential feature in the education of a student who is destined to a legal career. It is not "case law" with which he should burden his mind at the outset. But his first impulses should be to find the principles which govern the matters in hand,[2] which underlie the science he has resolved to study; and then, when he has succeeded in comprehending those principles which represent the touchstone by which particular decisions have been tried,[3] he will be able to approach the closer study of the decisions themselves, of the "case law" which he will require in practice, with an armoury which will render him a puissant adversary in many a later forensic contest.

False notion as to method of learning Jurisprudence.

3. In the course of a debate on the Bombay Revenue Jurisdiction Bill it was observed by the then Law Member of the Governor-General of India's Council[4] that "the only way he knew of learning principles of Jurisprudence, is to

[1] Dig. I. 1, 1.

[2] See the remarks on this subject by Mr. Justice John F. Dillon, U. S., in Vol. 19, *American Law Review*, p. 21.

[3] Per Sir F. Pollock in his eloquent Address on *The Vocation of the Common Law*, before the Harvard Law Association; *American Law Review*, Vol. 29, p. 600.

[4] Now Lord Hobhouse.

look at and see what is embodied in actual Laws."[1] Now Jurisprudence, as we shall presently see, *is* the Science of the Actual or Positive Law, and in a loose sense one may say that to learn Jurisprudence is to learn the Positive Law. But if the language of the learned Member was meant to convey more than a mere general indication of the scope of such a study, it is clearly open to criticism. It would certainly be misleading as a canon of legal education. For according to this method a student would first have to learn the whole body of any given system of Positive Law before he could set himself to learn the principles of Jurisprudence. But surely this could scarcely have been the meaning of so clear a thinker and lawyer? It would involve the singular plan of beginning to learn the elements of a science after you had completely mastered it, and would be open, therefore, to the serious objection of beginning at the wrong end. It would be just as incorrect as if one had said that the only way to learn the grammar of a language was to look at and see what was embodied in its literature; in other words, to study the literature first and the grammar afterwards. Now Jurisprudence is the grammar of Law, and must be taught in much the same way. The notion underlying the proposed method, if such a course of acquiring a knowledge of principles can be called a method, could only be the false and exploded one of regarding Law as a purely empirical branch of knowledge. This notion may, indeed, claim the credit of hoary antiquity in support of it, for in the days of Cicero the extent of legal capacity required from a Jurisconsult was a mere empirical knowledge of the Law current amongst private citizens, or the skill requisite in giving opinions, bringing actions, and guiding one's clients aright.[2] But this notion is subversive of all scientific study of Law, and could hardly be seriously asserted at the present day, except to

[1] Vol. XV., Proceedings of G.-G. of India, p. 126.
[2] *De Orat.* I. 48.

CHAP. I.

gain a point in the course of a lengthy debate. The credit of elevating Jurisprudence upon a loftier pedestal, and of showing that it is capable of being learnt as a science, which it truly is, was due to a small but distinguished roll of Roman Jurists, among whom the name of Ulpian deserves special mention, who claimed to be "the Priests of Justice, engaged in the pursuit of a philosophy that is truly such, and no counterfeit."[1] By the efforts of these cultivated intellects was evolved the notion of a legal science, which had an existence independent of the actual institutions of a particular country. The error, in fact, of saying in the nineteenth century that the way of learning the principles of Jurisprudence is to look at and see what is embodied in actual law, is that the statement ignores results which have already been obtained. It is no doubt quite true, as was observed by the Roman Jurist Paulus, "that the law is not to be deduced from the rule, but the rule from the law (*non ut ex regula jus sumatur, sed ex jure, quod est, regula fiat*)." But it must be remembered that it is only when science steps in and reduces the pre-existing law from a chaotic mass of undigested Customs and Usages into something like a system, that it is possible to extract fixed rules from it. And once this stage has been reached, it is only by comprehending these rules, and learning how to apply them to future cases, that a true knowledge of the existing law can be obtained. The labours of other workers have thus at this stage produced results which each student would otherwise have had to work out for himself. But, having these results at hand, he naturally turns to them in the *first* instance, and the scientific arrangement and classification of these results is called the *Science of Law* or *Jurisprudence*, which is a system founded on principles, sanctioned or protected by a political society called the State.[2]

[1] Dig. I. 1, 1, 1.

[2] Weiske's *Rechtslexicon*, Bd. IX., tit. *Recht*, p. 140.

Jurisprudence, or the science of Law.

This exact scope and definition difficult to be defined.

4. Although an appropriate name was early enough found for this science, yet the exact scope which ought to be assigned to it, or the definition which would most correctly express its true aim and object, has nevertheless been a subject of the keenest controversy down to the present time. To the Romans it was taught much in the same spirit as wisdom was represented to the Greeks by the Stoic philosophers, as the "Knowledge of things human and divine, the science of the just and unjust."[1] But this was to confound all distinction between Law and Morality, and it is the distinguishing feature of the School of Jurisprudence established by Austin, that it marks this distinction with the sharpest lines, by restricting the term Law to that which is set or imposed by men as political superiors, or by men as private persons, in pursuance of legal rights. Amongst German Jurists, Krause, perhaps, of all others up to his time (1780—1832), made the boldest and most successful attempt to separate Law from Morality. But even he could not completely free himself from the speculations of his predecessors, and in his system also we find an intimate union between law, morals, and religion everywhere insisted upon. Law becomes, in his view, the lever of progress of all the fundamental elements of human life and culture. It does not intervene to *limit*, but, above all, to *aid*, the intellectual, moral and physical activity of mankind. He considers the State as the special institute of Law, but not as absorbing man or society. Morals, religion, sciences, arts, industry and commerce, have each a distinctive organization, but the political organization of the State must be placed on the most intimate relation with the whole range of human activity. The State thus becomes, as it were, the mediator of the destiny of the individual as of society. The whole system of Krause, if it can be called an independent system, is an attempt to combine

The Roman view.

The modern German view.

[1] Dig. I. 1, 10.

and harmonise the theories of the historical school of Hugo with the idealism of Fichte, as modified by Schelling, and still later by the absolute idealism of Hegel.[1] More recently, it has been claimed for the German Common Law that, unlike the Roman, it has not been enacted nor commanded, but discovered and drawn from the fountain-springs of nature.[2] This recalls to our mind the celebrated passage of Demosthenes, where he says, "Laws are the gift of the gods, and the discovery of sages."[3] Since the end of all Law is the attainment of Justice, and since God is Himself the embodiment of Justice, the object of human laws, it is said, ought not to be to separate themselves from the foundation on which they are all built, *viz.*, the Divine Law, but to complete and develop it. Law, it is argued, is not something foreign to, or essentially different from, Morality; it has its ethical side and rests upon the moral order of the world. But all moral precepts are not appropriate to be regarded as legal principles, and many legal principles recognised by the Positive Law are prescribed more upon grounds of expediency or utility than upon moral considerations, and are, therefore, not moral, but exclusively legal, principles.[4]

General Continental view.

4*a*. Although this alleged but really nebulous relation between Morality and Law is a favourite theme with Continental writers, the difficulty of exactly defining it in words has led Ihering to designate it the Cape Horn of the Science of Law, to attempt to correctly solve which is to incur the risk of fatal shipwreck. This risk, as Ahrens observes,[5] can only be avoided by taking care to provide one's self with

[1] See an interesting criticism of Krause's views in Henri Ahrens' *Cours de Droit Naturel*, 8th ed., pp. 78—80.

[2] I. C. Bluntschli, *Gesammelte Kleine Schriften*, Vol. I., p. 29.

[3] Adv. Aristogeit, 1.

[4] Bluntschli, *Gesammelte Kleine Schriften*, Vol. I., p. 37. Cf. also Ahrens' *Philosophie des Rechts*, Vol. I., pp. 312 *et seq.*: Wien, 1870.

[5] *Philosophie des Rechts und des Staates*, Vol. I., § 37, p. 308: Wien, 1870.

a good compass, and by pursuing upon our scientific course the strict line which is indicated by sharp and very distinct notions. The subject is one which certainly has a peculiar fascination of its own, and it is one also which can hardly be avoided by a writer on Jurisprudence, because it is intimately mixed up with many of the most important materials of private and public law. In the discussion of such a question a wide scope is naturally afforded to philosophical speculation in demarcating the exact boundary lines between what is called the Philosophy of Law and the Philosophy of Morality, which will account for the variety of views we meet with in the literature on the subject. Thus a recent Italian Jurist[1] describes the difference between these various branches of social science as depending solely on the point of view from which we regard human actions. Starting from the broad principle that the object of all human action is (or ought to be) the attainment of Good,[2] Ethics, as the Science of Good, must, it is contended, be the common foundation of Law as well as of Morality. But while the Philosophy of Morality regards man, individually and socially, with reference to his ultimate destiny, subordinating all the good of life to the ultimate good of life itself, the Philosophy of Law studies conditional good in an external social relation, in so far as that good ought to be attributed to each one according to his respective title. The Philosophy of Law thus plays, as in the theory of Krause, a mere complementary *rôle*, or, as Lorimer expresses it, "the subordinate relation of species to genus."[3] It only affirms the ethical order of life and of institutions, distributing to them with equal measure their

[1] Professor Giovanni Abate Longo in his *Filosofia del Diritto*, Vol. I., pp. 18, 19 (1885): Catania.

[2] This, in other words, is the theory of the "inborn tendency to the good," which, according to Felice Toscano (*Filosofia del Diritto*, Napoli, 1860), is the first element and causal principle of every human operation, and the impulse by which God draws His creature to Himself.

[3] *Institutes of Law*, p. 281.

CHAP. I. respective good. Economical Science, again, regards human actions principally from the utilitarian point of view, concerning itself only with the satisfaction of human needs. So that while the Law considers the good in so far as it is the object of attribution, Economical Science looks at it with reference to the effort which man has to make to attain it, recognising as its fundamental principle that the larger economy lies in inverse ratio to the smaller expenditure. Ahrens endeavours to state the distinction between Morality and Law with still greater precision, but from a somewhat different standpoint. According to his notion, Morality regards the *motive* of an action, while Law regards the action in its outward or objective *results*. The precepts of Morality are absolute, unchangeable, and independent of time and place: those of Law are relative and changeable, because the conditions of existence and of progress differ according to time, place, education, and manners. Nevertheless the fundamental principle of Law is immutable and eternal, resting everywhere and in every age upon the obligation to secure to everyone the necessary means for his development. It is only the *means* themselves which change with the nature of individuals and nations. Finally, Morality is a subjective science, Law an objective science.[1] Vico, who, it is said, weds philosophy and philology, and opens the pathway to the *Scienza Nuova* (or New Science), travels over much the same ground, and his leading doctrine is expressed in the formula that Morality is the reason or motive, and Utility the occasion, of the law; or, as Romagnosi—the Italian Bentham—expresses it, "Right is a system of Utility conformable to Morality." And a distinguished countryman and follower of Vico's—I refer to Diodato Lioy—himself one of the acutest thinkers of Italy, sums up his review of

[1] *Philosophie des Rechts und des Staates*, Vol. I., pp. 309—312; also in his *Cours de Droit Naturel* (8th ed.), Vol. I., p. 161.

the various ideas of Law with the following observations: "Law is not separated from Morality, but is merely distinguishable from it. The profit of the community is its only limit, and its sphere widens or narrows itself for this reason according to the different stages of civilisation. At first, everything appears inseparable from Religion, but gradually Science, Art, Morality, Law disconnect themselves from it, without, however, losing their innate relation with it. . . . . Truth becomes the Good in Morals, Justice in Law: the purport is the same, the relations only change. . . . . If therefore the Law objectively is the expression of the relations of an ideal justice, it is subjectively the capacity or force whereby the individual or social man is enabled to realise those relations."[1] From all that has been said it would seem that the prevailing Continental view of the relation between Law and Morality amounts in substance to this—that there cannot be any such complete separation between the two as would exclude the latter from the sphere of the former; and that in all civilised countries the former must guarantee the latter.[2] It is certainly unquestionable that it is the supreme interest of the State to promote external Morality as far as possible. It is equally true that Morality and Law have the same end in view, namely, the perfection of man and of society;[3] and that the Law will never directly set itself in opposition to Morals is still recognised in the principle to be found in all modern systems, that contracts *contra bonos mores* (*i.e.*, contrary to good morals) are illegal, as being opposed to public policy. But the Student of the Science of Jurisprudence is after all not concerned with a system of Ethics or abstract Justice, but rather with that form of Justice which is realisable by means

[1] *The Philosophy of Law*, by Diodato Lioy, pp. 114—116. See p. 131, Vol. I., of Mr. Hastie's translation.

[2] *Filosofia del Diritto Privato*, per P. Cogliolo, p. 113; Firenze, 1888.

[3] *Cours de Droit Naturel*, 8th ed., p. 164.

Chap. I.

of rules of Law, and he will do well in this respect to follow the advice of Thomasius in regard to Theology, and not "put his sickle into such dread fields of speculation."[1]

Austin's view of Jurisprudence.

5. This last observation brings us directly to the narrower view propounded by Austin, according to which the Science of Jurisprudence is concerned with *Positive Laws* or with Laws strictly so called, as considered without regard to their goodness or badness. Austin further divides it into "general" and "particular" Jurisprudence, the latter being restricted to the science of any actual system of law or of any portion of it, while "the proper subject of the former is a description of such subjects or ends of law as are common to all systems, and of those resemblances between different systems which are bottomed in the common nature of man, or correspond to the resembling points in these several portions."[2] But this subdivision has been sharply criticised by Professor Holland, who—having regard to the circumstance that a science is a system of generalisations which, though they may be derived from observations extending over a limited area, will nevertheless hold good everywhere—refuses to admit the existence of a *particular science* of Law, which is as inconceivable as a *particular science* of Geology.[3] If, however, we admit that Jurisprudence itself is a science,—that is to say, a formal science, as Professor Holland understands it, of those relations of mankind which are generally recognised as having legal consequences,—it may be possible to speak of a branch of that science which treats of how those human relations are regulated in the laws of any individual country as a particular Jurisprudence. But it must be confessed that, even in this restricted sense, the phraseology is not marked by that scrupulous exactitude which is so charac-

"Particular" and "General" Jurisprudence.

This terminology criticised by Professor Holland.

Professor Holland's own definition of Jurisprudence.

[1] *Inst. Jur. Div.*, lib. i. c. 1, § 163.

[2] *Student's Austin*, by R. Campbell, p. 151.

[3] *Jurisprudence*, pp. 9—10.

teristic of Austin's writings. Professor Holland's own definition of Jurisprudence as a *formal* science has, in turn, been pronounced by a later English writer[1] as a mistake if applied to general Jurisprudence, whose object is not only to arrive at general distinctions but at general principles, and cannot therefore be correctly called a *formal* science. This writer would himself prefer a different terminology, distinguishing between Pure, General, and Applied Jurisprudence. It is in the elementary stage of pure Jurisprudence that we have to consider the relation which the Science of Law bears to the Science of Ethics or Morality, and to Politics or the Science of Government. In a more advanced stage of the Science we have nothing further to do with abstract Justice, but our object is then to expound the principles and distinctions which prevail generally in most bodies of law, and to facilitate the knowledge and improvement of particular bodies of law. We then reach the last and final stage, when we have to apply the classification we have invented and the principles we have discovered to a given system of law, for the double purpose of learning the law and of improving it. This is called the "Science of Applied Jurisprudence," while Jurisprudence, as a whole, is defined as the "Science of the attainment of Justice by means of rules of Law,"[2] just as Cicero long ago defined Justice itself as "obedience to the laws" (*Justitia est obtemperatio legibus*).

Criticised in turn by Mr. Lightwood.

6. Having thus briefly indicated the different attempts which have been made to define the Science of Jurisprudence, and the objections which have been raised to each of those definitions, it will be sufficient if I now state that the meaning which I shall ascribe to the term in the following pages is the "Science of the actual or positive Law."

Definition accepted for the present purpose.

[1] *The Nature of Positive Law*, by John M. Lightwood, 1883.

[2] *The Nature of Positive Law*, p. 24.

CHAP. I.

Subjects which fall within the scope of Jurisprudence.

7. Thus understood, the subjects which fall immediately within the scope of this science are of a two-fold character:—

(i) The nature of Law.

(ii) The nature and fundamental distinctions of Rights and Duties.

But the full import of this scope cannot be completely realised until we fix in our own minds the exact meanings which we wish to convey by the terms "Law," "Right," and "Duty." It is obvious also that we cannot construct a science unless we can adopt terms to which a precise and invariable meaning can be ascribed.

CHAPTER II.

LAW, RIGHT, AND DUTY.

Definition of the term "Law."

8. It would be useless in a treatise intended for beginners to enter upon any examination of the various interpretations which have been given by the Roman, English, and Continental Jurists of the term "Law." For the mere student it is immaterial whether Law arose, as Grotius contends, from a social instinct (or *appetitus societatis*), or from a fear of a war of all against all (*bellum omnium contra omnes*), as Hobbes maintains, or from a desire of happiness, according to Thomasius, or from a craving after perfection, as Wolff thinks. It is sufficient for his purpose to know that Law develops itself *pari passu* with the notion of authority, which naturally inspires a respect for it,[1] and that the different words used by the various leading races of antiquity to indicate Law, all agree in embodying in the conception the idea of *command*, *authority*, *protection*, *bond*, or *aid*, which is also characteristic of the terminology adopted by the nations of modern Europe, as illustrated by the terms *diritto*, *droit*, *recht*, *derecho*, *right*.[2] So the Greek word νόμος, as well as the Latin *lex*, expressed strictly the commands of the State founded upon human dispositions;[3] and it was in the same sense that Demosthenes defined Law as "the common institution of the State according to the determination of which every man who lives in the State must order his life."[4] The

[1] *La Filosofia del Diritto*, per Professor Giovanni Abate Longo, p. 54 (1885).

[2] *Saggi di Filosofia Giuridica*, per Ferdinando Puglia, pp. 21, 22, 2nd edizione; Weiske's *Rechtslexicon*, Bd. IX., tit. *Recht*, p. 140.

[3] *Theory of Law and Civil Society*, by Augustus Pulszky, p. 335; London.

[4] As quoted by Marcian, Digest, I. 3, 2.

CHAP. II. question indeed, What is Law? can only be likened, as Bluntschli observes, to that larger and more celebrated question, What is Truth? and no completely satisfactory answer is perhaps possible. But the fundamental notion which is now generally accepted as underlying the idea of Law in Jurisprudence, and which is sufficiently exact to enable us to construct our science, is that of "a rule which, in the complex relations of society, is required to regulate the actions of the individual members."[1] Or, expressed in the terser and more technical language of Professor Holland, a Law, in the proper sense of the term,—that is to say, as applied to Law prevailing in a modern State as first conceived by Bodin and a century later by Hobbes,—is "a general rule of external human action enforced by a sovereign political authority."[2] In this conception coercion constantly forms the reserve and background of existing law, to which it should be possible at any time, and on any occasion, to appeal.[3] Some writers add to the definition that the rule must be *permanent*. But if by this expression it is meant that the rule must be perpetual, as Suarez seems to think, although he hastens to explain that he only means perpetual in a *negative* sense,—that is to say, as excluding a rule established *ad certum ac definitum tempus* (for a fixed and definite time),[4]—the addition would not be in harmony with actual practice, for there are many general rules enforced by a sovereign political authority which are only enacted for a fixed and definite time, which are nevertheless laws in the truest sense of the expression. Thus, for example, an income tax may be introduced, as it was in India, for a specified time.[5] During this limited period the will of

[1] *The Nature of Positive Law*, p. 269.

[2] *Jurisprudence*, p. 37.

[3] *Theory of Law and Civil Society*, by Augustus Pulszky, p. 326.

[4] *De Legibus*, 1, x.

[5] *Vide* sect. 249 of Act XXXII. of 1860, which was to continue in force from the 31st July, 1860, until the 1st August, 1865, *and no longer*.

the Legislature would undoubtedly have the force of a Law. If, on the other hand, the term *permanent* is only intended to imply that the rule ought to be *stable*,—that is to say, that it shall receive a general application for a period more or less long,—the addition is not necessary; for a command that vanishes the moment it has been obeyed once, cannot be correctly spoken of as a *rule*, which of itself implies that which is prescribed as a guide to conduct or action and having a certain duration.[1] It involves, in short, the idea of repetition or recurrence.

Distinction between rule of Law and rules of Morality, &c.

9. It is this element of enforcement by a sovereign political authority which, in the opinion of Austin and his followers, distinguishes the rule of Law from all those other rules which, like the principles of Morality and the so-called laws of honour and of fashion, are enforced by an indeterminate authority, as well as from all those rules which are enforced by a determinate authority, which is either, on the one hand, superhuman, or, on the other hand, politically subordinate.[2] Rules of the former kind, established in an independent political community by the authority of its sovereign or supreme government, are called Positive Laws. The ideal notion of Morality, on the other hand, presents itself as the sum of those desirable rules, the realisation of which cannot be expected, even under abstract conditions answering this ideal, through coercion on the part of the State.[3]

Objections to Austin's theory.

10. But if we accept the limitation of Laws properly so called to *commands* proceeding from a *determinate* source, we are not only led, as Professor Robertson remarks,[4] to the apparent paralogism of admitting the bye-laws of a private

[1] *Les Principes Fondamentaux du Droit*, par Le Comte Vareilles Sommieres, pp. 9—12; Paris (1889).

[2] *Jurisprudence*, p. 38.

[3] *Theory of Law and Civil Society*, by Augustus Pulszky, p. 331.

[4] See article "Law" *Ency. Britannica.*

CHAP. II.

club, if made in pursuance of a legal right, to be Laws properly so called, while the whole mass of International Jurisprudence is mere opinion improperly called Law—a conclusion which is calculated to shock our sense of the proprieties of expression. But we have a further difficulty to contend against. As applied to a political community answering to the modern notion of a civilised State, in which Legislation tends to become the only true source of new Law, Austin's theory of resting the obligation of Law upon the existence of political sovereignty is strictly accurate. But before Laws were thus made, there were, as Montesquieu remarks,[1] "relations of possible justice," or what Italian writers term "*bio-ethical* relations," which were recognised as necessary conditions for the co-existence of individuals in society.[2] And it was probably not within the range of Austin's knowledge that societies existed, notably in India, prior to the advent of British rule, in which human actions were undoubtedly governed by rules as absolute as any set by a political superior, but which nevertheless were not Laws within his conception of the term. To describe, however, such rules as mere rules of Morality, would be to misunderstand their nature and to misuse language. By those who are acquainted with the force of Customary Laws relating to inheritance, the alienation of property, the right to levy customary fees, or the use and partition of common waste lands as they exist, for instance, in village communities in the Punjab, the Austinian conception of Law must be received with a distinct qualification—a qualification which would limit its application to new laws in a civilised State of the modern type. So the older written Hindu Law would not strictly correspond with Austin's conception of a Law, even if the system of penances for the breach of their precepts could be accepted as

Customary Law of the Punjab outside that theory.

[1] *Spirit of Laws*, Book I., section 1.

[2] *Saggi di Filosofia Giuridica*, per Ferdinando Puglia, Professore di Diritto nell' Universita di Messina, pp. 14—15.

equivalent to the sanction of the political authority required by Austin. It is not indeed until we come to the comparatively late period of Manu's *Institutes* that we find any trace of even an ideal tribunal for the punishment of those who have transgressed the precepts of the written law; and the provisions which are contained in that book for the construction of a tribunal, composed of the king with learned Brahmins as assessors, were in all probability purely idealistic, and not taken from the actual administration of Law in any Hindu Kingdom which then existed.[1] The character of Hindu Jurisprudence is, in fact, altogether different from that of any of the European systems. The Hindu Rishis who composed the *Sanhitas* had no temporal power, and the rules they prescribed did not at their origin owe their authority to the sanction of any temporal sovereign or administrator, but to the veneration in which the sages themselves were held.[2] And one cannot but admire the practical good sense which these lawgivers showed in their manner of prescribing rules. They did not profess to lay down arbitrary laws of their own invention. On the contrary, they assumed to compile their rules from the ordinances of the Vedas, which were represented as too vast to be mastered by ordinary mortals. The Rishis only claimed to be the exponents of this divine law, eternal in its source and immutable in its character, or interpreters of the approved customs and usages of the past. And to this position they clung even when introducing the most radical reforms. They did not by a stroke of the pen seek to eradicate the barbarous institutions of a more primitive age, for they knew very well "that the power of age and custom

Character of Hindu Jurisprudence.

[1] In the Vedic period mention is made of *Sabhās*, or Assemblies in which the elders of village communities settled their internal affairs. The Vedic *Sabha*, or Council of Elders, bears some resemblance to the βουλὴ γερόντων of the ancient Greeks, and, in its original inception also, to the Roman Senate, as the Supreme Council of Elders (Cic. *De Senec.* VI., 19). Cf. Leist, *Alt-Arisches Jus Gentium*, p. 530.

[2] Leist, *Alt-Arisches Jus Gentium*, p. 458.

CHAP. II.

is exceedingly great."[1] When they wished to abolish some prevailing practice or custom, they did not do so by an express injunction, but, by pretending to regulate the practice, they subjected it to so many conditions and ceremonial requirements, as in reality to render its observance impossible. Thus it has happened that, although these Rishis were neither elected by the people nor appointed by a political sovereign to make laws, their precepts have continued to the present time to be generally obeyed as commands, and to retain the same vitality as they had in the old days of Brahminical ascendancy. It is also noteworthy, as further illustrating the worldly wisdom of these ancient Hindu lawgivers, that they recognised as a fundamental maxim that custom or usage was "transcendent law," and denounced a practice which, though legal, was abhorred by the world, as one that secured no celestial bliss, and was not fit to be followed. By such wise maxims the authors gave to their codes an elasticity which has not rendered them obsolete despite the lapse of centuries. So, again, the customary rules I have referred to were enforced, prior to the establishment of British power, not in consequence of any sanction, expressed or implied, of the dominant political authority for the time being, but in deference to that "plainest counsel of common sense," not to neglect the results of our predecessors' experience in a like matter.[2] In other words, from an inveterate regard for precedent, which exercises as great an influence in England and on the Continent at the present time as it ever did in India or in ancient Rome, and which was as much recognised and respected (or at least ostensibly so) by the Homeric gods on Olympus as it is now by the humble peasants of an agricultural village in the Punjab,

Inveterate regard for precedent.

[1] Cicero, *De Amicitia*, XIX. 68: *Maxima est enim vis vetustatis et consuetudinis.*

[2] Pollock's *Essays in Jurisprudence and Ethics*, p. 52; Jenk's *Law and Politics in the Middle Ages*, p. 57.

who see in the practice and usages of their forefathers the guiding rule for their own conduct—a rule which by long familiarity has come to be looked upon as the most natural one to observe, and therefore the right rule, to transgress which would shock the public sense of propriety. For usages and customs, no less than religions, undoubtedly descend by inheritance; and Lord Melbourne, although he may have incurred the ridicule of philosophers for saying that he should adhere to the English Church *because* it was the religion of his fathers, really only uttered, as Walter Bagehot aptly says,[1] one of the most firm and accepted maxims of old times, based upon that principle of ancestor-worship which in early stages of society formulates as law the rule of the dead over the living. This rule is primarily concerned in regulating personal conditions only, and hence it is that the movement of progressive societies has been characterised by Sir Henry Maine as a movement from *status* to *contract*.[2] Succeeding generations follow the same rule, true to the imitative faculty which is the leading trait in the character of archaic peoples as it is of children, who live by what they see and hear, and cannot help imitating what comes before them. In course of time these inherited usages eventuate, as Herbert Spencer[3] observes, in a rigid set of customs, restraining men's action in a greater degree than could any rules having a more formal and artificial origin. For custom is lord of all.[4] But inasmuch as the construction of rules which will adequately sum up the general current opinion upon any given class of rights requires two distinct faculties —the faculty of observation and the faculty of expression[5]— and these faculties are in a more or less undeveloped condition

Usages and customs descend by inheritance.

Progress from *status* to *contract*.

[1] *Physics and Politics*, p. 99, 5th ed.

[2] *Ancient Law*, Chapter V., p. 170.

[3] *Political Institutions*, section 535, p. 535.

[4] Herod. III. 38, quoting from Pindar.

[5] Ihering, *Der Geist des Römischen Rechts*, 1, 28.

in communities still existing under primitive organisations, it naturally follows also that these inherited usages, crystallised into later Customary Laws, are, for the most part, restricted to matters of frequent occurrence in the community, and are handed down by tradition in the simplest possible forms.

Law has its own history.

10*a*. Law, in fact, has its history, like every other science. For since Law is the manifestation of the majesty of a State, and no State (*i.e.*, a portion of mankind viewed as an organised unit)[1] is conceivable which has not been the product of a keen conflict of opposing interests; so it follows that where there has been no conflict there is no history, which after all is but the record of how that conflict came about, and where there is no history there can be no Law, for a pre-historic State or a pre-historic Law has not yet been discovered, and is really a contradiction in terms.[2] Law is thus, like a State, the product of history, and the period of barbaric liberty and self-help permits and promotes the development of the one as well as the other.[3] We may say, further, that there is no branch of the Law which has not its own peculiar history, and this will become evident as we proceed. For the present it will be sufficient for our purpose if we briefly trace the growth of that archaic body of first principles known as the *Jus Gentium* of the ancients. Amongst all Aryan nations—the Hindus, the Greeks, and the Romans—it appears to have undergone three distinct stages of development. In the first stage the conception of Law is that of a Divine but humanly (by *Brahmans*, *Exegetai*, or *Pontifices*) interpreted unwritten (*agrapha* or *jus non scriptum*) rule of conduct, the *dharma* and *rita* of the ancient

Growth of the *Jus Gentium*.

[1] Bluntschli, *Lehre vom Modernen Stat.*, Bd. I. s. 24.

[2] *Sommario della Storia del Diritto in Italia*, Professor Giovanni Bovio, p. 34; Napoli, 1883.

[3] Burgess, *Political Science and Constitutional Law*, Vol. I., Chap. II., pp. 59—67.

Hindus, the φύσις and θέμις of the ancient Greeks, and the *fas* and *ritus* of the ancient Romans.[1] Its key is to be found in the domestic regulation of the powers and duties of the Householder—the *grihin* of the Hindus, the *oikonomos* of the Greeks, and the *pater familias* of the Romans—for the Household was organised on strictly monarchical principles. He has particularly to observe the *ăcăra* or holy usage,[2] or the ἱερὰ καὶ ὅσια of his ancestors, which among the Hindus mainly consisted of four religious (*mahayajna*) and five moral duties (*manava*),[3] which have their exact counterparts also among the Greeks and Romans. But as in course of time individual households become incorporated into larger communities, the power of the *grihin* or *oikonomos* becomes subject to a higher authority, and in the slow but steady development of city life, with the introduction of a wider range of social and a completely new class of public duties, we gradually reach the second stage *legibus et moribus inductum*, in which we observe that human experience has enlarged and intercourse between different cities has supervened. In the maturity of this stage the world-wide conquests of Alexander the Great, followed by those of Rome, naturally spread far and wide the civilization of the two great Empires of the West, producing, as was to be expected, a large imitation, in the first instance, of Hellenistic, and, subsequently, of Roman institutions. It is not a matter of very great surprise, therefore, that it thus became possible in the classical period of Roman jurisprudence to construct a fresh body of principles which the Roman Jurist Ulpian could reasonably describe in his day as generally accepted by mankind (*quo gentes humanæ utuntur*). These principles were in fact to be found in the system of Equity administered in distant provinces under

[1] Leist, *Alt-Arisches Jus-Gentium*, p. 527.

[2] *Institutes of Vishnu*, translated by Julius Jolly, Vol. VII., Sacred Bks. (19—23).

[3] See Leist, *Alt-Arisches Jus-Gentium*, pp. 174, 247, 381.

Greek and Roman governors. But we must remember that the transition of the legal ideas of the first stage into those of the second was the product of a long and tedious development, and this will explain how the influence of the early holy *dharma*, θεμις and *fas* has never been completely eradicated, and is still visible in the modern notion of the intimate relation between Law, Religion and Morality, which, we have seen, has permeated all schools of thought. The third and last stage is only a more advanced development of the second, in which the City has everywhere expanded into a State, which can henceforth alone prescribe what shall be the Law for all persons residing within its territorial limits. These three periods of internal growth of the Law correspond to Ulpian's view of a triple division, *ex naturalibus præceptis aut gentium aut civilibus.*[1] The first of these divisions is characterised by the rules of the *Jus Naturale*, which are believed to be common to all animals (human beings as well as others)—*quod natura omnia animalia docuit;* the second by those of the *Jus Gentium*, the governing principle of which is the *naturalis ratio* derived from the customs and usages of mankind alone;[2] and the third, by the rules prescribed by the State itself.

Complexity the characterristic feature of the later law.

10*b*. But one of the most striking and external characteristics in the process of the historical development of law is this, that its provisions steadily advance from original simplicity and strictness to increasing complexity and elasticity. And it is a remarkable fact that the older the period which comes under our observation the more certain are we to find that its Law bears the character of a *Strictum Jus*. The history of the Roman Law, for instance, is for the most part a continuous process of development from the *jus strictum* to the *jus aequum et bonum*[3]—a process which in every country goes hand in hand with the expansion of the

[1] Dig. I. 1, 1, § 2, [2] Dig. IX. 1, 1. [3] Baron, *Pandekten*, § 13, p. 25.

relations and necessities of life, and therefore with the more manifold development of the material which reacts upon the Law, and which Law has to master and control.[1] Thus Law as a branch of the national life can never be stable. It is always gathering, so to speak, new material, and approximating itself by a more or less rough process to an ideal which is never attained. It has consequently no moment of absolute cessation, but it develops with the people, and attaches itself to the national character at its different stages of culture, adapting itself to the changing wants and requirements of the people.[2] It has its roots dug deep into the past, and can never be rightly understood without reference to the customs and usages out of which it has arisen. But while consecrating a spirit of continuity in its institutions, it at the same time develops from within by an impulsion of the national life, and thus brings itself into harmony with existing needs.[3] So that as new legal principles manifest themselves the Law naturally undergoes change, and the most essential influence determining this process of change lies in the position which a people assumes as a member of the whole of mankind. In the absence of any legislative machinery the immediate conviction of the people is necessarily the primary source of all Law, and in the conviction that the prevailing usage is right lies the binding force of Customary Law.[4] Now this period of youth of nations, in which Law exists, as we have seen, in the consciousness of the people, may be characterised as poor in ideas, but, as Savigny observes, it nevertheless enjoys a clear perception of its relations and circumstances, and feels and brings the whole of them into play. Customs may

[1] Puchta, *Cursus der Inst.*, section 19, ed. 1, p. 41: Leipzig, 1865. See para. 197.

[2] *Ibid.*, p. 40; Hastie's *Outlines of the Science of Jurisprudence*, p. 57 (1887); Pollock's *First Book of Jurisprudence*, p. 41.

[3] *Cours de Droit Naturel*, per Henri Ahrens, pp. 57—58.

[4] Windscheid's *Lehrbuch des Pandektenrechts*, Vol. I., section 15, p. 42, 5th ed.

indeed appear from their gradual growth to arise spontaneously, and may be rarely traceable to premeditation; but Lorimer is unquestionably right in saying that "they must always have rested on a previous conception of an object to be attained and of the means of attaining it."[1] Nor is a custom ever a pure mistake. On the contrary, there is, as we have seen, a close organic connection of Law with the being and character of the people, which manifests itself also in the progress of the times, and is subject to the same movement and development as any other popular tendency. For Law is essentially a principle of life and movement and follows the evolutions of life in society. "Fire," said Aristotle, "burns both in Hellas and in Persia; but men's ideas of right and wrong vary from place to place."[2] The progress in the formation of Law accordingly keeps pace with the progress in the knowledge of the people of the facts which they observe,[3] and hence it is that Law has its provincialisms no less marked than Language.[4] So that Law grows with the growth and strengthens with the strength of a people,[5] and its standard of excellence will generally be found, at any given period, to be in complete harmony with the prevailing ideas of the best class of citizens.

Customary law as the immanent rule of conduct.

11. The Customary Law thus gradually formed, the *jus non scriptum* (or unwritten law), becomes now the immanent rule of conduct which flourishes at its fullest in the youthful life of peoples and in the still undeveloped State. In its earliest beginnings its rules depend doubtless largely upon natural intuitions, increasing with the experience of what is

[1] *Institutes of the Law of Nations*, Vol. I., p. 28.

[2] *Eth. Nic.* V., 7, § 2.

[3] *Trattato delle Leggi*, per l'Avv. Professore G. Saredo, p. 20: Firenze, 1886.

[4] Puchta, *Cursus der Inst.*, section 10, p. 22.

[5] Savigny, *The Vocation of Our Age*, translated by Abraham Hayward, pp. 25, 27.

useful and what injurious. Thus we may surmise that a long course of sufferings and deaths must have generated a body of direct usages to alleviate evil and to promote good. But it was only by a very gradual process that such usages were moulded into existence, and their extension in other directions was probably again marked by as slow a development as the transition from barbarism to civilization. So, for example, even what now seems to us the very simple knowledge of how to kindle a fire, or to cultivate the field, or to make bread, was probably only as slowly discovered as the respect due to the right of property or the necessity of punishing evil-doers. Gradually, however, the sphere of knowledge in the childhood of peoples widens and expands, the usages and practices of the past become sanctified by constant observance, and at length they are deemed to constitute a body of Customary Laws, the violation of which is at once an offence against the community and also against its tutelary deities.[1] And as in the case of Language, so in that of Customary Law, the father gives the law to the family, the family to the tribe or clan, and the tribe or clan to the community. But in the process of formation those rules which directly and irrespective of authority conduce to social welfare, initiated by the consensus, as it has been termed,[2] of individual interests, precede the kind of law initiated by political authority. Equality is the essential principle of the former, as Inequality of the latter. It is the coercive sense of ingrained usage in the former which in early stages of social organisms keeps men from thinking what they have not before thought, and from doing what they have not before done.[3]

A "legal right" defined.

11*a*. We have thus seen where the weak point of the Austinian conception of Law lies. But viewed in its modern

[1] *Filosofia del Diritto Privato*, per P. Cogliolo, pp. 25, 30.

[2] *Political Institutions*, by H. Spencer, p. 528.

[3] Bagehot's *Postulates of English Political Eco.*, p. 44.

and matured development, we may very well accept Austin's definition of Jurisprudence as the Science of the Positive Law; and since the immediate objects of Law are the creation and protection of legal Rights, the next thing we have to consider is, what is meant by the expression a Legal Right? It has been defined by Austin as a "faculty" which resides in a determinate party or parties by virtue of a given law, and which avails against a party or parties (or answers to a duty lying on a party or parties) other than the party or parties in whom it resides.[1] More briefly it may be said to be the capacity or power residing in a person (whether a natural or an artificial person) of controlling, with the assent and assistance of the State, the actions of others.[2] And in this sense it may exist without being exercised, consciously or unconsciously.

The term contrasted with "might" and "moral right."

12. The exact meaning of the term can best, perhaps, be understood by contrasting it with the expressions "might" and "moral right." This has been admirably done by Professor Holland in the following passages, which are borrowed from his excellent work on Jurisprudence:[3]—

"If a man by his own force or persuasion can carry out his wishes, either by his own acts, or by influencing the acts of others, he has the 'might' so to carry out his wishes.

"If, irrespectively of having, or not having, this might, public opinion would view with approval, or at least with acquiescence, his so carrying out his wishes, and with disapproval any resistance made to his so doing, then he has a 'moral right' so to carry out his wishes.

"If, irrespectively of his having, or not having, either the might or moral right on his side, the power of the State will

[1] *Student's Austin*, by R. Campbell, p. 118 (note).

[2] Gondsmit's *Pandects*, Ch. II., § 17, p. 38 (1); Holland's *Jurisprudence*, p. 70; Pollock's *Essays on Jurisprudence and Ethics*, p. 11.

[3] Pages 72, 73.

protect him in so carrying out his wishes, and will compel such acts or forbearances on the part of other people as may be necessary in order that his wishes may be so carried out, then he has a 'legal right' so to carry out his wishes.

"If it is a question of might, all depends upon a man's own powers of force or persuasion. If it is a question of moral right, all depends on the readiness of the public opinion to express itself upon his side. If it is a question of legal right, all depends upon the readiness of the State to exert its force on his behalf. It is hence obvious that a moral and a legal right are so far from being identical that they may easily be opposed to one another. Moral rights have, in general, but a subjective support, legal rights have the objective support of the physical force of the State." Thus the immediate activity and movement of the principles of Legal Right and Moral Conduct fall into two different spheres, the former being embodied in the external relations of persons, the latter in the inner sentiment and disposition of the individual. But the main difference, it will be seen, lies in the sanctions attached to them respectively.[1] So that Moral Rights are those rights the violation of which only incurs the disapprobation of the society in which the offender lives and its social consequences, whereas the violation of a Legal Right is repressed, directly or indirectly, by the State and its agents.

Jurisprudence only concerned with legal rights.

13. Thus the only kind of right which Jurisprudence is concerned with, is one that may be enforced by the person in whom it resides with the assistance of the State. It is, as Bentham says, in its proper sense, a creature of Law properly so called.[2] Or, as a German Jurist expresses the notion, "it is a legally protected interest."[3] This Right may or may

[1] *Elements of Politics*, by Henry Sidgwick, Ch. XIII., p. 191.

[2] *Theory of Legislation*, Hildreth's trans., p. 84.

[3] *Geist des Römischen Rechts*, Volume III., section 60.

not correspond with an antecedent Moral Right, or it may be more or less extensive than the latter. But in all cases it draws its validity solely from its enforcement by the supreme political power in a State.[1] Just so far then as the aid of the public force is given a man (or more correctly speaking a person, whether physical or artificial), he has a Legal Right, and this Right is the same whether his claim is founded in righteousness or iniquity.[2] Again, it is essentially a false notion that *Law cannot avail against Natural Right.*[3] Employed in this anti-legal sense, Bentham is surely justified in saying that the word *right* becomes "the greatest enemy of reason, and the most terrible destroyer of governments. For there is no reasoning with fanatics armed with *Natural Rights*, which each one understands as he pleases, and applies as he sees fit."[4] The reverence for such rights as are supposed to be based on a law of nature may have exercised a beneficial influence in simplifying French Law and rescuing it from the chaos into which it had fallen prior to the Great Revolution; and it may also be conceded that there are certain *natural instincts* or tendencies in human nature which every legislature conducted on wise principles would respect. It is probably in this sense alone that Mr. Herbert Spencer speaks of the folly of trying "to repeal by Act of Parliament a law of Nature."[5] But when we speak of *legal rights* we now mean those Rights the measure of which is not the absolute one of Truth but the relative one of Purpose;[6] and it is only this Purpose which the State deems it proper to clothe with its sanction or autho-

[1] *The Science of Law*, by Sheldon Amos, p. 95.

[2] *The Common Law*, by O. W. Holmes, iv., p. 214.

[3] Thus, Suarez (*De Legibus*, III. c. 19) contends that an unjust law is not only not to be obeyed, but that it is not to be regarded as a law at all: *lex injusta non est lex.*

[4] *Theory of Legislation*, Hildreth's trans., p. 85.

[5] *Ethics*, Part III., p. 546.

[6] Ihering, *Der Zweck im Recht*, Vol. I., p. 439 (1884 ed.).

rity, and to the realization of which it thus lends its compulsory force, that can lay the foundation of a Legal Right. Hence it follows that what may be regarded as a Legal Right in one country may not be so regarded in another; because the individual legal propositions which together form the Right of a people stand in an organic connection with one another, and in this fundamental relation the Right of a people may again be compared to its language, which likewise rests upon certain principles and rules existing unexpressed within itself, and which are brought into light and consciousness by science.[1] We can thus only fix the abstract notion of what a Legal Right should correspond to; but it would be as vain and foolish to attempt to go further, and prescribe what shall be regarded as universal Legal Rights for all peoples and for all time, as it would be to prescribe a universal remedy for all the diseases to which humanity is subject.[2]

Origin of rights.

14. Bearing in mind the above definition, it follows that Rights, in a legal sense, spring from certain Facts supposed to be true of the person who is entitled to such Rights, to which the law attaches certain consequences; and whenever the Law gives anyone special Rights not shared by the body of people, it does so on the ground that special Facts, not true of the rest of the world, are true of him.[3]

Function of rights.

14*a*. The function of a Right, viewed as to its object, may be indicated by saying that it has to determine the relation of persons as such to one another.[4]

Parties to legal rights.

15. According to Austin,[5] there are three parties to every Legal Right; the sovereign government of one or a number

[1] *Cursus der Inst.*, von G. F. Puchta, section 15, ed. 1, p. 32: Leipzig, 1865.

[2] Ihering, *Der Zweck im Recht*, Vol. I., p. 440.

[3] *Ibid.*

[4] *Cursus der Inst.*, by Puchta, section 21, p. 45.

[5] *Student's Austin*, p. 117.

CHAP. II.

which sets the Positive Law, and which, through the Positive Law, confers the Legal Right and imposes the relative Duties: the person or persons on whom the Right is conferred: the person or persons on whom the Duty is imposed, or to whom the Positive Law is set or directed.

A sovereign government has no legal rights against its own subjects.

16. But it is important to notice that in Austin's view a sovereign government has no Legal Rights against, and consequently lies under no Legal Duties towards, its own subjects. This notion proceeds upon the broad principle that a man is no more able to confer a Right on himself than he is to impose on himself a Law or a Duty. Consequently, if a sovereign government had Legal Rights against its own subjects, those Rights would be the creators of Positive Laws set to its own subjects by a third person or body, who must therefore be sovereign over them.[1] The community would, therefore, be subject to two different sovereign authorities, which is contrary to the true definition of sovereignty, which implies an independent political society, having a single sovereign authority as the ultimate source of laws and institutions as they exist.[2] In practice, however, in most civilized countries, the sovereign government does submit itself to appear in the character of a defendant before tribunals of its own creation, and it also claims, on the other hand, to pursue its rights judicially as a demandant. This course was adopted by the British Government in India from a very early period (*vide* Regulation III. of 1793, Section II.), and at the present day the courts are frequently engaged in the disposal of suits by or against Government. But the rights which are pursued against the State, and also the rights which it pursues before tribunals of its own, are merely *analogous* to Legal Rights (in the proper acceptation of the term). They are in short *quasi*

Instance of this in India.

[1] Professor Holland maintains, on the contrary, that a State has rights and is subject to duties: *Jurisprudence*, pp. 110—111.

[2] Pollock's *Science of Politics*, p. 103.

Legal Rights; and thus in England the object of the plaintiff's claim against the sovereign is not demanded as of right (as it is in India by virtue of a formal legislative submission on the part of Government to be sued), but is begged of the sovereign defendant as a grace or favour in the form of a *Petition of Right.* And no engagement made by the Crown with any of its military or naval officers in respect of services either present, past, or future, can be enforced in any court of law.[1] It must also be recollected that the *Secretary of State for India in Council,* in whose name all actions by or against the Government of India must be brought, is a purely artificial person created by the British Parliament (21 & 22 Vict. c. 106, s. 65), and invested with the capacity of suing and being sued in an ordinary action.

Ihering's view of Law in its final development.

17. The practice just indicated more truly corresponds, moreover, with that final stage in the development of Law where legal order is made the basis and aim of government, and which, in the opinion of Rudolph von Ihering, can only be fitly designated as the condition of Law (*Rechtszustand*). Now the distinguishing feature of a true condition of legal order (*Rechtsordnung*) is, that the State itself respects the laws which it enacts for its subjects. Law, in this complete sense of the expression, is therefore the reciprocal binding force of the Statutes, the special subjection of the political power in the State itself to the Statutes issued by it.[2]

Different classes of rights.

18. Rights, again, may be divided into primary (or antecedent), or secondary (or remedial), according as they exist independently of, or in connection with, a wrong having been committed.[3] A right of the former kind is said to be an exceptional advantage granted to the person who is clothed

[1] *Mitchell* v. *The Queen,* (1896) 1 Q. B. 121 *n.* See *post,* as to the real nature of a claim by Petition of Right.

[2] *Der Zweck im Recht,* Vol. I., pp. 357, 358.

[3] Holland's *Jurisprudence,* pp. 141, 142; Pollock's *Essays,* p. 15.

Chap. II.

with it, while a right of the latter kind is one which is given by way of compensation when an antecedent or primary right is violated. The German Jurists again draw a distinction between "primitive" (*Urrechte*) and "acquired Rights" (*erwerbliche Rechte*). The former are inborn and natural, which every human being possesses independently of any act of his own. The latter are in their nature derivative or accidental, depending upon the free act of the person entitled to them.[1] But the demarcating line between these two classes of Rights is not easy to fix, and in the following pages the classification first mentioned will be adopted.

Analysis of a right.

19. If we now analyse the elements into which a Right may be resolved, we find, as Professor Holland points out,[2] that they consist of a series of four terms, namely:—

The person entitled;
The object;
The act or forbearance;
The person obliged.

But it is not to be understood that all these four elements must necessarily co-exist in every Right, for it is possible to conceive Rights which have no determinate object, as, for example, the right of a man to his good name. Rights of this description are said, therefore, to be Rights to acts or forbearances merely, which the person in whom the Right resides is entitled to exact. An illustration suggested by Professor Holland will serve to explain the above analysis. A testator leaves to his daughter a silver teapot. Here the daughter is "the person entitled," also called by Professor Holland "the person of inherence," *i.e.*, in whom the right resides; the teapot is the "object" of the right; the delivery of the teapot to the daughter is the "act" to which her Right entitles her; and the executor is "the person of incidence," *i.e.*, the person obliged or against whom her Right is avail-

[1] Ahrens, Bd. I., p. 365, § 47.

[2] Holland's *Jurisprudence*, p. 78.

able. A further illustration will explain the application of the terms in the case of a Right which has no determinate object. A. is B.'s servant. Here B. is the "person of inherence," reasonable service is the "act" to which he is entitled, and A. is the "person of incidence" against whom the Right is available.

Explanation of the term duty.

20. In the above analysis of a Right it will be noticed that one of the four elements which are requisite to complete the notion is the act or forbearance to which the person of inherence is entitled. Whenever anyone is entitled to such active or passive furtherance on the part of others, such furtherance is called their Duty. This Duty is, therefore, the correlative of Right, by which it is called into being,[1] and when it is to do an act it is called "positive," and when to forbear from doing an act it is called "negative." Duties may again be divided into "relative" and "absolute,"[2] and "primary" and "secondary." Absolute Duties are said to be those to which there is no corresponding Right belonging to any determinate person or body of persons, as the duty to pay taxes. Relative Duties are those to which there is a corresponding Right in some person or definite body of persons, as the duty to pay one's debts.[3] Primary Duties are those which exist *per se*, and independently of any other duty. "Secondary" or "Sanctioning Duties" are those which have no independent existence, but only exist for the sake of enforcing other Duties. The duty to forbear from personal injury is an instance of the former; that of paying damages for the injury inflicted an instance of the latter.[4]

Absolute and relative duties.

Primary and secondary duties.

Conflicting duties.

20*a*. In view of two conflicting Duties, the question which should be sacrificed when both cannot be fulfilled, may be

[1] Weiske's *Rechtslexicon*, Bd. IX., tit. *Recht*, p. 140.

[2] *Student's Austin*, p. 161.

[3] *Ibid.*, p. 194.

[4] Markby's *Elements of Law*, section 183, p. 102.

CHAP. II. answered generally with reference to two leading principles :—

(a) Among Duties of the same class, the relative importance of the Duties depends upon the importance of their objects, and in case of conflict the best object should be chosen;

(b) As between different classes of Duties (other things being equal), the importance of the Duty depends on the extent of the group to which it applies.[1]

Thus, to give an example of the first rule, it has been pointed out that it is a primary Duty to forbear from personal injury. But it is equally a Duty to protect the body of another person or one's own body against an offence affecting the human body; and having regard to the importance of protecting society against such acts of violence, the object of the latter Duty is relatively more important than that of the former. Hence, if Z. under the influence of madness attacks A. and attempts to kill him in the presence of B., here B. would be justified in defending A., and, under certain conditions, of even causing the death of Z.[2] So it is the duty of a soldier to obey the command of his superior officer; but it is also his duty, as an armed citizen, to obey the laws of his country, and the importance of the former is as nothing compared to that of the latter. Consequently, if the command of the superior officer is *plainly* unlawful, as for instance, to shoot another person merely because he is disobeying an order of the officer, the soldier is bound by his duty to obey the law of the land (not to commit murder) and to sacrifice his duty of blind obedience to his military superior.[3] Or, again, to take an example from the Civil

[1] *Theory of Morals*, by Paul Janet, p. 245. Cf. Ahrens' *Philosophie des Rechts*, 6th ed., Vol. I., pp. 331, 332.

[2] *Vide* sections 97 and 100, Indian Penal Code. Cf. also §§ 15, 16, 24, 25, 26, *Romagnosi's Genesis of the Criminal Law*, Vol. I. of the German Translation by Heinrich Luden, Jena, pp. 22—26.

[3] *R.* v. *Thomas*, 1 Russ. 823; No. 17, Punjab Record, 1883; *Dawkins* v.

Law, suppose A. contracts to take in cargo for B. at a foreign port. A.'s Government afterwards declares war against the country in which the port is situated; here by the declaration of hostilities the performance by A. of his contract becomes unlawful, and, since the observance of the law is a higher duty than that of performing his contract, the law will relieve him from all liability for non-performance.[1] As an illustration of the second rule, it will suffice to refer to a simple application of the well-known maxim *salus populi (vel reipublicæ) suprema lex* (the welfare of the people [or the State] is the highest law). Thus, since the public welfare is the first and highest consideration imposed on a citizen, it follows that although we owe a duty to every individual to respect his right of property, we also owe, on the other hand, a still higher duty to protect the public welfare; and accordingly, we may lawfully destroy or injure the house of a private person for the purpose of checking a fire which might otherwise spread to the injury of the town, because individual interests must yield to the public welfare, and regard for the latter would justify what would otherwise be an illegal and unjustifiable interference with private property.

20*b*. From a moralist's point of view, the rules we have been considering are not inaptly summed up in that saying of Fenelon's, "I owe more to humanity than to my country, to my country than to my family, to my family than to my friends, to my friends than to myself."[2] It is precisely on the same principle of the relative importance of conflicting duties determining the obligation of obedience, that Grotius,[3] Blackstone,[4] and other writers[5] assert that human laws are of

Lord Rokeby, 4 F. & F. 806; and *Marks* v. *Frogley*, (1898) 1 Q. B. 388; confer, however, *R.* v. *Hutchinson*, 9 Cox, Cr. 555.

[1] Section 56, Illust. (*d*) Indian Contract Act.

[2] Quoted by Paul Janet in his *Theory of Morals*, p. 245.

[3] *De J. B. ac P.*, ii. 3, 6.

[4] *Comment. Introd.*, p. 43, Vol. I.

[5] Suarez, for instance, in the passage above quoted, p. 21.

CHAP. II. no avail if contrary to the Law of Nature, which, according to Blackstone, "is binding all over the globe in all countries and at all times." But this last quotation is only here made to warn the student of law that this old woman's theory of a supposed Law of Nature (or Natural Law as it is sometimes called), implanted in the human heart and common to all men, has long since been abandoned as standing in open contradiction to the well-established fact that there are millions of human beings still immersed in barbarism to whom such an imaginary law is unknown, and amongst whom there are some who honour and worship animals while they murder and abandon their own offspring with impunity. We are now more accustomed to regard those principles of justice which writers of an idealistic school were wont to teach as coeval with humanity as in reality the product of a slow and very gradual elaboration of the human intellect, and it is the study of this evolution of fundamental juridical notions that constitutes the objective side of the philosophy of law.[1] So that in the history of law, as in that of every other science, we are constantly reminded of what the poet says:—

> "The heights great men reached and kept—
> Were not attained by sudden flight,
> But they while their companions slept,
> Were toiling upwards in the night."

It is, moreover, a perfectly inadmissible proposition to permit the undefined and undefinable principles of the so-called Law of Nature to ride supreme over the Positive Law. For, as Bentham justly observes, in the immense varieties of ideas respecting Natural and Divine Law, cannot some reason be found for resisting all human laws if such a proposition as Blackstone asserts were once recognised?[2] It would be to arm every fanatic against all government. All that can be conceded from a juridical point of view is, that there are

[1] *Saggi di Filosofia Juridica*, per Ferdinando Puglia, p. 64.

[2] *Theory of Legislation*, Hildreth's trans., p. 86.

certain rights that are proper to man even when external things may be wanting—attributes as it were of his human personality—which no well-ordered government can refuse to guarantee. And it may be added, that no government could hope to maintain the stability of its authority which arbitrarily violated such rights. But nevertheless in theory there is nothing to prevent the legislature from making laws with all the license of caprice, and such laws derive their force from the authority of the legislature, and not from the principles upon which they are based.[1]

[1] *Filosofia del diritto privato*, p. 57.

CHAPTER III.

THE OBJECTS OF RIGHTS, AND HEREIN OF PERSONS AND THINGS.

CHAP. III.

Objects of rights.

21. THE Objects of Rights may be Persons and Things, hence the well-known division of Law into the Law of Persons and the Law of Things. But remembering the analysis already given of a Right, it will be obvious that a Right cannot itself be the Object of a Right, for that would involve the absurdity of one of the constituent parts being itself the whole.

Persons and Things defined.

22. Again, when we speak of Persons and Things as being the Objects of Rights, we are obliged to use the terms in a natural as well as in an artificial sense. In a legal sense a Person, as the subject of a Right or of a Duty, may either be a "natural person," *i.e.*, a living human being, whether actually born or still *in ventre sa mère*, provided he is regarded by Law as capable of Rights or Duties; or he may be an artificial or "juristical person" upon whom the law has conferred a legal "status," and who is thus capable of sustaining the mask of personality, having the same capacity for Rights and liability to Duties as a natural person.[1]

Status.

23. In early writers we find the term "Status" distinguished by "Status Civiles" (which was again subdivided

[1] Windscheid, *Lehrbuch des Pandektenrechts*, Vol. I., p. 152 (1882). In the Roman Law a child in the mother's womb was not regarded as a separate being but as a part of its mother (*mulieris portio*, Dig. xxv., 4, 1, 1). If, however, the child was born alive, had a human form, and was capable of living, its rights dated back to the time of its conception in the mother's womb.—*Windscheid*, Vol. I., pp. 131, 132.

into the *tria capita* of (*a*) "libertatis," (*b*) "civitatis," and (*c*) "familiæ"), and "Status Naturales" (*i.e.*, *sexus*, *ætatis*, *&c.*).[1] But it is now employed to mean any aggregate of Rights and Duties which are attached to a person either as a member of the community or as one of a class. Inasmuch, however, as there is a tendency to bring all Rights and Duties attached to individuals as members of a class more and more under the control of those upon whose assent they come into existence, it is usual to call those Rights and Duties which are capable of being altered, terminated, or otherwise affected at the desire of the persons entitled or subject to them, "mere matters of contract."[2] And if we desire to speak with accuracy we do not use the word *status* to express such matters. The term applies more correctly to those cases where a *permanent* relation, not capable of being changed, prolonged or ended at the desire of the parties, is created by the law: such as parent and child, husband and wife. "The status of an individual, used as a legal term," said Brett, L.J., in *Niboyet* v. *Niboyet*,[3] "means the legal position of the individual in or with regard to the rest of a community"; and he then proceeds to point out that "that relation between the parties, and that status of each of them with regard to the community, which are constituted upon marriage *are not imposed or defined by contract or agreement, but by law.*" Under the Roman law actions relating to *status* belonged to the so-called "*actiones prejudiciales*," the object of which was to obtain, not the condemnation of the defendant, but merely a judicial acknowledgment of a legal relation, such as liberty or paternity. Under the Indian Specific Relief Act (I. of 1877, § 42), a person claiming a legal character or *status* which is denied to him, may sue for a mere declaration that he is so entitled.

1 *Windscheid*, Vol. I., p. 140, note.
2 Markby's *Elements of Law*, pp. 177—180.
3 4 P. D. (1878), at p. 11.

Chap. III.

Artificial persons.

24. Artificial or Juristical Persons are said[1] to be of two kinds—

(1.) *Universitates personarum*, such as the State itself; *Collegia*, such as the University of Oxford or the University of the Punjab; Churches, and Parishes.

(2.) *Universitates bonorum*, such as funds left to "pious uses" without a trustee; the estate of an intestate before administration, the estate of a Bankrupt.

Requisites of.

25. In the case of groups of persons or a mass of property falling under the first category, such, for instance, as corporations for commercial purposes, or educational institutions like the Universities of Oxford or of the Punjab, it is requisite that the legal status of a person should be conferred upon them either by a general or a special act of sovereign power. For instance, the Indian Companies Act of 1882 confers the privileges of a corporation upon any association of seven persons who fulfil the conditions prescribed by that Act. The University of the Punjab, on the other hand, is incorporated under a special Act of the Indian Legislature, namely, XIX. of 1882.

In the second group it is only by a figurative turn of expression that the term "juristical person" is applied, which is intended merely to indicate the legal situation, but not to fully or accurately describe it.[2] It is a peculiarity of all *Universitates* that their identity is independent of any change in their component parts.[3] Thus in a corporation (like a Joint Stock Company or a Municipality) there may be a continual change of Members, but the corporation remains the same.

[1] Holland's *Jurisprudence*, p. 83. See also Windscheid's *Pandektenrechts*, Vol. I., pp. 148—152.

[2] *Windscheid*, Vol. I., p. 148, note 2.

[3] Markby's *Elements of Law*, section 139, p. 85.

Extinction of.

26. A *universitas personarum* may cease to exist in several ways:[1]—

(1.) By failure of its component parts. Thus in the case of a corporation registered under Act VI. of 1882, by the number of its members being reduced below seven (*vide* Section 73 of the Indian Companies Act, and Section 48 of 25 & 26 Vict. c. 89).

(2.) By a valid resolution on the part of the group of persons constituting it, as a special resolution to wind up a Joint Stock Company voluntarily (*vide* Section 173 (*b*), and Section 174 of the Indian Companies Act, and Sections 129 and 130 of 25 & 26 Vict. c. 89).

(3.) By expiry of the period fixed for its duration (Section 173 (*a*) of the Indian Companies Act).

(4.) By a forfeiture of its privileges, as was alleged in the case of the revocation of the Charter of the City of London by Charles II., or as may happen under the Punjab Municipal Act, 1891.

(5.) By a surrender of its franchises, such as took place in the case of the London College of Advocates in pursuance of 20 & 21 Vict. c. 77.

Things divided into two kinds.

27. Precisely as in the case of Persons so in that of Things, the Science of Law recognises a two-fold description, for which various terms are used, such as corporeal (*res corporales*) or incorporeal (*res incorporales*), physical or intellectual. The distinction aimed at in each form of terminology is that between material or physical objects, perceptible again and again, or repeatedly by the external organs of sense, such as a house or a horse, on the one hand, and artificial or purely intellectual objects, such as a copyright, a trade mark, a patent, on the other.

[1] Holland's *Jurisprudence*, pp. 83, 84; *Windscheid*, Vol. I., p. 163, section 61.

CHAP. III.

Further classification of things.

28. Again, things may be classified into—

(*a*) moveable and immoveable;

(*b*) fungible or non-fungible;

(*c*) consumable and non-consumable;

(*d*) divisible and non-divisible;

(*e*) principal or accessory;

(*f*) *res in commercio* and *extra commercium*.

CHAPTER IV.

ACTS.

29. Having in the previous Chapters defined the exact limits and scope of the Science of Jurisprudence, and determined that the immediate objects of Law are the creation and protection of "Legal Rights"; and having further fixed the meaning of the terms Right, Duty, Person, and Thing, we can now enter upon the important relation of Acts in the creation, extinction, or modification of "Legal Rights."

CHAP. IV.

Acts.

30. Matters of fact (*Thatsachen*) are mere transient causes of sensation, but those upon which the creation, extinction, or alteration of Rights depend are called Juristical Facts (*juristische Thatsachen*). Facts may be either "Events" or "Acts."

Juristical Facts.

31. "Events" are movements of external nature which are not ordinarily under human control, such as a landslip, death, or an accidental fire. "Acts" (*Handlungen*) on the other hand, in the widest sense of the term, are movements of the will, and, therefore, Events regarded as under human control.[1] Ihering distinguishes between an Event (*Ereigniss*) and an Act (*Handlung*) by saying that the groundwork of every Act is a Purpose—where there is no Purpose there is no Act, but only an Event—and illustrates this distinction by the following examples: "He jumped down from the tower, because he wished to kill himself." Here the muscular movement of

"Events."

"Acts."

[1] Windscheid's *Pandekten*, Vol. I., section 67, p. 172; Henri Ahrens, *Cours de Droit Naturel*, 8th ed., Vol. I., p. 190; Baron, *Pandekten*, § 47, p. 75; Zweite Auflage, Leipzig, 1876.

CHAP. IV.

jumping is an Act, and it is done with a Purpose (*Zweck*). But "he has lost his life, because he fell from the tower"; here the falling from the tower is an Event, not an Act, because it was not a bodily movement which followed upon volition.[1]

"Inward" and "outward" Acts.

32. Mere movements of the will are called "inward Acts," that is to say, they are as yet in that inner stage which ends with the determination to which the Act is guided by a given Purpose (*Zweck*). But when the determination of the will has produced its effect upon the external world we have an "outward Act," and it is with Acts of the latter description that Jurisprudence is alone concerned.[2]

Analysis of an Act.

33. In common language an Act (*Handlung*) is spoken of as expressing both the movement following upon a determination of the will and the consequences resulting from it. But this use of the word is not strictly accurate. The Act by itself, *i.e.*, the movement which follows upon a volition, is nothing more than a mere "voluntary muscular contraction." The chain of physical sequences which it sets in motion is no part of it. Thus, if I kill a person with a pistol, my only Act is to contract the muscles of my arm and forefinger in a certain way whereby I am enabled to raise the weapon, point it at his body, and pull the trigger. What follows upon my Act, and in connection with it, are its consequences; but while I *will* the Act I do not *will* those consequences, although I may *intend* them. The distinction between the *will* and *intention* will be stated presently. Again, it is important to recollect that between the Act and its consequences many other natural causes, and even human beings,

[1] *Der Zweck im Recht*, Vol. I., p. 15 (1884 ed.). Austin also says that "events which are not *willed* are not *acts*."—*Student's Austin*, p. 204. See also Sheldon Amos's *Science of Law*, pp. 102, 103.

[2] Ahrens, *Cours de Droit Naturel*, Vol. I., p. 190; Ihering's *Der Zweck im Recht*, Vol. I., p. 22; Markby's *Elements of Law*, sections 213, 214; *Student's Austin*, p. 174; Holland's *Jurisprudence*, p. 90.

may intervene and produce effects which would not have happened but for such intervention. Hence arises the rule of law that a man is only liable for the natural and ordinary consequences of his deliberate Acts. The reason for this limitation of liability is, that if the intervening events are of such a kind that no foresight could have expected to look out for them, the defendant is obviously not to blame for having failed to do so.[1]

Forbearance.

34. If the effect intended by the determination of the will is of a negative character, that is to say, the *not* doing some given external Act *in consequence of a determination of the will*, the proper term to express this form of volition is "Forbearance."[2]

Essentials of an Act.

(*a*) Exertion of the will.

35. It results from what has already been said that one of the first essentials of an Act is the exertion of the will, that is to say, the *willing* of the particular muscular movement which follows immediately upon a volition. An Act of Will has been defined as "that inward state which, as experience informs us, is always succeeded by motion, while the body is in its normal condition," *i.e.*, not paralysed.[3]

(*b*) State of consciousness.

Every Act is prompted by a purpose or motive.

36. But to Act and to Act for a given purpose are synonymous, for it is impossible to conceive an act of volition without connecting it with some purpose to the attainment of which it is directed. In other words, an Act without a Purpose is as impossible as an Effect without a Cause.[4] This incentive to a determination of the will is, therefore, the motive or purpose of its exercise, and involves a state of consciousness on the part of the doer of the Act. Here,

[1] *The Common Law*, by O. W. Holmes, pp. 91, 92; Markby's *Elements of Law*, section 215; *Student's Austin*, p. 202. Cf. *Carter* v. *M'Laren*, L. R. 2 H. L. (Sc.) 120, 126.

[2] *Student's Austin*, p. 174; Markby's *Elements of Law*, section 215*a*; Holland's *Jurisprudence*, p. 90.

[3] Sir J. F. Stephen's General View of the Criminal Law, p. 76.

[4] Ihering, *Der Zweck im Recht*, Vol. I., p. 14.

When an *intention* may be imputed to the doer of an Act.

then, we have the second essential element of an Act. When this state of consciousness accompanies the determination of the will, it is said that the doer *intends* the consequences which, in the ordinary course of things, are known to follow from a similar muscular movement. "The intent," says Mr. Holmes, "which is meant when spoken of as an element of legal liability is an intent directed toward the harm complained of, or at least toward harm."[1] Here we see the distinction between the *will* and *intention*. The *will* may imply *intention*, but the latter does not imply *will*. The *will* has to do with *Acts*, the intention with the *consequences* of Acts.[2]

Degrees of consciousness.

37. The state of consciousness may, however, be possessed in very different degrees by different classes of persons, and at different times. It may also be regulated by the Law itself. Thus it is wholly absent in lunatics, and consequently the Law recognises the physiological fact (*furiosi nulla voluntas est*), and often refuses to attach any legal consequences to any Act of such a person, whether it may happen to be favourable to or against his interest (*furiosum sive stipuletur sive promittat nihil agere natura manifestum est*—from the nature of the case it is manifest that a *furiosus*, whether he stipulates or whether he promises, his act is a nullity).[3] In like manner a child under the age of seven years is supposed to have no will, and consequently has no legal capacity[4] (*qui fari non potest*). Thus the Indian Penal Code has a general exception to the effect that "nothing is an offence which is done by a child under seven years of age."[5] Having no understanding-will the defect cannot

[1] *The Common Law*, p. 132. [2] *Student's Austin*, pp. 204, 205.

[3] Windscheid's *Pandekten*, Vol. I., p. 182. This rule is somewhat modified by the Indian Contract Act, which allows a claim to be enforced for necessaries supplied to a lunatic suitable to his condition in life: section 68, illustration (*a*).

[4] Dig. XLIV. 7, 1, 12, 13. [5] Section 82.

ordinarily be supplied by the authority of a tutor or guardian (*auctoritate tutoris*).[1] Beyond the age of seven years the degree of consciousness is deemed to vary according as the person has or has not attained the age of puberty, and the Positive Law generally regulates the period at which this age commences. Thus *impubertas* according to the Roman Law ceased in the case of males on the completion of the fourteenth year, and in case of females of the twelfth year.[2] The Indian Penal Code (sect. 83) enacts that "nothing is an offence which is done by a child above seven years of age and under twelve, who has not attained sufficient maturity of understanding to judge of the nature and consequence of his conduct on that occasion." Here it will be observed that the question of the degree of understanding in the case of a person within the limit of ages specified is one to be determined in each case. Again, in some systems of law,[3] women, decreed prodigals, and minors are deemed to have imperfect understanding, which may, however, be supplied by an express provision of the law. According to the Law prevailing in the Punjab and some other parts of India, persons who have been declared incapable of managing their own estates are placed under the superintendence of Courts of Wards, and are pronounced incapable of charging their estates.[4] The Indian Contract Act[5] only recognises those persons as competent to contract, who have attained the age of majority according to their personal law, who are of sound mind, and who are not disqualified from contracting by any law to which they are subject.

[1] Dig. XXVI. 7, 1, 2. For an exception to this rule, see Dig. XLI. 2, 32, 2. See *Windscheid*, Vol. I., section 155, Note 13.

[2] *Windscheid*, Vol. I., section 54, p. 136.

[3] For instance, the old Roman Law (Ulp. XI., 27; Gai. I., 189—193; and the old German Law (Kraut, *Vormendschaft*, II., 291; Stobbe, *Deutsch. Privatr*. I., pp. 239, 240).

[4] Section 4, Act XII. of 1878.

[5] Section 11.

CHAP. IV.

Other causes affecting consciousness. Drunkenness or temporary delirium.

38. But a conscious determination of the will may be affected also by a temporary suspension of the intellectual faculties, namely, by drunkenness, or temporary delirium, in the case, for instance, of a sane person who is delirious from fever, or of a person who is usually of sound mind, but occasionally of unsound mind. In such cases the Civil Law regards the person so affected as incapable of understanding or of forming a rational judgment as to the effect of his determination of the will upon his interests. In England contracts by a person in a state of drunkenness are only voidable and may be ratified when the contractor is sober.[1] But according to the Indian Contract Act they are wholly void, and consequently incapable of such ratification.[2] In the Criminal Law of India drunkenness is only a valid excuse if the thing which caused the intoxication was administered to the person without his knowledge or against his will.[3]

Error or mistake.

39. Again the legal result of Acts may be affected either by error or mistake, that is to say, either by ignorance or misapprehension. In such cases, however, the error or mistake is not, strictly speaking, the ground for the nullity of the outward expression of the will, but the true reason is that the outward expression when influenced by error corresponds to no real determination of the will.[4] It is in this sense that the phrase *nulla voluntas errantis, i.e.*, that a person under the influence of error has no will, is perhaps to be understood. It simply means that the existence of error excludes that agreement between the will and its outward expression, which underlies all legal liability for the consequences of an Act. From the existence of error we conclude the absence of unlawful intention or inadvertence. Thus the

[1] *Matthews* v. *Baxter*, L. R., VIII. Exch. 132.
[2] Section 12.
[3] Section 85, Indian Penal Code.
[4] *Windscheid*, Vol. I., section 76, p. 204.

Indian Penal Code lays down that "nothing is an offence which is done by a person who is, or who by reason of a mistake of fact, and not by reason of a mistake of law, in good faith believes himself to be, bound by law to do it."[1]

CHAP. IV.

Ignorance of fact and Law.

40. The distinction which the passage just cited draws between mistake or ignorance of fact and ignorance of Law, is one which has been handed down from the Roman Law,[2] but unfortunately without the modifications which in that system rendered the stringency of the rule less oppressive than it has become in ours. The general rule is expressed by Paulus: *Regula est, juris ignorantiam cuique nocere:*[3] the rule is, that ignorance of Law injures everyone. The reason assigned in the Digest for the inexcusability of ignorance of Law is, that "law both can and should be limited in extent (*jus finitum et possit et debeat*),"[4] and it is therefore presumed to be possible for every person of discretion, as Blackstone says, to know the Law. "The law," said Tindal, C. J., in *McNaghten's case*, "is administered upon the principle that everyone must be taken conclusively to know it without proof that he does know it."[5] But this *pretiosa ratio*, as Austin calls it, is obviously unsatisfactory, and Austin himself more approaches the true ground, at all events the only ground upon which the rule in question can be rationally supported, when he bases it on expediency. "If," as he says, "ignorance of law were admitted as a ground of exemption, the Courts would be involved in questions which it were scarcely possible to solve, and which would render the administration of justice next to impracticable."[6] This reasoning may not be convincing, but it is at least intelligible. It is not convincing, because the Courts are often concerned as it

[1] Section 76. Cf. as to alleged mistake of Law, I. L. R. XVI. Allah. 212.

[2] See the Title *de juris et facti ignorantia* in the Digest (XXII. 6) and Code (1, 18).

[3] Dig. XXII. 6, 2.

[4] *Ibid.*

[5] 10 Cl. & F. 210.

[6] Student's ed., pp. 238, 239.

CHAP. IV.

is with questions of intention, and many alleged errors of fact are as difficult to investigate as alleged errors of law. But, on the whole, the rule would be salutary if it were less stringently insisted upon. The English Law acknowledges only a single exception to it, and that only to a partial extent. "Yet England," as Sir Frederick Pollock well observes, "is the one country in Western Europe where it is most difficult for a man, who is not a lawyer by profession, to have any clear notion of the laws he lives under, and where the chances are greatest that matters of serious importance will turn out to be provided for inadequately or not at all."[1] The partial exception to which allusion has been made may be best expressed in the words of Mr. R. Campbell, the able editor of *Austin*. "If I sell land, and it turns out that I have no title, I am not liable to pay *substantial* damages for the loss of the land bargained for, but only the costs occasioned by the abortive transaction. The reason is said to be that the pitfalls in English title to land are so notorious that no one can be presumed to know whether he has a good title or not."[2] But these pitfalls are only some of those which are scattered along the path of our every-day life, which remain open "merely because it is nobody's business, until the mischief is done, to see they are filled up." If we turn from the English to the Roman Law, we find that the practical sense of the Roman Jurists soon recognized the injustice of assuming a general knowledge of Law which was entirely contrary to the actual fact; and they accordingly exempted certain classes of persons, *quibus permissum est jus ignorare* (to whom it is permitted to be ignorant of Law), from the operation of the rule, because it was vain to expect in their case a knowledge of the Civil Law, of which it was notorious they were ignorant. The classes so exempted were soldiers, women, rustics, and minors. But the exemption did not extend to excuse ignorance of those parts of the Law

[1] *Essays*, p. 63.

[2] See the note, *Student's Austin*, p. 239.

which were derived from the *jus gentium*,[1] and which were presumed to be knowable *naturali ratione*, nor, according to Labeo, if the Law might have been conjectured, or if good legal advice was available.[2] This last proviso was also waived if the point of law was so doubtful or so disputed that an absolutely certain opinion was not to be obtained.[3] Whether a somewhat similar exemption might not now be made in administering the Law amongst a people like the agricultural inhabitants of the Punjab, whose familiarity with Courts of Justice or any definite system of Law dates back only to a little less than fifty years ago, and whose intellectual capacity is of the lowest degree, may well be considered by the Indian Legislature. Meantime, the Courts are often induced to exclude the operation of the rule upon grounds which are more specious than logical, in order to meet the plain requirements of justice. As an instance of this kind may be cited a case which occurred in the Chief Court of the Punjab, and which is reported as No. 81 of the *Punjab Record* for 1886.[4] In England, also, an attempt has been made to limit the operation of the rule by restricting it to *jus* in the sense of the general principles of Law, so that an error in regard to a private right would stand on the same footing as an error of fact.[5]

[1] This term meant in the Roman Law, from which it is borrowed, the principles of law generally accepted among mankind, and in accordance with which the Roman magistrates decided cases in which the parties were not both Roman citizens, and in which, therefore, the *jus civile* was regarded as inapplicable.

[2] Dig. XXII. 6, 9.

[3] Cf. *Wächter*, II., section 21, note 21; Savigny's *System*, III., sections 336 *et seq.*

[4] So in *Brij Mohan Das* v. *Mannu Bibi* (1897), the High Court held that a person was entitled to the benefit of sect. 14 of Act XV. of 1877 (*the Limitation Act for India*), if his mistake was a *bonâ fide* mistake of law. In supporting this view the learned C. J. (*Sir John Edge*) said, "that a mistake of law can be made in good faith most judges would probably admit from their own personal experience on the bench." I. L. R. XVI. All. 212.

[5] Per Lord Westbury in *Cooper* v. *Phibbs*, L. R. 2 App. 170. Cf. Savigny's *System*, VIII. p. 327 (note *c*).

CHAP. IV. And in a leading American case,[1] it is laid down that while "a mere mistake of law, stripped of all other circumstances, constitutes no ground for the reformation of written contracts, the rule that an admitted or clearly established misapprehension of the law *does* create a basis for the interference of Courts of Equity, *resting on discretion and to be exercised only in the most unquestionable and flagrant cases*, is certainly more in consonance with the best considered and best reasoned cases upon this point, both English and American."[1] This statement of the law was approved by the majority of the Supreme Court, United States, in the case of *Griswold* v. *Hazard.*[2] But *Brown*, J., dissented, citing in support of his view the English case of *Powell* v. *Smith*,[3] where the defendant endeavoured to defeat the enforcement of an agreement to give a lease upon the ground that he was mistaken as to the legal meaning and effect of an important provision. In that case the Master of the Rolls, in overruling the defence, said: "All those cases which have been cited during the argument are cases where there was either a dispute and doubt as to the thing sold, or where the words of the agreement expressed certain things in an ambiguous manner, which might be misunderstood by one of the parties. In all these cases the Court has held that it must look at the evidence, and if the mistake is sufficiently proved the Court will then set aside the agreement. But here the words of the agreement are quite certain, *and the only thing that was not understood was the legal effect of certain words which it contained. Now that is no ground of mistake at all. It is a question upon the construction of an agreement agreed to by everybody concerned.*"[4]

The Indian Legislature has adopted the rule in all its stringency in regard to contracts, which cannot be avoided

[1] *Snell* v. *Insurance Co.*, 98 U. S. 85, 90, 92.

[2] 141 U. S. Rep. 284.

[3] L. R. 14 Eq. 85, 90.

[4] Cf. also *Beauchamp (Earl)* v. *Winn*, L. R. 6 H. L. 223; 22 W. R. 193.

on the mere ground of a mistake as to any law in force in British India. But a mistake as to any law not so in force is declared to have the same effect as a mistake of fact.[1] And, in regard to contracts, it is also important to bear in mind that a contract is not voidable merely because it was caused by one of the parties to it being under a mistake as to a matter of fact.[2]

Error of fact must be material.

41. It is not, moreover, every error of fact which is sufficient to show that there was no conscious determination of the will. In order to render an error of fact a valid excuse for an Act, or to justify its rescission, it is necessary that the error should affect the whole scope of the Act, or at least in some material respect (*error in substantia*). If, on the other hand, the error only concerns some immaterial element in the determination and expression of the will, the law refuses to attach any importance to it. For instance, an error in regard to the mere name of a person or thing, when there is no doubt as to the person or thing intended, would be an immaterial error. But if it related to the very nature of the jural relation intended to be created or affected by the Act, or to the person in reference to whom the will was declared,[3] assuming that the doer of the Act had a particular person, and only that person, in view, the error in such and similar cases would be sufficient to deprive the Act of any legal effect.[4] "Whenever the consideration of the person with

[1] Section 21 of the Contract Act.

[2] Section 22 of the Contract Act.

[3] *Windscheid*, section 76, pp. 205—209; Markby's *Elements of Law*, section 262.

[4] The case of *Cundy* v. *Lindsay*, L. R. 3 App. Cases, 459, is a good illustration of the principle laid down in the text. That was a case in which A., by fraudulently stating that he was X., induced B. & Co. to sell him some goods. The House of Lords held there was no contract. "Of him (A.)," said Lord Cairns, "they (B. and Co.) never thought. With him they never intended to deal. Their minds never for an instant rested on him, and as between him and them there was no consensus of mind which could lead to any agreement or contract whatever." As Sir W. Markby observes, the ground of the decision is, not that because of error the liability on the con-

Chap. IV.

whom I contract," says Pothier,[1] "is an ingredient of the contract which I intend to make, an error respecting the person destroys my consent, and consequently annuls the agreement; for instance, if with the intention of giving or lending a thing to Peter, I give or lend it to Paul, whom I mistake for Peter, the gift or loan is void for want of my consent, for I did not intend either to give or lend the thing to Paul, but only to Peter; a consideration of the person of Peter was an ingredient in the contract that I intended to make." This passage was quoted with approval by Fry, J., and acted upon in *Smith* v. *Wheatcroft*.[2]

Responsibility of doer of Act for consequences not intended by him.

42. We have hitherto dealt with the responsibility of the doer of an Act for the consequences which he *intends* to follow from it. But it is of course conceivable that consequences may follow *without* being intended. Here the responsibility of the doer of the Act depends upon a variety of considerations which will now be discussed.

Accident or chance.

43. Suppose, for instance, that owing to the operation of causes which the doer of the Act *had no opportunity of taking into account*, the consequences which he anticipated as likely to follow did not follow, but that consequences of a very different character followed in their stead, which he neither desired nor expected. Here the consequences are attributable to "nobody's fault"[3] but to mere *accident* or *chance*, for which the doer is not held to be legally responsible. "Nothing," says the Indian Penal Code, "is an offence which is done by accident or misfortune without any criminal intention or knowledge in the doing of a lawful act in a lawful manner, by lawful means, and with proper care and caution."[4] The general principle of the English

tract must be set aside, but that because of the error there was no *consensus* such as would make a contract. Section 746, p. 358, *Elements of Law*.

[1] Vol. I., p. 13, Eng. trans. by W. O. Evans, London, 1806.

[2] (1878), 9 Ch. D. at p. 230.

[3] *Hamilton, Fraser & Co.* v. *Pandorf & Co.* (1887), 12 App. Cas. 518, 526.

[4] Section 80.

Law is likewise that "loss from accident must lie where it falls, and this principle is not affected by the fact that a human being is the instrument of misfortune."[1] Thus, where the defendant, who was one of a sporting party, fired at a pheasant, and a pellet from his gun glanced off the bough of a tree and wounded the plaintiff, who was engaged in carrying cartridges and game for the party, it was held, in the absence of negligence, the defendant was not liable in damages.[2]

Where result might have been foreseen if reasonable forethought exercised.

44. Or, again, if the consequences are such as, although neither desired nor expected, might have been foreseen if the forethought of a reasonably prudent man had been exercised, the legal result is affected according as the doer of the Act is guilty of "rashness," "heedlessness," or "negligence."

"Rashness" defined.

45. "Rashness" is the quality attributed to an Act which is done on the insufficient assumption that consequences which may follow from an Act, will not follow in the given instance.

"Heedlessness" and "negligence" defined.

46. "Heedlessness" and "negligence" are closely allied; in each the party is inadvertent of consequences. But the former state of mind is represented by an Act which is done without adverting to its probable consequences; while "negligence" is the inadvertent omission to act as one ought. Both states of mind suppose unconsciousness. The "heedless" man *acts* as he does because he does *not* think of the consequences. The "negligent" man *omits* to act because he does *not* think of it. They are both distinguished from the "rash" man, inasmuch as the latter is *conscious* of the risk he runs, but he thinks (for a reason which he examines insufficiently) that the mischief will probably be averted in the given instance.[3]

Contrasted with rashness.

1 Holmes, *The Common Law*, p. 94.

2 *Stanley* v. *Powell*, W. N., 18th Nov. 1890, p. 182.

3 *Student's Austin*, pp. 208—210; Holland's *Jurisprudence*, p. 94; Markby's

CHAP. IV.

Other circumstances affecting the determination of the will.

47. We have now seen the influence which ignorance and certain other mental conditions exercise upon the legal effects of Acts. But there still remains another class of cases to be considered, where the determination of the will, although consciously exercised, is really influenced by means of "physical compulsion," "fear," "undue influence," "fraud," or "misrepresentation." These terms need, therefore, a brief explanation.

"Physical compulsion" and "fear."

48. "Physical compulsion" is said, for instance, but, of course, only as an illustration, to be used when the hand of a person is forcibly guided by another person in making a signature to a document.[1] "Fear" is the condition in which a man is placed who is threatened by another with injury to his person or property. It is noteworthy that the Indian Contract Act[2] goes beyond the English Law in defining what constitutes "coercion," a term which includes both "physical compulsion" and "fear" (*vis metusve* of the Roman Edict, or *duress* and *menace* of the English Common Law). It does so inasmuch as it does not require that the coercion should be exercised by or even known to the other party, nor that the person coerced should be the party whose consent is to be obtained, or in any way related to him.[3] In the former respect the Indian Act agrees with the Roman Law, which rescinded, with one exception, all obligations contracted by violence, from whomsoever the violence proceeded.[4] The

Elements of Law, sections 226—228. Sir F. Pollock considers these distinctions not only useless for practical purposes, but devoid of any philosophical merit (*vide* Remarks on section 62 of *Civil Wrongs Bill*). They are retained in the text because they are generally employed by writers on Jurisprudence, and it is as well that students should be acquainted with them.

[1] *Windscheid*, section 80, p. 216, note (1). As to modern English cases of compulsion, reference may be made to *Scott* v. *Sebright* (1886), 12 P. D. 21; and *Ford* v. *Stier*, (1896) Prob. 1.

[2] Section 15.

[3] *Pollock on Contracts*, p. 701.

[4] Dig. IV. 2, 9, 1; Pothier, *Law of Obligations*, Eng. trans, Vol. I., pp. 16, 17.

exception referred to the case put by Pomponius of a man falling into the hands of robbers and offering a passer-by a reward for his assistance to effect a rescue.[1] On the other hand, the Roman differed from the Indian and agreed with the English Law,[2] in refusing to recognize force or threats directed against a *stranger* to the contract as affording a ground for avoiding it. The threat by the Roman Law must have been applied to the person forced into a contract, either in regard to his own person or to that of some member of his family.[3] And so in English Law, threats against the tranquility or honour of a man's family vitiates the consent.[4]

"Undue influence," "fraud," and "misrepresentation" defined.

49. For an explanation of the other terms, the following definitions taken from the Indian Contract Act will suffice for the Indian student:—

"Undue influence"[5] is said to be employed in the following cases:—

(1.)—When a person in whom confidence is reposed by another, or who holds a real or apparent authority over that other, makes use of such confidence or authority for the purpose of obtaining an advantage over that other, which, but for such confidence or authority, he could not have obtained;

(2.)—When a person whose mind is enfeebled by old age, illness, or mental or bodily distress, is so treated as to make him consent to that to which, but for such treatment, he would not have consented, although such treatment may not amount to coercion.

"Fraud"[6] means and includes any of the following acts committed by a party to a contract, or with his connivance, or by his agent, with

[1] Dig. IV. 2, 9, 1.

[2] *Anson on Contracts*, Ch. IV., § 4, p. 174, 6th ed.

[3] Dig. IV. 2, 8, 3; Pothier, Vol. I., p. 17.

[4] *Williams* v. *Bayley*, L. R. 1 H. L. 200.

[5] Cf. Holland's *Jurisprudence*, p. 223, 4th ed. In connection with cases of "undue influence" oppressive dealings with "expectant heirs," or other persons in distressed circumstances may be referred to. See, for instance, *O'Rorke* v. *Bolingbroke* (1877), 2 App. Cas. 814; *Fry* v. *Lane* (1888), 40 Ch. D. 312; and *Raja Mokham Singh* v. *Raja Rup Singh* (1893), L. R. 20 Ind. App. 127.

[6] Cf. *Ibid.*, p. 195.

CHAP. IV.

intent to deceive another party thereto or his agent, or to induce him to enter into the contract:—

"(1.)—The suggestion, as a fact, of that which is not true, by one who does not believe it to be true;

(2.)—The active concealment of a fact by one having knowledge or belief of the fact;

(3.)—A promise made without any intention of performing it;

(4.)—Any other act fitted to deceive;

(5.)—Any such act or omission as the law specially declares to be fraudulent."

"Misrepresentation" means and includes—

(1) the positive assertion, in a manner not warranted by the information of the person making it, of that which is not true, though he believes it to be true;

(2) any breach of duty which, without an intent to deceive, gains an advantage to the person committing it, or any one claiming under him, by misleading another to his prejudice or to the prejudice of anyone claiming under him.

(3) causing, however innocently, a party to an agreement, to make a mistake as to the substance of the thing which is the subject of the agreement.

True ground for relief in such cases is absence of free consent.

50. In all the above cases the effect of the Act is not necessarily nullified by the compulsion, fear, undue influence, fraud, or misrepresentation to which the doer has been subjected. In each case there has been a real determination of the will, and the act is as much the act of the doer as any other act done under a different motive. *Coacta voluntas, voluntas est:* a consent extorted by violence is still a consent. But the law will not hold the doer responsible for the *consequences* of an act when done under circumstances such as those to which reference has been made, if he chooses to repudiate it; and the true ground for relief is that there has been no free consent on the part of the doer.[1] This is well put by Paulus in a passage which is often quoted. "If," says the Roman Jurist, "I have accepted an inheritance under the influence of fear, I am of opinion that I become heir, because

[1] *Windscheid*, Vol. I., section 80, pp. 215—217; Markby's *Elements of Law*, sections 254, 255.

although, if I had been free, I should have refused, yet I did consent, though under compulsion (*coactus volui*). But the Praetor will give me relief."[1] Where, however, a man is not physically constrained, as, for instance, where he can at his free option do a thing or not, the maxim *volenti non fit injuria* (to one consenting no wrong is done) applies.[2] So, also, it is no fraud in the eye of the law, as affording a ground for relief, to deceive the deceiver (*fraus non est fallere fallentem*). This maxim was acted upon in a case where a debtor combined with one of his creditors in fraud upon the others, and the creditor subsequently broke trust.[3]

(c) Third essential element of an Act. Manifestation of the will.

51. The third essential element of an act is the manifestation or expression of the will, which may be express or tacit, and may be manifested or expressed by the party willing himself, or through the agency of a third person, in which case the act of the agent is regarded as the act of his principal (*qui facit per alium facit per se:* he who does anything by the instrumentality of another, does it by himself). The manifestation may also be formal or informal, and the Law frequently prescribes the exact form in which the manifestation or expression shall take place. Where such a provision of the Law exists, no other form of manifestation can be regarded as producing legal results. Thus, according to sect. 54 of the Transfer of Property Act, 1882, for India, in the case of a sale of immovable property of the value of Rs. 100 or upwards, and in the case of a sale of a reversion or other intangible thing, there must be a writing, which must also be registered under Act III. of 1877. In the case of a tacit manifestation the surrounding circumstances have to be looked at to see what light they throw upon the action.

May be formal or informal.

[1] Dig. IV. 3, 21.

[2] Per Lord Bramwell in *Membery* v. *G. W. Ry. Co.*, 14 App. Cases, 179. But see note (5), par. 57, *ante*, as regards oppressive bargains with expectant heirs and persons in distressed circumstances.

[3] *Woodford* v. *Multon*, Cary, 13.

CHAP. IV.

Juristic Acts.

52. Where the legal result follows because that result was itself contemplated, the Act is variously called by English writers a "Juristic Act," or "act in the law." It is defined by Windscheid as "a manifestation of the will of a private individual directed to the origin, extinction, or modification of rights."[1]

Requisites of.

53. These "Juristic Acts" must exhibit, in common with all acts (*Handlungen*) which we have previously considered, the characteristics of an act of will. There must be a conscious determination of the will, and there must be a strict agreement between the will and its expression. The legal result is also nullified or modified by the existence of error, compulsion, fear, fraud, or any circumstance preventing the free exertion of the will. These "Juristic Acts" may also be performed, for the most part, by representatives or agents, and may either be unilateral, where the will of one party only is active, or bilateral, where there is a concurrence of two or more wills to produce the effect of the act. The form of the act must conform to any special provision of the law on the subject, but where no form is prescribed the determination of the will may be expressed by a mere course of conduct. The capacity to perform a "Juristic Act" may also be restricted by the law, as in the case of persons under a certain age.[2]

"Void" or "voidable" Acts.

54. "Juristic Acts" which are wanting in the essential requirements of such acts are a mere nullity (*Nichtigkeit*), and are regarded for all legal purposes as void from the beginning. Where, however, the deficiency is one which may be supplied

[1] *Pandekten*, Vol. I., section 69, p. 176.

[2] Cf. Holland's *Jurisprudence*, pp. 97—99. Thus, also, under the Code of Civil Procedure for British India (Act XIV. of 1882), an agreement to give time for the satisfaction of a judgment debt is declared to be *void*, even if made for consideration, unless made with the *sanction* of the Court which passed the decree: sect. 257A. And see *Dan Bahadar Singh* v. *Anandi Prasand*, 18 Allah. 435.

by a subsequent change of circumstance, as where the defective authority of an agent is subsequently rectified, or which may be waived by the party to be bound, as in the case of fraud or compulsion, the Act is not absolutely void (*i.e.*, fails, as Windscheid says, to realise the legal effect contemplated, just as if it had never taken place), but is only voidable; that is to say, open to attack (*Anfechtbarkeit*) by the party sought to be bound by it.[1]

"Voidable Acts" may be subsequently ratified.

55. "Voidable Acts" in the above sense are Acts which may be deprived of their legal effect at the option of a party who is intended to be affected by them. But a person who has an option to do a thing is not bound to do it. Thus, a person who, if he chooses to take the proper steps for that purpose, may counteract or modify the legal results of a "voidable act," chooses rather to affirm or recognise it as a valid act, is perfectly competent to do so. This subsequent affirmation or recognition of an act which was originally "voidable" is called ratification, the effect of which is to give validity to the Act from its inception (*omnis ratihabitio retrotrahitur et mandato priori æquiparatur:* every ratification relates back and is equal to a prior command).[2] But where an act is not merely "voidable," but "void," it is regarded in law as if it had never taken place; and it is consequently incapable of being validated by subsequent ratification, in accordance with the maxim *quod ab initio non valet in tractu temporis non convalescit:* that which is bad (or invalid) from the beginning is not cured (or rendered convalescent) by length of time. "Convalescence," as defined by Savigny, is the aspect which an Act assumes when, by the removal of an intervening hindrance or impediment, it is entitled to its full legal effect. In this connection there are two important legal

"Ratification" explained.

[1] Windscheid's *Pandekten*, Vol. I., section 82, pp. 220—228.

[2] It has been doubted whether this maxim applies in the case of a will. *Mills* v. *Millward*, 15 P. D. 20; 59 L. J. 23; *Boulton* v. *Lambert*, 41 Ch. D. 295; 58 L. J. Ch. 425.

CHAP. IV.

maxims to be borne in mind. Thus, it is said, *confirmatio est nulla ubi donum præcedens est invalidum*: confirmation is of no avail where the original grant is invalid. But, on the other hand, there is this rule: *confirmatio omnis supplet defectus, licet id quod actum est ab initio non valuit*: confirmation supplies all defects, although that which had been done was not originally of avail. What has been said above will explain how these rules are to be applied.

"Juristic Acts" are constituted of different facts.

56. The will manifested or expressed in a "Juristic Act" may be concerned with various matters of fact (called the *Inhalt* or "purport of the will") which may either be "essential," "accidental," or "natural" (*essentialia, accidentalia*, or *naturalia negotii*).[1]

"Essential facts."

57. The *essentialia negotii* are those facts which constitute the very essence of the Act, without which it could not exist; for instance, in the case of a sale contract, that the purchaser shall have a given thing at a given price.[2] The Roman Law styled such conditions, *juris conditiones*, or *conditiones quae tacite*, or *ri ipsa negotio insunt*.

"Accidental facts."

58. The *accidentalia negotii* are those facts which are not essential and which must be proved, as, for instance, that the purchase-money in a sale contract shall be payable with interest from the date of the conclusion of the contract.[3]

"Natural facts."

59. The *naturalia negotii* are those facts which the Law itself presumes from the Act, and which the parties would have presumably expressed in the same sense had their

1 Windscheid's *Pandekten*, Vol. I., section 85, p. 237.

2 *Ibid.*, note 1; Ahrens' *Philosophie des Rechts*, Bd. I., p. 359: Wein, 1870; Holland's *Jurisprudence*, p. 103, 4th ed.

3 Windscheid's *Pandekten*, Vol. I., section 85, p. 237, note 1. As regards the general law regulating the allowance of interest, the Indian student must refer to Act XXXII. of 1839. Cf. also section 55 (4, *b*) of the Transfer of Property Act, IV. of 1882.

minds been directed to the subject: *e.g.*, according to the Roman Law, that the property in goods did not pass till the price had been paid.[1]

CHAP. IV.

"Resolutive" and "suspensive" or "inherent" conditions.

60. The legal effect of the act may also be controlled by the will of the parties to it, by the addition, for instance, of a condition upon which the effect of the act is made to depend. The condition may refer to the origin, extinction, or alteration of the Juristic Act itself, or to the annulment of another cotemporaneous act. In the last-named instance, the condition, according to Windscheid and many other German Jurists, is called a "resolutive condition" (*negotium sub condicione resolvitur*), and all other conditions are called "suspensive" (*negotium condicione suspenditur*) or "precedent."[2] The effect of the former is to make an obligation cease when it is accomplished, and that of the latter to suspend the obligation until the accomplishment of the condition in question.[3] Lord Justice James is responsible for naming another class of conditions which "qualify, restrain, or charge an estate" as "conditions inherent."[4]

Conditions may be past, present, or future.

61. The condition may also refer to something in the past, present, or future. Thus, "if Titius was Consul," or "if Mævius lives," or "if Titius will become Consul." It may also contemplate something which must happen, or which is impossible. In the former case the legal result would follow upon the happening of the contemplated event; in the latter the act itself would be devoid of all legal effect (*si impossibilis condicio obligationibus adjiciatur, nihil valet stipulatio*: if an impossible condition is annexed to the obligation, the stipulation is invalid).[5] A condition may be impossible

Impossible conditions.

[1] Windscheid's *Pandekten*, Vol. I., section 85, p. 237, note 1.

[2] *Ibid.*, section 86, pp. 241, 242; Ahrens, p. 360.

[3] *Pothier*, Eng. trans., p. 129; Puchta, *Institutionen*, Vol. II., § 204, pp. 566, 567, 5th ed.; Baron, *Pandekten*, § 53, s. 87.

[4] *Ex parte Collins* (1875), L. R. 10 Ch. at p. 372.

[5] Inst. 3, 19, 11. See *post*, §§ 209, 210, and 224.

CHAP. IV.

either with reference to natural Physical Laws, or to a provision of the Positive Law. Or, again, it may be so in an absolute or relative sense. Thus an estate bequeathed to A. on condition that he shall walk a hundred miles in an hour,[1] or that he shall touch the heavens with his finger,[2] are both void bequests on grounds of physical impossibility, and in an *absolute* sense. A condition is impossible in a *relative* sense if it is impossible only in given circumstances, as, for instance, if a horse I promised to sell was dead at the time of the promise.[3] But a bequest to B., on condition that he shall murder C. is void, because it is contrary to a provision of the Positive Law which forbids murder.[4] The Roman Law drew a distinction between impossible conditions when stipulated for between living persons, and those which were annexed to bequests. In the former case the expression of the will was devoid of all legal effect, and was treated as a nullity (*ad impossibilia nulla datur obligatio:* no obligation is attached to what is impossible). But in the case of bequests the impossible condition was simply ignored, and the bequest itself was maintained as if no such condition had been annexed to it (*impossibiles condiciones testamento adscriptas pro nullis habendas:* impossible conditions annexed to a testament are held to be invalid).[5] This distinction is no longer preserved, as we have seen, in the Indian Succession Act.

While condition is in suspense, Act is binding on parties.

62. While the condition is still in suspense the rights and liabilities of the parties affected by the Juristic Act are simply in abeyance (*pendente conditione nondum debetur, sed spes est debitum iri*). If the act has not already produced a

[1] The Indian Succession Act, section 113 (*Illustration* (*a*)). See also section 25, Indian *Transfer of Property Act*, 1882.

[2] Just. *Inst.* 3, 19, 11.

[3] *Ibid.*, 3, 19, 1.

[4] Indian Succession Act, section 14 (*Illustration* (*a*)).

[5] Dig. XXXV. 1, 3, 4; *Windscheid*, section 94, pp. 270, 271; Ahrens, Bd. I. p. 361.

legal effect there is at least a prospect of it doing so, and until the event happens upon which its legal operation depends, or the time fixed for its happening expires, the party who is to bear the consequences of that event cannot deprive the other party of the possible result arising from the fulfilment of the condition, by doing something meanwhile in derogation of his promise.[1] On the other hand, if the thing, which is the object of the conditional obligation, entirely perishes before the accomplishment of the condition, it will be to no purpose that the condition is accomplished afterwards; for the accomplishment of the condition cannot confirm the obligation which no longer subsists, for there cannot be any obligation without something which is the subject of it.[2] So, when a bargain is made for goods "on arrival" by a certain ship, if the ship is wrecked or arrives without the goods, without default of the seller, the bargain is at an end.[3] The principle underlying such cases was explained in *Taylor* v. *Caldwell*[4] thus: "Where from the nature of the contract it appears that the parties must, from the beginning, have known that it could not be fulfilled unless, when the time for the fulfilment of the contract arrived, some particular specified thing continued to exist, so that when entering into the contract they must have contemplated such continued existence as the foundation of what was to be done; then, in the absence of any express or implied warranty that the thing shall exist, the contract is not to be considered a positive contract, but subject to the implied condition that the parties shall be excused in case, before breach, performance becomes impossible from the perishing of the thing without default of the contractor,"[5] that is to say, by causes over which the contractor has no control. The

Where subject of obligation perishes before accomplishment of condition.

[1] Windscheid's *Pandekten*, Vol. I., section 89, pp. 248, 249.

[2] Pothier, *Law of Obligations*, Eng. trans., Vol. I., p. 127.

[3] *Boyd* v. *Siffkin* (1809), 2 Camp. 326.

[4] (1863), 32 L. J. Q. B. 164; followed in *Howell* v. *Coupland* (1876), 1 Q. B. D. 258.

[5] See *post*, § 224.

Indian Specific Relief Act, however, does not regard a contract as wholly impossible of performance because a portion of its subject-matter, *existing at its date*, has ceased to exist at the time of performance (§ 13).

Time.

63. Sometimes in consequence of a provision of the Law, or of a condition attached to the "Juristic Act," Rights or Duties come into existence (*terminus a quo*) or cease (*terminus ad quem*) after a certain time has elapsed.[1] Thus, under the Indian Contract Act,[2] where no time for performance of a promise is specified in the contract, the engagement *must* be performed within a *reasonable* time. What constitutes a reasonable time is a question of fact to be determined by the Court in each particular case. So also under the Indian Limitation Act, at the determination of the period limited to any person by that Act for instituting a suit for possession of any property, his right to such property is deemed to be extinguished.[3] Or again, I may agree to sell a horse to B., and B. may promise to pay me the price of the animal one month after delivery. Here my Right to demand payment of the price, and B.'s Duty to make it, will arise at the determination of the period agreed upon.

Measurements of time, how computed.

64. In calculating measurements of time for juridical purposes, fractions of a day are generally disregarded (*dies coeptus pro completo habetur*),[4] and the day is limited to the usual hours of business prevailing at the place where performance

[1] Markby's *Elements of Law*, section 280, p. 144; Ahrens, Bd. I., p. 362.

[2] Section 46.

[3] Section 28.

[4] For some purposes a Court will consider fractions of a day. *Ex parte Farquhar*, Mont. & McA. 7. Where, for instance, it is necessary to show which of two events first took place; therefore the Court will regard the particular hour at which a defendant dies, so as to see whether execution issued previously to his demise. *Clinch* v. *Smith*, 8 D. P. C. 337. So also, in support of a commission of bankruptcy, by admitting evidence, that the act of bankruptcy, though on same day, was previously to the issuing, *i.e.*, awarding and sealing commission. *Wydown's Case*, 14 Ves. 80.

is to be made. Thus, if A. promises to deliver goods at B.'s warehouse on the 1st January, and on that day A. brings the goods to B.'s warehouse, but after the usual hour for closing it, and they are refused; here A. will not be deemed to have performed his promise.[1] But if A. were bound to pay a sum of money to B. three days after notice, and notice were given to B. at ten o'clock in the morning of the third, it would not be necessary for A. to make payment by ten o'clock of the morning of the 6th. He could make the payment at any time during business hours on the 6th.[2] Moreover, in reckoning days when Rights or Duties are made conditional upon the lapse of a certain period of time after a certain event, the day on which the event happens is now generally excluded.[3] In the Roman law the day when the event happened was considered the first of the prescribed period, and the last was reckoned by counting from, and inclusive of the first. In a case in which the expiration of the time conferred a right or a capacity, it was sufficient that the day had begun (*dies coeptus pro completo habetur*). Thus in the case of a person born on the 1st January, he acquired a capacity to execute a will on the commencement of the 31st day of December of the year in which he completed his fourteenth year. But when the expiration of the time caused the loss of a right by reason of non-usage, it was necessary that the day should have ended. So a *bonorum possessio* was only deemed to be lost if the right had not been exercised during the *whole* of the last day of the period prescribed for its exercise.[4]

[1] Section 47, Indian Contract Act (*Illustration*).

[2] Markby's *Elements of Law*, section 284, p. 145.

[3] *Ibid.*, section 286. The student who desires to make himself acquainted with the historical development of the juridical notion of the *civil day*, would find much interesting information collected in G. Bilfinger's *Der bürgerliche Tag*, Stuttgart, 1888. But this *brochure* should be read with the criticism by Hölder upon it, published in the 14th vol. of the *Kritische Vierteljahresschrift für Gesetzgebung und Rechtswissenschaft*, p. 321.

[4] Baron, *Pandekten*, § 74, p. 125.

CHAP. IV.

Meaning of "month" and "year."

65. The word "month" or "year" is now understood to mean a calendar month or year; and this is the rule which the Indian Legislature has adopted in the interpretation of similar words occurring in legislative enactments.[1] In modern legislation and practice, the movable month is counted from such a day of one month of the calendar to the day bearing the same date in the following month, or in the month in which a specified term expires.[2] So a period of time is usually treated as a continuous or consecutive series of years, months, or days,[3] each day comprised in the period being reckoned, without considering what acts it was possible or impossible to execute on such or such a given day. But in the Roman Law there were exceptions for certain judicial acts, in regard to which the time fixed by law for their accomplishment (one year at most) was composed exclusively of days on which the person interested was in a condition to act.[4] Even in England, prior to the Rules of 1875 passed under the Judicature Acts, in reckoning the days within which an appeal had to be entered, Sundays were excluded from the computation.[5] But since the Rules of 1875 Sundays are not excluded.[6] In India if the last day for filing a suit, appeal, or application falls on a Sunday or a *dies non*, that day is to be excluded from the computation.

[1] Section 3, clauses 29 and 59, Act X. of 1897.

[2] *The Pandects*, by J. E. Goudsmit, LL.D., translated by R. de Tracy-Gould, § 78, p. 219, note (*z*); Baron, *Pandekten*, § 74, p. 125.

[3] *Brown* v. *Johnson*, Car. & M. 440; 10 M. & W. 331.

[4] Dig. 38, 15, 2; 44, 3, 1.

[5] *Ex parte Hicks, In re Ball*, L. R. 20 Eq. 143; 44 L. J. Bk. 106; *Ex parte Hall, In re Alven*, 16 Ch. D. 501; 50 L. J. Ch. 400.

[6] *Ex parte Viney, In re Gilbert*, 4 Ch. D. 794; 46 L. J. Bk. 80.

CHAPTER V.

THE SOURCES OF LAW.

66. In order to know the Law, it is necessary that the student should know how to discover it and where to discover it. He should be able to comprehend not only what constitutes Law, but from what sources that Law is to be ascertained (*fontes e quibus juris notitia hauritur*). The first branch of this knowledge has already been discussed. It now remains to consider the second.

Legislation the primary source of law in modern States.

67. From the definition of Law which has been previously given, it is natural that, in civilised States of the modern type, we should look to Legislation as the primary form in which the sovereign authority of any independent political community declares its will as Law. This function of sovereignty may be either exercised directly or delegated to a subordinate body. The Indian Councils Act of 1861 may be cited as a notable instance of the direct exercise of legislative functions by the supreme authority of the British Parliament with respect to India.

Examples of subordinate legislatures.

68. Examples of legislative functions being delegated are afforded by the Colonial and Indian Legislatures, which derived their authority by delegation from the supreme sovereignty of England. But in the Colonies, although theoretically the supreme authority of the Queen and British Parliament is not denied, any active interference on the part of the latter in matters of Colonial legislation is practically unknown, and would probably lead to complications if

CHAP. V.

attempted to be enforced. Hence it is that powers of the most general kind are conferred upon most of the Colonial Legislative Assemblies, as, for instance, upon that of the Dominion of Canada,[1] and the tendency of English judges is to hold that no Act of the Imperial Parliament is intended to extend to the whole of the British Empire, a rule of construction which is only to be departed from when the contrary intention is unmistakeably expressed.[2] In regard to India, the functions of the Council of the Governor-General are expressly limited by Act of Parliament, and, apart from the control which the British Parliament has thus reserved to itself,[3] the supreme sovereignty of England is recognised by the provision empowering Her Majesty, through the Secretary of State for India in Council, to express her disallowance of any legislative enactment passed in India (24 & 25 Vict. c. 67, s. 21). In practice no legislative measure of any general importance is introduced into the Governor-General's Council without the previous sanction of the Secretary of State for India in Council.

Subordinate legislatures frequently allowed to delegate their functions.

69. As a delegated authority cannot, without express permission, re-delegate its authority to another (*delegatus non potest delegare*), so a subordinate Legislative Assembly must exercise its powers itself, unless it has received permission from the supreme sovereign authority to delegate them to any other person or body of persons.[4] In India such a power of delegation has been conferred upon the Governor-General in Council subject to the previous assent of the Crown, and thus, while the Council of the Governor-General

[1] 3 & 4 Vict. c. 35.

[2] Cf. *The New Zealand Loan Co.* v. *Morrison*, (1898) A. C. 349.

[3] *Vide* 3 & 4 Will. IV. c. 85, section 51.

[4] See the remarks of the Privy Council in the leading Indian case of *The Queen* v. *Burah*, L. R. V. Indian App. 178 (see p. 194). This case is also important as showing how far Courts of Justice can question the exercise of legislative functions by a subordinate legislature (see pp. 193, 194).

of India can legislate for all British India, there are also Provincial Councils which possess legislative functions within their respective territorial limits. At the present moment there are six such councils, namely, those of Madras, Bombay, Calcutta, the North-Western Provinces and Oudh, the Punjab and Burma. These subordinate bodies are aptly styled by Austin "reservoirs fed from the source of all Law, the Supreme Legislature, and again emitting the borrowed waters which they received from that Fountain of Law."

Quasi legislative functions exercised by Municipal Committees and other bodies.

70. *Quasi* legislative functions are also at times exercised by particular persons or a particular body of persons by virtue of a provision contained in some special Act of the Legislature. Thus in India the Lieutenant-Governor of a Province is frequently authorised by an Act of the Indian Legislature to make Rules consistent with its general provisions,[1] and Municipal bodies constituted under Act XIII. of 1884 enjoy the same privilege within certain prescribed limits and subject to certain specified conditions.[2] The Chief Court of the Punjab, under Act XVIII. of 1884 (§ 14), and the various Chartered High Courts under their Charters, possess a similar power of framing rules.[3] When a *quasi* legislative power of this kind is exercised in the manner and within the limits prescribed by the sovereign authority, the rules so framed acquire the full force of law, precisely as if they had been embodied in the legislative enactments under which they are made.[4]

[1] *Vide* section 50, Act IV. of 1872; sections 2 and 3, Act XV. of 1875; section 55, Act I. of 1879; section 25, Act III. of 1880; section 55 (2), Act XX. of 1883; section 154 of Act XIII. of 1884; and section 17, Act XVII. of 1887.

[2] *Vide* sections 119—122.

[3] See also section 254 of Act VI. of 1882.

[4] In many Acts empowering Rules to be framed this is expressly stated (*vide* section 10, Act VII. of 1875; section 30, Act VIII. of 1875; and section 57, Act I. of 1879). But even where no such express provision is made, the same effect would follow, provided the Rules were consistent with

CHAP. V.

Legislation only characteristic of political communities of advanced type.

71. But the creation of Laws by means of Legislation is only characteristic of political societies of an advanced type, where Law ceases to be a bundle of Customs or Traditions, and becomes a Science.[1] In earlier archaic societies we would look in vain for this source of Law. In them the rules which, for all practical purposes, possess the force of Law in the true sense of the term, as regulating human actions so far as those actions are intended to create Rights or impose Duties, are generated in a very different way.

Growth of Custom.

72. Law, in the sense of the English Analytical Jurists (Bentham and Austin), involves the idea of a Command emanating from a Sovereign. And we have seen[2] that the different terms used to express Law amongst the leading races of antiquity as well as of modern Europe all embody the same fundamental notion of *command*, *protection*, or *authority*. But in the early stages of civilisation we find nothing exactly corresponding to this notion. The idea of a sovereign authority issuing commands to its subjects regulating their private Rights and Duties *inter se*, is in truth a development of a much later age. In primitive times men grouped themselves together into communities for

the enactment under which they were made, and fulfilled the other conditions prescribed by that enactment. *Hardcastle on the Construction of Statutes*, p. 153; *Jurisdiction of Courts* by Horace Hawes, section 7, p. 10. *Cf.* No. 8, *Punjab Record*, 1887, Cr. Rulings. The reasonableness of Rules so framed, provided they are strictly confined to the purpose for which they are authorised to be made, is not examinable by the Judges, and the Rules will be binding whether they are reasonable and proper Rules or not. *Bailey* v. *Williamson*, L. R. VIII. Q. B. 118. For instances where Rules have been declared to be *ultra vires* of the Act under which they purported to be framed, see No. 65, *Punjab Record*, 1882; No. 40, *Punjab Record*, 1884. See also *Hardcastle on the Construction of Statutes*, 150. It is important to bear in mind that when authority is given by any Statute to make a By-Law or Rule, and the Statute is subsequently repealed, the By-Law or Rule ceases to be operative. If it be intended to re-enact the Statutes, it is necessary to keep the By-Law or Rule in force by express provision. Lumley *On By-Laws*, p. 65.

[1] The *Law of Contracts*, by J. I. Clarke-Hare, Boston, 1887, p. 4.

[2] Page 13.

purposes of mutual protection, and the fear of aggression induced concert for defence.[1] In such communities the common-sense principle, that the interests of the individual must be subordinated to those of the community in which he lives, receives naturally very early expression. The individual is thus looked upon as a mere member of that group or body which constitutes the Whole. But to preserve the whole, a proper equilibrium of the Parts must be maintained, and to do this a certain order has to be observed. It would be impossible for any community to be preserved for any length of time if this were not the case. But the spirit of cohesion which draws men together, teaches them also to submit to a certain control of their actions, although at first this control may be of the most shadowy description. By degrees that which, in its inception, was almost imperceptible, becomes by constant usage and practice so impressed upon the public mind, that it is looked upon as a binding rule of conduct, an infraction of which would be sure to meet with strong disapproval in the community of which the person committing a breach may be a member. In small communities such a disapproval on the part of the general body, or a major part of that body, cannot be disregarded; and thus the rule established in this imperceptible way acquires, in course of time, a force which is simply irresistible. "The Law," as Adolf Trendelenburg says, "is in the Moral Whole the sum of those general rules of action by which it happens that the Moral Whole and its constituent members can be maintained and further developed."[2] In fact, it is only when a mastery has been established over Inequalities and Individuals, that the road is cleared for the establishment of Law.[3] It is thus also that customs affecting private Rights grow up. What has been done once supplies a rule

[1] The *Law of Contracts*, by J. I. Clarke-Hare, Boston, 1887, p. 2.

[2] *Naturrecht*, section 46, p. 83.

[3] Puchta, *Cursus der Institutionen* 1, section IX. p. 17.

CHAP. V.

of action for another occasion, and people are prone, especially in archaic societies, to adopt a rule which has already been applied under similar circumstances, rather than undergo the labour of thinking out a new one for themselves.[1] The rule gains strength and sanctity by gradual repetition, and when at length it is matured and approved by a long past (*antiquitus probata et servata tenaciter consuetudo*),[2] it is dignified into a Custom, which may thus be said to be truly the "unconcious result of instinctive preferences and inarticulate convictions."[3] It is this long usage (*longævus usus*) hardened into a custom which reflects the conviction of the people that what they do is law, and in this conviction lies the reason of the binding force of Customary Law.[4] In the formation of a particular Custom, conflicting interests may at times have struggled for the mastery, and the theory of a painless development of Right evolved by Puchta may be open to the sharp criticism of his countryman Ihering, who pronounces it to be in truth a mere romantic idea, resting upon a false idealisation of past conditions.[5] But the credit of recognising custom as a source, and, in early stages of civilisation, the only source of law, is nevertheless due to the historical school of Germany, of which Savigny and Puchta are the two most celebrated representatives.

Importance of Custom in India.

73. The importance of giving due effect to Custom in India, and especially in provinces like the Punjab, where the people are extremely simple in their habits, and where a large proportion of the inhabitants are agriculturists, to whom the Hindu and Muhammadan Laws are more or less foreign,

[1] We may illustrate this with reference to the Homeric *Themistes*, a body of precedents founded upon a series of individual decisions—the word *themis* meaning "what has been laid down," that is, a decision in a particular case. Jebb's *Introduction to Homer*, Chapter II., section 10.

[2] Dig. I. 3, 32, 33, 35.

[3] Holmes's *Common Law*, p. 36.

[4] *Windscheid*, Vol. I., section 15, p. 42.

[5] *Battle for Right*, p. 21, Mr. Ashworth's translation.

cannot be over-estimated. It was Sir Henry Maine who first drew attention to the phase which custom had assumed in India, and to the impossibility of applying the Austinian conception of Law to the state of facts which were there found to exist, especially in the Punjab, at the period of our conquest. Indeed, under his interesting treatment of the subject, Customary Law assumed an entirely new garb, and became in truth "a new phenomenon in the juristic sky."[1] It is now well known that the written Hindu Law itself gives the most unqualified recognition to Customary Law, which it pronounces to be "transcendental law." The king who knows the revealed Law is enjoined by the Code of Manu "to inquire into the particular usage of trades and the rules of certain families, and to establish their particular laws."[2] Indeed, the Brahminical Law itself is mainly based on Custom, interpreted, it is true, from a Brahminical point of view. And if the Muhammadan Law of the Sharah does not expressly recognize custom, actual practice in this respect has overridden the written law. Thus, even amongst Muhammadan noblemen of otherwise unquestionable orthodoxy, we find the rules of the Koran as to Inheritance departed from, and females are at times entirely excluded from inheritance, while in other cases the widow in default of male issue takes a life interest in the entire estate of her deceased husband, rather than a specified fractional share thereof, as prescribed by the Koran.[3] In short, Jurisprudence in India, and particularly in the Punjab, may be described as a mosaic in which the maxims and principles of several Systems of Law—the English, Muhammadan, and Hindu—alternate with the Customs and Usages of towns and villages.

[1] Kant's *Philosophy of Law*, p. 237.

[2] *Manu*, Chapter IX., section 104; and Cf. Chapter VIII., section 416.

[3] No. 13, *Punjab Record*, 1875; No. 1, *Punjab Record*, 1876; No. 17, *Punjab Record*, 1882; No. 64, *Punjab Record*, 1884; No. 89, *Punjab Record*, 1886.

CHAP. V.

Essentials of a valid Custom.

74. To constitute a valid Custom, it is now generally held that the usage which goes to support it must be ancient, invariable and reasonable, and, being in derogation of the general rules of Law, it must be construed strictly.[1] But the "reasonableness" of a Custom does not mean that it must be judged according to our modern views of suitability. Many customs which may not be in accord with our individual notions of suitability may and are constantly still enforced. Thus the custom of "Gavelkind," which prevails in parts of Kent, in England, would probably not be regarded by many of us as very reasonable in this broad sense; and the same might be said of some mercantile customs in England and of many village customs existing in India. But what is really meant when it is said that a Custom must be reasonable is, that it must not be opposed to the fundamental laws of morality or of the State in which it is asserted to exist.[2]

At what moment a Custom becomes Law.

75. It has been a matter of controversy at what moment a Custom becomes Law. Consistently with the general principle that Custom is only transmuted into Positive Law when it is adopted as such, either by being expressly embodied in Statutes promulgated by the sovereign authority, or implicitly by decisions of the Courts of Justice which are enforced by the power of the State,[3] Austin's view was that Customary Laws are not Positive Laws *until their existence as such is declared by the decisions of the Courts.*[4] But this view is clearly erroneous. Courts of Justice do not *make* Laws; their province is to *ascertain* and *declare* what the Law is. They have recourse, therefore, to the written Law where such exists, and where it does not, or where it

[1] *Hur Pershad* v. *Sheo Dyal* (1876), *Privy Council Judgments*, compiled by Baldeva Ram Dave, p. 51.

[2] *Windscheid*, Vol. I., sect. 16, p. 46; Weiske's *Rechtslexicon*, Bd. IV., p. 846 (7), tit. *Gewohnheitsrecht*; see also sect. 7 of Act IV. of 1872, otherwise called the "Punjab Laws Act."

[3] Student's edition, p. 19.

[4] *Ibid.*, p. 270.

fails to supply a rule of decision for the particular case, Courts are obliged to resort to the other recognized sources from which a knowledge of the Law is to be obtained. Now one of these sources, as we have seen, is Custom; and when a Court finds a Custom to exist and to fulfil the general requirements of a valid custom, it acts upon it, not because it is convinced that it *ought* to constitute the Law for the future, but because it is satisfied that it *is* the Law which has hitherto prevailed on the subject, and which, therefore, being ancient, invariable, and reasonable, ought to be maintained as Law for the future. The judicial decision in any given case merely manifests *what* is the Custom, and thereby brings it home to the "consciousness of the people." But it does not transmute the Custom into Law for the first time.[1]

76. In addition to the two sources we have mentioned above, there are others which are generally considered under the heads of "Judiciary Law," "Scientific Law," "Equity and Good Conscience." But I think it would be more convenient to consider these sources as falling more appropriately under one or other of the heads *Oblique Legislation* or *Supplementary Legislation*.[2] Other sources of Law.

77. Under "Oblique Legislation" I would include most of the so-called Judge-made Law. It is "an oblique" form of law-making, because Judges never profess to *make* Laws directly. But frequently gaps occur in the Laws of most countries; and where Judges are unable to discover a distinct rule of Law applicable to the case before them, they are obliged to invent a rule, either by analogy to some other recognised rule of Law, or by having recourse to what are styled the "rules of equity and good conscience," constituting Oblique Legislation.

[1] Cf. Holland's *Jurisprudence*, pp. 53, 54; Weiske's *Rechtslexicon*, Bd. IV., pp. 847, 848.

[2] Lightwood's *Nature of Positive Law*, pp. 412, 413.

CHAP. V. the fourth root of Law according to the classification of Manu,[1] and which supply a fertile and inexhaustible source of invention.[2] Judges in India are particularly enjoined by the Legislature to have recourse to these so-called "rules"; but where they are to be discovered is conveniently left to the Courts themselves to find out—precisely as Selden cynically observed, the Equity of English Courts was measured by the length of the Chancellor's foot.[3] We may say, however, in the language of Hindu lawyers, that "they must satisfy our sense of equity, and be acceptable to reason,"[4] and this is, perhaps, as near as we can approach to any definite statement on the subject. The Justice, however, which a Judge is required to dispense in dispensing Equity is not, be it remembered, of a different kind from that on which Law reposes. Legal Justice and Equity are not opposed to each other, but identical. The Judge may apply to exceptional circumstances an exceptional Law, but the Justice he is to administer is the ordinary Justice of the case.[5] In the technical language of English lawyers, *Equity follows the Law* and does not *subvert* it.[6] Thus, in its concurrent jurisdiction, in matters affecting *legal* estates, rights, and interests, Courts of Equity were strictly bound by the rules of Law and could

[1] *Institutes*, 2, 6.

[2] "The best measure of justice, equity and good conscience," said Sir J. F. Stephen in his speech on the Native Marriage Bill, "with which I am acquainted, and the one which is always resorted to by Indian Courts, is to be found in those parts of the decisions of English Courts, and they are very numerous, which deal not with technicalities peculiar to English Law and English Courts, but with broad and general principles founded on human nature itself, and recognised with various degrees of distinctness by all or nearly all civilised nations."—*Gazette of India*, 27th January, 1872. Kant looked at Equity from another standpoint, "as a dumb goddess who cannot claim a hearing of Right."—*Philosophy of Law*, p. 51.

[3] *Table Talk*, article "Equity."

[4] Tagore Law Lectures for 1880, p. 137.

[5] Lorimer's *Institutes of Law*, p. 219.

[6] Snell's *Equity Jurisprudence*, p. 17, 4th edition. The same thing was said of the Prætorian Law (*Dig.* xxii. 5, 14).

not deviate from them. So also in regard to *equitable* estates, rights, and interests, although not strictly *bound* by the rules of Law, they acted in analogy to these rules, wherever the analogy existed.[1]

Origin of Equity.

77a. There is indeed hardly any subject which has given rise to more controversy than the attempts to define the origin of an equitable jurisdiction as distinct from that exercised by the ordinary legal tribunals. The two great systems of Law in which this separation is most distinctively marked are the Roman and the English, and in both the same general causes operated to produce it. A lofty sense of self-consciousness, a veneration of a past of which either nation was justly proud, a contempt and scorn for foreign customs and usages, and a jealous attachment to existing principles and institutions, resting upon the recollection that the latter were the outcome of a long contest for political freedom, coupled with the publicity of political life and the general participation of the people in politics, were some of the principal factors which produced in Rome as in England that peculiar trait of national character which clings to established principles and institutions, even when they have ceased to correspond to the progress of the times.[2] We see this spirit of ingrained conservatism underlying the outward respect still paid to Laws which have grown too old for the actual needs of the people, and which are allowed to be circumvented, toned away, supplemented, and hedged in by fictions, constructions, and adaptations, although their place in the statute roll, consecrated by a hoary antiquity, is transmitted from generation to generation, untouched and unaltered. Thus in Rome the Twelve Tables survived down to a time when their very language ceased to be intelligently

[1] Snell's *Equity Jurisprudence*, p. 17, 4th edition.

[2] *Die Lehre vom Jus Naturale*, &c., Dr. Moritz Voigt, Vol. I., section 4, p. 26.

CHAP. V. understood; and so in England we find that trial by battle was only formally abolished by 59 Geo. 3, c. 46, after two unsuccessful attempts in 1768 and 1774, although the right to appeal to this procedure had not been resorted to for a considerable period.[1] But in Rome, as in England, while the Law in the abstract furnished the governing rule of decision, the Magistrates and Judges brought to the determination of concrete cases the application of principles deduced, or professing to be deduced, by a process of analogical reasoning from the established rules of law, which were at the same time in harmony with the popular sense of justice, and which expressed that spirit of *levelling* which, according to Sir Henry Maine, was the true tendency of the Roman "Equity."[2] The Roman Prætor administered this Equity as the keeper of the conscience of the Roman people, just as in the English system the Lord Chancellor did so as the keeper of the King's conscience; and in the exercise of this unique jurisdiction the Prætor, like the Lord Chancellor, arrogated to himself the discretional power of determining in what cases the strict Law was to give way to natural Equity. The Equity thus administered was intended to represent the most recent phase of the popular sense of Right; and under the attractive guise of giving effect to the spirit rather than to the letter of the Law, an elasticity and vigour were given to the administration of the Law which made it harmonize with existing needs, and thus to a large extent obviated the necessity of corrective legislation, at all times distasteful to the Roman people, by a fiction which the people had no desire to criticise too closely, that the justice administered by the Prætor was substantially in accord with the rules of the Civil Law when correctly interpreted. Thus the Prætorian Equity, no less than the Equity of the English Court of Chancery, may be

[1] Fitzjames Stephen's *History of the Criminal Law*, Vol. I., p. 249.

[2] *Ancient Law*, Chapter III., p. 59.

said, and with the same modicum of truth, to have *followed the law*. Chap. V.

77*b*. In granting or withholding relief an English Court of Equity acts in accordance with certain fixed rules,[1] and the three following golden maxims occur so frequently in practice that a few words may be said concerning them for the benefit of the Indian student. Leading maxims of Equity.

A.—He who seeks Equity must do Equity.

In illustration of this maxim may be mentioned the case which is frequently met with where a person having title to an estate stands by and knowingly suffers some third person who is ignorant of his title to expend money upon the estate either in buildings or in other improvements, and then afterwards asserts his title to the estate, together with the buildings or improvements. Here the third person, if he acted in *bonâ fide* ignorance of the other's title, would be entitled to be indemnified for his expenditure.[2] Applications of this rule are to be found in the Roman Law,[3] from whence indeed the rule was derived, and in the Indian Case Law.[4] But it must not be extended so as to affect matters unconnected with the transaction in respect of which the relief is sought.[5]

[1] The doctrines of this Court," said Lord Eldon, "ought to be as well settled and made as uniform, almost, as those of the Common Law, laying down fixed principles, but taking care that they are to be applied according to the circumstances of each case."—*Gee* v. *Pritchard*, 2 Swanst. 414.

[2] *Ramsden* v. *Dyson*, L. R. 1 H. L. 129; *Hallett* v. *Martin*, 24 Ch. D. 624.

[3] Just. *Inst.* II., 1, 30; *Dig.* 42, 1, 7, 12.

[4] Beng. L. Repts. Suppl., p. 595; IV. Mad. H. C. Repts. 312; No. 42 P. R. 1866; Cf. No. 2 P. R. 1885; 25 W. R. 205; *Ibid.*, 211; III. Cal. Law Repts., at p. 196; I. L. R. XV. Bom. 71. The principle has also been recognized by the Indian Legislature in Act XI. of 1855.

[5] *Wilkinson* v. *Fowkes*, 9 Hare, 592; *United States of America* v. *McRea*, L. R. 3 Ch. 79; 37 L. J. Ch. 129; *Gibson* v. *Goldsmid*, 24 L. J. Ch. 279; 3 Eq. Rep. 106.

CHAP. V.

B.—He who comes into Equity must come with clean hands.

The case of *Overton* v. *Banister*[1] is usually cited under this rule. That was a case where an infant, fraudulently concealing his age, obtained from his trustees part of a sum to which he was entitled on coming of age; and when of age, a few months after, he applied for and received the residue, and then afterwards instituted a suit to compel the trustees to pay over again the portion improperly paid during minority. But the Court held that the concealment of age was a fraud on the part of the infant, and that neither he nor his assignees could enforce payment over again by the trustees of the sum they had paid during the minority. It is upon the like principle that a party cannot come into Court and seek relief from his own fraud or from that of his ancestor.[2] But the rule does not prevent a person against whom an agreement is sought to be enforced from showing what the real circumstances were under which the agreement was entered into, even though it discloses the fraud of his own ancestor.[3]

C.—Delay defeats Equities; or Equity aids the vigilant, not the indolent.

The reason of this rule is best explained in the words of Lord Camden in *Smith* v. *Clay*:[4]—"A Court of Equity, which is never active in relief against conscience or public convenience, has always refused its aid to stale demands where the party has slept upon his rights for a great length of time. Nothing can call forth into activity but conscience, good faith, and reasonable diligence." Thus, in an Indian case where a *solehnama* in 1847 to which were parties the sons, daughters, and widow of a deceased Muhammadan proprietor, transferred the shares of two minor daughters in their

[1] Hare, 503. Cf. also *Nelson* v. *Stocker*, 4 De G. & J. 458, 464.

[2] 6 Suth. W. R. 287; 1 Hay's Repts. 528; 2 *Ibid.* 499; 3 Suth. W. R. 30; 4 Suth. W. R. 37; 15 Suth. W. R. 273.

[3] 19 Suth. W. R. 238. Cf. 20 *Ibid.* 112.

[4] 3 Bro. C. C. 640, note.

father's estate, having been executed by their mother, the widow, on their behalf; on the question whether the *solehnama* should be set aside, at the instance of the two daughters, on the ground of its having been beyond their mother's power to bind them, and of the instrument having been prejudicial to their interests, the evidence showed that it had been acted on and followed by possession, and that the daughters had, after attaining full age, allowed a lengthened period of twenty years to elapse without taking proceedings to dispute it. The Privy Council held that, if the mother had exceeded her powers in executing the *solehnama* on their behalf, and if they might, at one time, have had it set aside, their long acquiescence was sufficient to show ratification of the transaction, and the *solehnama* was upheld.[1]

Equity leans on side of fair dealing.

77*c*. But there is a class of case, by no means unfrequent, in which a well-known principle of law is difficult of application by reason of the facts of the case bringing it, so to say, on the disputed border land. It is here that a court of equity possesses a wide discretion in dispensing justice. "I have always thought," said Sir George Jessel, the late Master of the Rolls, referring to this class, "that in those cases where the Court is satisfied of the *bona fides* of a transaction, and its entire freedom from the mischief which the established principle of law intended to prevent, the Court should lean on the side of fair dealing, and should not so apply the principle of law as to make it comprise a case not within the mischief which it was intended to prevent without absolute necessity, the necessity being that of preserving the principle untouched for the guidance of mankind in their ordinary transactions."[2]

Supplementary Legislation.

78. "Supplementary Legislation" is also a form of Judge-made Law, and includes two sources, namely, *Interpretation*

[1] L. R. XV. Ind. App. 220.

[2] *Albion Steel and Wire Co.* v. *Martin*, 1 Ch. Div. at p. 584.

CHAP. V.

and the *Expression of Judiciary Law in Subsidiary Rules.* Owing to the natural imperfections of language it is often difficult for the Legislature to so express its intention as to place its meaning beyond all doubt. Here the task of the Judge begins. He has to extract, if possible, the true intention of the Legislature from the language employed by it. In doing so he does not, strictly speaking, either extend or modify the Law: he merely declares what is the true meaning of the Law. The less distinct Statutory Law is, the more difficult and the more important becomes the office of interpretation.

Interpretation.

79. To aid Judges in their often extremely difficult task certain rules of interpretation were laid down by the Roman Jurists which are still generally observed.[1] Thus the primary rule of all is, that the meaning of the legislator is to be sought in the actual words used by him, which are to be interpreted in their ordinary and natural meaning,[2] for *maledicta expositio quæ corrumpit textum* (that is a bad exposition which corrupts the text). This is called "Grammatical Interpretation," and where there is no ambiguity in the language employed, no other form of interpretation is permissible: as Paulus says—*quum in verbis nulla ambiguitas est, non debet admitti voluntatis quæstio:* when there is no ambiguity in the words, the question of intention ought not to be admitted.[3] But where the "Grammatical Interpretation" fails to meet the case—where, for instance, the words, either in themselves or in connection with the context, are ambiguous, or where they are capable of two distinct inter-

[1] It is perhaps right in this place to warn the reader in regard to the use of legal maxims. The terse form in which they are usually expressed is sometimes misleading, and at times, if literally understood, they might be held to include something which is really not intended to be included in them. See on this point the remarks of Lord Esher, late Master of the Rolls, in *Yarmouth* v. *France*, 19 Q. B. D. 653; 57 L. J. Q. B. 7.

[2] *Student's Austin*, p. 316.

[3] Dig. XXXII. 25, section 1; and *Ibid.* 69.

pretations each at variance with the other—it is obvious that we must call in some other aid; for *in verbis non verba sed res et ratio quærenda est* (in words, not the words but the thing and the meaning are to be inquired after). This aid is furnished by what is called "Logical Interpretation," which teaches us to observe the relation in which different portions of a law stand to each other: *ex antecedentibus et consequentibus fit optima interpretatio* (from that which goes before, and from that which follows, is derived the best interpretation);[1] the phraseology which is characteristic of the lawgiver; and how far the expressions used by him in one enactment may serve to explain similar expressions in a later enactment *in pari materiâ:* for *ubi eadem ratio ibi eadem lex* (where there is the same reason, there is the same law). In this form of interpretation there are two principal rules to be observed, both of which are taken from the Roman Law. The first is, that where the words of a law are ambiguous, that rendering is to be most preferred which would operate to some effect and prevent the law from becoming a dead letter (*in ambigua voce legis ea potissimum significatio accipienda est, quæ vitio caret*).[2] The second rule is, that where two interpretations are possible, that meaning should be preferred which is best suited to accomplish the object which the Legislature presumably or expressly had in view (*quotiens idem sermo duas sententias exprimit, ea potissimum accipiatur, quæ rei gerendæ aptior est*).[3] Lastly, when the language of a written law is doubtful, its meaning may be made clear by reference to, and consideration of, the circumstances attending its original enactment. This is called "Historical Interpretation," and the rule to be observed here is best stated by Lord Coke. The interpreter must consider what was the condition of the law before the new law was passed, what was the mischief or defect intended to be remedied, and what was the remedy which the Legisla-

[1] 2 Coke's Inst. 317. [2] Dig. I. 3, 19. [3] Dig. I. 17, 67.

ture had resolved to adopt to cure the mischief or defect. The true reason and remedy of the new law being ascertained, such a construction should be made as will suppress the mischief and advance the remedy; avoiding and suppressing subtle inventions and evasions, and giving life and vigour to the remedy proposed. Again, where a contemporaneous construction has been applied to a law, that construction is generally adopted as most likely to be in accordance with the intention of the Legislature: *contemporanea expositio est optima et fortissima in lege* (a contemporaneous exposition is the best and strongest in law).[1]

Expression of Judiciary Law in subsidiary rules.

80. The second form of "Supplementary Legislation" is found in the *Expression of Judiciary Law in Subsidiary Rules.* But where the "Subsidiary Rules" are made in the exercise of direct powers of legislation conferred by the Legislature upon the Judges of a specified Court, they are more appropriately considered as falling under the head of "Subordinate Legislation," in regard to which some remarks have already been made in paragraph 70, *ante.* The "Subsidiary Rules" which are here more particularly referred to are those which Judges are in the habit of abstracting from decided cases. This process has been called by Paley the "competition of opposite analogies,"[2] but the phrase has been sharply criticised by Sir Samuel Romilly[3] and Austin. "If the rule of law," says Austin, "has been inferred from one decided case, it cannot have been founded on *opposite* analogies. If it was established by several decided cases, it was founded on the *resembling* and not on the *different* properties of those several cases."[4] But as Austin himself subsequently points out, in the application of the rule to the case awaiting solution, a middle course may have to be followed. Thus the new case may in some points resemble the one which is the subject of

[1] 2 Coke's Inst. 11.

[2] *Moral Philosophy*, Vol. II., p. 259.

[3] *Edinburgh Review*, Vol. XXIX., p. 224.

[4] Student's edition, p. 320.

the rule proposed to be applied. It may in other points resemble a case which forms the subject of a different rule. Here there are certainly "competing analogies" from a due consideration of which it may be possible to extract a rule applicable to the case before the Court.[1] In England and in India considerable weight is attached to previous decisions of a co-ordinate Court, while those of a superior Court are regarded as authoritative. But under the Law of the Roman Empire no Judge or arbitrator was bound to follow a decision which did not commend itself to his mind as correct, and the Prussian *Landrecht* goes further and enacts that the "opinions of law Professors and the views taken by prior Judges shall not be in any way considered in future decisions."[2] The French Civil Code also denies any authoritative force to ordinary Judicial Interpretation.[3]

Influence of Commentators in forming such rules.

81. In the formation of such "Subsidiary Rules" the works of Commentators and Text Writers exercise an important influence, and are frequently referred to by Courts. But by themselves such works, as a general rule, have no binding force, although the reputation of the author may be such as to attach to his opinions even greater weight than would be commanded by the decision of a Judge. In India the Commentaries known as the *Mitacshara*, the *Dyabhaga*, the *Vivadachintamani*, the *Smritichandrika*, and the *Vyavaharamayukha*, as repertories of the Hindu Law prevailing in Benares, Bengal, Mithila, Madras, and Bombay respectively; and the *Hidayah*, the *Fatwa Alumgiri*, and *Fatwa Kazi Khan*, as similar repertories of the Muhammadan Law, may be mentioned as works of this description, which have still retained an almost conclusive authority, and are constantly quoted and relied upon by Courts of Justice in support of their decisions on questions relating to the Hindu or Muhammadan Law.

[1] Student's edition, p. 320.

[2] *Allgem. Landrecht*, Introduction, section 6.

[3] Article 5.

CHAP. V.

History of Codification.

81*a*. The Codification of the Law,[1] of which several attempts have been made in various countries at different times, requires brief mention as representing, perhaps, the ultimate form in which the Positive Law of a nation tends to transmute and perpetuate itself. When a nation has advanced to a certain stage of civilisation, when its judicial institutions have become deeply rooted and matured, and especially when a concurrence of political causes determines the commencement of a new period in its history, the need begins to be felt of collecting together the undigested laws, of reducing them to some order and method, of harmonising their provisions, and of publishing the result in a compact form, easy of reference, and in language at once simple and concise, capable of being understood by the people at large. It was under such conditions, brought about by the French Revolution, that the French Civil Code was enacted, in the composition of which the political element had a greater influence than the technical.[2] Previous to the Revolution France was, for juridical purposes, divided into two great Departments, the one, and that the more considerable in extent, governed by local statutes and custom (whence called *pays de droit coutumier*), the other governed by the Roman Law (whence called *pays de droit écrit*). Now one of the main objects of the Revolution was to unify French legislation, and to have a common law for all Frenchmen. This led to the immediate preparation of a Code, and a decree of the 24th Thermidor, in the year VIII., appointed a commission consisting of Trouchet, Bigot-Préameneu, Portalis, and Malleville to submit a project for such a Code. So indefatigably was the work carried on, that in four months the Commission completed its labours; and after undergoing certain modifications in the Council of State, the compilation was eventually promulgated under the

[1] It is said in Murray's *Dictionary* that Bentham introduced the term into the English language, and we ought to be grateful to him for it.

[2] Savigny's *Avocation of Our Age*, p. 70.

title of the *Civil Code of France*, for which the title of the *Code Napoléon* was substituted when the first Emperor had extended his empire over the greater part of Europe.[1] So again in Italy, the events which brought about the unification of the kingdom by the popular vote of 1860 and 1861, may be said to have necessitated also the unification of the laws; and the first care of the newly-established government under Victor Emmanuel was to introduce a project for a general Civil Code. This work was approved by the Senate on the 29th March, 1865, sanctioned by the King on the 2nd April, 1865, and by the Ordinance of the 25th June it was introduced throughout the kingdom from the 1st January, 1866. Tracing back the history of Codification to early times, Rome furnishes a unique attempt of the kind in the compilation of the Twelve Tables, bearing the official title of *Lex XII. Tabularum* (303 U.C.), which became the basis of the bulk of the Civil Law (*Jus Civile*) of Rome.[2] As time went on, and manners and customs changed, this primitive Code was found an insufficient guide; and although, under the supplementary jurisdiction of the Prætors, the inconvenience of an inadequate Civil Law was, as we have seen, to some extent remedied, there was a general desire towards the close of the Republic to have the Civil Law placed on a more satisfactory footing. Had Cæsar lived, he would have added the codification of the enormous mass of materials which had accumulated for centuries, and from which the law on any given point had to be extracted, to the other great benefits which he had already, in his too brief period of power, conferred upon his country. For we know

[1] *Cf. Saredo's Trattato delle Leggi*, p. 97. This writer gives a most interesting account of the part Codification plays in the history of Law, and much that is stated in the text is borrowed from this work. I trust this general acknowledgment will be accepted as sufficient for the obligation I am under to that learned author in this part of my own work.

[2] Livy III. 34; Diodor. XII. 26.

CHAP. V.

from his biographer that he had such a work in his mind when the misguided zeal of a would-be patriot[1] deprived Rome of her greatest genius.[2] His untimely death and the political troubles which followed upon it turned public attention into other channels, and it was not until the reign of the Emperor Hadrian that any serious attempt was made to consolidate even a portion of the laws. The Prætorian Law (the *Jus Honorarium*) had by this time assumed proportions which no human memory could be expected to master, and the Emperor Hadrian wisely resolved to refashion this branch of the law, and to give it another and a more permanent shape. He accordingly commissioned a Jurist of the period, named *Salvius Julianus*, who held the office of Urban Prætor, to revise and recast it. The work appears to have been satisfactorily accomplished, although it is unfortunately no longer extant, and was promulgated under the express sanction of the Senate and with the approval of the Emperor. From this period the law thus enacted was no longer liable to alteration or addition at the hands of the Prætor. For two centuries we hear of no further projects of Codification, but quite at the end of the third century, probably in the reign of Diocletian, a collection of imperial rescripts (with a few edicts) was made by one Gregorianus, which was followed by that of

[1] M. Junius Brutus, much celebrated for his virtue and integrity, but who appears to have been in reality an unconscionable usurer, who was not unwilling to resort to unworthy means to enforce his inequitable demands. He appears to have employed a business agent named Scaptius, and it is said that this individual lent money for his principal to the citizens of Salamis in Cyprus at 48 per cent. when the legal interest was fixed at 12 per cent. Scaptius endeavoured to enforce this agreement in the most arbitrary and oppressive way, and when Cicero, then Pro-consul of Cilicia (51 B.C.), was compelled on the representation of the Salamisans to interfere, Brutus wrote privately to him to try and persuade him to leave Scaptius alone. Römische Staatsverwaltung, von Joachim Marquardt, I. p. 542, 2nd Auflage.

[2] Suetonius, *Cæsar*, 44.

Hermogenianus in the year 365 A.D. But it is in the reign of Theodosius II. that we first meet with a real, methodical, and systematic effort to codify the existing law. Struck, as the Emperor says in a constitution in which he explains the motives that had actuated him to undertake the work, by the poverty-stricken condition of Jurisprudence, and how very few men there were who were able to make themselves familiar with the whole range of law, he resolved to compile a single code from materials derived alike from the writings of the Jurists, the Gregorian and Hermogenian collections, and the edictal laws from the time of Constantine downwards. The work when finished was to be a complete exponent of the existing law, and to supersede everything of an earlier date. No complete copy of this compilation has come down to us, and its latest editor (Haenel) estimates that about 450 constitutions of the first five books have been lost. Between the date of this Code and the later legislation of Justinian, we have three collections of laws compiled in Western Europe after it had thrown off the sovereignty of Rome, namely, (*a*) the *Edictum Theodorici*, compiled at the instance of Theodoric, King of the Ostrogoths, during his residence in Rome in the year 500 A.D.; (*b*) the *Lex Romana Visigothorum* or *Breviarium Alaricianum*, a larger and more important collection compiled by commissioners appointed by Alaric II., King of the Western Goths, with the approval of the bishops and nobles, and published at Aire in Gascony in the year 506 A.D.; and (*c*) the *Lex Romana Burgundionum*, which was prepared for the use of the Roman subjects of the kingdom either in the reign of King Gundbald or of his son Sigismund, probably in that of the latter about the year 534.[1] We then pass again to the Eastern Roman Empire, and arrive at the period when the collection and consolidation of

CHAP. V.

[1] *Trattato, delle Leggi*, per Giuseppe Saredo, Firenze, 1886, pp. 67, 68; Muirhead's *Law of Rome*, pp. 397—399.

CHAP. V.

the law was planned and carried out by the Emperor Justinian very soon after he succeeded his uncle and adoptive father, the Emperor Justin (527 A.D.). The urgent need of the reformation of Roman Jurisprudence at this period may be judged from the fact that the infinite variety of the laws and legal opinions filled many thousand volumes, which, as Gibbon forcibly puts it, "no fortune could purchase and no capacity could digest."[1] Within six months after the death of the latter, the new Emperor appointed a commission to prepare a new Code on the basis of the three preceding Codes—the Gregorian, Hermogenian, and Theodosian—and to embody in it the imperial constitutions which had been ordained since the last of those Codes had been confirmed. The commissioners, at whose head was the famous Tribonian —the Quæstor of the Royal Palace, who assisted Justinian in all his legislative reforms—compiled the new Code within fourteen months (on the 7th April, 529 A.D.); but a new edition was soon rendered necessary by some new constitutions and rescripts of the Emperor, and it is this second edition published on the 16th November, 534 A.D., that we now possess. Between the publication of the first and revised edition of his Code, Justinian had also caused the preparation of two other very important compilations, the one entitled *Institutiones*, intended for the use of students studying the law, and the other entitled *Digesta*, consisting of excerpts from the writings of the Jurists. By these three great works, whatever their literary defects may be, Justinian has earned the lasting gratitude of succeeding generations, even if we reject his boast of having "transmuted brass into gold."[2] The Roman law under his wise and enlightened efforts, although even he found it necessary[3] "to purify his own

[1] *Decline and Fall*, Ch. XLIV., p. 760 (1860 ed.).

[2] 1st *Præfat. ad Pandect.*

[3] Gibson's *Decline and Fall*, p. 763.

gold from the mixture of base alloy," became in truth a universal law, which has supplied the materials for all later legislation of a similar kind. Putting aside the *Decretum* of Gratian, a Benedictine monk of Bologna, the *Decretals* of Pope Gregory IX., "who sought the fame and received the title of the Justinian of the Church,"[1] the *Sext.* of Boniface VIII., and the *Clementines* of Clement V., in regard to ecclesiastical laws, which with a few other compilations collectively constitute the source of the *Corpus Juris Canonici*, and which are not properly Codes in the modern sense; and the *Constitutio Criminalis Carolina* of the Emperor Charles V. (1532 A.D.), one of the earliest attempts to provide a Criminal Law for a whole Empire; it is not until we come down late into the last century that we find the legislative activity of European nations again directed with any renewed energy in the direction of the codification of laws. The *Costituzioni* (of 1723 A.D.) of King Vittor Amadeo II. of Sardinia; the *Leggi e Costituzioni* promulgated by his son Charles Emmanuel in April 1770, which continued in force until the epoch of the French domination, and was again re-introduced after that domination ceased to exist, and which then remained in full force and vigour down to the promulgation of the several *Codici Albertini;* the Code of Laws published by command of Francis III., Duke of Modena, in 1771; the Code of Frederick II. of Prussia, compiled by Cocceius in 1750, and his new Code, or *Landrecht*, published on the 5th February, 1794, which came into operation on the 1st June of the same year; were at this period some of the principal products of this great movement, actuated by the desire of having a concise, clear, and yet comprehensive (*brevis, clarus, sufficiens*, as Leibnitz expressed it) manual of the laws prevailing in each independent State. In the

[1] Bryce's *Holy Roman Empire*, 5th ed. p. 102.

CHAP. V.

present century the principal Codes that have been compiled are those of France (the *Code Napoléon; Code de Commerce* of 1807; *Code Pénal* of 1810); of Italy (*Codice Civile; Codice Penale; Codice di Commercio*); of Austria (Civil Code of the 7th July, 1810); of Germany (the *Handelsgesetzbuch*, and the Penal Code of 1872, and the Civil Code of 1896 for the German Empire); the *Civil Code* for Japan of 1898; the New Dutch Code of 1866; the Civil Code of Lower Canada; the New York Codes; the Penal Codes of Louisiana; the trilingual Swiss Code of Obligations, which came into operation from the 1st of January, 1883; the *Code Civil Ottoman;* and lastly, though not the least successful, the Indian Penal Code (the monumental work of Lord Macaulay) and the Codes of Civil and Criminal Procedure.

Motive underlying all codification.

81*b*. The above brief and necessarily imperfect sketch is merely intended to give the student a general idea of what has been accomplished in the direction of Codification up to the present time. The motive which underlies all these previously-mentioned legislative attempts is the very laudable one of making the laws of a country as accessible and as intelligible as possible. But the weak point throughout has been in dealing with the whole mass of law at one time as a single undertaking. Such a work is too stupendously difficult to be ever successfully accomplished; and thus it is that though Theodosius, Justinian, and the framers of the *Code Napoléon* intended that their codes should be complete and embody the final expression of the law, a very short experience proved that such an anticipation was illusory, and that in each case the "final word" was very far from having been spoken. Napoleon is said to have remarked when the first commentary upon his Code—that by Malleville—one of its compilers—was shown to him—"My Code is lost!" (*mon Code est perdu*); and indeed no Code has had more commentators, and none has received more additions and modifi-

Weak points in previous attempts.

cations, than his. It is probable that if success in this department of legislation is to be obtained in the future, it will be by adopting the practice of the Indian Legislature and codifying at intervals distinct parts of the law—such as Contracts, Succession, and Trusts—independently of each other.[1] It is not meant of course that these parts of the law should be codified without relation to some general scheme, and without keeping in view the ultimate object of constituting a complete Civil Code. For it must be remembered, as Sir James Fitzjames Stephen well observes, that no one great department of law is *absolutely* unconnected with any other. For instance, bigamy is a crime; but, in order to know whether a person has committed bigamy, it is necessary to know whether his first marriage was valid. Thus the definition of the crime of bigamy cannot be completely understood by any one who is unacquainted with the law relating to marriage.[2] In this sense the great leading branches of the law, although to a great extent distinct from each other, and capable of separate codification, must have a certain inter-relation. But so long as this relation of the parts to some general scheme is maintained, the several leading branches of the law can most conveniently be dealt with separately. Even then it would be advisable to make a provision for the revision of the Code after a certain period—say ten years—when defects could be remedied, and judicial interpretations or new laws worked into the Code. By this means the usual objections to a Code of want of flexibility and elasticity would be overcome; and withal the opinion may be hazarded, that an imperfect Code is, on the whole,

The Indian practice preferable.

Need of constant revision.

[1] The British Parliament has also produced several consolidated enactments, such as the Bills of Exchange Act, 1882, the Partnership Act, 1890, and the Sale of Goods Act, 1893, and the Merchant Shipping Act, 1894.

[2] *Hist. of the Criminal Law of England*, Vol. III., p. 350. A good illustration of what is stated in the text is supplied by the recent decision of the High Court of Bengal, reported in I. L. R. XVIII. Cal. 264.

preferable to a condition of law the sources of which consist of thousands of statutes and countless reports of decided cases, which would require a lifetime to read through, and which no lawyer even can ever pretend to master. Such a condition of the law may claim the praise of elasticity. But it stands condemned on the score of uncertainty. For a law that is not certain is a snare, and causes incalculable mischief.

CHAPTER VI.

THE CAUSES WHICH INVEST OR DIVEST RIGHTS.

82. THE nature and scope of rights have already been considered. This chapter will be confined to the causes which originate or terminate the connection of a given right with the person in whom it resides. They are considered by Professor Holland under the title "Rights at Rest and in Motion." The arrangement of treating these causes in a separate Chapter is a convenient one, but the title itself is scarcely simple enough for mere students. It is, moreover, hardly appropriate. A "Right at Rest" means, if it means anything, a Right which is in a condition of being peacefully enjoyed by the person in whom it resides. But Professor Holland's Chapter does not deal with Rights from this point of view at all. The first part of the Chapter, which professes to deal with "Rights at Rest," really discusses the various causes which lead to an infringement of Rights, and the second part is devoted to "Rights in Motion." Of course, to understand what constitutes an infringement of a Right you must first have a clear conception of what constitutes a Right, and of the advantages which are conferred by its enjoyment. Thus, the former branch of the subject is only a natural sequel to the latter, but as such it is capable of separate treatment. For this reason, and in order to lead the student gradually to a fuller knowledge of the general theory of Rights, he has in this treatise been first instructed as to the elements of a Right, and it is presumed that he is now able to comprehend what has to be said about the "infringement" of a Chap. VI.

Right, and of Rights being set in motion. Some repetition may perhaps be noticed, but it is not easy to avoid it, and it is better to incur this objection than to leave the student in a state of fog.

Causes which originate Rights.

83. Now the causes which originate Rights are due, as we have previously seen, to either one of two species of facts, *e.g.*, "events" or "acts." But the technical term proposed by Austin for a fact which gives rise to a Right, or imposes or withdraws a Duty, is "Title," which Bentham proposes to call a "*dispositive fact.*" "Investitive" is the name given by Bentham to the whole class of facts by the intervention of which Rights or Duties come into existence, which he divides again into *collative* (those conferring Rights) and *impositive* (those imposing Duties). "Divestitive" facts are those which put an end to the Right or Duty, and are divided into *destructive* or *privitive*, which put an end to Rights, and *exonerative* which extinguish or relieve from Duties.[1]

Infringement of a Right.

84. By the "infringement of a Right" is meant that the enjoyment of those advantages which a Right confers upon the person in whom it resides is interfered with by the act, omission, or forbearance of another. Every such "infringement" denotes that an injury or wrong has been committed, which is imputable to the person by whose act, omission, or forbearance it has resulted.

Imputability defined.

85. But the notion of imputability does not consist in the mere act, omission, or forbearance[2] from which a particular injurious consequence has resulted. It is compounded also of the intention, negligence, heedlessness, or rashness[3] by which the act, omission, or forbearance is preceded or accompanied. The latter constitutes as much an ingredient of the notion of imputability as the former, but is not of *itself*

[1] *Austin*, Student's ed. 434, 435.

[2] These terms have been previously explained. See paras. 33—35, *ante*.

[3] See paras. 45, 46, *ante*.

injury or wrong, and will not place the party in the predicament of imputability. Thus, in order that the party may be placed in the predicament of imputability, his intention, negligence, heedlessness, or rashness must be referred to an act, omission, or forbearance of which it was the *cause.*[1] How far this imputability may be excused by certain abnormal conditions of the party has already been explained.[2]

Cause.

86. Before an act, omission, or forbearance can be regarded in law as the true cause of a result, it must be shown to be the "proximate" and not the "remote" *cause* thereof: *in jure non remota causa, sed proxima, spectatur:*[3] in law the proximate, and not the remote, cause is to be regarded. Where, however, the act and the resulting injury can be "concentrated as cause and effect,"[4] there the law regards the original mover in the injury as responsible for all the natural consequences of his act. The case of *Scott* v. *Shephard*[5] well illustrates this principle. That was a case where the defendant threw a lighted squib into a market-place during a fair, and the squib fell upon a stall, and the stall-keeper, to protect himself, threw the squib across the market-place, where it fell upon another stall, and was again thrown, and exploded near the plaintiff's eye and blinded him. Here it was held that the original thrower was responsible for the injury sustained by the plaintiff. "He who does the first wrong," it was said, "is answerable for all the consequential damages." All that was done subsequently to the original throwing "was a continuation of the first force and first act, which will continue till the squib was spent by bursting, and any innocent person removing the danger from

[1] *Student's Austin*, pp. 224, 225.
[2] *Ante*, paras. 37, 38.
[3] Bac. Max. Reg. 1.
[4] *Gerhard* v. *Bates*, 2 Ell. & B. 490.
[5] Wm. Bl. 892.

CHAP. VI. himself to another is justifiable." The case of *Gibbons* v. *Pepper*[1] supplies an illustration of a different kind. There it was decided that if a man's horse is frightened by accident or a third person, and runs away with him and injures a person who is walking in the street, the rider is not responsible. In that case the injury could, indeed, have been referred *remotely* to the act of mounting and taking the horse out into the street. But the possibility of being run away with when riding quietly, though not an unknown thing to happen, is comparatively slight. Inasmuch, therefore, as the law will not look at the remote cause, but only at the proximate, the rider was not held to be responsible for consequences which, as an average man of ordinary intelligence and prudence, he could not have contemplated. But suppose the horse had been unruly, and had been taken into a frequented place for the purpose of being broken, the result of the decision would have been very different. In such a case it would be the fault of the rider to bring a wild or unruly horse into a place where mischief might probably be done.[2] Again, to borrow an instance from the Roman Law, where cattle are driven violently along a narrow way, on either side of which there is a deep precipice, and some of the animals fall down the precipice and are killed, here the act and damage are sufficiently connected as cause and effect.

Contributory negligence.

87. In determining how far a given act is the *cause* of a result, the law will also take into consideration any conduct of the party injured or wronged which may have immediately contributed to that result. This is upon the principle of what has been termed "culpa-compensation," where the "culpa" on one side compensates for the "culpa" on the other; and the reason for admitting it is, that the causal connection between the act and damage is interrupted by

[1] 1 Ld. Raym. 38.
[2] Holmes's *The Common Law*, p. 94.

the "culpa," or negligent conduct of the injured party.[1] Where such conduct can be proved, the party will be considered in law to be the author of his own wrong, and it will be fatal to any action on his part based on the injury. Because the rule of Law is, that a person who suffers a damage by his own fault is really not deemed to have suffered any legal damage: *quod quis ex culpa sua damnum sentit, non intelligitur damnum sentire.*[2] Thus, if a person irritates an animal, which injures him in consequence, he has no action either against the owner or against the keeper.[3] So, where a passenger was removed by the servants of a railway company, under circumstances which did not justify the removal, he was held not entitled to recover the value of a pair of race-glasses which he *negligently* left in the carriage, and which were lost.[4] So, again, where A. placed lime rubbish in the highway which, blowing into the face of B.'s horse, frightened it, so that it nearly dashed against a passing waggon, and, in his efforts to avoid it, B. *unskilfully* drove against another heap of rubbish, and was overset and hurt, it was held that he could not recover against A.[5] But it must be carefully borne in mind that a plea of "contributory negligence" will not avail a wrongdoer, although there may have been some negligence on the part of the injured person, unless the latter might, by the exercise of ordinary care, have avoided the consequence of the other's negligence. It is only when the injured person might have avoided that consequence that the Law will regard him as the author of his own wrong.[6] Another limitation on the effect of "contributory negligence" is, that where the immediate cause of

[1] *The Lex Aquilia*, by Erwin Grueber, 1886, p. 228. *Cf. Wharton on Negligence*, section 300, and remarks thereon in Beach's *Law of Contributory Negligence*, p. 13, New York, 1885.

[2] Dig. L. 17, 203.

[3] Paulus, *Sentent.* I. 15, 3.

[4] *Glover* v. *London & S. W. R. Co.*, L. R. 3 Q. B. 118.

[5] Mayne's *Law of Damages*, p. 37, 2nd edition.

[6] *Rudley* v. *London & N. W. R. Co.* (1876), 1 App. Cas. 759.

the accident is the defendant's fault, so that without it the accident could not have happened at all, it is no answer that, only for the plaintiff's negligence in something collateral to the immediate cause of the injury, it or part of it might have been avoided.[1] Thus, when two omnibuses were racing, and one struck against the other, it appeared that if the omnibus in which the plaintiff was riding had been driven slower, it might have been pulled up *after* a collision and the accident prevented; but this was held to be no answer.[2] Nor, again, will the plea of "contributory negligence" be allowed if the party complained of might, by the exercise of due care on his part, have avoided the consequences of the carelessness on the part of the plaintiff. Thus, where a man negligently left an ass in a public highway, tied together by the forefeet, and the defendant carelessly drove over and killed it, in the daytime, the ass being unable to get out of the way; it was held that the misconduct of the plaintiff in leaving the ass in the highway was no answer to the action, the defendant being bound to go along the road with care; as, were it otherwise, a man might justify driving over goods left in the street, or over a man lying there asleep, or against a carriage going on what is called the wrong side of the road.[3] The question of the privity in negligence between a passenger and carrier, for a long time (since 1849) governed in England by the supposed rule of "identification," established by the case of *Thorogood* v. *Bryan*,[4] has more recently undergone a resettlement in better harmony with sound sense and justice. It had often been doubted whether the decision in *Thorogood* v. *Bryan*, whereby a passenger was deemed to be identified with the carriage or vessel he was travelling in, so as to be disentitled from recovering damages from the owner of another vessel or

[1] *Rigby* v. *Hewitt*, 5 Exch. 240.

[2] *Plower* v. *Adams*, 2 Taunt. 314.

[3] Wharton's *Legal Maxims*, p. 198; and *Rudley's Case*, cited above.

[4] 8 C. B. 115, see p. 130.

carriage for injuries received in a collision caused by the joint negligence of those having the control of both vehicles, was one that rested on any sound principle; and the theory of agency on which it was founded had been abandoned, even in those cases (like that of *Armstrong* v. *Lancashire Railway Company*[1]) where it had been followed. In America the current of Authority appears to have run, though not uniformly, against the English rule; and it was there held, with apparently better reason, that as the passenger is a perfectly innocent party, having no control over the conveyance in which he is for the moment travelling, he ought to be able to sustain an action against the employer of the wrong-doer.[2] But at length in *The Bernina case*[3] the English Court of Appeal has taken the opportunity to review the whole law on the subject, with the result that both *Thorogood* v. *Bryan* and *Armstrong* v. *Lancashire Railway Company* have been distinctly overruled; and the true rule has been established that where damage is sustained by the concurrent negligence of two or more persons, there is a right of action against all or any of them at the plaintiff's option, and the exception of contributory negligence extends only to acts and defaults of the plaintiff himself or those who are really his servants or agents. But it is to be observed that privity in negligence between a public carrier and a shipper of *goods* stands upon a different footing, and may be said to be firmly established both in England and America. The reason for the distinction between the carrier of goods and the carrier of passengers is said to be (*a*) that the former is an insurer, the latter is not; and (*b*) the former acts as the agent of the shipper, whereas there is no contract of bailment or agency between the latter and the passengers he carries.[4]

[1] L. R. 20 Exch. 47.

[2] Beach's *Contributory Negligence*, pp. 114, 118: New York, 1885.

[3] 11 P. D. 58; *Mills* v. *Armstrong* (1887—88), 13 App. Cas. 1.

[4] Beach's *Contributory Negligence*, pp. 118, 119.

CHAP. VI.

Volenti non fit injuria.

88. In connection with the effect of contributory negligence we may also consider the maxim *volenti non fit injuria*, the meaning of which is that the law will not consider that an injury to which a man consents. This maxim, borrowed originally from the Civil Law, has lost some of its significance (for instance, in cases arising out of a statutory duty),[1] but like most other rules formulated by Roman Jurists, is nevertheless founded on good sense and justice. An injury of a purely private nature is a matter for which the law gives a redress in the interests of the person injured; and if he chooses not to regard it as such, or not to avail himself of the remedies which the Law places at his disposal, it is his business, and the Law will not compel him to assert his rights against his will, on the principle of the maxim just quoted, and of another to the effect *quilibet potest renunciare juri pro se introducto*:[2] every one is able to renounce a right introduced for himself. Thus, to quote an illustration from the Indian *Transfer of Property Act*, A., the lessor, gives B., the lessee, notice to quit the property leased. The notice expires. B. tenders, and A. accepts, rent which has become due in respect of the property since the expiration of the notice. The notice is waived.[3] In its application to questions between employer and employed, the maxim as now used generally imports that the workman had either expressly or by implication agreed to take upon himself the risks attendant upon the particular work which he was engaged to perform, and from which he has suffered injury. Accordingly, where a person undertakes to do work which is intrinsically dangerous, notwithstanding that reasonable care has been taken to render it as little dangerous as possible, he no doubt voluntarily subjects himself to the risks inevitably accompanying it, and

[1] *Baddeley* v. *Granville* (*Earl*), L. R. 19 Q. B. D. 423; 56 L. J. Q. B. 501.

[2] See another application of this maxim in *Carlill* v. *Carbolic Smoke Co.*, (1893) 1 Q. B. 256.

[3] As defined in section 320.

cannot, if he suffers, be permitted to complain that a wrong has been done him, even though the cause from which he suffers might give to others a right of action. Where, however, a risk to the employed, which may or may not result in injury, has been created or enhanced by the negligence of the employer, the mere continuance in service, with knowledge of the risk, will not preclude the employed, if he suffers from such negligence, from recovering in respect of his employer's breach of duty. In such a case the employer cannot invoke the aid of the maxim, *volenti non fit injuria*, to protect him from liability for his wrong.[1] The maxim is also, to some extent, recognised in the Criminal Law. Thus, under the Indian Penal Code, an act not intended and not known to be likely to cause death or grievous hurt,[2] if done by consent, is not an offence by reason of any harm which it may cause, or be intended by the doer to cause, to any person above the age of eighteen years. The consent must, however, be a free consent. It is only where a man is not physically constrained, that is to say, where he can at his option do a thing, or not, that the maxim *volenti non fit injuria* applies.[3]

Actus Curiæ neminem gravabit.

89. The law also refuses to recognise any "infringement of a Right" where the alleged injury is the consequence of an Act of a Court of Justice or of God. Thus, a man's liberty is one of the most precious Rights that he possesses. But if he is arrested in execution of a decree of a Civil Court he is deemed to have suffered no injury, though the judgment of the Court may be wrong: for *executio juris non habet injuriam:* the execution of the process of the Law does no injury. So if a constable executes a warrant of arrest issued by a competent Court, no action will lie against the constable: for *actus Curiæ neminem gravabit:* an Act of the Court

[1] *Smith* v. *Baker & Sons*, (1891) App. Cas. 325, at pp. 355, 360, 362.
[2] Section 87.
[3] *Membery* v. *G. W. R. Co.*, 14 App. Cas. 179.

injures no one. In all such cases it is not the use, but the abuse of the process of the Law which makes an injury, and the misuser of the process of the Law is a question of damages merely between the parties.[1] The most ordinary case in which the last-mentioned maxim is applied is where a defendant dies pending the argument on a point reserved on which judgment is afterwards given in his favour. In such a case judgment is entered up *nunc pro tunc.* The importance of such an application of the maxim will be best understood by the following illustration. A. sued B. for pre-emption of property, and after the trial was concluded, but pending judgment, B. died. Here under the then existing Law of procedure for India, A. was bound to apply within sixty days of B.'s death, to have his legal representatives substituted in his stead. But he failed to make the application within the prescribed time, and judgment was pronounced in his favour long after it had expired. Here, as the delay was attributable to the Court in not delivering judgment at once, A. was held not to be prejudiced, and judgment, when pronounced, was delivered *nunc pro tunc.*[2]

Actus Dei nemini facit injuriam.

90. In like manner the Act of God injures no one (*actus Dei nemini facit injuriam*). Thus, under the English Law, if the judgment-debtor taken in execution were afterwards set at liberty by the judgment-creditor, this was deemed to be a discharge of the debt. But if the judgment-debtor died while undergoing imprisonment, no such result ensued, and the creditor could have a new execution by *elegit* or *fieri facias.*[3]

How Rights may be connected with or disconnected from a person.

91. We now come to the way in which Rights may be connected with or disconnected from the persons who are the subjects of such Rights. The connection may arise in con-

[1] Wharton's *Law Maxims*, p. 67.

[2] *Nunna Mal* v. *Sheo Nath*, No. 46, *Punjab Record*, 1887. Cf. also I. L. R. XVIII. Cal. 631.

[3] Wharton's *Legal Maxims*, p. 7.

sequence of an exceptional grant made by the sovereign power in favour of a specifically determined person or a corporate body, called a "privilegium" or "beneficium juris," or by reason of the intervention of some fact distinguishable from the Law conferring the Right which brings a particular instance within the operation of a general Law.[1] Thus a patent to manufacture and sell a particular article, a monopoly to sell opium within a certain district, or to have the exclusive right of constructing a railway, is a *privilegium*.[2] But a sale giving rise to a right of pre-emption, under the Punjab Laws Act of 1872, would be a fact of the second kind. So would the acquisition of a Right of Occupancy, under the Punjab or Bengal Tenancy Act, or of an Easement, under section 26 of the Indian Limitation Act of 1877. The right in such cases would be acquired not because the acquirer was specially determined, but agreeably to the provision of a general law which annexes the Right to a fact or a series of facts of a particular description. The proper term for an investitive fact of this kind is, as previously stated, a *Title*.

Rights resulting from "voluntary acts" or *ex lege immediate*.

92. Again the Right or Duty may arise or be divested as the result of a voluntary act, or *ex lege immediate*. In the

[1] *Austin*, Student's ed., pp. 431, 433; Holland's *Jurisprudence*, p. 134.

[2] Modern Jurists are in the habit of speaking of "favourable privileges" (*privilegia favorabilia*), when they confer anomalous Rights, and of "*odious privileges*" (*privilegia odiosa*) when they impose anomalous obligations or inflict anomalous punishments. But, as Windscheid points out, this use of the term *privilegium* does not appear to be sanctioned by the Sources of the Roman Law (Vol. I., section 29, p. 73, note 4), and is certainly not in accordance with present English usage, which recognises only *favourable* privileges. A privilege may be conferred by a direct act of the legislature, as in the case of a law of Wurtemburg of 1839, which conferred an exclusive copyright in Schiller's works on the heirs of the poet, or as in the case of an *arrogatio per populum* under the old Roman law. Or it may be conferred by a political authority in exercise of a power granted by the legislature, as, for instance, an exemption from personal appearance in a Court of Justice, granted by a Local Government under the provisions of section 641 of the Indian Code of Civil Procedure of 1882.

Chap. VI.

latter case the Right or Duty is invested or divested by operation of law, and not by a title, which may consist of or comprise any act of the invested or divested person. Thus an heir *ab intestato*, under the Indian Succession Act (X. of 1865), takes the heritage *ex lege immediate*. But a Right which passes by a contract of sale or *ex testamento* is the result of a voluntary act.[1]

Assignatus utitur jure auctoris.

93. When a Right is divested from one person and invested in another, as the result of a voluntary act, it is presumed, unless the contrary appears, that it embraces everything incident to the Right which the divested person enjoyed. This rule is expressed in the maxim *assignatus utitur jure auctoris:* that which is assigned takes with it for its use the rights of the assignor. The person divesting himself may, of course, transfer by his act less than he possesses, as a part of his estate, or a right of property apart from the property itself, as in the case of a mortgage or pledge. But where he makes no such reservation, in that case, inasmuch as two persons cannot possess one thing in its entirety (*duo non possunt in solido unam rem possidere*), he is deemed to have transferred his rights as a whole. And thus also it is presumed that he grants that without which the thing granted would be useless:—*cuicunque aliquis quid concedit, concedere videtur et id sine quo res ipsa esse non potuit.* Thus, if A. sells to B. a piece of land in the middle of other land of his, he is presumed at the same time to impliedly grant a way to it, and the grantee may cross the grantor's land for that purpose without being liable to an action for trespass.

An assignor cannot transfer a greater Right than he himself has.

94. As a corollary from the maxim *assignatus utitur jure auctoris* it follows that the condition of the assignee cannot be better than that of his assignor (*non debeo melioris condi-*

[1] *Austin*, Student's ed., p. 439.

tionis esse quam auctor meus a quo jus in me transit).[1] In other words, although an assignor may transfer a *less* Right than he possesses, he cannot confer a *larger* Right upon his assignee: *nemo potest plus juris ad alium transferre quam ipse habet* (no one can transfer a greater Right to another than he himself has).[2]

Succession.

95. When the very Right itself is granted, the "title" is spoken of as one of "Succession." But the "Succession" may be limited to a single Right, as the ownership of an estate, when it is called "Singular"; or it may extend to that entire bundle of Rights and Duties which the Roman Jurists included in a man's *jus*, and to which the name *juris universitas* has been given. This *juris universitas* constitutes, as it were, what Sir Henry Maine happily calls, "the legal clothing of some given individual,"[3] and it devolves by succession on an executor or administrator, or on a trustee in Bankruptcy.

Intestate.

96. In regard to the transfer (*translatio*) of the Rights of a deceased person to his heirs, this may result by mere operation of law, as in the case of his death intestate, or by reason of a declaration of his will in the form of a testament. In early times the notion prevailed that the existence of the ancestor was continued in that of the heir, and the transition of his property to the heir was but the natural sequence of ideas. This notion was familiar to most nations of antiquity, and certainly to the Hindus. The son and daughter of a man, according to Manu, were even as himself,[4] while the right of the widow to succeed was based on the fiction that in her half the body of her husband survived.[5] The author of the *Mitacshara* asserts the same notion in distinct terms. "Woman's property," he says, "goes to her daughters

[1] Dig. L. 17, 175, section 1.
[2] Dig. L. 17, 177. But see para. 151.
[3] *Ancient Law*, p. 50.
[4] Chap. IX., verse 130.
[5] *Dayabhaga*, Chap. 11, section 1, verse 2.

CHAP. VI.

because portions of her abound in her female children; and the father's estate goes to his sons, *because portions of him abound in his male children.*"[1] This important passage not only supplies us with clear evidence that the right of Succession was based on the theory of the continuation of the existence of the ancestor in the person of the heir, but also with the key for the solution of the question, as to the rule by which the right of the heir is to be determined. It was clearly by that of propinquity or nearness of kinship to the deceased, with a preference of males in the succession to males, and of females in the succession to females. Thus the son succeeds the father because he is deemed to be a portion of the father, and for precisely a similar reason a daughter is allowed to succeed her mother. In Bengal, under Brahminical manipulation, a further rule of spiritual benefits was developed as a natural consequence of the rule that accumulated wealth was only intended for religious purposes.[2] But even in that system the extent of the benefit depends on the propinquity of relationship to the deceased, allowing a certain preference of males to females.

Testamentary Succession.

97. The other form of Succession, *i.e.*, by a Testamentary Disposition (*dispositio ultimæ voluntatis*) was a later provision, and could only have been devised when individual ownership was firmly established. It was so completely recognised in the Law of Rome, even at so early a period as the publication of the Twelve Tables, that the rule that every citizen could dispose of his property as he liked, stood in the forefront of that Law.[3] Kant, indeed, asserts that "Inheritance is inconceivable in the State of Nature without a Testamentary Disposition."[4] But we know that there were nations of antiquity among whom Testaments were unknown. Thus,

[1] Chap. I., section 3, verse 10.

[2] *Dayabhaga*, Chap. XI.

[3] *Uti legassit suæ rei, ita jus esto:* "as a man shall settle in reference to his estate, so shall it be law." Gai. II. 224; Just. *Inst.*, II. 22 pr.

[4] *Philosophy of Law*, p. 136.

there was no such thing in Sparta. They were introduced in Athens by the legislation of Solon,[1] and there is no mention of them in the old Hindu law books.[2] Yet the Spartans, Athenians, and Hindus distinctly recognised a law of Inheritance. In Rome, indeed, Testaments made in the Comitia of the Curies (*Calatis Comitiis*) and in presence of the army on the eve of battle (*in procinctu*),[3] date back to a remote antiquity. But in the story of the grant by Romulus of little homesteads that were "to follow the heir," we probably have an indication of the introduction of a rule of Succession before any testamentary dispositions were known. Moreover, as regards Comitial Testaments, it is highly probable that originally they were legislative acts, whereby the testator's peers, for reasons which they and the presiding Pontiffs thought sufficient, sanctioned in the particular case a departure from the ordinary rules of Succession; while those made by soldiers on the eve of battle were nothing more than an apportionment of the testator's belongings amongst his proper heirs.[4] Voluntary dispositions in a man's lifetime stand of course on a different footing. The power of making such dispositions followed naturally the segregation of the individual from the family, and according to the *Tattiria Brahmana* Manu himself is supposed to have "divided his wealth among his sons."[5] But in earlier times, when the family property was vested in the family corporation, and when members had nothing more than a right of usufruct, the idea that any individual could exercise a power of disposal *to commence after his own death* would have been a contradiction in terms.[6]

[1] Muirhead's *Law of Rome*, 47.

[3] Gai. II. 101.

[2] *Vide* Tagore Law Lectures for 1880, pp. 243, 244. The practice of making Wills of some sort appears to have been in vogue in Arabia in the time of Muhammad. *Kinship and Marriage in Early Arabia*, by Robertson Smith, p. 99.

[4] Muirhead's *Law of Rome*, pp. 47, 166.

[5] *Tagore Law Lectures* for 1880, p. 243.

[6] Mayne's *Hindu Law*, section 336.

CHAP. VI.

Testaments among Hindus.

98. The execution of written Testaments by Hindus dates from a period long subsequent to the time when the *Dayabhaga*, for instance, was written.[1] They owe their origin to the Customary Law, and were not improbably known before the advent of British rule. The Supreme Court of Calcutta granted probate of a Will so early as 1776; and the Will of the famous Omichand was dated 1758 A.D. Wills were also expressly recognised in the case of Hindus by the Indian legislature so long ago as 1779,[2] and their validity generally has been sanctioned by the Privy Council.[3] In the decision referred to, the Privy Council deal with a Will as "a continuous act of gift up to the moment of death," when it begins to operate. But the notion that the law of Wills is simply a logical development of the law of Gifts has been doubted;[4] and the description of a Will as a continuous act of gift up to the moment of death, when it begins to operate, is also open to criticism. The *Translatio* of the property of the deceased, that is to say, the acquisition of the appointed heir who takes the estate, and the relinquishment of the testator who leaves it, may take place in the same moment of time, *i.e.*, *in articulo mortis;* but the transfer itself cannot be complete without the consent or acceptance of the beneficiary. As Kant long ago pointed out, "by a mere unilateral act of will, nothing can in fact be transmitted to another person, as in addition to the Promise of the one party (*e.g.*, of the testator to transfer his estate to the person named in the Will after his death) there is required Acceptance on the part of the other, and a simultaneous bilateral act of will, which is here wanting."[5] Until acceptance the *heredium* or estate was called in Roman Law a *hæreditas jacens*, and the

[1] *Tagore Law Lectures* for 1884-85, p. 632.

[2] Regulation 5 of that year, sections 1 and 2.

[3] *Bengal Law Reports*, Vol. IX. p. 377.

[4] Markby's *Elements of Law*, section 792, p. 385.

[5] *The Philosophy of Law*, p. 137.

CHAP. VI.

right of the heir was a mere *jus in re jacente*, that is to say, a right of choice as to whether he would actually make the estate bequeathed to him his own or not. By the mere *institutio hæredis*, or institution as heir by the Will, the heir did not acquire any of the property of the testator. But by his act of acceptance the property was deemed to pass without interruption to the heir, precisely as under the Indian Succession Act (and the English Law is the same), the testator's estate does not necessarily, and in all cases, vest in the executor at the moment of the testator's death, for the executor has the option of refusing to act as such, and, if he does so refuse, the inheritance never vests in him at all. Acceptance on his part is, therefore, as much necessary as it was in the case of an heir under the Roman Law; but the effect of the acceptance is to carry the relation of his title back to the death of the testator.[1]

[1] *Vide* sections 187, 188, 194, 196 of Act X. of 1865; Broom's *Commentaries*, p. 616 (1st ed.), and Markby's *Elements of Law*, sections 802—804.

PART II.

CHAPTER VII.

PRIVATE RIGHTS.

CHAP. VII.

99. IN the present Chapter we begin the second branch of our general subject. The preceding Chapters were intended as an introduction to the Science of Law in which the fundamental principles of that Science were briefly stated. The student has thus learnt to understand the general characteristics of Law and of Rights. He can now enter upon a wider field where the Science of Right will be subjected to a more detailed examination. This can best be done by adopting the sub-division of Private Right and Public Right, which was borrowed from the Roman Law by Immanuel Kant and other Continental writers.

"Private" and "Public Right" defined and contrasted.

100. The former sub-division embraces all Rights which subsist between Subject and Subject, while the latter refers to those which subsist between the State and its Subjects. Or, put in other words, the one class of Rights is given in the interests of the Individual, the other in the interests of the State.[1] Private Rights again require no external promulgation, whereas the term Public Right embraces all those Laws that are requisite for a people as a multitude of men, forming an independent community, and require to be universally promulgated in order to produce a juridical state

[1] Stahl's *Die Philosophie des Rechts*, Vol. II., section 39, p. 242.

of society.[1] Private Rights may be modified by conventions; Public Rights are those which cannot be so modified: *jus publicum privatorum pactis mutari non potest; privata conventio juri publico nihil derogat.* The former include the integrity and freedom of the Person, Property, and Family. The latter are those which affect the State or the Church, and include, besides the law of Political Conditions and of Crimes, the law relating to Criminal and Civil Procedure,[2] and, according to Continental Jurists, International Law (*Volkerrecht*).[3] From the Austinian standpoint the inclusion of this last branch of Law, which is not Law properly so called, is the greatest logical error which is involved in this double classification, which is said to rest upon no intelligible basis.[4] Austin's chief objection to this classification is, that every part of the Law is in a certain sense public, and every part of it is in a certain sense private also, and that, therefore, it is impossible to maintain any sharp distinction between private and public rights.[5] This is so far true, and undoubtedly, as Stahl says, man is the central point of both classes of rights.[6] But the classification does not necessarily rest on any such sharp distinction, and it has not only obtained the recognition of the Roman and Continental Jurists, but there is much to be said in its favour. It was regarded by Lord Bacon as a true and received division in his time, the one comprehending "the sinews of Property, and the other of Government;"[7] and it is convenient as separating into two broad and distinct groups the Laws which affect the one from those which concern the other.

[1] Kant's *Philosophy of Law*, section 43, p. 161. *Cf.* Stahl's *Philosophie des Rechts*, Vol. II., section 36, p. 239.

[2] *Publicum jus in sacris, in sacerdotibus, in magistratibus consistit*, Dig. I. 1, 1, 2.

[3] Stahl's *Die Philosophie des Rechts*, II., section 36, pp. 239, 240.

[4] *Student's Austin*, p. 372.

[5] *Ibid.* 369.

[6] *Die Philosophie des Rechts*, section 38, p. 241.

[7] Works, VII. 731.

The one group postulates the *utilitas privatorum* (*i.e.*, utility in the interest of private persons), the other the *vigor publicæ disciplinæ* (the vigour of public discipline),[1] and without some such severance the Law relating to Crime would find no satisfactory position assigned to it in any system of Law.

"Private Rights" fall under three heads.

"Antecedent" and "Remedial Rights."

101. Now all private rights may be said to fall under one or other of three groups: (1) those relating to the protection and freedom of action of the person; (2) those relating to property; and (3) those relating to the family.[2] Every right falling within these several groups may also be considered from a two-fold aspect, (*a*) as a right existing independently of any wrong having been committed, when, as we have previously seen, it may be called an "Antecedent Right"; and (*b*) as furnishing the ground for a remedial action for compensation, when it has been infringed or violated.

Rights relating to the protection and freedom of the Person.

102. Adopting the above grouping, and dealing with each group in the first instance as constituting "Antecedent Rights," we begin with those Rights which relate to the protection and freedom of action of the person.

What they consist of.

103. The rights which may be embraced within this first group are those upon which the very existence of a man's personality depends, and include the protection of life and limb, freedom of action, the right to a good repute, legal capacity, and protection in the possession of Acquired Rights.[3]

Distinction between "Rights *in Rem*" and "Rights *in Personam*."

104. All the above Rights are Rights which are available against the whole world, and are, therefore, usually classified under the category of Rights "in Rem" (*jura in rem*). Most of them may also be combined with Rights "in Personam" (*jura in personam*), that is to say, available against determinate

[1] Dig. XXXIX. IV. 9, 5.

[2] Stahl's *Die Philosophie des Rechts*, Vol. II. bk. 3, section 1, p. 255.

[3] *Ibid.* section 2, p. 257.

individuals.[1] In the present Chapter we shall only deal with them in the former category.

Rights relating to personal safety and freedom of action.

105. The first class of Rights which we have to consider includes all those Rights which relate to "Personal Safety" and "Freedom of Action." In civilised countries Rights of this description are held to be the birth-right of a free man, and are hence called "Innate Rights," or Rights which belong to every one by Nature, independent of all Juridical Acts.[2]

Instances of former description of Rights.

106. Instances of the former description of Rights are the following:—

(*a*) Not to sustain personal injury, directly or indirectly, at the hands of another.

"Direct personal injuries" are those which are the result of direct violence, such as hurt or an assault.

"Indirect injuries" are those which result from the negligent exercise on the part of others of their own rights, as, for example, in keeping a vicious animal or allowing the existence of a house in bad repair.

(*b*) Not to be subjected to a threat or menace of injury, or to intentional insult.

Thus, the Indian Penal Code defines criminal intimidation as the threatening another with any injury to his person, reputation, or property, if done with intent to cause alarm; and this offence is punishable with two years' imprisonment, or with fine, or with both.[3] In like manner the same Code regards an "Intentional Insult" as a criminal offence, if done with intent to provoke a breach of the peace.[4]

(*c*) In the case of women not to have their virtue assailed against their will, nor to have their modesty insulted even by gestures.

Thus the Indian Penal Code punishes Rape or an Attempt

[1] *Student's Austin*, pp. 176, 185, 381.

[2] Kant's *Philosophy of Law*, p. 55.

[3] Sections 503 and 506.

[4] Section 504.

CHAP. VII.

to commit Rape,[1] and also the uttering of any word or the making of any gesture calculated to insult the modesty of any woman.[2]

The above Rights die with the Person.

107. But although the above rights are such as may be asserted by the injured person against the whole world, they are nevertheless Rights that are *personal* to him. And thus if a party who has received any personal injury dies before he receives any compensation, his Right dies with him in accordance with the maxim of law: *actio personalis moritur cum persona:* a personal action dies with the person. The English, Canadian, American, and Indian legislatures have, however, introduced an exception to this rule; and an action may now be maintained by the executor or administrator of any person whose death has been caused by the wrongful act, neglect, or default of any other person, if the act is such as would (if death had not ensued) have entitled the party injured to sue.[3] But the action can only be brought according to the English and Indian Law for the benefit of the wife, husband, parent, and child of the deceased, and, if none of these persons exists, the above maxim still applies.[4] The Rights we have been considering may therefore be said, subject to the statutory exception mentioned, to live and die with the person in whom they reside.

An exception to the rule introduced by Statute Law.

Right to "freedom of action" explained.

108. The right to "Freedom of Action" is a Right to act according to one's own will and pleasure, that is to say, independent of the compulsory will of another. But this

[1] Sections 376 and 511. [2] Section 509.

[3] Stat. 9 & 10 Vict. c. 93, and Act XIII. of 1855 of the Indian Legislature; see also section 268 of the Indian Succession Act. In Canada, the Statute Law on the subject is based on Lord Campbell's Act; and in several States of the United States, Statutes of like effect are now in force, a list of which, with their material provisions, is given in Patterson's *Railway Accident Law*, p. 404: Philadelphia, 1886.

[4] In some of the American States the personal representatives or the heir at Law can claim the benefit of the action. *Vide* Patterson's *Railway Accident Law*, p. 404.

Right must co-exist with the like Freedom of the rest of the community according to a Universal Law, which compels a man to respect the Rights of others while he exercises his own.[1] Freedom, in this restricted sense, has been called "the Innate Right of common action on the part of every man so that he may do towards others what does not infringe their Rights or take away anything that is theirs unless they are willing to appropriate it."[2] There is in fact an innate Equality belonging to every man, which consists in his Right to be independent of being bound by others to anything more than that to which he may also reciprocally bind them.[3]

The "infringement" of this Right is actionable.

109. Accordingly, whoever prevents a man from exercising this Right of Freedom, for example, of going where he pleases so long as he does not interfere with the rights of others, commits a wrong for which the Law allows a remedy. The Civil Law gives him an action for damages, while the Criminal Law punishes every one who voluntarily obstructs another so as to prevent him from proceeding in any direction in which he has a right to proceed.[4] And if the restraint is of such a kind as to prevent the person restrained from proceeding beyond certain circumscribing limits, the offence is deemed to be one of "wrongful confinement," for which a much heavier punishment is provided.[5]

But may be justified in certain cases.

110. But the infringement of a Right of "Freedom of Action" may be justified on the ground of the execution of legal process, for, as we have already seen, *executio juris non habet injuriam.* Other grounds of justification are the Right of Private Defence of person or property, or the preservation of the Peace.

[1] Stahl's *Die Philosophie des Rechts*, Vol. II., bk. 3, section 4, pp. 259, 260.

[2] Kant's *Philosophy of Law*, p. 56.

[3] *Ibid.*

[4] The Indian Penal Code, sections 339, 341.

[5] *Ibid.*, sections 340, 342.

CHAP. VII.

Right of action for infringement does not survive.

111. The Right is also a purely personal right which lives and dies with the person. Thus, no action for false imprisonment would survive to a man's executors or administrators.[1]

Right to a good repute.

112. A man's Honour is another Right which falls within the same category. It represents his moral worth in the political community of which he is a member, and he is entitled to have it respected by every other person within the same community. Like the preceding Rights of "Personal Safety" and "Freedom," the Right to a good repute is common to all men and may be asserted against all men. But like them also it is personal and dies with the person in whom it resides.

Is personal, and dies with the person of inherence.

Defamation defined.

113. Now, subject to what is stated in the next paragraph, any statement which conveys concerning a person any imputation tending to bring him into hatred, contempt, or ridicule, or, being made concerning him in the way of his office, profession, or calling, tends to injure him in respect thereof is deemed to defame that person.[2] And if that statement is either made to a third person directly, or is so published or made known that its purport is communicated to persons generally, it becomes actionable. But if the statement is merely made to the person concerned himself, inasmuch as it cannot operate to lessen the esteem to which he is held by others, it is deemed to do no wrong, and is therefore not actionable.[3] The statement may be made by spoken or written words or by signs, or by pictorial or other representations or symbols,[4] and either directly or by in-

[1] Indian Succession Act, section 268.

[2] See section 32 of Sir F. Pollock's *Civil Wrongs Bill.*

[3] *Muhammad Ismail Khan* v. *Muhammad Tahir*, 6 N.-W. P. Rep. 38.

[4] See the case of *Pitumbar Das* v. *Dwarka Pershad*, 2 N.-W. P. Rep. 437. The English distinction between libel and slander is not based on any intelligible principle, and in practice it is disregarded by Courts in British India in suits between natives. *Cf.* XV. Beng. L. Reps. 151; VII. Bomb. H. C. Reps. (A. C.) 17; and I. L. R. VIII. Mad. 175.

sinuation or irony. And it is no excuse that the statement was a mere repetition of a rumour.[1]

CHAP. VII.

When defamatory statement may be justified.

114. The Law acting in the interests of the general public will hold a statement which might otherwise be defamatory to be justified under certain circumstances. Thus, in order to secure the efficient discharge of public functions, and to encourage a wholesome attention to public affairs on the part of the general public, it is held not to be defamation to make or publish in good faith (*i.e.*, with the exercise of due care and caution) any *fair comment* on matters of public interest, or matter otherwise fairly open to public comment. In this way the conduct of a person in the exercise of any public office, the conduct of local authorities in local administration, a published book or paper, a work of art publicly exhibited or offered for sale, a public building, or publicly exhibited architectural design, a new invention or discovery publicly described or advertised, a public performance or entertainment, and the conduct of persons in public places, are all matters open to public criticism.[2] In like manner, in order to promote the impartial discharge of judicial and legislative duties, and to give the utmost publicity to proceedings in Courts and Legislative Assemblies, it is held that *fair* public reports of such proceedings are not defamation. In the case of judicial proceedings, it is immaterial whether the proceedings are preliminary or final, whether contested or *ex parte*, and also whether the Court has actually jurisdiction or not, so long as the proceedings are in due course.[3]

"Privileged communications."

115. Again the Law recognises statements made on certain occasions as privileged, that is to say, they do not then

[1] *Watkin* v. *Hall*, L. R. 3 Q. B. 396.

[2] See the Illustrations to section 35 of Sir F. Pollock's *Civil Wrongs Bill.*

[3] *Usill* v. *Hales*, 3 C. P. D. 319; *Lewis* v. *Levey*, 27 L. J. Q. B. 282; *Abdull Hakim* v. *Tej Chander Mukarji*, I. L. R. III. Allah. 815; *Watson* v. *Walter*, L. R. 4 Q. B. 73.

CHAP. VII.

amount to defamation, provided they are made in good faith, although their purport may be defamatory. These have been summarised as follows, by Sir F. Pollock in his draft *Civil Wrongs Bill*,[1] and may be accepted as embodying the results of English Case Law:—

(*i.*) In discharge of a legal, moral, and social duty existing, or by the person making the statement believed in good faith to exist, of giving information in the matter of the statement to the person to whom it is made; or—

(*ii.*) To a public servant, or other person in authority, in a subject-matter reasonably believed to be within his competence, with a view to the prevention or punishment of an offence or redress of a public grievance; or—

(*iii.*) With a view to the reasonably necessary protection of some interest of the person making the statement; or—

(*iv.*) With a view to the reasonably necessary protection of an interest, or the proper performance of a duty, common to the person making the statement and the person to whom it is made.

No statement defamatory if true.

116. But it is necessary to bear in mind that the Right to a good name can only be said to be a "legal right," when it rests on a solid foundation of truth. A person has no Right, for instance, to a fictitious reputation,[2] and he cannot therefore be said to be defamed if a reputation to which he has no real claim is exposed. Hence it is that the Law allows the truth of a statement to be pleaded as a complete defence in an action for defamation, provided the party relying on the truth of it proves the substantial truth of it as a whole and

[1] Section 38.

[2] Dresch, *Naturrecht*, p. 158; Pollock's *Law of Torts*, p. 223.

of every material part of it.[1] This is called the *exceptio veritatis*.[2] Chap. VII.

117. A Jural Capacity, that is to say, a General Capacity for being the Subject of Rights (*Rechtsfähigkeit*), is another of those Innate Rights which every Man is now deemed to possess in all civilised States. This Capacity signifies that in the eye of the Law all Men, without distinction, are entitled to avail themselves of, and are equally subject to, its general provisions. But it does not mean an absolute unconditional Equality, which involves the abolition of all distinctions, and the levelling of all ranks of society. This unobtainable Equality was, indeed, the boasted product of the French Revolution. But a product destructive of the very fabric of a State could not in the nature of things be permanently maintained, and France at the present day, although governed as a Republic, recognises those distinctions which wealth, education, and position confer upon the individual, and which must prevail in every State where Order and Rights are respected and enforced. We have already seen that a person's Jural Capacity may be restricted in various ways, by age, by sex, by mental conditions. He may also be deprived of it as a consequence of certain Punishments, or by entering into a Religious Order, which involves an abandonment of the world and its affairs.[3] Thus the Roman Law attached the loss of Freedom and Citizenship to the two higher forms of *Capitis Deminutio*, which were, therefore, often assimilated by Roman lawyers to Death.[4] So, also, according to the French Civil Code, persons condemned to Death or to certain other punish-

Capacity for Rights innate to man's nature.

Restriction of Jural Capacity.

Effect of Civil Death.

[1] But in a criminal proceeding for defamation, the truth of the defamatory statement only affords a good defence when it can be shown that the statement was published for the public good. First exception, § 499, I. P. C.

[2] Stahl's *Die Philosophie des Rechts*, Vol. II., bk. 3, section 5, p. 262. *Cf.* Odger's *Libel and Slander*, p. 179.

[3] This was the old English Law, *see* Coke's Reports, Vol. II., p. 48.

[4] Savigny's *System*, Vol. II., pp. 68, 69.

CHAP. VII.

ments (extended by the *Code Pénal* to Penal Servitude for Life on the Galleys and to Deportation) are deemed to be "civilly dead," and for the future incapable of all Civil Rights (*droits civils*). Their entire existing estate passes at the very moment of such an occurrence to their Intestate Heirs, and whatever they may acquire during the period of their Civil Death falls to the State on their Natural Death. During this period also they are incapable of receiving or giving Donations; they are incapable of contracting a valid Marriage, and their existing Marriage is dissolved in regard to all civil effects.[1] So also, although there is no such thing now in English Law as Civil Death, and the fact of a man's entering into a Religious Order (in which Rights of Property are not recognised) no longer deprives him of Rights to which he would otherwise be entitled,[2] it is otherwise in India. Here a person by abandoning worldly affairs and entering a strictly religious or ascetic Order becomes "civilly dead," and forfeits all rights of Inheritance.[3] This principle has been applied by Courts in the Punjab to mendicants of the *Udasi* sect.[4]

No longer recognised in English Law.

But otherwise in India.

Rights and privileges attaching to a man's condition as a Citizen enforceable against every one.

118. But where the natural Capacity for Rights is not specially restricted, every person is held in law to be entitled to all the Rights and Privileges which attach to his position as a Citizen of the State to which he belongs. No one can interfere with his enjoyment of those Rights and Privileges without being answerable in damages, on the principle of "no injury without damage." In such a case there is at least *injuria*, although it may be *sine damno*, which means that the person has suffered what in the eye of the law is looked

[1] Articles 23—25, 33, *Code Civil.* See also Savigny's *System*, Vol. II., section 75, pp. 113 and 114 of my translation.

[2] As to the former English Law, *see* Blackstone's Commentaries, Vol. I., p. 132, and Coke's Reports, Vol. II., p. 48.

[3] Rattigan's *Digest of Civil Law*, p. 34, para. 30, 5th edition.

[4] No. 1, Punjab Record, 1868; No. 15, Punjab Record, 1874. *Cf.* No. 82, P. R. 1883.

upon as a legal injury, and even though he has suffered no actual harm, he must have a corresponding right of action.[1] The celebrated case of *Ashby* v. *White*[2] may be cited in illustration of this important principle. That was an action against a returning officer for maliciously refusing to receive the plaintiff's vote at the election of burgesses to serve in Parliament. It was held by Lord Holt, C. J., and by the House of Lords, that the action was maintainable, although the candidates, in whose favour the vote had been tendered, were in fact elected. The *ratio decidendi* was, that the plaintiff had a legal right to give his vote; and that, having been disturbed in the enjoyment of such right, he could maintain an action[3] against the party causing the disturbance. A somewhat similar case arose under the Bengal Municipal Act (III. of 1884), where an action was held maintainable for a declaration of a right to vote and stand as a candidate for election.[4] So also it has been held in Madras that where a person holds a public Office like that of a Municipal Commissioner, to which no fees or emoluments are attached, but from which he is only removeable on proof of misconduct, an action for damages will lie against the Secretary of State for India in Council if he is removed without proof of misconduct.[5] This was so held under the *Towns Improvement Act of Madras* (No. III. of 1871). But it is to be noticed that the Municipal Act for the Punjab (XX. of 1891) gives the Local Government much larger powers of discretion in judging whether misconduct is established or not than the Madras Act.[6]

Ashby v. White.

119. Protection in the enjoyment of Acquired Rights is the last of those Rights which fall under the first subdivision

Protection of Acquired Rights.

[1] *Kali Kishen Tagore* v. *Judoo Lall Mullick* (1879), *Privy Council Judgments*, by Baldeva Ram Dare, p. 289.

[2] 2 Ld. Raym. 953.

[3] Broom's *Commentaries on the Common Law*, pp. 86, 87. But see Week's *Doctrine of Damnum absque Injuria*, p. 3 (2).

[4] *Sabhapat Singh* v. *Abdul Gaffur* (1896), I. L. Rep. XXIV., Cal. series, 107.

[5] I. L. Reps. VII., Madras series, p. 466.

[6] *Vide* section 11.

CHAP. VII.

of Private Rights, as directly involved in the very notion of a Person, and inseparable from his Personality.[1] As "Acquired Rights" they are distinguishable from those which are regarded as "Innate." But the protection of such Rights is itself an Innate Right. Man, as a sentient Being, is a Being destined to a life of action, and his activities in the direction of the acquisition of Rights are but a natural development of a progressive social existence. It is a form of Activity which the Law must therefore protect, or suffer the very foundations of Society to be overthrown.

Examples.

120. Thus every man has a Right to the unmolested pursuit of the profession or occupation by which he gains his living, provided it is not of an immoral character or contrary to Law; and if this Right is maliciously or violently infringed, under such circumstances as to make the infringement a legal wrong, in other words, if the person is illegally disturbed in carrying on his trade by the employment of unlawful means, an action lies against the wrongdoer.[2] Thus, if a person is compelled by serious threats of personal violence to give up his employment, that would be a case of legal coercion which would give him a good ground for an action against the person who used the threats.[3] So also the Law, in its anxiety to quiet titles to property, will not compel a man to wait until he is actually ejected or forcibly dispossessed. If his title to any character or right is denied by any person, he is entitled to an immediate remedy by way of a suit for a declaration of title.[4]

[1] Stahl's *Die Philosophie des Rechts*, Vol. II., bk. 3, section 7, p. 266.

[2] *Keeble* v. *Hickersgill*, 2 East, 576. This case has been much considered by the House of Lords in the case of *Allen* v. *Flood*, (1898) A. C. 1. The qualification in the text is based on the judgment of Lord Watson, at p. 101.

[3] Per Lord Watson, in *Allen* v. *Flood*, at p. 105. It has more recently been held by the Appeal Court that this decision does not shelter those who take part in "watching and besetting" a man's house or place of business for purposes of indirect coercion. *Lyons & Co.* v. *Wilkins and others*, TIMES, 21st Dec., 1898.

[4] Section 42, Indian Specific Relief Act. See *post*, para. 128.

CHAP. VII.

Where profession is immoral the Law will not recognise it.

121. But if the profession or calling is of an immoral character, such, for instance, as that of prostitution, the Law will do nothing which would give it a legal recognition.[1] Indeed, the Law will go further, and, acting for the protection of minors, it will even render the selling, letting to hire, or otherwise disposing of a minor under a certain age (sixteen years under the Indian Penal Code), with intent that such minor will be employed or used for the purposes of prostitution, a heinous criminal offence.[2] But care must be taken, especially in India, not to extend the application of the rule refusing recognition to immoral professions to other professions, such as that of dancing girls, in which prostitution is neither the *essential* condition nor *necessary* consequence of its practice, but merely an incident due to social influences. Thus it has been held that an adoption of a daughter by a *Naikin*, or dancing girl, can be recognised by the Civil Courts, and does confer rights on the adopted girl.[3]

Certain professions confer no right to remuneration.

122. There are also certain learned professions like that of a Barrister, and till recently that of a Physician,[4] which by a fiction are deemed to be practised without any object of gain. Thus a Barrister in England,[5] and also in India if he has been enrolled as an Advocate of any of the High Courts, is incapable of validly contracting to be paid for his professional services; and, on the other hand, he cannot be sued in regard to any matter in which the relation of counsel and client exists. The rule of incapacity for entering into any contract for hiring with respect to his services as an Advocate is one of the few provisions of the ancient Roman Law[6] which have been

[1] I. L. Repts. I. Mad. 168. [2] Section 372, I. P. C.
[3] I. L. R. XI. Mad. 393. *Cf.* I. L. R. XIV. Bomb. 90.
[4] *Vide* 21 & 22 Vict. c. 90, sect. 31, known as "*The Medical Act*"; *Gibbon* v. *Budd*, 2 H. & C. 92; 32 L. J. Ex. 182. *Cf.* 31 & 32 Vict. c. 29.
[5] *Kennedy* v. *Brown*, 32 L. J. C. P. 137; *Robertson* v. *McDonough*, 14 Cox, C. C. 469; *Hobart* v. *Butler*, 9 Ir. C. L. R. Ex. 127; *Morris* v. *Hunt*, 1 Chit. 544.
[6] Enacted by the *Lex Cincia* in the year of the city 550, modified by Claudius, restored by Nero, and again modified by Trojan. Weiske's *Rechtslexicon*, tit. Advocat, Bd. I., 173.

CHAP. VII.

preserved in England; and when applied to India, where the conditions of practice are altogether different, the rule is clearly anomalous. But it has nevertheless been held by high judicial authority[1] to be applicable to India, and cannot therefore be ignored. It applies to Barristers in India as part of the Law affecting their bar, or professional status.[2] Of course the rule in question is only applicable to *professional* services rendered by a Barrister, or when the relation of counsel and client exists. For other work performed by a Barrister he stands on the same footing as any other individual. Thus it has been held that he can recover remuneration for acting as returning officer at an election,[3] and that he has also a lien for fees on a commission.[4] Even fees to Counsel's clerks are mere gratuities, for which they have no legal demand.[5] A Barrister has, however, been allowed to prove for fees in bankruptcy where the solicitor, the bankrupt, had actually received them before his bankruptcy.[6]

The Right of the individual may also be sacrificed in the interests of the State.

123. The Right to a peaceful enjoyment of one's acquisitions is also subject to the higher Right which belongs to the State, of sacrificing the interests of the individual for the benefit of the general public, when a real necessity for this sacrifice arises. In such cases we have an application of the maxim *salus reipublicæ suprema lex*: "the welfare of the State is supreme Law."[7] Thus, if a man's house be on fire, both it and other property not on fire may be pulled down to prevent the fire spreading to other more valuable property. In such a case a *jus aliquod in re aliena* is conceded even to

[1] 3 N.-W. P. H. C. Reps. 83; I. L. R. VII. Mad. 138. *Cf.* 25 Suth. W. R. 332, as to services rendered *beyond* those of a Barrister, *e.g.*, acting as an attorney in the Mofussil.

[2] *Queen* v. *Doutre* (1884), 9 App. Cas. 745; and No. 51 P. R. 1895.

[3] *Reg.* v. *Kensington Union Guardians*, 3 Q. B. 935, n.

[4] *Smith* v. *Haken*, 2 F. & F. 678.

[5] *Ex parte Cotton*, 9 Beav. 107; 10 Jur. 84.

[6] *In re Hall*, 2 Jur. N. S. 1076.

[7] Stahl's *Die Philosophie des Rechts*, Vol. II., bk. 3, section 7, pp. 268—272.

Chap. VII.

private persons on the ground of an extreme urgent physical necessity (*summa necessitas*).[1] So in time of war, every man's property may be taken for the defence or preservation of the State generally.[2] In like manner a man may be compelled on payment of compensation to give up his private property, no matter how much he may prize and desire to keep it, if it is required for some public purpose such as that of a line of railway or some town improvement, although the general rule of Law is to the effect that "no man shall be compelled to sell his property even at a fair price" (*nemo cogitur rem suam vendere, etiam justo pretio*).[3]

Rights of Property.

124. We now come to Rights of Property the subjects of which are Things, understood in the wide legal sense of the expression, as embracing the two-fold classification of *material* or *physical* objects perceptible by the external organs of sense, and artificial or purely intellectual objects which have no tangible external existence.[4] In this connection a curious question may be raised whether a dead body of a human being is the subject of a right of property? By the Law of England the answer to this question would require to be in the negative, for by that Law there can be no right of property in a dead body, nor can a man dispose of his body by will, although a Court would very naturally be disposed to give effect to the reasonable wishes of the deceased.[5] Until burial the executors of a deceased have, however, a right to the custody and possession of the body, and when it is buried in consecrated ground it remains under the protection of the Ecclesiastical Court of the diocese, and cannot be removed from the grave, or vault, or mausoleum in which it

[1] Grotius, *De Jure Belli ac Pac.* lib. III. c. 20, section 7.

[2] Wharton's *Law Maxims*, 177.

[3] *Vide* Act X. of 1870.

[4] *Vide* para. 26, *ante*.

[5] Cf. the judgment of the Consistory Court of London, in the matter of the cremation of the remains of Lieut.-Col. Dixon, reported in the *Times* of 30th July, 1892.

CHAP. VII.

has been placed, except under a faculty granted by an Ecclesiastical Court, and then only to another grave or vault in consecrated ground.[1]

The meaning of "mine" by Right.

125. Speaking generally, Thing may be said to be "*mine*" by *Right* when I am so connected with it, that if any other person should make use of it without my consent, he would do me a lesion or injury.[2] It follows, therefore, that the possibility of excluding every other person from the Possession or private Use of a Thing is the fundamental element which constitutes my Right in that Thing. Hence, as Kant truly says, a man entirely alone upon the earth could properly neither have nor acquire any external Thing as his own.[3] Because between him, as a person, and all external objects, as Things, there could be no relation of obligation. It is this relation, then, between the possessor and other people which he can exclude from the Thing, that furnishes the necessary condition for the foundation of a Right.

Gradual development of the notion of Possession.

126. But in the childhood of the history of mankind, a natural instinct led men to appropriate for their own use objects in the external world which were necessary for their bare existence. Thus they plucked roots or fruits, caught or killed wild beasts, with the skins of which they clothed themselves, and broke off branches from trees with which they constructed a rude shelter. In short, the necessities of personal existence drove man in a state of Nature to seize physical objects within his grasp. He thus learnt to recognise his mastery over them, and to realize that they were intended for his use. In this way the individual became master of his prey, of his care, of his female. At first he

[1] *Williams* v. *Williams*, L. R. 20 Ch. D. 659.

[2] Kant's *Philosophy of Law*, p. 61.

[3] *Ibid.* p. 86. There cannot be personality without community, whence the aphorism *unus homo, nullus homo.* *Vide* D. Lioy's *Philosophy of Right*, by Hastie, Vol. II., p. 6.

contented himself with what was necessary for his daily consumption. This was the period of "occupation" which Schäffle assimilates to that of wild beasts (*thierähnliche Okkupation*).[1] But by degrees men began to see the necessity of reserving a store for future use; and the same necessity impelled them to guard that store from external attack. Here then the first traces of the value of Possession begin to show themselves. Primitive man knows nothing indeed of Ownership as distinguished from Possession. But he fully comprehends that while a thing is in his possession it is in his power, and he can use it. When it has passed from his possession into that of another, it ceases to be his.[2] Bentham may scoff at this primitive form of possession and call it "wretched and precarious,"[3] which it was. But it was nevertheless the first step towards the evolution of a Right of Property, and in this light it is interesting to the student of Jurisprudence.

The notion of Ownership follows upon that of Possession.

127. Once in fact we reach the stage of social progress where the value of Possession is recognised, we may be assured that the process of evolution of the idea of Ownership has already commenced; for, as Lubbock rightly says, the latter idea must develop itself from the notion of simple Possession.[4] The transition from a nomadic to a partially settled condition has then surely begun, and the individualisation of property now becomes at once marked and positive, although it is as yet associated, not with immoveable estate, but, as Mommsen observes, with estate in slaves and cattle (*familia pecuniaque*).[5] Hence it may be said that the close of the earlier stage, which ends with the knowledge of the notion

[1] *Bau und Leben des sozialen Körpers*, III. 404.

[2] Bluntschli, *Gesammelte Kleine Schriften*, Vol. I., pp. 184, 185.

[3] *Principes du Code Civil*, par Dumont, c. IX.

[4] *Origin of Civilisation*, p. 394; see also Adolph Samter's *Das Eigenthum* (1879), p. 80.

[5] *Römische Geschichte*, Vol. I., p. 184, siebente Auflage: Berlin, 1881.

of Possession, marks the commencement of the later period, in which the idea of Ownership is gradually developed. The process of evolution was doubtless a long one, marked by streaks of blood through centuries of contest. But the final triumph of the idea was inseparable from the destinies of organised Society; and if at the present day we have seen its highest development carried to a point of altitude which gives some colour to the objection that the institution of Property is a cruel injustice, it is notwithstanding an idea which lies at the basis of all good government, and is a legacy which can never be completely abandoned, although it may receive a certain modification in the future. What that modification shall be, or what direction it shall take, is one of the burning questions which agitate, as Lassalle says,[1] the heart of the modern world, but it is one which happily lies outside the scope of the present work.

Distinction between Possession and Ownership recognised in Roman and Hindu Law.

128. The distinction between Possession and Ownership was first clearly indicated in the Roman Law. Down to the time of Servius no *dominium* or Quiritarian Ownership, except perhaps in the case of captured slaves or cattle, existed in moveables. But the protection of their Possession against theft or violence was secured by Interdicts, while the remedy for true Ownership or *dominium* was by a real action (*rei vindicatio, actio negatoria*). By the reforms which were introduced by Servius certain moveables came to be classed along with lands and houses as *res mancipi* (*i.e.*, transferable by mancipation or surrender in Court) and then became objects of Quiritarian Right.[2] But at this period the inhabitants of Rome had passed from a pastoral to an agricultural community, and the cultivation of the vine and the olive had, for the most part, supplanted the former occupation of grazing flocks and rearing cattle. The staff of the herdsman

[1] *Acquired Rights*, Preface, p. vii.

[2] Muirhead's *Law of Rome*, 42 and note.

was now laid aside for the ploughshare of the agriculturist, which for the second time, as Mommsen eloquently observes, secured to the Roman what he had originally acquired by the lance.[1] This transition from a pastoral to an agricultural economy naturally facilitated the development of ideas of Ownership of the soil which was cultivated. So long as men were huntsmen or herdsmen they were naturally nomadic in character, and had no settled habitations.[2] Like the Indians in the pristine forests of Brazil, they either lived on trees or in wattled huts constructed of branches twined together like bee-hives, and had no sense of Ownership in land. But with the planting of trees and the cultivation of the soil, the sentiment of a local home and the notion of Ownership begin to develop themselves. Trees take years to grow up and become fruit-bearing, and meantime require constant care and watchfulness, which can only be adequately given by those who are on the spot. This leads to the construction of dwellings and the change from a nomadic to a settled life. Then, again, the necessity of hedging round the vineyards and orchards, as a protection from the ravages of wild beasts and other external enemies, produces the notion of individual Right, which is the basis of what in a more advanced stage of Society we call Ownership.[3] The history of the Ownership of land is thus for the most part the history of Civilisation.[4] It is curious to notice that in the ancient Hindu Law also we have clear evidence of the distinction between physical Possession and full Ownership. Thus, both *Manu*[5] and *Yajnyawalkya*[6] recognise a title by prescription in the case of immoveables if the possession extends for a period of *twenty* years, and in the case of moveables for a period of *ten* years.

[1] Mommsen, *Römische Geschichte*, I., p. 183; Dickson's English translation, Vol. I., p. 193.

[2] Bluntschli, *Gesammelte Kleine Schriften*, Vol. I., p. 189.

[3] Hehn, *Kulturplanzen und Hausthiere*, p. 104.

[4] Bluntschli, *Gesammelte Kleine Schriften*, Vol. I., p. 189.

[5] VIII. 147.

[6] II. 24.

CHAP. VII.

Such a provision obviously implies that the physical fact may be ripened into an absolute Right by lapse of time; and furnishes fresh evidence of the truth of the theory that, although, as we shall see, Possession may exist apart from Ownership, the latter is but a development of the former. It is in Ownership, however, that the doctrine of Mine and Thine finds at last its fullest and most complete expression.

Physical Possession is itself a Right.

129. As the influence of Law began to be felt, that which before was a mere physical condition, began to assume a more formal character. And thus, even before a mere Possession is converted by prescription into a right of Ownership, it is in itself a right which, both according to the old Roman Law and the present Law of British India, is protected by special summary remedies. The Indian Specific Relief Act accordingly provides that, if any person is dispossessed without his consent of immoveable property, otherwise than in due course of Law, he, or any person claiming through him, may, by suit instituted within six months from the date of the dispossession, recover possession thereof, notwithstanding any other title that may be set up in such suit.[1] It has also been decided by a Full Bench of the Bombay High Court, that a person may even claim (under section 42 of the Specific Relief Act) a declaration of his Right to retain Possession against another person who cannot

[1] Section 9. The Roman Law also restored a man by means of Interdict to the position *quo ante* from which he had been illegally disturbed (*a*). Windscheid thinks that this protection of Possession rests on the same ground as protection against *injuria*, that is, that every one is the equal of every other in the State, and no one shall raise himself over the other. But he hastens to explain that this does not mean, as Bruns wrongly assumes, that Possession is protected by reason of the injury which underlies its disturbance—but rather, that the same notion of Right which lies at the foundation of the punishment of injury has led to the recognition of a Right to be restored to the factitious condition from which one has been removed by an arbitrary exercise of power (*b*).

(*a*) Windscheid, *Pandektenrecht*, Vol. I., Section 148, p. 445.
(*b*) *Ibid.*, note 6.

CHAP. VII.

show a better title, and who denies or is interested to deny his Right—founded on the mere fact of Possession—irrespective of whether the latter has continued for a sufficiently long period to confer an absolute title upon him under section 28 of the Limitation Act.[1] But this decision has been dissented from by a majority of a Bench of three Judges of the Chief Court of the Punjab.[2] The question must, however, be taken as settled contrary to the view of the Chief Court decision by the judgment of the Privy Council in *Ismail Ariff* v. *Mahomed Gous*,[3] in which it was held that lawful possession (though only extending over six years) is sufficient to entitle a person to a declaration of title against another who had no title and was a mere trespasser.

Elements constituting a Right of Possession.

130. This Right of Possession is called "*jus possessionis,*" and involves in its conception both a physical and mental element. Stahl contends, in controverting the opposite theory of Gans,[4] that Possession is not, strictly speaking, a Right, but only a "legally protected factitious condition," because it requires the existence of that condition for its continuance: when the condition ceases, the protection attached to it ceases also.[5] But as a Right has already been defined[6] to be "the capacity residing in a person of controlling, with the assent and assistance of the State, the actions of others," or, as Ihering has otherwise defined it, "a legally protected interest," it is difficult to appreciate the distinction between a right in this sense and a "legally protected factitious condition." As admirably observed by a well-known American Judge and writer, in a passage already quoted,[7] "just so far as the aid of the public force is given a man, he has a legal right." And just so far as

[1] I. L. R. VII. Bomb. 291.

[2] *Budreddin* v. *Abul Kasim and others*, No. 12 P. R. 1888.

[3] I. L. R. (1893), 20 Cal. 834.

[4] *Grundlage des Besitzes*, p. 33.

[5] *Die Philosophie des Rechts*, p. 313, Vol. II.

[6] *Ante*, para. 11 (a), p. 26.

[7] See *ante*, p. 28.

Possession is protected, it is as much a source of legal Right as Ownership is when it secures the same protection.[1] The truth is that Stahl and others after him have viewed Possession too exclusively as a physical condition. But the mere physical or factitious condition is not sufficient to constitute Possession in a juridical sense. There must still be added to it the mental element or intention to hold the Possession against all comers, except perhaps the true owner, should he ever happen to make his appearance. In other words, there must be an intent to appropriate it, to make it part of one's self, or one's own.[2] We must also distinguish the simple "right of possession"—the *jus possessionis*, derived from the mere physical fact of possession—from the "right of possessing," or the "right to possess" (the *jus possidendi*). Thus, the owner of a thing has the right of possessing it (the *jus possidendi*), although, as a fact, he may not have the actual physical possession of the thing. On the other hand, even a robber has a "right of possession" (*jus possessionis*) arising from the mere physical fact of possession, which he

[1] O. W. Holmes, Jr., *The Common Law*, p. 214; compare *Windscheid*, Vol. I., section 180, pp. 455—457. Professor Odoardo Ruggieri, in his learned work *Il Possesso e gl'Istituti di Diritto Prossimi ad Esso*, &c., Firenze, 1880, concludes a lengthy examination of the texts of the Roman Law concerning Possession by maintaining that according to the primitive and simple notion of the expression, which was never abandoned by the Roman Law, it meant the physical detention of a thing whereby man exercises his activity upon the same exclusively, and not momentarily. In a broader sense, viewed with reference to the principal considerations from which the positive law regards it, it is the physical detention or other condition of fact recognised by the law as equivalent, through which man exercises in reality or potentially his activity upon a thing, exclusively and not momentarily, and to which the law itself accords efficacity and protection. And as regards this protection, it is not derived from the mere simple nature of possession, but directly from the positive law in view of its external effects and general convenience. Vol. I., section 84, p. 115.

[2] As Kant says, there must be the empirical fact of taking possession (*apprehensio*) conjoined with the Will to have an external object as one's 'own." *Philosophy of Law*, p. 96. *Cf. Windscheid*, Vol. I., section 149, p. 450.

can assert against every one, but the true owner, who arbitrarily interferes with its exercise.[1] So, again, if I give a servant a purse filled with money to keep for me, he has no legal Right to the purse or its contents, although he has *physical* or actual possession of it (*i.e.*, a *jus possessionis* as distinguished from a *jus possidendi*): the reason being that I have not relinquished the physical Possession of the purse with the intention of losing control over it, nor, if the servant is honest, can he have the intention of exercising control over it upon his own behalf.[2] The celebrated case of *Armory* v. *Delamirie*[3] may also be cited in illustration of this doctrine. There the finder of a jewel, who took it to a jeweller to ask his opinion respecting it, was held to have an action of trover against the jeweller for tortiously retaining it. It was held that, although the plaintiff by finding the jewel did not acquire an absolute property or Ownership in it, yet the bare Possession constituted a sufficient title to enable the party enjoying it to obtain a legal remedy, if he chose to claim it, against all but the rightful owner. Now the fact that the plaintiff asserted this remedy was conclusive proof that he intended to derive all the benefit which the law gave him from the physical condition of Possession; and this element, added to the physical condition, completed his right to redress against the wrongdoer without a title.[4]

Physical contact not essential.

131. It is by no means necessary, however, that the physical element should consist in the actual control of the

[1] Savigny *Das Recht des Besitzes*, 6th ed., section 5, note 1, p. 25; section 6, p. 34; *Istituzioni di Diritto Romano, di Filippo Serafini*, Vol. I., p. 182. *Cf.* also Austin's *Jurisprudence*, Vol. I., p. 53, 3rd ed.; Ahrens' *Philosophie des Rechts, &c.*, Vol. II., section 72, p. 120.

[2] Markby's *Elements of Law*, sections 367—369. As Paulus says: "*Animo nostro, corpore etiam alieno possidemus.*" See also *Windscheid*, Vol. I., section 155, pp. 470, 471.

[3] 1 Smith's L. Cases, 6th ed., 315.

[4] As Windscheid remarks, the Will to appropriate as one's own may be either expressly declared, or deduced from one's act: Vol. I., section 154, p. 467.

CHAP. VII.

thing, whether it happens to be immoveable or moveable. All that is necessary is for the possessor to have the physical power of dealing with the Thing exclusively as his own. Thus, if money is locked up in a box, and the box is conveyed to my house, the key being placed in my hands, it cannot be doubted that Possession has been completely transferred to me, although I have had no actual corporal contact with the box. Or, to give a more homely illustration mentioned by the framers of the Indian Penal Code in their Report, "it will not be doubted that, when a person gives a dinner, his silver forks, while in the hands of his guests, are still in his Possession."[1] So in the case of a sale of a large estate, if I pay the price, and the title deeds are duly registered and delivered to me, and the buyer then takes me to the estate and formally makes over possession of the same to me, here also the transfer of Possession is complete, although I may not have come into physical contact with every part of the estate. In each of these examples, notwithstanding the absence of physical contact, the Possession is held to be complete, because the possibility exists of being able to deal with the property exclusively as one's own.[2] So again, where Government placed guards round a swamp in which salt was spontaneously formed, it was held by the Madras High Court that such Possession of the salt had been taken as would cause its removal from the swamp against the will of Government, and with the intention of obtaining an unlawful gain, to be theft.[3]

Distinction between Possession of domestic and wild animals.

132. The above principle may be further illustrated with reference to the Possession of live animals. In the case of

[1] Stokes's *Anglo-Indian Codes*, Vol. I., p. 55.

[2] Markby's *Elements of Law*, sections 354—358; Holland's *Jurisprudence*, p. 160.

[3] *Queen* v. *Tamma Ghaeirtayya*, I. L. R. IV. Mad. 228. In connection with this case reference may be made, as illustrating section 22 of the Indian Penal Code, to I. L. R. X. Mad. 255, and I. L. R. XV. Bomb. 702. *Cf.* also 10 Bomb. H. C. Reps. 74.

domesticated animals, the rule which applies to moveable property generally, is also applicable to them, subject to the same liberal construction. But in the case of wild animals, birds, fish, and all other animals which live either in the sea, the air, or on the earth, and which are *feræ naturæ*, a more stringent application of the rule is rendered necessary. In either case, what the Law requires to constitute a legal Possession is the possibility of exercising physical control over the object; that is to say, of dealing with it as one's own (*pro suo habendi*). In the case of an animal in a domestic state, my physical control over it would not be deemed to be lost merely because I could not for the moment lay my hand upon it. Thus in the case of a house dog, it would be absurd to suppose that I had lost Possession because the animal had gone from my house into the street or the open fields surrounding my house. Animals of a domestic nature, like a house dog, are accustomed to return to the place where they are fed and kept, and are hence presumed to have an *animus revertendi*.[1] But in the case of a wild animal which I have captured, no such presumption can be drawn. Accordingly, so soon as it has regained its natural liberty by escaping out of my sight or control, it ceases to be mine, and again becomes what it was before my capture, a *res nullius*, *i.e.*, a thing which has no owner, and which, therefore, becomes the property of him who next captures it.[2] Upon the same principle that complete captivity is necessary to constitute possession of *feræ naturæ*, the better opinion appears to have been in Rome, and it was subsequently adopted by Justinian,[3] that if a wild beast is badly wounded and pursued, it does not become the property of the pursuer until he has actually captured it. So it has been held in America, that an action does not lie against a person for

[1] Dig. XII. I. 415, section 4; Savigny's *Das Recht des Besitzes*, section 31, p. 400.

[2] Just. *Inst.*, II. 1, 12.

[3] *Inst.*, II. 1, 13.

CHAP. VII.

killing and taking a fox which had been pursued by another, and was then actually in the view of the person who had originally found, started, and chased it.[1] In India the question of the Possession of fish in tanks has more than once engaged the attention of the Civil Courts. Thus it has been held that fish in a creek,[2] or in the ordinary open irrigation tanks of Southern India,[3] or in navigable rivers,[4] are not in the possession of the person entitled to the ordinary *jalkar* rights of fishery. But where fish are kept in an *enclosed* tank, from which they are unable to escape, and are therefore "restrained of their natural liberty," they are held to be in the Possession of the owner of the tank.[5] On the other hand, where a bull has been set at large in accordance with Hindu usage, the animal, it is said, becomes *res nullius*, and therefore not property in respect to which any determinate person has Possession or in respect to which theft can be committed.[6] But this position has been doubted,[7] and it has been elsewhere held that a bull dedicated to an idol and allowed to roam at large is not *fera bestia* and therefore *res nullius*, but *primâ facie* the trustee of the temple, where the idol is worshipped, has the rights and liabilities attaching to its ownership.[8]

Representative Possession.

133. We have already seen that a servant who has the custody of a thing on behalf of his master, is not deemed in Law to have a "right of possessing" it (*jus possidendi*), although he may have a *jus possessionis* and may be com-

[1] Holmes's *The Common Law*, p. 217.

[2] *Queen* v. *Reva Pothadu*, I. L. R. V. Mad. 390.

[3] *Ibid.*, p. 391, note. *Cf.* I. L. R. XV. Cal. 402.

[4] *Hurri Mote Mohorell* v. *Dino Nath*, 19 W. R., 15 Cr. R.; *Bhusan Perin* v. *Dino Nath Banerjee*, 20 W. R., 15 Cr. R. *Cf.* also I. L. R. XV. Cal. 388.

[5] *Queen* v. *Shaik Adam*, I. L. R. X. Bomb. 193; *Maya Ram Surma* v. *Nichala Katani* (1888), I. L. R. XV. Cal. 402.

[6] I. L. R. VIII. Allah. 51; and IX. *Ibid.* 348. These decisions were followed by Norris and Macpherson, JJ., in *Romesh Chandar* v. *Hiru Mandal*, I. L. R. XVII. Cal. 842.

[7] *Vide* No. 34, P. R. 1888, Cr.

[8] I. L. R. XI. Mad. 145.

monly spoken of as "*in possessione esse.*" The former Right involves, as we have also seen, the intention on the part of the person in whom it resides *pro suo habendi*, and is characteristic of a proprietary possession. But the servant, if he is faithful to his trust, has no such intention; and the Law refuses to let him derive any advantage from his fraudulent act, if he subsequently determines to assume control on his own behalf. In contemplation of Law, two persons cannot at the same time fully and completely possess the same thing;[1] and as the servant has no such complete right by reason of the want of "animus," while the master has never relinquished the "animus" to maintain his own "right," the Law regards the legal possession as still vested in the master. This sort of Possession is called "Representative" or "Constructive Possession," and is also applied in the case of infants and persons of unsound mind. These persons, although themselves incapable of making any determination of the will, have their mental incapacity supplied by their parents, guardians, or curators, and through them they can legally exercise a Right of Possession.

Distinguished from Derivative.

134. The representative himself has no Possession of the thing in his physical control; the real possession is that of his principal. This is the element which distinguishes "Representative" from "Derivative Possession." The latter is true legal Possession, because the holder of the thing combines in his person both the physical and mental elements which are necessary to constitute it. He holds the physical control over the thing, and he intends to hold it as his own. Thus a creditor has a "Derivative Possession"[2] of the articles pledged with him, the bailee of the goods bailed, a pawnbroker of the goods pawned, and a watchmaker of the watch entrusted to him for repair, so long as anything is due

[1] Dig. XLI. 2, 3, 5.

[2] See Illustrations (*j*) and (*k*) of section 378, *Indian Penal Code*.

CHAP. VII. to him for his labour. In each of these the derivative holder has a special qualified Right transferred to him, which is in the nature of a *Jus in re aliena*, and available against all the world.[1] Indeed, the owner himself may commit a theft if he dishonestly removes the property out of the Possession of the derivative possessor. Thus, to take the instance of the watchmaker, to whom money is owed for repairing a watch. Here by law he is entitled to retain the watch as security for the debt due to him,[2] and if the owner of the watch were to take the watch out of his Possession with the intention of depriving him of the property as a security for his debt, he would commit theft.[3] The Roman Law indeed did not recognise the bailee or a tenant or fructuary as a legal possessor, and assimilated his position to that of a servant.[4] But the framers of the Indian Penal Code evidently dissented from this view, for, in illustration (*e*) of section 378 of that Code, they distinctly recognized the Possession of bailed goods as vested in the bailee, and by analogy they would doubtless have held the same with regard to a tenant and fructuary. And in the Indian Contract Act the Legislature has acted upon the same view of the law. Thus, if a third person wrongfully deprives the bailee of the use or possession of the goods bailed, or does any injury, the bailee is entitled to use such remedies as the owner might have used in the like case if no bailment had been made.[5]

Possession of co-owners.

135. It has been stated above that in contemplation of

[1] Markby's *Elements of Law*, sections 382—390; Holland's *Jurisprudence*, pp. 162—164.

[2] *Vide* section 170, *Indian Contract Act.*

[3] *Vide* Illustration (*j*), section 378, *Indian Penal Code.*

[4] Savigny's *Recht des Besitzes*, sections 9, 23. But at the same time the Roman Law permitted an *actio furti* to be brought by any one who was interested in the safety of the thing, although he was not the owner, provided the thing had been delivered to, and was or had been in his Possession. Gaius, iii. 203; Just. *Inst.*, IV. 1, 13, 14 and 15.

[5] Section 180, *Indian Contract Act.*

Law only one person can be in complete Possession of a corporeal thing at a time. But when corporeal property belongs to two or more persons as co-owners in certain defined shares, and they have a like power over their own shares, and intend to exercise, if necessary, that power on their own behalf, each of them is deemed to be in Possession of his share of the property.[1] Thus the Privy Council decided in the celebrated case of *Appovier* v. *Ramsubhai Aiyan*,[2] that under the Hindu Law of the *Mitacshara* school "when the members of an undivided family agree among themselves with regard to particular property, that it shall thenceforth be the subject of ownership in certain defined shares, then the character of undivided property and joint enjoyment is taken away from the subject-matter so agreed to be dealt with, and in the estate each member has henceforth a definite and certain share which he may claim a right to receive and enjoy in severalty, although the property itself has not been actually severed and divided." Under the Bengal school of Hindu Law, which has been called the school of "fractional ownership,"[3] there is no such thing as "Joint Ownership" in the sense of the two unities, *i.e.*, of Right and Possession. By that Law each co-owner has a definite share, and his right "is fastened upon one particular portion, which portion remains in an unidentifiable condition before partition, and becomes identifiable after partition."[4]

Quasi-possessio.

136. Since the legal idea of Possession depends on the possibility of exercising physical control over the thing, apart from Ownership, and does not necessarily require physical contact, there would appear to be no reason why a Right over a Thing should not be the subject of Possession. But as in

[1] Markby's *Elements of Law*, section 399; Stokes's *Anglo-Indian Codes*, Vol. I., p. 56.

[2] 2 Moore's *Indian Appeals*, 75. *Cf.* No. 2 Punjab Record, 1892.

[3] *Tagore Law Lectures* for 1884-85, p. 173.

[4] *Ibid.*, p. 171.

ordinary language we can hardly speak of the Possession of an incorporeal (*i.e.*, intangible) Thing, the position of a person who exercises a mere Right over that Thing is described by the term *quasi-possessio.*[1] In this sense the Roman lawyers included all Rights over estates short of Ownership, under the denomination of *servitutes*. These Rights conferred various privileges or advantages upon the person of inherence (*i.e.*, in whom they resided), or imposed burthens on the person obliged; as, for instance, that a person has to support the weight of the adjoining house, that a neighbour has the right of inserting a beam into his wall, that he is not to raise his house higher, or not to obstruct his neighbour's lights.[2] Such Rights, the nature of which will be more fully explained presently, would now for the most part be called Easements, while Servitudes with a right to make a profit out of the substance of the neighbouring tenement, such as to dig for minerals or sand, are termed in English law *Profits à prendre*. Thus a Right to take water from a spring on my neighbour's land would be an Easement; but the right to take gravel or grass would be a *Profit à prendre*. The distinction is a very slender one, and is not maintained by the Indian Legislature.[3]

Loss of Possession.

137. Possession ceases so soon as one of the elements which have been declared to be necessary for its constitution has ceased to be operative.[4] But once the mental element, for example, has been declared by the will, it is not necessary that it should be maintained in constant activity. It will be presumed to continue so long as it is not negatived by a new act of will opposed to that by which Possession was acquired: (*ita nulla amittatur, nisi in qua utrumque in contrarium actum*

[1] Sandars' *Justinian*, ii. 2, p. 195, 3rd ed.; Markby's *Elements of Law*, sections 391, 392; Holland's *Jurisprudence*, p. 167.

[2] Just., *Inst.* iii. 3, 1.

[3] Section 4, *Explanation*, *Indian Easements Act*, 1882.

[4] *Possessionem amitti vel animo vel etiam corpore.* Dig XLIV. 2.

est).[1] Nor, again, would it be sufficient to break the continuity of the possessory relation, if the corporal element was not actually existing at any given moment. Thus the person in Possession of a house may shut it up and go elsewhere for a time without meaning to abandon it, or to surrender his Possession. Or, a person may bury treasure in a place, and may afterwards momentarily forget where he buried it. In such, and analogous cases, there is no loss of Possession, because the power of reproducing the relation at will exists.[2] Again, the Law assumes that everything in my house or garden is in my Possession by reason of the complete and exclusive dominion I have over it.[3] By an application of this principle, it is held that if I drop a coin or ring in my garden, and cannot on searching find it, I do not by that circumstance lose my Legal Possession of the article.

CHAP. VII.

Ownership.

138. The transition of legal thought from Possession to Ownership runs historically parallel with the transition of primitive man from the condition of a Huntsman to that of a Shepherd, and from that of a Shepherd to an Agriculturist. As a Huntsman his wants were few, and these were supplied by the skill of his arm and the swiftness of his foot, and each day's supply was but sufficient for the day's consumption. He had as yet no higher sense of a Right of Property than that which the cravings of nature prompted him to assert.

> "Pride then was not, nor arts that pride to aid;
> Man walk'd with beast, joint tenant of the shade;
> The same his table, and the same his bed,
> No murder cloath'd him, and no murder fed."[4]

He was prepared, indeed, to maintain his hold of the beast of the forest or the fruits of trees which fell into his hands,

[1] Dig. L. 17, 1.

[2] Windscheid, *Pandektenrecht*, Vol. I., section 156, pp. 478, 479; Markby's *Elements of Law*, section 362; Holland's *Jurisprudence*, pp. 148, 149.

[3] Savigny, *Das Recht des Besitzes*, section 17, p. 25; section 313, p. 39.

[4] Pope's *Essay on Man*, III., 151 *seq.*

because his self-existence depended on his doing so. So long as such articles of consumption were within his grasp and under his immediate control, the fact of his Physical Possession gave him a rude sense of Right. The animals he had killed and captured, or the fruits he had plucked or gathered, were his by his actual mastery over them. But this glimmering sense of Right depended *ex hypothesi* on the maintenance of the physical condition. If that condition ceased to exist, the notion of Right, which depended upon it, vanished immediately. Here then Possession was deemed to confer a Right, but Ownership, as expressing the condition of a person in whom the virtual legal power over a Thing is vested,[1] and which may exist apart from actual or physical Possession, was not within the primitive Huntsman's conception. But when the Huntsman gradually merged into the Shepherd, and he began to tend and rear flocks, his idea of what constituted Possession naturally expanded. He could now understand that a thing which was not actually in his hand might still be in his Possession. His sheep and goats while they grazed in the forest or on the hill-side might often wander beyond his sight. But these animals were no longer in the condition of *feræ naturæ* or wild beasts, of which the primitive Huntsman had alone experience, and he knew they would return at his call. He therefore regarded them as still in his Possession, not only when they were herded together, but also when they were out for pasture. And lastly, when the Shepherd either combines with his pastoral the conditions of agricultural-life, or abandons the former for the latter, his ideas of the Right which Possession confers undergo a further development. The land which he now occupies, and from which he hopes to derive his subsistence, will not yield its produce without labour. He has first to plough the land, then to scatter the seed over it, and when, after a period of

[1] Ahrens' *Philosophie des Rechts*, &c., Vol. II., section 69, p. 114.

patient waiting, the seed at length begins to germinate, this need of vigilance becomes greater and continues until the crop has ripened and the harvest has been collected. During the intervening period of anxiety and hope, between the ploughing of the land and the reaping of the harvest, the agriculturist continues to regard the cultivated area as in his Possession. And as year by year he goes through the same process of ploughing, sowing, and reaping, his Possession acquires a fixity in his mind which is indistinguishable from pure Ownership. Thus, then, when we examine the conditions of primitive life, and trace it from a purely nomadic to a settled existence, we find the proof of what was previously stated, that Ownership is but a natural development of an earlier Right of Possession. It is consequently not a product of Nature but of human culture. In the most primitive condition of human life, when men were still Huntsmen, we perceive the Right of Possession in its earliest and rudest stage; in that of the Shepherd it has been more clearly realized, but is still confined for the most part to moveables; while in that of the Agriculturist it has extended itself to immoveables, and has acquired a fixity and permanence which assimilate it to Ownership.[1] At this stage it is felt that the use of the sling, the bow, or the carbine may be good, but that of the plough is better; a wigwam may afford a better shelter than the branches of a tree, but a barn and a house are better still.[2]

Earliest form of Ownership.

139. There can hardly be any doubt that the earliest form of Ownership gradually evolved, as we have seen,[3] from the primitive notion of "personal occupation" of "cave," "hut," or "prey," was that of Corporate or Family Ownership.

[1] Adolph Samter, *Das Eigenthum*, pp. 87—90; Bluntschli, *Gesammelte Kleine Schriften*, Vol. I., pp. 181—184.

[2] *Cf.* the speech of Kareihunsta, an Oneida Indian, quoted by Samter, *Das Eigenthum*, p. 89.

[3] Para. 126, *ante*.

CHAP. VII. The more wild and waste the condition of the earth's surface, the more need there was for men to co-operate to reclaim it by joint cultivation and joint labour. The notion, too, of communal or family tenures is but the natural sequence of the habits and sentiments of an earlier nomadic stage, in which the wandering horde, compelled to seek its subsistence on wild food, must continue to make joint use of the area which it temporarily inhabits. The habits and sentiments thus engendered survive after the transition to a partially settled life. And, again, common use of the greater part of the occupied area must long continue from mere inability to set up effectual divisions, and from the incentives to exclusive individual possession being small while the impediments to its peaceable enjoyment are great.[1] Hence it follows that the more archaic the society, the more certain are we to find the principle of joint Ownership preserved intact, with little or no trace of the individualisation of property. Thus, even at the present day the purest type of an Indian Village Community is that where joint and undivided Ownership is the prevailing tenure. Separate Ownership is a still later development, which presupposes a settled order of government, sufficiently strong to protect the individual in the enjoyment of his separate Rights. It was naturally a form of proprietary Right which developed itself under the influence of Rome's universal and iron sway. From Rome the theory was transmitted to other European nations, until it assumed a generality in the West which has since become almost universal. In India, likewise, we find that individual property was preceded by collective property in the land.[2] Joint possession of all property under the presidency of a House Father (*dampati=domus patres*) was the characteristic feature of the ancient *gotra* groups, which subsequently expanded

[1] Herbert Spencer, *Political Institutions*, pp. 541, 542 (1885).

[2] *Tagore Law Lectures*, for 1884-85, p. 90.

themselves into a number of class divisions known as Castes. Usanus, one of the early promulgators of the Hindu Law, enumerates amongst impartible things the field (*kshetra*), vehicles (*pattra*, translated *documents* by Colebroke), prepared food, water and women.[1] But under Brahminical influences the principle of collective-Ownership gradually weakened. The restrictions inseparable from a system of joint households were not conducive to the aggrandisement of wealth by the priestly class. Manu accordingly inculcated the doctrine that partition was conducive to the growth of religion, because religious rites are multiplied by there being several households in place of one.[2] And thus it is that in provinces like Bengal, where Brahminical influences operated to a larger extent than in others like the Punjab, which the advancing Aryans had left behind them in their onward march, the spread of individual Ownership was more rapid and more general than in the latter. It is noteworthy, for instance, that in the *Dayabhaga*, the leading authority on questions of Inheritance in the Bengal School, far greater prominence is given to individual property than to the proprietorship of a joint family, which is insisted upon in the *Mitacshara*, the leading authority of the North-Western School, which is undoubtedly of more ancient date than the former treatise.[3] At the present day the disintegration of Hindu families in most parts of India is slowly but steadily taking place; and the picture of a large group of persons living within one enclosure, ordinarily taking their meals together, having a common fund and common means of support, a common religion and a common ancestor worship, which were the distinguishing features of the ancient Hindu *Kutumba*, is now scarcely to be met with, at least in all its completeness.

[1] *Mitacshara*, Ch. I., section 4, para. 26. See translation given of the text in *Tagore Law Lectures* for 1884-85, p. 72.

[2] Ch. IX., III.

[3] *Tagore Law Lectures* for 1884-85.

CHAP. VII.

Ownership defined.

140. Ownership may be of a Thing or of a Right (*Jus in re*, as a Copyright or a Patent),[1] and implies that the person in whom it resides can possess or enjoy it to the exclusion of all others. It is defined by Austin as a "right over a determinate Thing, indefinite in point of user, unrestricted in point of disposition, and unlimited in point of duration."[2] It is an original and independent Right, whereas other material Rights over a Thing, such as a right of way, a right of pasturage, a right to draw water from a spring, and the like, pre-suppose that some other person possesses the Ownership of the Thing.[3] Hence it is said a person cannot have a Servitude over his own property (*nemini res sua servit*). The superior Right in this case would involve every other subordinate Right of which the property was capable, which had not otherwise, by operation of Law or Contract, been detached from it. Such detached Rights are called *jura in re aliena*. The two main attributes of Ownership are (*a*) peaceful enjoyment of the object, and (*b*) a right of disposition over it.

Restrictions on the powers of an Owner.

141. But both these attributes may be restricted by agreement or by operation of Law. Thus the Owner may surrender the actual enjoyment of his land for a specific period, or he may create an Easement over it in favour of some third person which would materially curtail his enjoyment of the full Rights of Ownership. Again, like all other Rights, the Right of Ownership is subject to the limitation

[1] Some writers deny that there can be Ownership of a Right. Windscheid, for instance, says that a legal Right may reside in a person, but to say that he has Ownership of it is to lead one to believe that all the rules applicable to Ownership are also applicable to intangible Rights, which is not the case; Vol. II., section 168, p. 521. See also Dernburg, *Pandekten*, T. 451 (n. 5). But the opposite view is taken by many other German Jurists, and is also found in the Roman Law (*dominium usufructus*, Dig. VII. 6, 3). The English Law distinctly recognises Ownership of things which have no corporal existence, as a patent, copyright, trade mark, &c.

[2] *Jurisprudence*, Vol. II., p. 477.

[3] Stahl, *Die Philosophie des Rechts*, Vol. II., bk. 3, section 21, p. 294.

that the owner must not thereby interfere with the Rights of others. This principle is the foundation of the well-known maxim *sic utere tuo ut alienum non lædas* (so use your own property as not to injure your neighbour's), and of that other analogous maxim *ædificare in tuo proprio solo non licet quod alteri noceat* (it is not lawful to build upon your own land to the injury of another). It was in accordance with the first-named maxim that a Burial Board was held responsible for the value of a horse which, while feeding in an adjoining meadow, ate of that portion of a yew tree, planted by the Board on their own land and about four feet from their boundary railings, and died of the poison contained in it.[1] And as an application of the second maxim, it may be said that, since houses are necessary for the habitation of civilised man, and the chief object of a house is that it should be fit for habitation, my neighbour will not be permitted to erect anything on his land which will materially interfere with the physical comfort and convenience, or tend to depreciate the value of my property. Nor will he be allowed to obstruct my ancient lights, or the flow of water from a stream running through his land if I have had an uninterrupted enjoyment of the water, as of right, for a period of twenty years. So again, in many systems of Law, the power of disposition over property, whether by gift *inter vivos*, or by a testament, is restricted. Thus, by the Muhammadan Law of the orthodox or Sunni sect, a man cannot dispose of more than a third of his property to a stranger by will or a death-bed gift, while a bequest of any portion of his estate to one or some of his heirs is not valid, except when consented to by the rest of the heirs.[2] Nor can a Hindu, governed by the

[1] *Crowhurst* v. *Amersham Burial Board*, 4 Ex. D. 5; 48 L. J. Ex. 109. See also *Whalley* v. *Lancashire and Yorkshire Railway*, 13 Q. B. D. 131; 53 L. J. Q. B. 285; *Black* v. *Christchurch Finance Co.*, (1894) A. C. 48; 63 L. J. P. C. 32; *Reinhardt* v. *Mentasti*, 42 Ch. D. 685; 58 L. J. Ch. 787. *Cf.* also para. 252.

[2] *Tagore Law Lectures* for 1874, pp. 18, 43, 45.

CHAP. VII.

Mitacshara school, alienate ancestral immoveables in the presence of a son or a grandson without his consent, except for pressing necessity, such as the maintenance of his family, the marriage of a son or a daughter, or the performance of indispensable religious duties.[1] In like manner the Customary Law of the Punjab imposes various restrictions on the power of a landowner to alienate his estate.[2]

Limited Ownership.

142. Ownership as hitherto described is full Ownership. But there may also exist a limited form of the Right. Thus an estate may be held for life only, in which case the limited owner is called in English Law a "life-tenant." Or there may be a still more modified form of Ownership, which for certain purposes may partake of the qualities of full Ownership, and in other respects may be restricted in point of duration. This peculiar form occurs in Hindu Law, and also in the Customary Law of the Punjab.[3] Thus a Hindu widow, or the widow of an agriculturalist, is ordinarily only allowed to succeed to the estate of her sonless husband for the period of her widowhood. But her position is essentially different from that of a life-tenant as understood in the English Law. The latter by no possibility can charge or alienate the estate beyond his own life. The Hindu widow, on the contrary, represents the entire estate, which under certain circumstances, for example, in order to meet a "legal necessity," she can dispose of absolutely.

Conditional Ownership.

143. Ownership may also be conditional. Thus all landholders in India, unless specially exempted, are liable to pay the Ruling Power a certain annual sum as revenue; and any default in the payment of such a charge may involve a sale of the defaulter's estate.[4] So also a Hindu widow, who

[1] *Mitacshara*, Chap. I., section 1, paras. 27—30. See also *Ibid.*, section 5, paras. 9 and 10.

[2] See my *Digest of Civil Law*, Chap. IV., paras. 58, 59, 61.

[3] *Ibid.*, paras. 64, 65.

[4] Sections 75 *et seq.* of the Punjab Land Revenue Act (XVII. of 1887).

succeeds to her husband's estate, does so on the condition of preserving her widowhood, and she forfeits all her rights in it if she re-marries.[1] So a right of Ownership may be created to take effect on the happening of an uncertain event, or if a specified uncertain event shall not happen, or upon the fulfilment of a specified condition.[2] Thus if A. transfers an estate or a sum of money to B., on condition that he shall marry with consent of C., the transfer is conditional, and the estate does not vest in B. until he has fulfilled the condition.[3] Again, property may be transferred with the condition superadded that, in case a specified uncertain event shall happen, such interest shall pass to another person, or that in case a specified uncertain event shall not happen, such interest shall pass to another person. For example, an ulterior conditional disposition may be made to operate in case the person in whom the property primarily vests changes his religion, or adopts a professed religious life, or dies not having attained a certain age.[4]

Two principal forms of Acquisition.

144. There are two principal forms of acquisition of Ownership, which are called "Original" and "Derivative." The former is the consequence of some independent personal act of the acquirer himself, the latter is a derivation of the Rights of a former owner, either by means of a conveyance *inter vivos*,[5] or by a legacy or a *donatio mortis causa*.

Sub-division of "Original Ownership."

145. "Original Ownership" may again be considered from a threefold aspect, according as it is acquired over a previously ownerless object (*i.e.*, *res nullius*), in which case it is called

[1] Section 2, Act XV. of 1856; see also my *Digest of Civil Law*, Chap. II., para. 32.

[2] Sections 21, 25, *Transfer of Property Act*, 1882, for India.

[3] *Vide* section 26, *ibid.*

[4] *Transfer of Property Act*, 1882, for India, section 28; Shepherd's Commentary, pp. 40, 41.

[5] Stahl, *Die Philosophie des Rechts*, Vol. II., bk. 3, section 24, p. 297. The term *donatio mortis causa* will be explained *post*.

CHAP. VII.

"Absolute," or, as it causes the extinction of a previous Ownership by an independent adverse act on the part of the acquirer, in which case it is called "Extinctive"; or, as it is the result of "accession," in which case it is called "Accessory."[1]

Occupation of Ownerless Things.

146. In the case of Ownerless Things, the general rule is founded, as Justinian says, on natural reason, that the first occupier becomes the owner.[2] For this mode of acquisition the actual physical control of the thing, or Occupation, is essential. Amongst things which may be acquired in this way are wild animals or birds, fish in public rivers,[3] bees until they are hived, and precious stones, gems, and other things found upon the sea-shore.[4] But, according to English Law, wild animals and fish are held to be in the possession of the person in whose land they happen to be, and when killed or captured they belong to the landowner and not to the captor. In Bengal, however, it would appear that the Zamindar does not *necessarily* enjoy *jalkar* or a right of fishery over *jheels* in his zamindari. His right thereto is said to be contingent on it having been separately assessed by Government at the time of the Permanent Settlement. Where this is not the case, the Government has assumed to resume the *jalkar* under the operation of Regulation II. of 1819, as in the case of the Kotwalipara Pargana of the Faridpur District.[5] But then the Zamindar in Bengal is a creature of our own making, who was recognised at the time of the Permanent Settlement as the landowner, although in

[1] Stahl, *Ibid.*, pp. 298—301.

[2] Inst. II. 1, 12: *Quod enim ante nullius est, id naturali ratione occupanti conceditur:* for natural reason gives to the first occupant that which had no previous owner.

[3] The *Jalkar*, or right of fishery, in a navigable river is not affected by reason of the river having changed its course. I. L. R. XVII. Cal. 963.

[4] Just. *Inst.* II. 1, 12, 14, 15, 18.

[5] See an able letter signed "*Justice*" on *Fishery Rights in Bengal* in the *Pioneer* of the 29th August, 1887.

the majority of cases the individual to whom this status was conceded had no proprietary right in the soil. It was competent, therefore, to the Government to attach any restrictions to his tenure which it thought fit to prescribe. In exercise of its *dominium eminens*, which has always been conceded to the State, the Government of India has also asserted its right to all mines of metal or coal and all earth-ore and gold washings;[1] and by virtue of the same inherent right, it formerly prescribed, with the aid of the legislature, special rules for determining the Rights of Government and of individuals with respect to hidden treasure.[2] But the existing law with regard to Treasure Trove in British India is contained in Act VI. of 1878. By that enactment, anything of any value hidden in the soil, or in anything affixed thereto, is deemed to be "treasure."[3] If any such "treasure," exceeding in amount or value ten rupees, is found, and no one is able to prove that it was hidden by him or by some other person under whom he claims, within one hundred years before the date of the finding, the Collector may declare the treasure to be "ownerless." When such a declaration has been made, the owner of the place where the treasure was found, if he appears and asserts his claim in the manner prescribed by the Act, is entitled to one-fourth, and the finder to the residue. If the owner of the place does not appear and assert his claim, the finder is entitled to the whole. But the Act also gives the Collector the power to acquire any such treasure on behalf of the Government, by paying to the persons otherwise entitled thereto a sum equal to the value of the materials of such treasure, together with one-fifth of such value.[4] In England, treasure trove belongs to

[1] Section 41, *Punjab Land Revenue Act* (XVII., 1887).

[2] *Vide* Bengal Regulation V. of 1817, and Madras Regulation XI. of 1832.

[3] This was also the meaning of *thesaurus* in the Roman Law. Dig. X. 2, 22; X. 4, 15; XLI. 2, 44.

[4] Section 16.

CHAP. VII. the Crown. According to the Roman Law, the finder, and the owner of the place where it was found, divided the treasure trove equally,[1] and this rule generally prevails on the continent of Europe.

Specificatio. 147. Another mode of acquiring absolute Original Ownership is by means of what the Roman Jurists termed "Specificatio," that is to say, the working up of materials belonging to another into a new product (*nova species*).[2] Before Justinian's time two opposite views were held as to Ownership of things so manufactured. The followers of Proculus (hence called Proculians), a distinguished pupil of a famous Jurist named Labeo, asserted that the thing being newly made it could have had no former owner, and consequently its maker is the only true owner (*quia quod factum est, antea nullius fuerat*). The Sabinians (after Sabinus, a follower of Capito), on the other hand, said that the materials remain, although their form is changed, and their proprietor is the owner of the thing made. The Emperor Justinian adopted a middle opinion, based on the following distinction. If the thing made can be reduced to its former rude materials, then the owner of the materials is also considered the owner of the thing made; but, if the thing cannot be so reduced, then he who made it is the owner of it.[3] But as Stahl[4] pertinently observes, this criterion is hardly satisfactory; for take the case of a celebrated sculptor who has modelled a statue from clay belonging to another. Here the statue can certainly be reduced to the rude material from which it was made, but the chief value of the thing made consists in its form, and to leave this element out of consideration, and to regard the owner of the rude material as the owner also of the statue,

[1] Windscheid, *Pandektenrecht*, Vol. I., section 184, p. 587.

[2] *Ex aliena materia speciem aliquam facere.* Windscheid, *Pandektenrecht*, Vol. I., section 187, p. 599.

[3] Inst. II. 1, 25.

[4] *Die Philosophie des Rechts*, Vol. II., p. 300 (*n*).

would scarcely be consistent with the dictates of justice. In English Law the question can scarcely arise, for the rule is that if I take another man's goods and mix them with my own, I am liable to pay for the value of the goods, and damages for their detention.[1]

Extinctive Acquisition.

148. The second form of Original Ownership is that which results from what is called Extinctive Acquisition. This term is applied to acquisitions which follow from a long and continuous possession of a thing as owner (*animo rem sibi habendi*); that is to say, by *prescription*. Thus, by the Law of the Twelve Tables, a person acquired an indefeasible title to moveables by a *bonâ fide* possession of one year, and to immoveables if the possession continued for two years.[2] Under the later Law of Justinian, in the case of moveables, the period for an extinctive acquisition was increased to *three* years, and, in the case of immoveables, to *ten* years for persons living in the same province, and to *twenty* years for persons living in different provinces.[3] So under 3 & 4 Will. 4, c. 27, after the determination of the period limited by the Act, the *Right* of a person to recover land of which he has been out of possession is *extinguished*.[4] The Indian Legislature has gone even further in the same direction, for by section 28 of the Limitation Act of 1877, at the determination of the period limited by the Act to any person for instituting a suit for *possession* of *any* property (therefore

[1] Markby's *Elements of Law*, section 495.

[2] In *Gautama's* Institutes it is interesting to notice that, in the case of moveables, adverse possession *inter præsentes* for a period of *ten* years created, subject to certain exceptions, an indefeasible title in the possessor (12, 37); while in the case of (*Bhumi*) immoveables *Yajnyawalkya* states the rule of Extinctive Acquisition as resulting after twenty years (2, 24). See *Tagore Law Lectures* for 1882, pp. 19 *et seq.*

[3] *Inst.* II. 6.

[4] *Dawkins* v. *Lord Penrhyn* (1878), 4 App. Cas. 51, at p. 58. *Cf.* I. L. R. XI. Allah. 438.

CHAP. VII.

moveables as well as immoveables[1]) his right to such property is extinguished. The practical effect of the "extinction" of the title in the former owner is the "acquisition" of it by the new possessor, whose title, if his own possession has continued for twelve years in the case of immoveable property, becomes absolute and indefeasible. This mode of Acquisition is therefore called Extinctive.[2]

Accession.

149. Lastly, Original Ownership may also be acquired by means of "Accessio." Thus, if a tree bears fruit, or a domestic animal bears offspring, the produce belongs to the owner of the tree or animal, unless he has parted with the Right to the same. So also crops are inseparable from the soil in which they are planted, and things which are annexed to a building, and which do not come within the definition of fixtures, are deemed in law to become part of it, in accordance with the maxim *quidquid plantatur solo, solo cedit* (whatever is affixed to the soil, belongs to the soil).[3] A more familiar instance of the application of this principle of acquisition is afforded by the disjunction or junction of land which so frequently occurs in India by rivers changing their course. Where such changes occur, the Rights of persons affected by it are primarily regulated by Custom, if it can be clearly and definitely ascertained.[4] In the Punjab many special customs of this kind have been proved to exist, such as the *Kishti-banna* (or deep-stream rule), the *Ru-gardani* (or face-revolv-

[1] *Cf.* I. L. R. IV. Cal. 297; V. *Ibid.*, 949; IX. *Ibid.*, 651; No. 106, P. R. 1883; I. L. R. XIII. Mad. 491; I. L. R. III. Allah. 435.

[2] Stahl, *Die Philosophie des Rechts*, Vol. II., p. 301.

[3] But compare section 108 (*h*) of the *Transfer of Property Act* of 1882 for India. By that section the lessee may remove, at any time during the continuance of the lease, *all things which he has attached to the earth*, a phrase which has a very wide meaning given to it in the "Interpretation Clause" (section 3).

[4] Here we have another clear instance where the Indian Legislature has distinctly recognised the force of Customary Law. See section 2 of Reg. XI. of 1825.

ing, referring to the change produced by the altered course of a river, whereby what was once the *face* becomes the *back*, and *vice versâ*), and the *Warpar* or *kuch-much* (according to which the original area is alone looked to, and whether in the bed of the river or out of it, the lands comprised within these limits remain for ever a part of the estate). Where, however, no special Custom is proved to exist, the transfer of Ownership by alluvion and diluvion is determined by the provisions of Bengal Regulation XI. of 1825. But the Privy Council has ruled that the principle of "Accession" in such cases cannot be carried further than the provisions of the Regulation clearly sanction. Thus, land washed away and afterwards identified as re-formed in the old recognised site, is not land "gained by gradual accession" within the meaning of that enactment; but, when so re-formed or identified, remains the property of the former owner, and all Rights with respect thereto, existing at the time of its submersion, shall be deemed to be revived on the re-appearance of such land,[1] provided of course that no one else has acquired an indefeasible title to such re-formed land by long adverse possession.[2]

Who is entitled to "accession" on a transfer of the property.

150. The question who is entitled to the benefit of "accessions" which accrue during the interval between the execution of a deed of conveyance and the actual *traditio*, or taking possession of the property sold, depends on when the Law regards the alienatory contract complete, so as to effect the transfer of Ownership. By Roman Law delivery of possession was requisite.[3] But by the modern French Law and the English Law, the transfer is accomplished as soon as the

[1] V. Beng. Law Repts. 521, P. C.; 25 W. R. Cal. 242; No. 1, P. R. 1880; *Surab Surat Debia* v. *Soorjyakant Acharjya*, Privy C. Judts. by *Baldeva Ram Deva*, p. 3. *Cf.* Just. *Inst.* II. 1, 21.

[2] I. L. R. III. Cal. 796; Vol. VII. *Ibid.* p. 225, *Cf.* No. 83, *Punjab Record*, 1876.

[3] The German Civil Code adopts the same rule. Ernst Barre, *Vergleichende Darstellung*, p. 146.

CHAP. VII.

alienatory contract is complete.[1] The Indian Legislature has departed from the English Law only to this extent, that in the case of tangible immoveable property of the value of one hundred rupees and upwards, it refuses to recognise the transfer, unless it is effected by an instrument in writing duly registered under the law in force for the registration of deeds;[2] and in the case of similar property of a value less than one hundred rupees, unless the transfer is either made by a registered instrument or by delivery of the property.[3] Until, therefore, a deed of transfer is registered, or delivery (in the case of tangible immoveable property of less value than a hundred rupees) takes place, there is no completed act of transfer of Ownership, and consequently the transferee would neither be liable to bear the loss arising from the destruction, injury, or decrease in the value of the property not caused by the seller, nor, on the other hand, entitled to the benefit of any improvement in, or increase in value of, the property, or to the rents and profits thereof.[4] In the case of property leased, the lessee is entitled to any accession (subject to the law relating to alluvion for the time being in force) accruing during the continuance of the lease.[5]

Derivative Acquisition.

151. Derivative Acquisition we have seen takes place by a conveyance *inter vivos*, or by a legacy or a *donatio mortis causa*. It is called "Derivative" in contradistinction to "Original," because the acquirer derives thereby the rights

[1] Art. 1138, C. C. Stahl, *Die Philosophie des Rechts*, Vol. II., bk. 3, section 25, p. 303; Holland's *Jurisprudence*, p. 177. See also section 63 of the English *Conveyancing and Law of Property Act*, 1881 (44 & 45 Vict. c. 41). As regards the Indian Law relating to moveables, see section 78, *Indian Contract Act*, and para. 152, *post*.

[2] Act III. of 1877.

[3] Section 54 of Act IV. of 1882.

[4] Section 55 (5 *c*, *c*, 6, *a*) of Act. But under English Law from the date of a Contract which is capable of being specifically enforced, the property comprised in the Contract is deemed to belong to the purchaser. *Edwards* v. *West*, L. R. 7 Ch. D. 862.

[5] Section 108 (*d*), Act IV. of 1882.

of a former owner. The orbit of his right is limited by that of the person from whom he derives it, since no one, speaking generally, can transfer a greater right to another than he himself has (*nemo potest plus juris ad alium transferre quam ipse habet*). But this rule (perfectly sound as a general maxim of Jurisprudence) has been found in modern practice to be inconvenient to its full extent in commercial transactions, especially since the practice of advancing money upon the security of goods and merchandise came to be so important as it is.[1] Modifications of the rule have been introduced in England and Scotland by the Factors Act, and in India by the Contract Act,[2] which must be kept in view in considering its application to any given case. Where the acquisition is the result of a conveyance *inter vivos*, what has been said in the preceding paragraph in regard to the necessity of possession must also be borne in mind. In the case of a specific legacy, that is to say, a bequest of a specified part of the testator's property, the legatee is entitled to the clear produce thereof from the date of the testator's death; and the same rule holds good in the case of a general residuary bequest with respect to the produce of the residuary fund.[3] Delivery is not necessary to complete the acquisition of Ownership on the part of the legatee. Thus, if no time is fixed for the payment or delivery of the legacy, and the legatee dies after the testator, but before he has received the legacy, it passes to his representatives.[4] Donations *mortis causa* are gifts of moveables in contemplation of death, and do not take effect if the donor survives the donee. But in order to complete the acquisition by the donee there must be a delivery, either actual or con-

[1] Per Lord Blackburn in *City Bank* v. *Barrow*, V. App. Cas. (1880), at p. 678.

[2] Section 108, Except. I.; and section 178.

[3] Sections 309 and 310 of the *Indian Succession Act*, and Williams's *Law of Executors*, 1429.

[4] Section 91, *Indian Succession Act*.

CHAP. VII.

structive, *e.g.*, by the delivery of the key of a trunk or safe in which the subject of the gift is contained.[1]

Joint Ownership.

152. Precisely as in the case of Possession, so in that of Ownership it is not possible for two persons to possess or to own a thing *in solidum*.[2] But there is no reason why two or more persons may not enjoy the Ownership of a thing in common. This sort of enjoyment is termed Joint Ownership, of which there may be two kinds. In the one case the Joint-Owners (or Joint-Tenants, as they are called in English Law,) are seised, as it is said, *per my et per tout*, and each has the entire possession, as well of every parcel as of the whole. In respect of his companion, each Joint-Owner is seised of the whole, but for the purposes of alienation, and to forfeit, he is the Owner only of his undivided part or portion. The distinguishing incident in this tenure is that, on the death of any of the Joint-Tenants, the entire estate passes to the survivors by what is termed the *jus accrescendi*, or right of survivorship.[3] The case of *Narpat Singh* v. *Muhammad Ali Hassain Khan*, which was decided by the Privy Council, affords a good illustration of the application of this doctrine. There, the lands of three brothers having been confiscated, the Government afterwards assigned revenue-paying lands for the benefit, in certain proportions, of the minor son of the eldest brother, also of the widow, minor son and daughter, of the youngest brother. The grant did not define the rights assigned to each grantee, and it was held accordingly that the grant was to be construed as made to the persons named as joint-tenants and not as tenants in common, with the result that the widow of the youngest brother, on the deaths

[1] Section 178 and Illustration (*b*), *Indian Succession Act*. *Cf. Robson* v. *Hamilton*, 2 Ch. D. (1891), 559. *Cf. Mustapha* v. *Wedlake*, W. N. of 19th December, 1891, where the delivery of the key of a safe was held to complete gift of bonds in the safe.

[2] Dig. XIII. 6, 5, 15: *duorum . . . . in solidum dominium vel possessionem esse non posse.*

[3] Kent's *Commentaries*, Vol. IV. p. 405.

Chap. VII.

of his son and daughter, became by survivorship sole owner of the estate so assigned for their and her benefit.[1] In the other form of Joint-Ownership the co-owners have a defined share in the property, and there is no such thing as survivorship amongst them. This is a form of tenure which is called in English Law a "tenancy in common." Each of these forms is represented in the Hindu Law. The former has its counterpart in the "Aggregate Ownership" of the joint-family of the *Mitacshara* system, the latter in the "Fractional Ownership" of the joint-family of the *Dayabhaga*, or Bengal system.[2] Under the *Mitacshara* law, so long as a family is living in union and in possession of an undivided estate, without having come to an ascertainment and specification of their rights in it, so long no member of the family has any such proprietary right in it as he can alienate or encumber. The property, under such circumstances, belongs to all the members of the family jointly, as to a corporation; and no one of the individual members has any share in it which he can deal with as property.[3] In Bengal, on the other hand, as each co-parcener has a definite share in the undivided estate, so he can alienate that share as he pleases.[4] In

[1] I. L. R. XI. Cal. 1. See also No. 27, P. R. of 1891, in which the Chief Court followed the ruling quoted in the text.

[2] *Tagore Law Lectures* for 1884-85, pp. 53, 58; 170—175.

[3] *Mohabeer Pershad* v. *Ramyad Singh*, 20 W. R. 194; *Lala Nukched Lal* v. *Fatteh Bahadar Lal*, 24 W. R. 39; I. L. R. XVIII. Cal. 157. See also *Tagore Law Lectures* for 1884-85, pp. 196, 197. *Cf.* No. 153, *Punjab Record*, 1883; and No. 81, *ibid.*; I. L. R. V. Allah. 385. In Madras, however, the alienability of a single share in an undivided estate is admitted. I. Mad. H. C. Repts. 471; II. *ibid.* 416; V. *ibid.* 166. But not by a testamentary disposition, VIII. *ibid.* 13. The Bombay High Court has to a certain extent followed the Madras rule. X. Bomb. H. C. Repts. 139, 160, and at p. 380. But in that Presidency a co-parcener cannot by simple voluntary gift, or by devise, alienate his share to a stranger, so as to bind his surviving co-parceners after his decease; XI. *ibid.* 76. See the remarks of Mr. Nelson on the Madras decisions in Chap. VI., Part II., *Indian Usage and Judge-made Law in Madras.*

[4] *Tagore Law Lectures* for 1883-84, p. 483. *Cf.* No. 149, *Punjab Record* for 1884, where the interests of each co-sharer had been ascertained.

CHAP. VII.

regard to the common lands in villages in the Punjab, it has been held that none of the proprietors can do anything which alters the condition of the joint property without consent of all the co-sharers.[1] Nor in the absence of custom can the will of the majority of a village community prevail against that of the minority, when the question is one as to the disposal of the common property in such a way as to preclude all use of it by the owners.[2] By English Law co-owners of land are either joint tenants or tenants in common. In the former case they hold by the same title, in the latter by different titles. An alienation by a joint tenant effects a severance of the tenure for the alienee, who thus becomes a tenant in common with the other co-owner. The Indian Transfer of Property Act, 1882, provides that where one of two or more owners of immoveable property, legally competent in that behalf, transfers his share of such property or any interest therein, the transferee acquires, as to such share or interest, and so far as is necessary to give effect to the transfer, the transferor's right to joint possession or other common or part enjoyment of the property, and to enforce a partition of the same, but subject to the conditions and liabilities affecting, at the date of the transfer, the share or interest so transferred.[3] But the Act is careful to add a proviso, that where the transferee of a share of a dwelling-house belonging to an undivided family is not a member of

[1] See my *Digest of Civil Law*, section 225; No. 70, *Punjab Record*, 1866; No. 109, *ibid.* for 1879; No. 73, *ibid.* for 1882; Nos. 74 and 121, *ibid.* for 1885; No. 54, P. R. 1886. *Cf.* I. L. R. V. Cal. 188.

[2] No. 76, *Punjab Record*, 1873; No. 78, *ibid.* 1877. But where a building has been erected on common land without the permission of the co-sharers, and even in spite of their protests, the objecting co-sharers will not be entitled to obtain the demolition of the building unless they can show that the building has caused such material and substantial injury as could not be remedied on a partition of the joint land. I. L. R. VI. Allah. 661; I. L. R. XIV. Cal. 236; No. 54, P. R. 1888; No. 1328 of 1887 (M. S.); No. 187, P. R. 1889; No. 54, P. R. 1892. *Cf.* also I. L. R. XII. Allah. 436, and I. L. R. XVIII. Cal. 10.

[3] Section 44.

the family, nothing in this section shall be deemed to entitle him to joint possession or other common or part enjoyment of the house. Again, where several co-owners of immoveable property transfer a share therein, without specifying that the transfer is to take effect on any particular share or shares of the transferors, the transfer, as among such transferors, takes effect, according to the Indian Act, on such shares equally where the shares were equal, and, where they were unequal, proportionately to the extent of such shares.[1]

Priority of rights created by transfer *inter vivos*.

153. Another important point to bear in mind in connection with "Derivative Acquisition," by means of alienation *inter vivos*, is the question of priority of rights created or purporting to be created by the transfer. It not unfrequently happens that a person purports to create by transfer at different times rights over the same property which cannot all exist or be exercised to their full extent together. In such a case it is a matter of considerable importance to determine which of the transferees shall have priority. So long as actual delivery of the thing alienated was necessary to complete the transfer of Ownership, as it was under the Justinian legislation,[2] it was unimportant to lay down any rule on this point. But when the possibility of a transfer of Ownership by a mere alienatory contract between the parties, unaccompanied by a transfer of possession, was once admitted, the necessity for some rule determining the rights of successive transferees was immediately felt. Now the general rule, borrowed from the Roman Law, as applied to the case of a Pledge, which will be considered hereafter, is expressed in the maxim, *qui prior est tempore, potior est jure:* he who is first in time has the strongest claim in law. This rule may be modified by the superaddition of special formalities in certain

[1] Section 47.

[2] *Traditionibus et usucapionibus dominia rerum, non medio pacto transferuntur.* Cod. Just. 2, 3, 30.

CHAP. VII.

cases, the non-observance of which would invalidate the transfer irrespective of its chronological order. Thus the requirement of the English Law, that a grant of land must be under seal; or of the Indian Law, that if above a certain value, it can only be made by a registered instrument, and if under that value (*i.e.*, less than a hundred rupees), either by a registered instrument or by delivery of the property;[1] or of the French Law, that the presence of a Notary, and the transcription by him of the alienatory contract in a public register, are essential to its validity;[2] or of the Prussian Law, that the parties must apply to and obtain the assent of the Court, which then causes an entry of the transferee's name on the register.[3] In the case of ascertained moveables, the Indian Law regards the transfer as complete when the whole or part of the price, or when the earnest, is paid, or when the whole or part of the goods are delivered.[4] Subject, therefore, to any modification which the Law specially prescribes, the general rule as to priority of rights is that stated above, which has been adopted by the Indian Legislature.[5]

Loss of Ownership.

154. Loss of Ownership may take place as the result of a criminal punishment or by operation of law, or in consequence of a judicial process. Thus a conviction of certain offences may itself involve a forfeiture of the offender's property, while in other cases the penalty of forfeiture must be adjudged as part of the sentence. For example, under the Indian Penal Code, a conviction of waging war against the Queen, or attempting to wage such war, or abetting the

(*a*) By forfeiture.

[1] Section 54, *Transfer of Property Act*, 1882.

[2] Code Civil, Art. 2146. *Cf.* also Art. 939 as to transcription of gifts *inter vivos*.

[3] Rönne, *Staatsrecht der Preussischen Monarchie*, section 362; Dernburg, *Lehrb. d. Preuss. Priv. R.*, Vol. I., sections 193, 240.

[4] Section 78, Act IX. of 1872. Special rules are enacted in the case of goods yet to be ascertained, sections 79—84.

Section 48, *Transfer of Property Act*, 1882.

waging of such war,[1] or of collecting men, arms, or ammunition, or otherwise preparing to wage war, with the intention of either waging, or being prepared to wage war against the Queen,[2] carries with it, as a necessary consequence, a forfeiture of all the offender's property. But a Criminal Court may also adjudge a forfeiture of property whenever a person is convicted of an offence punishable with death; and whenever any person is convicted of any offence for which he is transported, or sentenced to imprisonment for a term of seven years or upwards, the Court may adjudge that the rents and profits of all his moveable and immoveable estate during the period of his transportation or imprisonment shall be forfeited to Government, subject to such provision for his family and dependants as the Government may think fit to allow during such period.[3] The same Code attaches the further consequence to the conviction of an offence for which the offender is *liable* to forfeiture of all his property, that the offender becomes incapable of acquiring any property, except for the benefit of Government, until he shall have undergone the punishment awarded, or the punishment to which it shall have been commuted, or until he shall have been pardoned.[4] But a forfeiture under the Indian Penal Code does not, as in English Law, corrupt the blood, and the Government takes nothing which the offender could not have assigned. When, therefore, a sentence of forfeiture is passed on the father of a Hindu undivided family subject to the *Mitacshara*, the rights of his sons who take as his co-heirs are not affected.[5] The Government, moreover, would take subject to all *bonâ fide* charges up to conviction; but a fraudulent transfer made in apprehension of conviction, and in order to defeat the right of Government, would be bad.[6]

[1] Section 121, I. P. Code.
[2] Section 122, I. P. Code.
[3] Section 62, *ibid.*
[4] Section 61, *ibid.*
[5] Stokes's *Anglo-Indian Codes*, Vol. I., pp. 21, 22, Introduction.
[6] *In re Sanders' Estate*, 9 Cox, Cr. C. 279.

CHAP. VII. A forfeiture may also take place for a breach of the Customs and other fiscal laws.[1] Thus, on conviction under section 9 of the Inland Salt Act (XII. of 1882), the convicting Magistrate, on the application of the Assistant Commissioner or Salt-revenue Officer, may declare to be confiscated all works, materials, and implements constructed or prepared for the purpose of manufacturing or refining salt or saltpetre contrary to the provisions of the Act or any rule made under it, and all salt or saltpetre so illicitly manufactured is also liable to confiscation (*vide* section 12). So, also, a second conviction of an unlicensed person for selling any spirituous liquor, wine, or intoxicating drug, to or for the use of any European soldier or soldier's wife, renders the offender liable to have all spirituous liquours, wines, or intoxicating drugs, within the cantonment limits in his possession, seized and confiscated.[2] The like penalty may be adjudged for every conviction under sections 3 and 4 of Act XVI. of 1863, for making special provision for the levy of the Excise duty payable on spirits used exclusively in Arts and Manufactures or in Chemistry;[3] and also for a conviction under section 34 of Act XII. of 1875, or section 9 of Act I. of 1878, or sections 11, 18, 19, 42, &c., of the Sea Customs Act (VIII. of 1878).

(*b*) By operation of law.

155. Transfer of Ownership as the result of the operation of law, apart from that attached as a consequence to the conviction of a criminal offence, may take place under the Bankruptcy Laws,[4] or, as we have seen, by Prescription, or again by the Law of Intestate Succession.

(*c*) By judicial process.

156. As the result of a judicial process a transfer of

[1] *Windscheid*, Vol. I., section 174, p. 555.

[2] Section 15, Act XIII. of 1889; and section 2, Act XVIII. of 1853 (still in force in Sindh).

[3] *Vide* section 9 of the Act.

[4] *Vide* sections 7 and 11 of 11 & 12 Vict. c. 21.

Ownership may take place either by a direct adjudication, or by a seizure and sale in execution of a decree of Court.[1]

CHAP. VII.

Ownership of intangible property.

157. It has already been stated[2] that a Right of Ownership may also exist in intangible property. Thus, for the purpose of encouraging learning and a taste for art, the legislature in most civilised countries has created what is called "literary and artistic property." This sort of property is acquired by producing and making public a work of literature or art, and is protected against any infringement or piracy after certain formalities of registration have been duly complied with. An international Copyright may exist by convention between different nations. The law on the subject in India is at present regulated by Act XX. of 1847, which is based mainly on the English Act 5 & 6 Vict. c. 45. A right of copyright is assignable, but the assignment to be effectual in law must be registered.[3] It was held under the Indian Act (which relates only to books) that copyright in designs, being a right created by the Statute Law of the United Kingdom and not thereby expressly extended to India, is a right that cannot be recognized and enforced by the Courts of Law in British India.[4] But this decision led to the Indian legislature passing an Act which had the effect of securing to any new and original design or pattern, or the application thereof to any substance or article of manufacture, the exclusive privilege of making, selling, or using the same for a period of three years.[5] Inventors of new manufactures in India may also acquire a protection for their inventions by obtaining leave from the Governor-General in Council to file a specification thereof. Upon the specification being filed (after leave obtained) the petitioner obtains an exclusive

Copyright.

Patents.

[1] *Cf. Windscheid*, Vol. I., section 173, p. 553.

[2] *Vide* para. 140.

[3] Sections 5 and 14 of Act XX. of 1847.

[4] 16 W. R. 90.

[5] *Vide* sections 2, 3, and 4 of Act XIII. of 1872.

privilege of making, selling, and using the invention in British India for a period of fourteen years, which may subsequently be extended to a further period of fourteen years under certain conditions.[1] It is competent, however, for the Governor-General of India in Council to cause every such exclusive privilege to cease by declaring that the same, or the mode in which it is exercised, is mischievous to the State, or generally prejudicial to the public.[2] Exclusive privileges of the kind mentioned are called "Patents" and may be assigned, and are also transmissible to one's executors and administrators.

How a right in a Patent may cease.

Nuda proprietas.

158. We have now considered the different forms of Ownership and the various modes in which it may be acquired or lost. But, as we have previously seen,[3] it is possible that many subordinate elements which are included in the general notion of Ownership may be detached from the main Right, and may exist in other persons as independent Rights. When these subordinate Rights are so detached the residuary Right still remains in the Owner, and although called by the Romans a *nuda proprietas* (or naked Right) is a Right which possesses considerable legal importance. As Sir William Markby says,[4] "it enables the holder of it to assume a position of great advantage in all legal disputes. All (he can say) belongs to me which cannot be shown to belong to anyone else. Everyone who intermeddles is an intruder, unless he can establish his right to do so. Everybody also must take just what he is entitled to and no more. The presumption is always in favour of the owner."[5]

Roman nomenclature for such Rights.

159. Of these subordinate Rights the Roman Law recognised four distinct kinds, called respectively "Servitude," "Pledge," "Emphyteusis," and "Superficies." The nomen-

[1] Act XV. of 1859.

[2] Section 16, *ibid.*

[3] *Vide* para. 140.

[4] *Elements of Law*, section 319.

[5] *Cf.* section 110 of the Indian Evidence Act, and I. L. R. I. Allah. 194.

clature in regard to the two first-named Rights has been preserved to the present day: but although, as regards the two others, the Roman names have not survived, both the Continental and Indian systems of Law recognise certain jural relations which are practically governed by principles which are more or less analogous to those which regulated the "Emphyteusis" and "Superficies" of the Roman Law.[1] We shall, therefore, consider each of these Rights separately.

Origin of.

160. With the growth of notions of exclusive ownership it became necessary to adjust the relative Rights and Duties of adjoining owners. The transition from corporate to individual Ownership led to the same result. When persons, who had formerly been joint, separated and divided their fields, they had to come to some arrangement about rights of way, rights to take and convey water to their respective fields, rights to water and pasture cattle, and other rights of a similar kind without which the enjoyment of their respective holdings would have been rendered impracticable. We see this process still in active operation in village life in India, whenever a village held in common (called *Zemindari*) is partitioned into separate holdings and converted into either a *Pattidari* or a *Bhaiachara* tenure.[2] So, again, when people began to live in cities and towns, the importance was soon felt of securing to each householder a free and uninterrupted verticle passage of light and air, or the right to discharge rain water from his roof on to that of his neighbour, or to insert beams into his neighbour's wall, or to the lateral support of the adjoining house. So, also, in countries where the custom of secluding women is in vogue, we find any invasion of the privacy of a neighbour's house strictly guarded against.[3]

[1] *Windscheid*, Vol. I., section 218, pp. 697—699.

[2] For an explanation of these terms, which are familiar enough to Indian Students, see my *Digest of Civil Law*, para. 137, 5th ed.

[3] It was for this reason that the Indian Legislature recognised an Ease-

CHAP. VII.

The Romans by a metaphorical turn of expression called Rights of this kind *Servitutes*, because the existence of such Rights indicated a condition of non-freedom or subjection (*servitus*) of the *prædium* (*e.g.*, land or house) which was subject to them (called the *res serviens*).[1] And precisely as a man was only in a condition of subjection or non-freedom when he was liable to serve another, so a Servitude could only exist with respect to immoveable property belonging to another person. Hence the rule of law mentioned by Paulus that a man cannot have a Servitude over what already belongs to him as owner: *nulli res sua servit.*[2] Nor, on the other hand, could a Servitude exist of a Servitude: *servitus servitutis esse non potest.*[3]

Classification of "Servitudes."

161. Servitudes in the Roman Law were distinguished as either "positive" or "negative."[4] The former were those which enabled the entitled person to assert his will, that is to say, to act on, in, or in respect of a thing belonging to another, and bound the latter to acquiesce in that Act. A "Negative Servitude" was one that conferred a right on the entitled person to prevent the owner of a thing from doing something which, as owner, he might otherwise have done, and bound the owner to forbearance.[5] Another and more important classification was that of "Personal" and "Prædial

ment to restrain interference with privacy. Section 5, Illustration (*b*), Act V. of 1882. As to the conditions under which such a right may be enforced in the Punjab, see No. 19, *Punjab Record*, 1882.

[1] *Windscheid*, Vol. I., section 200, p. 636, note (1).

[2] Dig. VIII. 2, 26. The reason, as previously explained (para. 140), was that, as owner, every right which could possibly be deemed a Servitude was included in his superior right of Ownership. He therefore exercised every subordinate right, not as a Servitude, but as a *part* of his right of Ownership. *Cf.* also Dig. VII. I. 63.

[3] Dig. XXXIII. 2, 1. *Cf.* also Dig. VIII. 3, 33, 1.

[4] Dig. VIII. 1, 15, 1.

[5] *Windscheid*, Vol. I., section 201, p. 639; Salkowski's *Roman Private Law*, section 93, pp. 445, 446; Markby's *Elements of Law*, section 404.

(or real) Servitudes,"[1] which in English Law may be represented by the terms "in gross" and "appurtenant." "Personal Servitudes" were created in the interests of a person, as "*usus*" and "*usufruct*," and were consequently inalienable and died with him.[2] The Prædial existed in the interest of the land or other immoveable property (*prædium*) to which they were attached, and passed with it to the vendee in case of sale.[3] It was necessary that they should satisfy a permanent requirement (*perpetua causa*) of the dominant estate.[4] Lastly, Servitudes might be "continuous" or "discontinuous" (*servitutes continuæ—discontinuæ*), according as their enjoyment was dependent or not on the act of man;[5] and this terminology has been retained in the English and Indian Law,[6] and also in the French and Italian Civil Codes.[7]

English classification.

162. English lawyers classify the *jura in re* which a Roman Jurist would have called *Servitutes* into "Easements" and "*Profits à prendre.*" The distinction between these two descriptions of rights may be briefly stated. An "Easement" may be defined as a right by which a person, by virtue of his interest in a certain tenement, is entitled to claim by way of advantage or convenience to his tenement that the possessor of a neighbouring tenement shall submit to something being done by him affecting such neighbouring tenement, or shall forbear from doing something on such neighbouring tenement.[8] But this right does not entitle the

[1] Dig. VIII. 1, 1.

[2] Just. *Inst.* II. 4, 3; Dig. VII. 1, 47; Dig. VII. 4, 3, 3; Dig. X. 2, 15; *Windscheid*, Vol. I., section 201, p. 641; section 202, p. 644.

[3] Dig. VIII. 4, 12.

[4] Salkowski's *Roman Private Law*, section 94, p. 449.

[5] *Windscheid*, Vol. I., section 201, p. 641.

[6] Innes's *Digest of the English Law of Easements*, p. 3, 3rd ed. *The Indian Easements Act*, 1882, section 5.

[7] Arts. 688, 689, Civil Code; and Art. 617, *Codice Civile*.

[8] Innes's *Digest of the English Law of Easements*, p. 1, 3rd ed. *Cf. Gale on Easements*, p. 5. *Cf.* No. 14, P. R. 1897.

CHAP. VII. person in whom it resides to make any profit out of the substance of the neighbouring tenement, *e.g.*, to take turf or stones, or to dig for materials, or to hunt and shoot and take away game. The proper name for a right of the latter description is "*profit à prendre.*" The Indian Legislature has wisely disregarded this distinction,[1] which is based or supposed to be based on the somewhat slender ground that an "Easement" is for convenience only, whereas the latter right is for profit. But it is difficult to appreciate the value of a distinction which recognizes the right of a person to go on another's land to draw water as an Easement, although, as Sir William Markby observes, the water may be subsequently used for the manufacture of beer, which may be sold for profit, and yet refuses to recognise the right to cut wood from another's land as such.

Easements, appurtenant and in gross.

163. "Easements" are again divided into "appurtenant" and "in gross." The first are those where the benefit as well as the burden are attached to land; the second where the benefit is enjoyed by the inhabitants of a particular district or by persons carrying on a particular trade. An "easement in gross" can only be acquired by custom. But an "easement appurtenant" may be acquired in several ways, *e.g.*, (1) by express public grant by an Act of the Legislature; (2) by express private grant, (*a*) *inter vivos*, (*b*) by testament; (3) by implied grant, when the intention is implied to grant the Easement together with property which is *expressly* granted; (4) by prescription, which requires enjoyment as of right for a particular period.[2] In India the acquisition of

How acquired in England.

In India.

[1] *Vide* explanation to section 4 of the *Indian Easements Act*, 1882. This Act originally only extended to territories respectively administered by the Governor of Madras in Council, and the Chief Commissioner of the Central Provinces and Coorg. But by Act VIII. of 1891 it has been also extended to Bombay, the N.-W. P. and Oude. See also the definition of "easement" in section 3 of the *Indian Limitation Act*, 1877.

[2] Innes's *Digest of the English Law of Easements*, p. 3, 3rd ed.

Easements by prescription is regulated by the provisions of the Limitation Act.[1] But it has been ruled by the Privy Council that the Act is remedial in character, and was neither intended to be prohibitive, nor exhaustive.[2] Indeed, it would be impracticable to attempt to give a complete list of such Rights. Other modes of acquisition must, therefore, be regulated either by the provisions of the Indian Easements Act, 1882, where that Act is in force, or by custom, or by applying the principles of English Law, which in this department are more than ordinarily free from local peculiarities, having been borrowed for the most part from Roman Law. As an instance of an "easement in gross" being established by custom in the Punjab, may be mentioned that of the proprietors of a village having the right to cut brushwood from the lands of a neighbouring village for the purpose of repairing water-courses.[3] On the other hand, for an instance, where an alleged customary right "of piscary" on the part of the inhabitants of a *zemindari* in Bengal was held to be bad as unreasonable, reference may be made to the case of *Lutchmeeput Singh* v. *Sadaulla Nushyo*, decided by the High Court of Bengal.[4]

Dominant and servient heritages and owners.

164. The land for the beneficial enjoyment of which the right of Easement exists is called the "dominant heritage," and the owner or occupier thereof the "dominant owner." The land on which the liability is imposed is called the "servient heritage," and the owner or occupier thereof the "servient owner."[5]

Licenses.

165. A person may also acquire by grant (express or implied) from another, quite independently of any tenement of

[1] Section 26, Act XV. of 1877.

[2] *Rajrup Koer* v. *Abul Hussein*, I. L. R. VI. Cal. 394, folld. in I. L. R. VI. Bomb. 20; I. L. R. V. Madras, 226; *Ibid.* 253; and in the Punjab in an unreported case No. 404 of 1883.

[3] No. 31, *Punjab Record*, 1882.

[4] I. L. R. IX. Cal. 698.

[5] Section 4, *Indian Easements Act*, 1882.

which he is owner or occupier, a right to do or continue to do, in or upon the property of the grantor, something which would, in the absence of such right, be unlawful. Where this right exists in respect of immoveable property it is called a "License," but where it exists with respect to personal things, it is called a "Loan."[1] Thus a right to hunt in A.'s ground, and to carry away deer is a "License," but a permission to take a book out of B.'s library for the purpose of reading it is a "Loan." A "License" creates no interest, nor alters or transfers property in anything. It simply makes an action lawful which without it would be unlawful.[2] All licenses necessary for the enjoyment of any interest, or the exercise of any right, are implied in the constitution of such interest or right. Such licenses are called "accessory licenses." For example, A. sells the trees growing on his land, or the fruit thereof, to B. B.'s right to go on the land and take away the trees or fruit is an "accessory license" implied in the sale of A.'s interest to him.[3]

Accessory licenses.

Pledge.

166. Distinguished from all other *jura in re* which we have yet considered, both in its objects and scope, is the Right "*in re aliena*" to which the Romans gave the name of *Pignus* and which is known to English lawyers as "Pledge." In a juristical sense the object of this Right is the subsidiary one of securing to a creditor the satisfaction of his claim. It is distinguished from other Rights of the same class by its independent nature. Other Rights "*in re aliena*" exist for their own sake, that is to say, to enable the person in whom they reside to enjoy the physical qualities of the thing which is subject to them. But the object of a Pledge lies outside itself. The former class of Rights secures to the entitled person immediate mastery of his will over a thing, whereas a

How distinguished from other *jura in re.*

[1] Innes's *Digest of the English Law of Easements*, p. 77, 3rd ed.; *Indian Easements Act*, 1882, Chap. VI., section 52.

[2] *Thomas* v. *Sorrell*, Vaughan, 351.

[3] Section 55, *Indian Easements Act*. *Cf.* No. 14, P. R. 1897.

Pledge only secures this mastery at the end of a stipulated period with the view of enabling the entitled person to obtain satisfaction of another Right. A Pledge is also distinguished by its absolute restriction on the rights of the owner of the thing pledged. No other "*jus in re aliena*" justifies such an interference with those rights. Thus the pledgee may, in the exercise of his right of sale, completely extinguish the right of the owner in the thing, and transfer that right to a third person.[1] But a Pledge in its original inception is included among the "accessiones" of a Right *in personam*.[2] It is consequently an "accessory Right" which can only subsist so long as the Right to which it is accessory continues, and is subject to the conditions and limitations of the latter Right.[3] But there is an exception to this rule arising out of the circumstance that a natural obligation (*e.g.*, one that is not capable of being enforced by the Civil Law) is sufficient to sustain the Pledge.[4] Thus if the Pledgee has the subject of the Pledge in his possession, he can still retain and enforce his Pledge, although he may not be in a position to enforce the claim which it was intended to secure.[5]

167. The historical development of the doctrine of Pledge has to be traced back to the *nexum*,[6] and *sponsio tertiæ partis*[7] **History of.**

[1] See, generally, *Windscheid*, Vol. I., section 224, pp. 715—717.

[2] Dig. XLVI. 3, 43.

[3] *Windscheid*, Vol. I., section 225, pp. 718, 719. If the original claim is diminished by payment, or increased by the accumulation of interest, the pledge is affected accordingly. *Ibid.* p. 723. *Cf.* Salkowski's *Roman Private Law*, section 101, p. 486.

[4] Dig. XXXVI. 1, 59: *remanet propter pignus naturalis obligatio.*

[5] *Windscheid*, Vol. I., section 225, pp. 721, 722. Cod. VIII. 30 (31), 2.

[6] The earliest form of Roman Contract, entered into in the presence of six witnesses, all fellow-citizens, the effect of which was that in default of his engagement the debtor was made over to his creditor and practically became his slave by a summary process called *manus injectio*, that is to say, of apprehending the debtor, detaining him, and putting him to service until the loan was repaid. Muirhead's *Law of Rome*, section 31, pp. 149—155.

[7] An engagement by third persons in the form of a stipulation to be responsible for the performance of the principal debtor's obligation.

of the Roman Law, upon which, in the first half of the Republican Period of Roman History, the jurists of that period engrafted what was called the *lex fiduciæ*, or, for sake of brevity, simply *fiducia*. By this device, what was in form an absolute transfer was in reality only provisional. The transferee was vested with the legal right of property in the thing transferred to him, and in law entitled to deal with it as owner, in so far as he was not restrained by special agreements; but, at the same time, he was a trustee (*fiduciarius*), bound so to deal with it as not unduly to prejudice the interests of the transferor. The technicalities, however, attending the re-transfer of the property to the owner, when the object of the provisional transfer had been satisfied, led in course of time to the introduction of a new and simpler form of security, which was termed Pignus, from which the modern Pledge has been derived. The "*jus pignoris*," as the Right which this new device created in the creditor was called, did not effect any actual transfer of ownership in the thing pledged, as in the case of the *fiducia*, but merely entitled the creditor to the possession thereof as a security for the payment of the debt due to him. At first the pledgee had no power of sale, except by express agreement (*jure conventionis*), but the later law conferred both this power and a power of sub-pledging the thing.[1] If the thing yielded any produce, the profit derived from its use had first to be carried to interest, and then, if any balance remained, to the reduction of the capital debt. If, however, it was agreed that the produce should be taken in lieu of interest, the proper term for this arrangement was "*antichresis*."[2] But as intercourse and commerce extended, and agriculture increased, greater facilities were naturally demanded for the security of debts without the necessity of effecting a transfer

[1] Dig. XX. v.; Code VIII., 24.

[2] *Windscheid*, Vol. I., section 234, pp. 757, 758, note (5); Dig. XX., I., II., section 1.

of possession in every case to the creditor. The old principle of Roman Law, that a *mere* agreement conferred no rights on the person in whose favour it was made of demanding its enforcement, had now to yield to the exigencies of advancing civilisation. Farm tenants, as a rule, had nothing beyond their farm cattle and implements, and to have taken these away from them by means of a *fiducia* or *pignus* would have obviously disabled them from rendering the very service for which they were employed. Some security, on the other hand, was naturally required by the landlord for the due payment of his rent.[1] Hence arose the device of effecting a pledge by simple agreement, without any change of possession of the thing pledged, which was first recognised by the Prætor Salvius, and to which the technical name of "*hypotheca*" was given.[2] When first introduced, this new form of security was restricted to the conventional right of a landlord over the slaves, beasts, and implements of his farm tenant[3] for the realisation of the rent. But the convenience of such a device was very soon experienced, and it was rapidly extended to creditors generally, whatever the nature of their claims.[4] Thus, then, we see that before the law relating to securities reached its final development, it passed through several distinct stages. At first the creditor, in the rude form of *manus injectio*, laid hands on his defaulting debtor, and literally took his "pound of flesh" out of him. Next he obtained the personal security of certain fellow-citizens. But when property-security was first conceived, it was effected by a clumsy process. The creditor now obtained a provi-

[1] Muirhead's *Law of Rome*, pp. 150, 267; Markby's *Jurisprudence*, section 444.

[2] Ulpian distinguishes a "*pignus*" from a "*hypotheca*" as follows: "Proprie *pignus* dicimus, quod ad creditorem transit; *hypothecam*, cum non transit, nec possessio ad creditorem." Dig. XIII. 7, 9, 2.

[3] Included in the phrase *invecta et illata*, Dig. XX. 2, 2, 3, 6; *Windscheid*, Vol. I., section 231, p. 740, note (5).

[4] Muirhead's *Law of Rome*, pp. 267, 268.

sional transfer of the right of Ownership, upon trust to re-convey the property back to the owner when his claim was satisfied. In the next stage of development the Possession of the thing was alone transferred to him, while the right of Ownership continued in the debtor. And in the final stage he merely obtained hypothecation of the property as security for his claim without possession of the same. But it was still not for some time after the introduction of the "hypothec" that a power of sale (*distractio*) was conceded to the creditor. At first this right could only be exercised if it had been expressly stipulated for. But in Ulpian's time, the prevailing law was that the power of the secured creditor to sell the property was the very essence of his right as such. Indeed, at a still later period, even a stipulation to the contrary did not deprive the creditor of this right of sale.[1]

Indian Law of Pledge.

168. The Indian Law relating to the Bailment of Pledges is contained in Chapter IX. of the Indian Contract Act. The pledgee may retain the goods pledged not only for the payment of the debt or the performance of the promise, but for the interest of the debt, and all necessary expenses in respect of the possession or for the preservation of the goods pledged.[2] But he is bound to take as much care of the goods while they are in his possession as a man of ordinary prudence would, under similar circumstances, take of his own goods of the same bulk, quality, and value.[3] In the event of the pledgor making default, he can sell the thing pledged, on giving reasonable notice of the sale.[4] He can also pledge the goods or the documentary title to the goods in his pos-

[1] *Windscheid*, Vol. I., section 237, p. 767, note (1); Salkowski's *Roman Law*, section 100, pp. 482, 483.

[2] Section 173, Act IX. of 1872.

[3] Section 151, *ibid.*

[4] Section 176, *ibid.* But he cannot, without consent of pledgor, sell as to himself. I. L. R. XIX. Cal. 322, P. C.

session to the extent of his interest.[1] And if a third person deprives him of possession wrongfully, the pledgee is entitled to all the remedies the owner might use in the like case.[2]

Judicial hypothec.

169. Apart from the stipulation of the parties themselves a "hypothec" may be created by a judicial sentence or in execution of one. This form of hypothecatory assignment took place in the Roman system in numerous cases. Where, for instance, the heir refused to give the legatee a legacy which had been left to him. Or where an indemnity was refused by the owner of land, the condition of which threatened injury to a neighbour.[3] In such cases a hypothecary action (*per hypothecariam*) was given to the legatee or to the neighbour threatened with an injury. Judicial "hypothecs" have descended to our own times, and are not unknown to Indian Law. Thus where the execution of decrees is transferred to the Collector of a District for disposal, it is competent to the Collector to raise the amount and interest due under the decree, by mortgaging the whole or any part of the debtor's immoveable property.[4] A like power is given to the Insolvent Courts of Presidency Towns.[5]

Not unknown to Indian Law.

Tacit hypothec.

170. A hypothec may also arise by application of a rule of law, and it is then called a "tacit hypothec." Thus the State has a tacit right of this kind for all claims,[6] which takes precedence of all other claims due to private persons,[7] and is a prerogative which cannot be taken away without the consent of the Crown.[8] So under Justinian's legislation the

[1] Sections 178, 179, Act IX. of 1872. [2] Section 180, *ibid.*

[3] *Windscheid*, Vol. I., section 233, pp. 746—748; Just. *Inst.* II. 4, 2.

[4] Section 323, Act XIV. of 1882. *Cf.* also section 305, *ibid.*

[5] Section 32, 11 & 12 Vict. c. 21. For a similar provision of the Roman Law, see Cod. VIII. 14 (15), 2.

[6] The rule of the Roman Law was: *Fiscus semper habet jus pignoris*: "the Treasury always has a right of pledge." Dig. XLIX. 14, 46, 3; *Windscheid*, Vol. I., section 232, p. 741.

[7] 5 Bomb. H. C. Reps., p. 23, O. G. [8] I. L. R. I. Bomb. 7.

CHAP. VII.

wife had, as a personal privilege, an implied hypothec on the effects of her husband for the payment of her *dos*, or marriage portion, which took priority over all other incumbrances.[1]

So in India it was at one time held that a Muhammadan widow *in possession of her husband's property* must be treated in the light of a mortgagee or pawnee so far as her dower is concerned, and could not be deprived of possession until her claim for the same had been satisfied.[2] But the Privy Council has since expounded the law to be that there is no hypothecation of an estate for dower of a Muhammadan widow, but that her right, when in possession, is founded on her power as creditor to retain the property of her husband until her debt is satisfied.[3] But as a debt it is payable *pari passu* with the demands of other creditors.[4]

Simple Mortgage.

171. Closely analogous to the Roman and Continental "Hypothec" is what the Indian Transfer of Property Act, 1882, calls a "Simple Mortgage." That is a form of security where, without delivering possession of the mortgaged property, the mortgagor binds himself personally to pay the mortgage-money, and agrees, expressly or impliedly, that, in the event of his failing to pay according to his contract, the mortgagee shall have a right to cause the mortgaged property to be sold and the proceeds of sale to be applied, so far as may be necessary, in payment of the mortgage-money.[5] But the difference between the two forms of security is, that while the Indian Act confines the "mortgage" to "an interest in specific immoveable property," the Roman "hypothec" could embrace both moveables (if they were not *extra commercium*), and immoveables, and in fact everything which could be legally sold.[6]

[1] Just. *Inst.* IV. 6, 29.
[2] 14 W. R. 239.
[3] (1871), 17 W. R. 113, P. C.; 14 Moor. Ind. App. 377. *Cf.* 22 W. R. 118; I. L. R. XVII. Allah. p. 80; and p. 93.
[4] 17 W. R. 525.
[5] Section 58.
[6] Dig. XX. 3, 1, section 2. As to the hypothecation of future property, see I. L. R. X. Allah. 133; and *Story on Bailments*, section 294.

CHAP. VII.

Other forms of Mortgage recognised in India.

172. The Indian Act also recognises three other kinds of Mortgage, named respectively, the "Mortgage by Conditional Sale," the "Usufructuary Mortgage," and the "English Mortgage."

Mortgage by Conditional Sale.

173. The "Mortgage by Conditional Sale" resembles the *mortuum vadium* of the English Equity Courts, and in form is ostensibly a sale subject to a condition of the sale not becoming absolute unless and until default of payment of the mortgage-money by a certain date takes place.[1] Mortgages of this description are to be carefully distinguished from contracts for sale with a condition of repurchase by the vendor on certain terms. The distinction turns on a question of intention. But where the intention is to pass the property by a present sale, with a mere condition for repurchase, the transaction is not affected by the rules applicable to Mortgages.[2] In the case of a genuine "Mortgage by Conditional Sale" in the Provinces of Bengal, Behar, Orissa, and the N.-W. Provinces, created before the 1st day of July, 1882, and in the case of all similar transactions created in the Punjab, irrespective of date, the sale cannot be made absolute, except by adopting a certain prescribed procedure, which must be strictly followed.[3] In the other Provinces named,

[1] In the Roman Law a Pledge could be given upon the condition that, if the debt be not discharged within a certain time, the creditor shall by the title of purchaser possess the property, to be thereupon appraised according to its true value. Dig. XX. 1, 16, section 9.

[2] 7 Mad. H. C. Reps. 6; L. R. 10 Ind. App. 229; I. L. R. III. Allah. 369; VI. *ibid.* 37. *Cf.* an unpublished case in the Chief Court of the Punjab, No. 1128 of 1886.

[3] *Vide* Bengal Regulation XVII. of 1806, sections 7 and 8. The leading case on this subject is that of *Forbes* v. *Amirulnissa*, decided by the Privy Council, where the whole law of foreclosure is summed up: 5 W. R. 47, P. C. *Cf.* I. L. R. II. Cal. 311; VIII. Allah. 388; Nos. 21 and 42, *Punjab Record*, 1870; No. 76, P. R. 1877; Nos. 84, 139, and 171, P. R. 1882; Nos. 32, 55, and 75, P. R. 1883; Nos. 114 and 117, P. R. 1885; No. 16, P. R. 1888; No. 106, P. R. 1889; No. 123, P. R. 1894; and No. 24, P. R. 1895. This Regulation is still in force in the Punjab.

Chap. VII.

except the Punjab, Mortgages executed after 1st July, 1882, are governed by the Transfer of Property Act, which does not apply to the Punjab. In Madras and Bombay the Regulation of 1806 does not apply, and in the former Province the rule of decision will be guided in regard to Mortgages executed on or after the 1st July, 1882, by the Transfer of Property Act, and in the case of Mortgages executed before 1858, and not later than 1875, by the principles of the English Court of Chancery, while full effect will be given to the Conditional Sale in the case of deeds executed after 1875. In Bombay the doctrine of the Chancery Courts is still followed.[1]

Usufructuary Mortgage.

174. Where the mortgagor delivers possession of the mortgaged property to the mortgagee, and authorises him to retain such possession until payment of the mortgage-money, and to receive the rents and profits accruing from the property, and to appropriate them in lieu of interest, or in payment of the mortgage-money (in which case it would resemble the *vivum vadium*, or Welsh Mortgage), or partly in lieu of interest and partly in payment of the mortgage-money, the transaction is called a Usufructuary Mortgage.[2]

English Mortgage.

175. Lastly, there is what is called the "English Mortgage." This is a transaction where the Mortgagor binds himself to repay the mortgage-money on a certain date, and transfers the mortgaged property absolutely to the mortgagee, but subject to the proviso that he will re-transfer it to the mortgagor upon payment of the mortgage-money as agreed.[3]

Tacking.

176. By the Roman Law the benefit of a security ordinarily extended, where the contrary was not expressly agreed

[1] 9 Bomb. H. C. Reps. 69, 71, 72; *Ibid.* 79; I. L. R. II. Bomb. 230.

[2] *Transfer of Property Act*, 1882, section 58 (*d*).

[3] *Ibid.* 58 (*e*).

upon, to other claims of the same creditor against the debtor.[1] But the English Lawyers engrafted upon this provision a peculiar doctrine of their own. Thus where the legal mortgagee, not having notice of a second incumbrance, had made further advances on the same security; or where a third or later mortgagee had, without notice of the second or other intermediate mortgage, purchased the first mortgage; in either case the holder of the legal estate was allowed, as it was said, "to squeeze out and have satisfaction" before the second or intermediate incumbrancer.[2] This was called Tacking, and the doctrine arose from the notion that the first incumbrancer, having the legal estate and an additional claim in equity, should not be defeated by one possessed of an equitable estate only. "Where," it is said, "equity is equal, the law shall prevail; and he that hath only title in equity, shall not prevail against law and equity."[3] This doctrine, which was based on the distinction of legal and equitable estates peculiar to the English Law, has not been recognised in India,[4] and has been expressly abolished by the Transfer of Property Act, 1882.[5] The Indian Law on the other hand goes further than the English Law in allowing priority to a first over a second mortgagee with respect to further advances made after the second mortgage in the following case. Where, for instance, a mortgage is made to secure future advances, or the performance of an engagement, or the balance of a running account, and expresses the maximum sum to be secured thereby, a subsequent mortgage of the same property shall, if made with notice of the prior mortgage, be postponed to the prior mortgage in respect of

CHAP. VII.

Abolished in India.

Exceptional priority allowed for future advances.

[1] *Windscheid*, Vol. I., section 226, p. 724.

[2] The leading case on this doctrine is that of *Brace* v. *Duchess of Marlborough*, 2 P. W. 491.

[3] Fonblanque's Eq. 302, 5th ed.

[4] 2 Beng. L. Reps. 45, App.; 5 Beng. L. R. 463; I. L. R. III. Cal. 307; I. L. R. VII. Bomb. 526; I. L. R. VII. Allah. 573.

[5] Section 80, *Indian Transfer of Property Act*, 1882.

all advances or debits not exceeding the maximum, though made or allowed with notice of the subsequent mortgage.[1] By English Law if the first mortgagee knew of the second mortgage when making further advances he would be affected by notice, and, as to those advances, he would rank after the second mortgage.[2]

General rule as to ranking of securities.

177. But except in the case mentioned in the preceding paragraph, and where, through the fraud, misrepresentation, or gross neglect of a prior mortgagee, another person has been induced to advance money on the security of the mortgaged property—in which case the prior mortgagee is postponed to the subsequent mortgage[3]—the rule of law applicable to all securities between private persons is *qui prior est tempore, potior est jure:* he who is first in time has the better right. It is interesting to find this rule of Law, borrowed by ourselves from Roman Jurisprudence,[4] distinctly asserted by the Hindu sage *Yajnyawalkya.* "In the case of a pledge, a gift, or a sale," says the sage, "the prior contract has the greatest force."[5]

Marshalling securities.

178. Another important doctrine connected with the law of Mortgage is that of "Marshalling Securities." The general rule of law is that a first creditor having two securities might

[1] Section 79, *Indian Transfer of Property Act*, 1882. But as the Act defines a "mortgage" to be "the transfer of an interest in specific *immoveable* property," this section would not apply to transactions of a similar character relating to *moveable* property, which would then be governed by the principles of English Law. See remarks at p. 158 of Shephard and Brown's *Commentary*.

[2] *Hopkinson* v. *Holt*, 9 H. L. C. 514.

[3] Section 78, *Indian Transfer of Property Act*. For the definitions of fraud and misrepresentation, see para. 48, *ante*. As to effect of negligence, see the comparatively recent decision of the English Court of Appeal in *Northern Counties of England Fire Insurance Company* v. *Whipp*, 26 Ch. D. 482, where the authorities are all reviewed. *Cf.* also 4 Madras H. C. Reps. 369; and I. L. R. VIII. Mad. 200.

[4] Dig. XX. 4; see *Windscheid*, Vol. I., section 242, pp. 786—795.

[5] *Mitacshara*, Chap. III., section 2, para. 5.

enforce his claim against both or either of them. But, if by making one of the estates exclusively liable, he would defeat the second creditor, who has no security except that estate to which to resort, equity intervenes to restrain the first creditor from resorting to the latter security, until the former, which he alone possesses, is exhausted.[1] Thus, if A. has a charge on two estates called Ramnaggar and Bhownaggar, and if B. also has a charge on Bhownaggar only, A. must take payment primarily out of Ramnaggar only, and must leave Bhownaggar, so that B., the other creditor, may follow it and obtain payment of his debt out of it.[2] This doctrine has been acted upon by Courts in India,[3] and has been affirmed by the Indian Legislature in the Transfer of Property Act, 1882.[4] But the benefit of the doctrine can only be claimed by a second mortgagee who took his mortgage without notice of the prior mortgage; and the claim to marshal must not be suffered to prejudice the rights of the first mortgagee or of any other person having acquired for valuable consideration an interest in either property.[5]

Doctrine of Contribution.

179. Distinct from the doctrine just mentioned is that known as "Contribution." The former operates in the interests of incumbrancers; the latter in favour of the owners of incumbered estates. The effect of this doctrine is thus stated in the Indian Transfer of Property Act:—Where several properties, whether of one or several owners, are mortgaged to secure one debt, such properties are, in the absence of a contract to the contrary, liable to contribute rateably to the debt secured by the mortgage, after deducting

[1] Shephard and Brown's *Commentaries on the Transfer of Property Act*, p. 160.

[2] *Webb* v. *Smith*, L. R. 30 Ch. D. 200.

[3] 1 W. R. 353; I. L. R. VII. Allah. 711. *Cf.* I. L. R. XVIII. Bomb. 160.

[4] Section 81.

[5] *Ibid.* The doctrine, moreover, is only applicable to creditors of the same person having demands against the property of that person. I. L. R. XII. Mad. 255.

from the value of each property the amount of any other incumbrance to which it is subject at the date of the mortgage. So where, of two properties belonging to the same owner, one is mortgaged to secure one debt, and both are mortgaged to secure another debt, and the former debt is paid out of the former property, each property is, in the absence of a contract to the contrary, liable to contribute rateably to the latter debt, after deducting the amount of the former debt from the value of the property out of which it has been paid.[1] The Calcutta High Court has laid down that the true intention of this provision of the law is not to cause the lien of the mortgagee to be split up, but simply to determine the principle of contribution as between the various persons who may be liable with respect to the same debt.[2]

Lien.

180. We have seen[3] that in the case of a Pledge the pledgee is invested with a right to deal with the thing pledged as his own, if the debt be not paid and the thing redeemed at the appointed time. But the law also recognises a mere personal right of detention of a chattel, which is immediately lost on the possession being parted with.[4] This right is called a "Lien," and merely produces a pressure upon the will of the debtor arising from the inconvenience of being kept out of his property.[5]

Different kinds of—

181. There are two kinds of Liens, "General," or "Special." The former exists in favour of bankers, factors, wharfingers, attorneys of a High Court, and policy-brokers. "Special Liens" exist in favour of an unpaid seller of goods; a

[1] Section 82. So a mortgagee will not be allowed, without special reason, deliberately to execute his decree exclusively against one of the owners of the equity of redemption for the whole debt: I. L. R. IX. Cal. 406; and I. L. R. XIII. Bomb. 45.

[2] I. L. R. XVIII. Cal. 320.

[3] *Vide* paras. 166, 167, *ante*.

[4] Per Cockburn, L. C. J., in *Donald* v. *Suckling*, L. R. 1 Q. B. 612.

[5] Markby's *Elements of Law*, section 467.

bailee, who has "in accordance with the purpose of the bailment, rendered any services involving the exercise of labour or skill in respect of the goods bailed;" a finder of goods who has incurred trouble and expense in preserving the goods and finding out the owner; a finder of goods when the owner has offered a specific reward for their return; an agent who has sold his principal's goods; an agent entitled to be paid for commission, disbursements, and services; and lastly, partners on dissolution: then each partner has a Lien on the partnership property for the purpose of having it applied, first, in payment of the debts of the firm, and then in payment of his separate debts. The Government, too, has a Lien on land and crops for land revenue, quit-rents, *nazaranas*, road cess, on forest produce, and on goods imported or exported for unpaid duty.[1]

Other *jura in re.*

182. We have now exhausted the list of the most important species of Rights *in re aliena*. But there are still two other species which held a very important position in the Roman Law, and to which modern Western Jurisprudence (for instance, the German Law), and the Indian Law afford somewhat close analogies. These were "Emphyteusis" and "Superficies," both of which may usefully, therefore, be noticed briefly.

Emphyteusis.

183. The Emphyteusis was a grant of a limited interest in land which was largely utilized for bringing into cultivation extensive tracts of provincial land belonging to Municipalities, the Church, or private landowners, which were unproductive and unprofitable through want of supervision on the spot.[2] The *emphyteuta*, as the grantee of the land was called, did not become owner; the grantor still remained the *dominus*, or legal owner, but the right which the grantee

[1] Stokes's *Anglo-Indian Codes*, Vol. I., pp. 529, 530.

[2] Salkowski's *Roman Private Law*, section 99, p. 478, Whitfield's English translation.

enjoyed, although a mere *jus in re aliena*, was so extensive as to be hardly distinguishable from real Ownership. It conferred upon him and his heirs a perpetual right in the lands included in the grant, in consideration of a fixed annual payment to the lord and due observance of conventional conditions; he could transfer his right to another, or transmit it by his last will and testament; and he could protect his interest by a real action (*utilis rei petitio*) analogous to that enjoyed by the owner himself. On the other hand, the *emphyteuta* was bound to maintain the land (*fundus emphyteuticus*) in proper condition, to discharge all imposts chargeable on it, to pay the lord the annual sum agreed upon without deduction, and he could not abandon the land, nor could he free himself of the obligations he had undertaken, without the lord's consent.[1] The Indian Student scarcely needs to be reminded of the resemblance which this sort of tenure bears to the Ryotwari system. But it bears a still closer analogy to the Occupancy Tenures of the Punjab. In the early days of our occupation, when land was plentiful and agricultural labour scarce, the owner of a large tract of waste land, which he had probably obtained from the British Government as a reward for personal service, very often induced tenants to locate themselves on the land and to bring it under cultivation on condition of their having a permanent and hereditable estate therein, subject to a small annual payment to him, either in cash or kind, in recognition of his proprietary right.[2] Indeed, the importance of subordinate tenures of this kind, in a country where agricultural interests are numerous and very keenly

[1] Muirhead's *Roman Law*, 421; *Windscheid*, Vol. I., section 219, p. 700; Salkowski's *Roman Private Law*, section 99, p. 479; *Instituzioni di Diritto Romano*, Filippo Serafini, Firenze, 1888, Vol. I., section 87, pp. 291—294. Sir H. S. Maine has drawn attention to the similarity of the Teutonic "Beneficium," an assignment of land by a conquering king as the reward or price of military service, with the Roman Emphyteusis. *Early Law and Custom*, p. 345.

[2] See the Judgment of the Chief Court of the Punjab in No. 467 of 1885.

prized, has been so largely felt, especially in the Provinces of Bengal, the North-Western Provinces, and the Punjab, that the Indian Legislature has devoted considerable attention to the subject, and special enactments have been passed regulating the Rights and Obligations of different classes of agricultural tenants in those Provinces and in other parts of India.[1] But although the statutory Rights of Occupancy which have thus been conferred are not inferior to those involved in the Roman Emphyteusis, the landlord is still entitled to insist that the land shall be used for the purposes for which it was granted; and while a Court in such cases will be disposed to place a liberal interpretation on the rights of the tenant, it will not sanction a complete change in the mode of enjoyment.[2] So, also, a voluntary abandonment by a tenant of his holding for more than one year without arranging for its cultivation works a forfeiture of his estate.[3] Nor can he relinquish only a part of his holding.[4]

184. The "Superficies" differed from "Emphyteusis," mainly in this respect, that while the latter represented an interest in *land*, the former was the term used to indicate the Right which one person might acquire *quasi dominus* over a *building* erected on *land* belonging to another, and which, as it was said, *civili et naturali jure* (by Civil and Natural Law), belonged to him to whom the land belonged,[5] in accordance with the principle *quidquid plantatur solo, solo cedit* (whatever is affixed to the soil, belongs to the soil). The Rights and Duties of the "Superficiarius," as the person who enjoyed Superficies.

[1] See, for instance, the *Bengal Tenancy Act*, 1885; Act XVIII. of 1873; *N.-W. P. Rent Act*, 1881; the *Punjab Tenancy Act*, 1887; the *Central Provinces Revenue Act;* the *Oudh Rent Act*, 1886.

[2] I. L. R. III. Cal. 781.

[3] Section 21 of the *Oudh Rent Act*, 1886; section 38 of the *Punjab Tenancy Act*, 1887.

[4] Section 37, *Punjab Tenancy Act*, 1887; section 20 (3), *Oudh Rent Act*, 1886.

[5] Dig. XLIII. 18, 2.

the Right was called, were very similar to those of the Emphyteuta. He could transfer his right either by a disposition in his lifetime, or by a will to take effect upon his death; he could create Servitudes upon the building, pledge his Right, and he could prosecute it judicially against every one who interfered with his possession or enjoyment of the Right. On the other hand, like the Emphyteuta, he was bound to pay a yearly rent (called *solarium* or *pensio*) to the owner of the land. The Right might be created by a grant from the owner of the land, or by a judicial sentence, or by Prescription.[1]

Nothing precisely analogous in modern Law.

185. Nothing precisely similar to this Right of the "Superficiarius" has descended to our times, although it is said that in many respects this *jus superficiarium* bears a strong resemblance to the long building leases granted by landholders in England, in consideration of a rent, and under reservation of the ownership of the soil.[2] But our Courts are not unfrequently called upon to adjudicate as to the Rights of persons who erect buildings on land belonging to other persons. In such cases the ordinary rule is *quidquid plantatur solo, solo cedit.* But where the builder has acted in good faith, or where the owner of the land has stood by and permitted buildings to be erected on his land without protest or objection, the English and Indian Courts, as we have seen,[3] have acted upon equitable principles, and allowed the builder compensation, and in some cases to become the proprietor of the land on paying its value to the owner.[4] Again, agricultural

[1] *Instituzioni di Diritto Romano*, Filippo Serafini, Vol. I., section 90, pp. 299, 300.

[2] Lord Mackenzie's *Studies in Roman Law*, 6th ed., p. 193.

[3] Para. 77*b*, p. 81, *ante*.

[4] *Cf.* I. L. R. I. Allah. 82; I. L. R. V. Cal. 688; 6 W. R. 228; 10 W. R. 258; 11 W. R. 574; 12 W. R. 495; 15 W. R. 360; 16 W. R. 169; 17 W. R. 977 and 383; 20 W. R. 328; 25 W. R. 211; 6 Bomb. H. C. Reps. 10 (A. J.); 8 *Ibid.* 77 (o. c. j.). As to buildings erected on common land without the permission of the co-sharers, and under what conditions the co-sharers may

CHAP. VII.

tenants of a certain class are entitled to erect on their holdings such buildings as are required for the more convenient or profitable cultivation of the land included in their tenancy; and no such tenant can be ejected until he has received compensation, which may assume the form of a beneficial lease.[1] So where miners erected machinery and buildings necessary for the working of a mine, and which were from the first intended to be accessory to the mining, it was held that the maxim *quidquid plantatur solo, solo cedit* had no application, and that the miners were entitled to pull down and remove the buildings while their interest in the mine continued.[2] It may happen also that the owner of land may give a vacant site to a person in order that the latter may build a residence thereon at his own cost. In such a case the presumption, in the absence of any express stipulation or local custom to the contrary, is that both parties intend that the person building the house shall have a permanent right of occupancy.[3]

Family Rights *in rem*.

186. The next class of Rights *in rem* to which we must now turn our attention is that very important group which centres round the Family in its relations with the outside world. We thus exclude from immediate consideration the Rights which each individual member of a Family may have against the other members. These must be reserved for treatment with the other rights *in personam*, which will form the subject of the next Chapter.

obtain the removal of the same, reference may be made to I. L. R. IX. Allah. 661; XII. *ibid.* 436; I. L. R. XIV. Cal. 236; I. L. R. II. Bomb. 133; No. 54, P. R. 1888; No. 187, P. R. 1889; No. 82, P. R. 1890; No. 54, P. R. 1892.

[1] Sections 63, 68, and 73, *Punjab Tenancy Act*, 1887; and sections 22, 26, and 28, *Oudh Rent Act*, 1886; 6 W. R. 40 (Act X. Rulings). *Cf.* No. 70, P. R. 1891 (*Rev.*).

[2] *Wake* v. *Hall*, 8 App. Cas. 195; 52 L. J. Q. B. 494. See also *Ainslie, In re, Swinburne* v. *Ainslie*, 30 Ch. D. 485; 55 L. J. Ch. 615.

[3] No. 34, *Punjab Record*, 1882; No. 50, P. R. 1888. *Cf.* I. L. R. III. Cal. 210; I. L. R. IV. Mad. 371.

Chap. VII.

Development of Institution of Marriage.

187. Now the group of Rights with which we are here concerned embraces all those Rights which arise out of the Domestic Relations which are founded on Marriage. When we trace back this Institution, which has done so much to elevate man and to refine his nature, to its primitive forms, we meet with very much the same course of historical development as we do in regard to the notion of Property. Precisely as we have seen that the earliest form of a Right of Property, succeeding that of mere primitive "Occupation," was that of Corporate Ownership by a small group of persons who were associated together for purposes of mutual defence, so we find that in the same period these groups of persons lived in a state of promiscuity, having their wives like their property in common.[1] But with the development of the idea of individual property we enter upon the first steps in the ascending ladder of civilisation which marks the transition from absolute promiscuity to individual marriages. The intermediate stages, however, were gradual and progressive. From polyandrous arrangements in which the whole tribe shared, we pass, as in the Tibetan polyandry and in the polyandry of the *Mahabharat*, to a practice of a more advanced kind in which all the husbands are brothers, a practice which was no doubt indorsed from considerations of economy, the scarcity of women, or the advantage arising from the concentration of heritages in a single family. Here again, as the elder brother is generally regarded as the natural head of the Household, he gradually assumes the position of being in a special sense the husband of the

[1] The hypothesis of primitive promiscuity, as the initial type of the human family, upheld by McLennan, Bastian, Lubbock, Bachofen, Herbert Spencer, and others, has more recently been rejected by Edward Westermarck, the lecturer on Sociology at the University of Finland. This able writer maintains the opposite theory of primitive monogamy, based on biological principles, affiliating human marriage on the monogamous instincts of animals, and allowing full weight both to natural and sexual selection. *The Hist. of Human Marriage*, Macmillan, 1891. See, also, an interesting article on "*Man as a Member of Society*," in the *Monist* for July, 1897, p. 530, and Andrew Lang's *Custom and Myth*, 245—275.

woman and the protector and nurturer of the children born in the house or tent. The idea of individual fatherhood is thus rudely formed, but when this stage is reached the further progress to individual marriages is comparatively easy. "The eldest brother, or head of the polyandrous group, will begin to desire to have his wife to himself; to ensure this he must find another wife for his younger brothers, and so gradually the principle of individual marriage and fatherhood must be established."[1]

Natural basis of Marriage.

188. Marriage, then, is founded upon the natural Reciprocity or Inter-community of the sexes.[2] The end of producing and educating children may be regarded as always the end of Nature in implanting mutual desire and inclination of the sexes. But in modern times amongst Western nations it is not esteemed necessary for the rightfulness of Marriage that those who marry should set this before themselves as the end of their union, otherwise the marriage would be dissolved of itself when the production of children ceased.[3] In ancient times, however, there can be no doubt that a husband could repudiate a barren wife. This was the practice of the Romans, and it is related by Gellius that Sp. Carvilius Ruga, with the approval of the domestic council (*consilium domesticum*), put away the wife he fondly loved because she was barren, and he was consequently unable, with a safe conscience, to assure the Censors that he had a wife who would bear him children.[4] It was equally the practice amongst the ancient Germans, and apparently the wife had also the right of separating from her husband, if the unproductiveness of the Marriage was attributable to his incapacity (*Unvermögen*).[5] In India, although by Hindu Law Marriage is regarded as

[1] Robertson Smith's *Kinship and Marriage in Early Arabia*, p. 123.

[2] Kant's *Philosophy of Law*, p. 109.

[3] *Ibid.* 40; Stahl, *Die Philosophie des Rechts*, Vol. II. section 47, p. 336.

[4] Muirhead's *Law of Rome*, p. 248 (note 1).

[5] Grimm's *Deutsche Rechtsalterthümer*, pp. 443 (4), 454.

CHAP. VII.

a sacrament and indissoluble, the power of a husband to "supersede" a barren wife is distinctly conceded; and according to the *Mitacshara* the wife's claim upon the husband in such a case is limited to a sum equal to the expenses incurred in the second marriage. But in modern practice, a husband is not bound to do more than to maintain a superseded wife by providing her with food and raiment.[1] It has been held, however, in the Punjab, that a "superseded" wife does not forfeit her right of inheritance as a widow on the death of her husband.[2] This decision was based on the ground that the Hindu Law does not recognise a power of divorce. But where local custom sanctions such a practice it would, of course, be allowed to have the force of law.[3]

Marriage produces certain Rights *in rem*.

189. Marriage, therefore, as the juridical relation which results from the obligation that is formed by two persons of different sex entering into a union solely on the basis of a (life-long) reciprocal possession of their sexual faculties, produces externally, as against the whole world, certain Rights and Duties which are incapable of alienation or waiver. Thus it establishes the Right on the part of the husband to his wife's society, which he can enforce against everyone who seeks to deprive him of it by either forcing or inducing the wife to leave his protection, or by seducing her. This Right continues so long as the Marriage-relation lasts, and subsequently only ceases upon the death of one of the parties, or the Marriage being annulled by a sentence of a Court of competent jurisdiction.

Marital Right.

Parental Right.

190. Another Right which results from a valid Marriage is that of the parents to the custody and control of the offspring of the Marriage, and to the produce of their labour until they themselves arrive at an age when the law concedes

[1] Macnaghten's *Hindu Law*, Chap. 5.

[2] No. 16, *Punjab Record*, 1875.

[3] Section 5, Act IV. of 1872; and I. L. R. III. Cal. 305.

to them an independent capacity of acquisition.[1] According to the principles of the Roman Law, and in this respect the English Law is the same, children born in lawful wedlock (*ex justis nuptiis*) followed the condition and were in the power of the father,[2] while those who were born *sine legitimo matrimonio* followed that of the mother unless a special law provided otherwise.[3] The father was reckoned to be he whom the nuptials indicate (*pater est quem nuptiæ demonstrant*), and it is interesting to notice that a precisely similar rule is recognised in the fundamental doctrine of Muhammadan Law—*al-walad li' l-firash*—"the son is reckoned to the bed on which he is born."[4] Parental Right might also be acquired by adoption, which is an institution very familiar to Indian Students, for it is recognised by both the Hindu and Customary Law.[5] Any act which interferes with the proper exercise by the parents of the control and custody of their children, or which deprives them of their services, is an infringement of this Right, and is actionable.

CHAP. VII.

May result from lawful wedlock.

Or be acquired by adoption.

191. The Parental Right ceases with the death of the parent or child, or by the child being transferred by adoption to another family, when the Right is acquired by the adoptive father, or by the child attaining the age which the Law prescribes as that of majority, or as the result of a judicial sentence. In the case of a female child the Right is lost on her marriage, except in countries where infant marriages are customary, and where the child-wife is left with her parents until she attains the age of puberty.

Duration of Parental Right.

[1] Thus by Muhammadan Law, a father may pawn on account of *his own debt* the goods belonging to his minor son, who would not be able to annul the contract on attaining majority. *Tagore Law Lectures* for 1873, pp. 482, 483.

[2] Dig. I. 5, 12, 19; I. 6, 3.

[3] Dig. I. 5, 24.

[4] *Kinship and Marriage in Early Arabia*, by Robertson Smith, pp. 109, 110.

[5] As to the Customary Law of adoption in the Punjab, see my *Digest of Civil Law*, Chapter III.

CHAP. VII.

May be delegated.

192. Although the Parental Right ceases with the death of the parent, it is one that is capable of being delegated both in the lifetime of the parent, and by a testamentary disposition to take effect after his death. Thus it may be delegated to a schoolmaster or by apprenticing the child with another person in order to learn a trade or profession. So also the father is entitled to nominate a guardian for his minor children, and the mother has the same right on the father's death.

Testamentary guardian.

Other kinds of guardians.

193. But a guardian may also be appointed by a Court, as in cases governed by Act VIII. of 1890, or the responsibilities of the office may devolve by law upon certain defined relations of the deceased parent,[1] or it may be assumed by a Court itself, as in the case of minor land-holders by the Court of Wards, acting under the provisions of section 3 of Act XII. of 1878.

Contractual Family Rights.

194. Under the class of Family Rights may also be included those which are acquired by contract. Thus a master has the Right to the services of his servant, which he can enforce by an action for damages against anyone who deprives him of the benefit of those services. In like manner the Manager of an Opera or Theatre can claim damages from the Manager of a Rival House who entices away his actors or singers.[2]

[1] As to the Hindu Law on the subject, see Macnaghten's *Hindu Law*, Chap. VII. For the respective order of Guardians according to the Muhammadan Law of the Hanifa School, see *Tagore Law Lectures* for 1873, pp. 485—488; Syed Amir Ali's *Personal Law of the Muhammadans*, pp. 410—413.

[2] *Lumley* v. *Gye*, 2 E. & B. 216; and *Bowen* v. *Hall*, L. R. 6 Q. B. D. 333.

CHAPTER VIII.

RIGHTS "IN PERSONAM."

195. In this Chapter, all those Rights will be considered which arise out of Contract or which are annexed by Law. The former from the very nature of their origin can only avail against certain or determinate persons, and are, therefore, in the strictest sense, *jura in personam*. But many of the second class of Rights arise out of relations which may be regarded from a general or from a special point of view, either as creating Rights available against persons generally, in which respect they have already been discussed as appertaining to Rights *in rem*; or, as creating rights available against determinate persons, in which respect they are properly *jura in personam*, and will be considered in the present Chapter from the point of view of Antecedent Rights.

Chap. VIII.

Jura in personam.

Early history of Contract.

196. Nothing is more interesting to the Student of Jurisprudence than to trace the gradual growth of a Law of Contract, and to mark the stages by which that process of development is distinguished. In prosecuting this path of inquiry, we are in fact investigating the history of the transition from Status to Contract, of the natural community of interests, which is characteristic of the untutored human instinct, to that of individualisation; and each progressive step in our inquiry brings us closer to the realisation of the principle, which still awaits complete development, that the Rights and duties of individuals *inter se* must be brought closer and closer under their own control, and regulated by their mutual agreements. We see this tendency showing

itself throughout the history of every department of Law. We see it in the Law of Property in the gradual recognition of subordinate elements of proprietary Right in land, and particularly in the transition from Villenage as a personal Status to Villenage as a Tenure in the thirteenth century.[1] We see it again in the substitution of voluntary service of the domestic servant for the compulsory service of the domestic slave. We see it still more plainly at the present day in the growing tendency to regard the Marriage relation, and the Rights and Duties which arise out of it, as regulated by agreement of parties rather than by any absolute Divine Law attaching to the Mystic Union of two persons of different sex on the basis of a reciprocal possession of their sexual faculties (*usus facultatum sexualium alterius*). In primitive times, when intercourse outside the Family or the Tribe was unknown or extremely limited, there existed but few occasions which could give rise to anything resembling a contract in the modern sense. Exchange and barter were no doubt rudely practised, but these were transactions which were adjusted on the spot, by the instant exchange and delivery of one commodity against another, and obviously gave no occasion for the creation of any future obligation.[2] But as the influence of the individual over the external world increased, as social and commercial intercourse enlarged their sphere, it became necessary to provide for the contingency of one man doing something in the immediate present on the faith of another engaging to do something for him in the future. Now at a time when the institution of tribunals for the settlement of private disputes was unthought of, and when the conception of Right was still in its rudest form, it is obvious that the only guarantee one had for the fulfilment of an obligation undertaken by his neighbour was that of

[1] See the passage from Bracton, quoted at p. 333 of Sir H. Maine's *Early Law and Custom.*

[2] Muirhead's *Law of Rome*, p. 49.

reliance on his good faith and probity. The early Romans were very sensible of this, and they deified Fides, showing their reverence for this virtue by investing it with a special cult and building a temple in its honour, which stood forth as a monument of that *Fides Publica* for which the early Republic was remarkable, and of which it was so justly proud.[1] The violation of good faith, which was pledged by giving the right hand, the supposed seat of Fides,[2] involved the loss of reputation, which was attended with serious disqualifications; and the extreme rarity of failure to perform an undertaking entered into in sight and hearing of a deity, which is testified to by Aulus Gellius,[3] rendered it unnecessary until the relaxation of morals in the latter years of the Republic, to devise any formula as a remedy for fraud and deceit.[4] The practice mentioned by Dionysius,[5] of resorting to the altar of Hercules erected in the cattle market to bind each other by agreements, will remind the Indian Student of a somewhat similar practice which prevails in the East of solemnly concluding an important engagement in the precincts of a mosque or temple, or of settling a dispute in accordance with the oath of one of the parties if taken in a sacred building of that character. So, in ancient Egypt, the parties with their witnesses resorted to the door of some sacred temple, and there, in the presence of their witnesses, concluded their contract.[6] It is noteworthy also that the importance of having engagements entered into in the

[1] Thus Cicero speaks of *Fides—i.e.*, adhesion to, and truth of, things said and agreed—as the basis of all justice. *De Officiis*, i. 8, 23. And in *Aulus Gellius* we read: "Of all (virtues, the Roman people) primarily and chiefly cultivated *Fides*, and regarded it as sacred both in private and in public;" XX. I. 39, 40.

[2] *Ibid.*, p. 50 (note 2).

[3] *Noct. Att.* XI. 18, 1.

[4] This formula (*de dolo*) was devised by Aquilius, the colleague of Cicero in the Prætorship. *De Officiis*, iii. 14.

[5] Dion. Hal. i. 41.

[6] Professor Revillout's *Les Obligations en Droit Égyptien*, p. 16.

presence of witnesses, in order to ensure their publicity and to render them susceptible of proof, is no less characteristic of the Hindu and Anglo-Saxon Laws than it is of the early Roman. In the Roman system five witnesses, representing the different elements of the nation, besides the scale bearer (*libripens*), were required to be present at noxal contracts, which will presently be explained, and the Law of the Twelve Tables provided that if any of these witnesses refused to declare his testimony when required, he should be reckoned dishonourable (*improbus*) and be incapable in future of executing or being a witness to, or taking any benefit under, a deed requiring the testimony of witnesses.[1] So also Narada propounds the rule that at least *three* witnesses are requisite to prove a transaction;[2] and a contract of sale was not obligatory among the Anglo-Saxons unless it was made in the presence of two or three official witnesses who were appointed in each township for such purposes.[3] The virtue of truth-speaking on the part of these attesting witnesses is also rigorously insisted upon. "Thy ancestors," says the Hindu law-giver, "are in suspense when thou art come to give evidence, and ponder in their mind: 'Wilt thou deliver us from Hell or precipitate us into it?'"[4] And if in modern times the Hindu is not proverbial for his veracity, he can at all events point to the ancient sages of the Law to prove, that they at least taught that "truth is the soul of man." Indeed in primitive times, when people had to rely solely on the probity of those with whom they dealt, and when engagements were orally concluded, it is only natural to suppose that the virtue of good faith and veracity would be held in the highest esteem, and that falsehood would be

[1] Muirhead's *Law of Rome*, p. 69 (note 13).

[2] Quoted in the *Mitacshara*, Chap. VI., section 1, paras. 5 and 6.

[3] *Law of Contracts*, by J. I. Clark-Hare, p. 69; Holmes's *Common Law*, pp. 255, 256.

[4] Narada's *Institutes*, by Jolly, p. 42.

Chap. VIII.

branded as the greatest crime. In such an age everything, as Narada observes, "depends upon truth."[1] "Therefore," in the words of the Chinese philosopher Lan-Tsze, "the sage keeps the obligations of his contract and exacts not from others."[2] There was one and only one exception in which falsehood was regarded as justifiable in the Hindu Law.[3] With a pardonable weakness for their own class, the Brahmin compilers of the Institutes of Manu ordained that: "In case of a promise made for the preservation of a Brahmin, it is no deadly sin to take a light oath."

Early forms of Contract.

197. One of the earliest Contracts which the exigencies of human existence compel mankind to enter into is that which is based on the practice of borrowing—a practice which enables one man whose own resources are insufficient for his immediate wants to avail himself of the larger resources of his richer neighbour for a consideration. The Roman name for a transaction of this kind was *nexum*, and it was effected by weighing out the money, at first raw metal, by a *libripens* (or scale bearer) in the presence of five witnesses, under the obligation (*nexum*[4]) of repayment. But at an earlier period, when the use of metal had not yet superseded sheep and cattle as the standard of value, and when property mainly consisted in slaves and cattle (*familia pecuniaque*), a purchase was effected by the seller delivering the article purchased into the hand of the buyer (*mancipare* = to deliver by the hand), and the buyer at the same time paid the seller the stipulated price.[5] The thing thus acquired by purchase is *mancipium*, indicating that it is *taken by the hand*, as all property was

[1] Jolly's Translation, Chap. V., para. 86, pp. 42, 43.

[2] Translation of the *Tau-Teh-King*, published in the *Monist* for July, 1897, at p. 601.

[3] *Manu*, VIII. 112.

[4] From the Latin verb *nectere*=to tie, to bind together: as Virgil says: *Quo vincula nectitis?* "Why fetters tie?" Ecl. VI. 23.

[5] Mommsen I. 151, note. 7th German edition.

CHAP. VIII. originally taken by actual seizure from the enemy. But when with the progress of ideas the distinction between the contract and the sale was understood,[1] the old term *mancipium* readily suggested the coinage of a new word, *mancipatio*, to denote the sale or conveyance. A further progress of ideas develops new forms of contract which supersede the primitive *nexum*; thus the contract *verbis* or *stipulatio*[2] at first operates as an adjunct to the *nexum* or *mancipatio*, and finally it is detached from its root, and, under the abstract term *obligatio*,[3]

[1] In his interesting lectures on *Obligations in the Egyptian Law*, Professor Eugène Revillout points out how the ancient Egyptians of the classical period (*i.e.*, since the reforms of Bocchoris) resorted to two distinct and successive written instruments, when it was intended to constitute the transferee the complete master of the subject of the sale. The first instrument evidenced the payment of the entire purchase-money in lieu of the right of property; while the second, which was in the form of a relinquishment or renunciation of right on the part of the vendor, was directed to the placing of the property at the complete disposition and enjoyment of the new proprietor. Until the latter instrument was executed, the sale in all its elements was not deemed to be complete. *Les Obligations en Droit Égyptien*, pp. 3, 4. A thorough examination of the recently discovered *Petrie Papyri*, in regard to which Professor Mahaffy read an interesting paper at the International Oriental Congress Meeting of 9th September, 1892, will probably add much to our existing knowledge of Egyptian Contracts. A very interesting paper on Babylonian House Leases, by Bruno Meissner and Knut L. Tallquist, has been published in the *Vienna Oriental Journal*, Vol. IV., No. 2, p. 112.

[2] "The *verborum obligatio* of the Romans was contracted by uttering certain formal words of style, and interrogation being put by the one party and an answer being given by the other. These obligations were called stipulations, and were binding, although without consideration." Lord Mackenzie's *Studies in Roman Law*, 6th ed., p. 228. *Stipulatio*=*stipula*, a synonym for *festuca*, a rod, which, according to Gaius (IV. 16), was used, in proceedings *in rem* with *vindicatio*, instead of the spear (*quasi hastæ loco*). But in the *Digest* the term is said to be taken from *stipulum*, which meant something firm, and was perhaps originally derived from *stipes* (trunk of a tree). *Dig.* III. 15, 1 pr. It engendered a unilateral agreement, which probably owed its origin to the old promissory oath—*sponsio ad aram* (*maximam*)—and was thus of sacral origin. Salkowski's *Roman Law*, p. 556.

[3] Paulus, for instance, says "that every 'obligation' is equivalent to 'contract,' for whenever a person incurs an 'obligation' he is deemed 'to contract.'" *Dig.* V. 1, 20. But the term is not found in the earlier

it takes its place in the latest phase of the Roman Law, as illustrated in the legislation of Justinian, to indicate "the tie of law (*juris vinculum*)" which binds us to the rules of our Civil Law, to render something.[1] The farther back we go, the more rigorous we find the forms and solemnities with which agreements have to be clothed before they receive the *juris vinculum* which gives them a legal recognition. The *nexum* or the *mancipatio* required, as we have just seen, the presence of a prescribed number of persons, the *stipulatio* or *verbis* the exact repetition of a certain solemn form of words; the *vadimonium*, or engagement on the part of sureties (*vades*), was an essentially formal contract; the contract *literis* depended upon a system of book-keeping peculiar to Roman citizens;[2] and it is not until trade began to assume considerable importance and intercourse with foreigners became frequent, that Consensual Contracts, which had nothing of the peculiar characteristics of the old Civil Law of Rome, and which required nothing more to perfect them than the simple consent of the parties (*consensu fiunt obligationes*[3]), were permitted to be enforced by Prætorian actions, called *bonæ fidei*, in four of the most ordinary transactions of daily life, such as sale, location (letting), partnership, and mandate (agency). This law of development from an unbending *strictum jus* to a more elastic *jus æquum* in all matters of legal procedure and legal contract is characteristic of the growth of Law in almost all nations. Thus in England, even as late as the middle of the thirteenth century, purely

Roman Law, and certainly appertains to a period much later than the Law of the Twelve Tables, *vide* Maynz *Cours de Droit Roman*, Tom. ii., p. 3 (1870).

[1] Inst. iii. 13.

[2] "There was a custom for everyone to keep a household account day by day of all his doings, that it might appear what each had laid by from his returns, from his calling, gains, or profit, and on what day, and what also he had incurred of expenditure or of loss." Ps. Ascon in Cic. *in Verr.* ii., 1, section 60.

[3] *Gaius*, iii. 35.

CHAP. VIII. Consensual Contracts had acquired as little force as they originally possessed in Rome; and a further illustration of the same tendency towards simplification may be traced in the history of the action of debt in both the English and German Laws, a complete history of which has yet to be written, but an admirable sketch of which has been given by Mr. O. W. Holmes, Junior, in his work on the *Common Law*.[1] It is of the greatest importance that the Student of Jurisprudence should be conversant with this law of development, and that he should further understand that although the enormous advance of commerce in modern times has given rise to far greater complexity in commercial transactions than was characteristic of simpler times, the substantial principles which govern Commercial Law at the present day are not materially different from those which are embodied in Roman Jurisprudence. A natural law of growth has no doubt brought about changes to meet the necessities of time and place. The old faint outlines of the law of bailment have been filled up, and the law of promissory notes, bills of exchange, and of insurance have been added to Commercial Jurisprudence as understood by Roman Jurists. But the germ underlying the whole modern Law of Contract is derived from Rome, and its history is only an illustration of the truth of the saying: *nomina sunt mutabilia, res autem immobiles*.[2] Names, indeed, have changed, but the principles founded on reason and common sense, on good faith and equity, still survive, and constitute the foundations on which the modern Law of Contract has been constructed.

[1] Chap. VII., pp. 247—288. See also Clark-Hare's *Law of Contract*, Chap. VII., p. 117. As to the growth of Contract in English Law, see *Law and Politics in the Middle Ages*, by Ed. Jenks, Chap. VII., pp. 246—292.

[2] Rome again owed a large part of her jurisprudence to the *jus gentium*, and the Jurists, whose excerpts form the bulk of the Digest of Justinian, were those who made the largest use of that source of law, and who claimed, like Ulpian, a Phœnician origin (Dig. L. 15, 1). *Cf. Les Obligations en Droit Égyptien*, par Eugène Revillout, p. 9.

Chap. VIII.

Elements of a Contract.

198. If we analyse a Contract, which is the legal term for an "agreement enforceable by law,"[1] we shall find that the following are its constituent elements:—[2]

1. Several parties capable of contracting;
2. A bilateral act by which they express their agreement;
3. A matter agreed upon which is (*a*) possible, (*b*) lawful, and (*c*) of a nature to produce a result legally binding and affecting the relations of the parties to each other; and
4. Very generally, either a solemn form or some fact which affords a motive for the agreement.

Let us consider each of these separately.

Parties capable of contracting.

199. Since a "Contract is only a technical name for an "agreement enforceable by law," it is obvious that there must be at least two parties to it, between whom there must be an agreement or concurrence of their wills producing (or intended to produce) a modification of their Rights. A promise to make a payment to one's self, would obviously be destitute of any obligation in a legal sense.[3] Thus where the same Company had two departments, one for insurance and one for annuities, the latter it was held could not validly contract with the former.[4] Hence the necessity of there being at least two independent parties, a *promisor* and a *promisee.* But there is the further qualification that the parties must be "capable of contracting." Upon this point the Indian Contract Act enacts that "every person is competent to contract who is of the age of majority according to the Law to which he is subject, and who is of sound mind, and is not

[1] *Indian Contract Act*, section 2.

[2] Holland's *Jurisprudence*, 218; Stokes's *Anglo-Indian Codes*, Vol. I., 492. *Cf.* Stahl. *Die Philosophie des Rechts*, Vol. I., sections 35—37, pp. 319—324.

[3] "The covenant to my mind is senseless. I do not know what is meant in point of Law by a man paying himself." Per Pollock, C. B., in *Faulkner* v. *Lowe*, 2 Exch. 195. See also Clarke-Hare's *Law of Contracts*, p. 174. *Cf.* Just. *Inst.* III. 19, 22; Dig. XLV. 1, 82, pr.

[4] *Grey* v. *Ellison*, 1 Giff. 438.

CHAP. VIII. disqualified from contracting by any Law to which he is subject."[1]

A Bilateral Act.

200. Every Contract, regarded in itself *objectively* consists of two juridical Acts: the "proposal" on one side, called the *pollicitatio*, and its "acceptance" on the other.[2] One party expresses his willingness to do or to abstain from doing something, and the other party expresses his assent to such act or abstention.[3] When accepted the proposal becomes a "promise," and every "promise, and every set of promises forming the consideration for each other," is an "agreement," which, if enforceable by Law, is a Contract. In order to convert a proposal into a "promise" the "acceptance" must be absolute and unqualified, and must be expressed in some usual and reasonable manner, unless the proposal prescribes the manner in which it is to be accepted. If the proposal prescribes a manner in which it is to be accepted, and the acceptance is not made in such manner, the proposer may, within a reasonable time after the acceptance is communicated to him, insist that his proposal shall be accepted in the prescribed manner, and not otherwise; but if he fails to do so, he accepts the "acceptance."[4] Thus, where goods were ordered to be sent by an unusual route for a special reason, but the reason ceased to exist before the order could be executed, and the goods were sent by the usual route, it was held by the Queen's Bench that this being acquiesced in by

What constitutes Acceptance of a proposal.

[1] Section 11, Act IX. of 1872. A minor being thus incompetent to contract, agreements entered into by him are void and not voidable. No. 23, P. R. 1888; I. L. R. (1890) XXIV. Cal. 265. *Cf.* also No. 96, P. R. 1888. The defence of infancy cannot, however, be successfully set up in support of fraud. I. L. R. (1898); I. L. R. XXV. Cal. 371. Nor can a minor, representing himself as of full age, be heard afterwards to assert the contrary in a suit brought by him to set aside the transaction on the ground of minority. (1896) I. L. R. XXI. Bomb. 198.

[2] Kant's *Philosophy of Law*, p. 121.

[3] Stokes's *Anglo-Indian Codes*, Vol. I., p. 492.

[4] Section 7, Act IX. of 1872.

the buyer was a sufficient performance of the original contract, and not of a substituted contract, and therefore no special memorandum of such alleged substituted contract was required to satisfy the Statute of Frauds.[1]

Communication and revocation of proposals and acceptance.

201. The mere fact, however, of one party having made a proposal to another may prevent him from revoking it, and may consequently entitle the other party to insist upon its enforcement, although the proposer may not have heard of the other's acceptance at the time of revocation. The Indian Act accordingly lays down very clear rules as to when a communication of a "proposal" or an "acceptance" is deemed to be complete.[2] As to the former it is complete when it comes to the knowledge of the person to whom it is made; and as to the latter, as against the proposer, when it is put in a course of transmission to him, so as to be out of the power of the acceptor, or, as against the acceptor, when it comes to the knowledge of the proposer. Thus, where the parties form their contract by correspondence, the proposal is complete when the letter conveying it comes to the knowledge of the person to whom it is addressed; but in the case of an "acceptance," as against the proposer, when it is posted, and as against the acceptor, when the letter comes to the knowledge of the proposer. It may, therefore, happen that while a proposer is bound by an acceptance of which he has acquired no knowledge, the acceptor will be free from all liability arising from his acceptance.[3] On the other hand, a revocation of a proposal *despatched* before the posting of the acceptance is in time even though it reaches the acceptor *after* he has *posted* the acceptance. In England and America the rule is somewhat different; and the question there depends

[1] *Leather Cloth Co.* v. *Hieronimus*, L. R. 10 Q. B. 140.

[2] See a curious case of negotiation by telegram, where it was held that the acceptance of an offer must be express and could not be implied. *Harvey* v. *Facey*, (1893) A. C. 552.

[3] Stokes's *Anglo-Indian Codes*, Vol. I., p. 493.

on whether the revocation was *received* before the acceptance was put in the Post Office, and not whether it was first written or first mailed.[1] The Indian Act, in this instance, has adopted the rule of the old Civil Law, under which it was requisite that both parties should concur in a common purpose at the moment when the contract is completed by acceptance, and an offer could not be accepted after it had been withdrawn, although the revocation had not been actually communicated or made known.[2] And, as observed by the late Lord Justice Bowen,[3] there is this clear gloss to be made upon the doctrine that the acceptance of an offer must be notified; that, as notification of acceptance is required for the benefit of the person who makes the offer, the person who makes the offer may dispense with notice to himself if he thinks it desirable to do so; and if he, expressly or impliedly, intimates in his offer that it will be sufficient to act on the proposal without communicating acceptance of it to himself, performance of the condition is a sufficient acceptance without notification. Thus, where the defendants, the proprietors of a medical preparation called "The Carbolic Smoke Ball," issued an advertisement in which they offered to pay 100*l.* to any person who contracted the influenza after having used one of their smoke balls in a specified manner and for a specified period, it was held that it was not necessary to notify acceptance of the offer before performance of the condition, and that the condition being performed the notification was dispensed with.

Revocation, how made.

202. A proposal is revoked in one of the following ways: (1) by the communication of notice of revocation by the proposer to the other party; (2) by the lapse of the time pre-

[1] *The Law of Contracts*, by J. I. Clark-Hare, pp. 367, 368. *Cf. Byrne* v. *Van Tienhoven*, 5 C. P. D. 344.

[2] *Ibid.*, p. 368.

[3] *Carlill* v. *Carbolic Smoke Ball Co.*, (1893) 1 Q. B. 256, at p. 269.

scribed in such proposal for its acceptance, or, if no time is so prescribed, by the lapse of a reasonable time, without communication of the acceptance; (3) by the failure of the acceptor to fulfil a condition precedent to acceptance; or (4) by the death or insanity of the proposer, if the fact of his death or insanity comes to the knowledge of the acceptor before acceptance.[1]

Voidability of contracts without free consent.

203. But the bilateral act which is expressive of agreement must not have been induced by "coercion," "undue influence," "fraud," or "misrepresentation";[2] and the party whose consent was so caused may decline to be bound by the contract. Or, in case his consent was caused by "fraud" or "misrepresentation," he may, if he thinks fit, insist that the contract shall be performed, and that he shall be put in the position in which he would have been if the representations made had been true. There is, however, one exception to the first-named rule, and that is, that if the party whose consent was so caused had the means of discovering the truth with ordinary diligence, he loses his right to treat the contract as *voidable*.[3] Again, where both the parties to an agreement are under a mistake as to a matter of fact essential to the agreement, other than an erroneous opinion as to the value of the thing which forms the subject-matter of the agreement, the agreement is deemed by the Indian Law to be *void*.[4] The distinction to be drawn between these terms—*void* and *voidable* —may be thus explained:—The former term is intended to express an "*agreement not enforceable by law*"; whereas "*an agreement which is enforceable by law at the option of one or more of the parties thereto, but not at the option of the other or others*," is said to be "voidable."[5]

[1] *Indian Contract Act*, section 6.
[2] For an explanation of these terms, see para. 49, *ante*.
[3] Section 19, Act IX. of 1872.
[4] Section 20, *ibid.*; see also I. L. R. III. Cal. 602; VI. *ibid.* 706.
[5] *Indian Contract Act*, section 2. See *ante*, para. 55.

CHAP. VIII.

Agreement, how to be expressed.

204. It was quaintly said by Chief Justice Brian in the reign of Edward IV. to be "trite law" that the "thought of man is not triable," "for," proceeds the learned Judge, "the devil himself does not know what the thought of man is."[1] But as embodying a general proposition the remark is not quite accurate, inasmuch as Courts in criminal cases have very frequently to analyse the "thought of man" in order to ascertain whether he is actuated by a malicious, fraudulent, or dishonest *intent*. In this sense the "thought of man" *is* triable. The learned Chief Justice was, however, dealing with an unexpressed acceptance, and as applied to such a matter his language is undoubtedly both expressive and correct. The agreement which results from an accepted proposal must be made manifest to the external senses by means of words, signs, or a course of conduct. The question in every case will be the same. Have the terms of the offer been fully communicated to the acceptor, and accepted by him? In England the tendency of judicial decision is towards a general rule, that if a man accepts a document which purports to contain the terms of an offer, he is bound by all the terms, though he may not choose to inform himself of their tenor or even of their existence.[2] This rule may be illustrated by reference to the cases which frequently arise when a contract has been made with a Railway Company for the safe carriage of the plaintiff, or of his luggage, or for the deposit or bailment of luggage in a cloak room. The law applicable to such cases is thus summed up by Mellish, L.J.:— "If the person receiving the ticket did not see or know that there was any writing on the ticket, he is not bound by the conditions; if he knew there was writing, and knew or believed that the writing contained conditions, then he is bound by the conditions; if he knew there was writing on

[1] Quoted by Lord Blackburn in *Brogden* v. *Metropolitan Railway Co.*, L. R. 2 App. at p. 692; Holland's *Jurisprudence*, p. 223; Anson's *Law of Contracts*, 4th ed., p. 16.

[2] Anson's *Law of Contracts*, p. 18.

the ticket, but did not know or believe that the writing contained conditions, nevertheless he would be bound, if the delivering to him of the ticket, in such a manner that he could see there was writing upon it, was, in the opinion of the Jury, reasonable notice that the writing contained conditions."[1] The first class of cases referred to may be further illustrated by *Henderson* v. *Stevenson*,[2] and the second by *Harris* v. *South Eastern Railway Company*.[3] According to the Indian Contract Act, in so far as the proposal or acceptance of any promise is made in *words*, the promise is said to be *express*. If made otherwise than in words, the promise is said to be *implied*.[4] Thus an acceptance by "signs" by a dumb person would, under the Indian Law, only establish an *implied* promise, which is somewhat singular. The more correct use of the above classification of agreements into *express* and *implied* is to restrict the latter term to those agreements which are to be implied merely by a course of conduct, and to include all others under the term *express*.[5]

May be made by Agent.

205. The proposal and acceptance may again emanate not only directly from the parties themselves, but equally so from their duly authorised agents.[6] Here we have an application of the well-known rule of law *qui facit per alium facit per se:* he who does anything by another does it by himself. Accordingly, it is held that the act of the Agent is the act of the

[1] *Parker* v. *S. E. Railway Co.*, L. R. 2 C. P. D. 423.

[2] L. R. 2 H. L. Sc. App. 470.

[3] L. R. 1 Q. B. D. 515.

[4] Section 9.

[5] Holland's *Jurisprudence*, p. 223.

[6] In the earlier Roman Law, as in that of Egypt, representation, as a general rule, was inadmissible. Thus Ulpian says, "No one can proceed by *legis actio* in the name of another." (Dig. L. 17, 123.) But an exception was allowed in favour of the people, of freedom, and of guardianship. (Just. *Inst.* IV. 10, pr.) So, except in the case of persons under one's power, no other third person could enter into a valid stipulation for another. (*Gaius*, III. 103.) And this old principle of the Roman Law is found to be equally characteristic of the ancient Egyptian Law. (Revillout's *Les Obligations en Droit Égyptien*, p. 21.)

CHAP. VIII.

Principal for everything done within the scope of his authority. But even where the person professing to act as Agent was not authorised at the time of forming the contract to act for the person whom he professed to represent, he may be retrospectively made the agent of that person by subsequent ratification.[1] This is an instance of the application of the maxim *Omnis ratihabitio retrotrahitur et mandato priori æquiparatur*: every ratification of an act already done has a retrospective effect, and is equal to a previous request to do it. But there is one important exception to this rule. Where an act is done by one person on behalf of another without such other person's authority, which, if done with authority, would have the effect of subjecting a third person to damages, or of terminating any right or interest of a third person, it cannot, by ratification, be made to have such effect.[2] Thus, if A. holds a lease from B., terminable on three months' notice, and C., an unauthorized person, gives notice of termination to A. In such a case the notice cannot be ratified by B., so as to be binding on A.[3] Or, again, where A., who is no party to a Bill of Exchange, and is not otherwise authorised to give notice of the dishonour of the bill, gives such notice, the notice so given cannot be ratified so as to bind an indorser or drawer.[4]

Authority of Agent may be express or implied.

206. The authority of the Agent may be expressed or implied. It is said to be express when it is given by words spoken or written; and to be implied when it is to be inferred from the circumstances of the case.[5] But the Law frequently prescribes the mode of appointment for certain purposes, and of course where such provisions exist, they must be scrupulously followed. Provisions of this kind occur in the Indian

[1] Section 196, *Indian Contract Act.*

[2] Section 200, *Ibid.*

[3] *Ibid.*, Illust. (*b*).

[4] Story on *Agency*, section 247.

[5] *Indian Contract Act*, section 187.

Registration Act (sections 32 and 33); in the Civil Procedure Code (sections 37, 39, 41, 465); in the Indian Companies Act, 1882 (Table A., paras. 48—51), and in some other Acts. In the case of an Agent appointed to do a particular act, the authority extends to the doing of every lawful thing which is necessary in order to do such act, and in that of an agent having an authority to carry on a business, the authority extends to the doing of every lawful thing necessary for the purpose, or usually done in the course of conducting such business.[1] But in an emergency an Agent is deemed to have authority to do all such acts for the purpose of protecting his principal from loss as would be done by a person of ordinary prudence, in his own case, under similar circumstances.[2] Thus, the master of a ship and the acceptor of a bill for the honour of the drawer may, at an emergency, borrow money on account of his employer without express authority to do so.[3] The mere existence of necessity will not, however, *create* Agency. Thus, it has been held in England that a Railway Company is not liable for the fees of a Surgeon who has been called in by one of their Station Masters to attend to the sufferers from an accident.[4] A familiar instance of implied Agency is supplied by the relation of a wife in the management of her husband's domestic affairs. When the husband permits the wife to manage his household she presumably acts as his Agent in all such matters; and it is only by reason of the authority she thus derives from her husband that her acts are binding upon him. The English Courts have accordingly held that where the husband prohibits the wife to pledge his credit, and there is no establishment of which the wife can be said to be the domestic manager, the question of implied Agency is at

[1] *Indian Contract Act*, section 188.

[2] *Ibid.*, section 189.

[3] Stokes's *Anglo-Indian Codes*, Vol. I., p. 631 (note 1).

[4] *Cox* v. *Midland Railway Co.*, 3 Exch. 268.

CHAP. VIII. an end, and the husband's liability does not in such a case depend on whether notice of the fact has been communicated to the particular tradesman or not, or whether the goods supplied were suitable to the husband's position in life.[1] But in the leading case of *Debenham* v. *Mellon* in which this doctrine was laid down, the House of Lords was careful to point out that the question whether the wife has authority to pledge her husband's credit is to be treated as a question of fact, to be determined upon the circumstances of each particular case.[2] In the case then before their Lordships the husband and wife were both servants of hotel-keepers; they lived in the hotel; the whole of their board and lodging was found for them, and therefore there was no household to be managed; there was in point of fact no domestic management at all. It was to a wife living with her husband under such circumstances that the plaintiff gave credit; and it was very reasonably held that as it was impossible from the facts of the case to imply *ex necessitate* any authority on the part of the wife to bind her husband, and as the husband had actually forbidden the wife to pledge his credit, the husband could not be held bound by his wife's unauthorised act. Now the Indian Contract Act also leaves the wife's authority to be inferred from the "circumstances of the case;"[3] and if the husband permits the wife to assume the control of his household a tradesman might well presume, in the absence of any distinct notice to the contrary, that she has authority to pledge her husband's credit for necessaries suited to his condition in life. What the term "necessaries" would include cannot be absolutely defined; but

[1] *Jolly* v. *Rees*, 15 C. B. (N. S.) 628; S. C. 33 L. J. C. P. 177. The House of Lords subsequently affirmed the principle of this case in *Debenham* v. *Mellon*, L. R. 6 App. Cas. 24; S. C. 50 L. J. Q. B. 155.

[2] See the observations of the Lord Chancellor on *Jolly* v. *Rees*, at pp. 157, 158, and of Lord Blackburn at p. 161 of the Report published in Vol. 50, *Law Journal*.

[3] Section 187. *Vide* also section 68, *Ibid*.

speaking generally, it may be said to be "something reasonably required for the nourishment, clothing, lodging, education, and decent behaviour and appearance according to the station of the particular person."[1] The Hindu Law appears to rest upon very much the same grounds as the English Law. A person dealing with a Hindu wife and seeking to charge her husband must show either that the wife is living with her husband and managing the household affairs, in which case an implied Agency to buy necessaries is presumed, or he must show the existence of such a state of things as would warrant her in living apart from her husband and claiming support or separate maintenance—when, of course, the law would give her an implied authority to bind him for necessaries supplied to her during such separation, in the event of his not providing her with adequate maintenance.[2] Where, however, parties separate by mutual consent and make their own terms, the implied authority to bind the husband is excluded by the express terms of the arrangement.[3]

Agent alone cannot sue or be sued upon contracts entered into by him as such.

Exceptions to rule.

206a. Since an agreement entered into by an authorised Agent is regarded as the contract of his Principal, it follows that the Agent alone cannot sue or be sued upon it. To this general rule there are certain exceptions. As, for instance (*a*) where the contract is made by an Agent for the sale or purchase of goods for a merchant resident abroad (*i.e.*, out of British India); (*b*) when the Agent does not disclose the name of his Principal; and (*c*) when the Principal, though disclosed, cannot be sued.[4] The Principal may, however,

[1] Per Bramwell, B., in *Ryder* v. *Wombwell*, L. R. 3 Exch. 96.

[2] Per Scotland, C. J., in I. Mad. H. C. Reps., p. 377. *Cf.* also I. L. R. III. Allah. 122; Vol. II., Mac. *Hindu Law*, 281; Mayne's *Hindu Law*, section 289.

[3] *Eastland* v. *Burchell*, L. R. 3 Q. B. D. 432.

[4] Section 230, *Indian Contract Act*. *Cf.* Story on *Agency*, sections 55, 266, 268, 290, 291.

CHAP. VIII. require the performance of a contract made with his Agent, although the other party may not have known, nor had reason to suspect, that the person with whom he was dealing was his Agent. But in such a case the Principal can only obtain such performance subject to the rights and obligations subsisting between the Agent and the other party to the contract.[1] On the other hand, where A. enters into a contract with B., and afterwards discovers that B. was acting as agent for C., A. may sue either B. or C., or both, upon the contract.[2] Where a person untruly represents himself to be the authorised Agent of another, and thereby induces a third person to deal with him as such Agent, he is liable to make compensation to the other party in respect of any loss or damage which he has incurred by so doing.[3] But the person falsely contracting as Agent is not entitled to require the performance of the contract.[4]

Liability of pretended Agent.

Sub-Agents.

207. Upon the principle *delegatus non potest delegare* (a delegated power cannot be delegated) an Agent cannot ordinarily employ another to perform acts which he has expressly or impliedly undertaken to perform personally. But he may delegate his power if by the ordinary custom of trade, or from the nature of the Agency, such a course is permissible or incumbent upon him.[5] Where such a delegation properly takes place, the Principal, so far as regards third persons, is represented by the Sub-Agent, and is bound by and responsible for his acts, as if he were an Agent originally appointed by the Principal. But the Agent nevertheless continues to be responsible to the Principal for the acts of the Sub-Agent, who in turn is responsible to the Agent but not to the Principal, except in cases of fraud or wilful wrong.[6] An

[1] Section 232, *Indian Contract Act*. See also section 231, *Ibid*.

[2] Section 233, *Ibid*.

[3] Section 235, *Ibid*. As to the measure of damages, see Mayne on *Damages*, 4th ed., pp. 325, 526.

[4] Section 236, *Indian Contract Act*.

[5] Section 190, *Ibid*.

[6] Section 192, *Ibid*.

Agent may also be expressly authorised to name another person to act for the Principal in the business of the Agency, or such an authority may be vested in him by implication, as, for instance, to instruct a Solicitor to recover moneys due to his Principal. In either of these cases, the relation between the Principal and the person so appointed, is that of an Agent of the Principal for such part of the business of the Agency as is entrusted to him, and not that of a Sub-Agent.[1]

Termination of Agency.

208. An Agency may be terminated in any of the following ways[2]:—(*a*) By the Principal revoking his authority. But there are certain limitations on the exercise of such a power by the Principal. Thus, where the Agent has himself an interest in the subject-matter of the Agency, the Agency cannot, in the absence of an express contract, be terminated to the prejudice of such interest.[3] Again, where the authority has been partly exercised, the revocation cannot affect such acts and obligations as arise from acts already done in the Agency.[4] The mere circumstance, however, that there is an express or implied contract that the Agency should be continued for any period of time, does not prevent the principal from revoking his Agent's authority before the expiry of that period. But where such a previous revocation takes place without sufficient cause, the Principal must make compensation to the Agent.[5]

(*b*) By the Agent renouncing the business of the Agency. Where this renunciation takes place before the period expressly or impliedly contemplated for the continuance of the Agency, the Agent must make compensation to the principal.[6]

[1] Section 194, *Indian Contract Act*. [2] Section 201, *Ibid.*
[3] Section 202, *Ibid.* *Cf.* I. L. R. V. Bomb. 253, and VII. Bomb. H. C. Reps. 10 (*a* J).
[4] Section 204, *Indian Contract Act.* [5] Section 205, *Ibid.* [6] *Ibid.*

(*c*) By the business of the Agency being completed, or ceasing to exist.

(*d*) By either the Principal or Agent dying or becoming of unsound mind. But where a payment is made or act done in good faith in pursuance of a power of attorney, such payment or act shall not be invalid by reason that before the payment or act the donor of the power had died or become lunatic or insolvent, or had revoked the power, if the fact of death, lunacy, insolvency, or revocation was not known to the person making or doing the same.[1]

(*e*) By the Principal being adjudicated an Insolvent under the provisions of any Act for the time being in force for the relief of insolvent debtors.

Third essential element of a Contract.

209. The third essential constituent element of a Contract is that the matter agreed upon must be (*a*) possible, (*b*) legal, and (*c*) of a nature to produce a result legally binding and affecting the relations of the parties to each other. Something has already been said[2] on the subject of "impossible conditions." According to the Roman Law the impossibility (whether physical or legal) had to consist in the nature of the thing to be done (*impossibilitas rei*) and not in the inability of the party to do it (*impossibilitas facti*).[3] Thus, if

[1] *Powers of Attorney Act*, 1882, section 3.

[2] Para. 61, *ante*.

[3] As Paulus expresses it, *quod natura fieri non concedit*, *i.e.*, which is contrary to the course of nature, or *quod Leges fieri prohibent*, which the Laws forbid. *Dig.* XLV. 1, 35; *Ibid.* 137, sections 4—6. Savigny states the distinction very clearly: "Impossibility," he says, "may consist either in the nature of the action itself, or in the particular circumstances of the promisor. It is only the first or objective kind of impossibility that is recognised as such by the law. The second, or subjective kind, cannot be relied on by the promisor for any purpose, and does not release him from the ordinary consequences of a wilful non-performance of his contract. On this last point the most obvious example is that of the debtor who owes a certain sum, but has neither money nor credit. There is plenty of money in the world, and it is a matter wholly personal to the debtor if he cannot get the money he has bound himself to pay." *Das Obligationen-recht*, 384; Dernberg, *Pandekten*, II. s. 46.

the thing could be accomplished by any one with proper means and the requisite skill and knowledge, the promisor was not less answerable because it was impossible to him (*ad incommodum promissoris pertinet*). Under the English Common Law the rule was that a man who agrees to do that which is contrary to the nature of things, or insusceptible of being performed, as for instance to construct a "perpetual motion," or deliver a larger quantity of barley than the world contains, cannot rely on the impossibility of performance as a defence.[1] In the leading case of *Thornborow* v. *Whitacre*,[2] Lord Holt, in overruling the defendant's demurrer based on the impossibility of performance which was evident on the face of the agreement, observed: "If a man will for money undertake to do an impossible thing, an action shall lie against him for not performing it." So in a comparatively recent case it was said that "if people will bind themselves to absurd regulations as to matters that appear to be impossible to be performed within the time, they must take the consequences of it, and therefore if you make such a bargain it is clear you cannot imply a condition which is unconnected with it."[3] Inasmuch, however, as to warrant a recovery in the old English form of action of Assumpsit it must appear not only that the defendant promised, and the plaintiff took the course which the promise was calculated to induce, but that he did so in *reliance* on the defendant's word (*fidem adhibens assumptioni*), the Courts came gradually to pay regard to the nature of the promise. Accordingly, if it was one which no sane man, according to the knowledge of the day, could have credited, an essential element was wanting, and the action could not be sustained. So in *Clifford* v. *Watts*[4] Brett, J., laid down the Law on the subject as follows: "I think it is

[1] *The Law of Contracts*, by J. I. Clark-Hare, p. 649.

[2] 2 Lord Raymond, 1164.

[3] *Jones* v. *St. John's College*, L. R. 6 Q. B. 115, 124.

[4] L. R. 5 C. P. 588.

not competent to a defendant to say that there is no binding contract, merely because he has engaged to do something which is physically impossible. I think it will be found in all the cases where that has been said, that the thing stipulated for was, according to the state of knowledge of the day, so absurd that the parties cannot be supposed to have so contracted." But a thing is not necessarily impossible because not *known* to be possible. This was well stated by Willes, J., in the case just cited, and it is common knowledge that many things are now possible which were formerly regarded as wholly impossible.[1] The answer to the question whether the defence of impossibility can be sustained turns, therefore, on whether it is such that reasonable men in the position of the parties must treat it as impossible. Thus a line appears to have been drawn much in the same way as in the Roman Law,[2] between that which, judging from the nature of the thing and the knowledge of the day, cannot *be* (*objective impossibility*), and that which cannot be *accomplished* (*subjective impossibility*). In the former case the promise is treated as so absurd that the parties cannot be supposed to have so contracted; while an undertaking which falls within the latter category, as for instance, that it shall not rain to-morrow, or that the Pope shall be at Westminster by a certain day, is treated as not less valid, because there are insuperable obstacles to its fulfilment.[3] These obstacles refer only to what the Roman Jurist calls *ad facultatem dandi*, and are therefore difficulties of a subjective character which affect the promisor alone. The principle is the same whether the impossibility of performance arises from the want of any legal means of carrying the contract into effect

[1] See the remarks on this subject in Pollock on *Contracts*, pp. 353, 354, 4th edition.

[2] Dig. XLIV. 7, 31; XLV. 1, 35, pr.; *Windscheid*, Vol. II. section 264, pp. 55, 56.

[3] *The Law of Contract*, by J. I. Clark-Hare, 642.

or from any other cause; and a covenant to obtain or perfect a patent may consequently be valid, although the parties are aliens, and the right to such an exclusive privilege is confined by the Law to citizens.[1] So it has been held in England that it is not a defence for the non-fulfilment of a covenant to supply the master of a ship with the pass which will enable him to procure a cargo, that it is arbitrarily withheld by the Government of the country where the Contract is to be performed.[2] But there are a variety of cases where the Courts in England and America have implied a condition in the Contract itself, the effect of which was to relieve the party when the performance had, without his fault, become impossible. These cases, however, have more particular reference to the *discharge* of a contract which was *valid* in its inception, and must be considered in that connection,[3] and not with reference to the constituent elements of a contract.

Indian Law as to impossibility.

210. The Indian Law regards an agreement to do an act impossible in itself as void,[4] and by implication it seems to recognise the rule above stated that in judging of the impossibility of the act the parties must be presumed to have had the ordinary knowledge of reasonable men.[5] Thus, although in various parts of India people may be found who honestly believe in the existence of magic—which is surely not more surprising than many things which modern Theo-

[1] *The Law of Contract*, by J. I. Clark-Hare, 642.

[2] *Kirk* v. *Gibbs*, 1 H. & N. 810. So where intercourse with the port to which a ship was chartered was prohibited on account of an epidemic prevailing there, whereby the freighter was prevented from furnishing a cargo, it was held that this did not dissolve his obligation. *Barker* v. *Hodgson*, 3 M. & S. 267. So also if the goods are confiscated at a foreign port, that is no answer to an action against the shipowner for not delivering them. *Spence* v. *Chadwick*, 10 Q. B. 517.

[3] See *post*, para. 224.

[4] Section 56, *Indian Contract Act*, adopting the rule of the Roman Law *impossibilium nulla obligatio est*. Dig. L. 17, 185.

[5] See the remarks of Sir Frederick Pollock at p. 354 of his *Principles of Contract*, 4th ed.

CHAP. VIII. sophists of Madame Blavatsky's school believe—the Indian legislature has pronounced an agreement to discover treasure by magic to be void.[1] But where one person has promised to do something which he knew, or, with reasonable diligence, might have known, and which the promisor did not know, to be impossible or unlawful, such promisor must make compensation to such promisee for any loss which such promisee sustains through the non-performance of the promise.[2] A Contract to do an act which, after the Contract is made, becomes impossible, or, by reason of some event which the promisor could not prevent, unlawful, becomes void when the act becomes impossible or unlawful.[3] But according to the Specific Relief Act of 1877,[4] a contract is not wholly impossible of performance because a portion of its subject-matter, existing at its date, has ceased to exist at the time of the performance. Thus, where A. contracts to sell a house to B. for a lakh of rupees, and the day after the contract is made, the house is destroyed by a cyclone, B. may nevertheless be compelled to perform his part of the contract by paying the purchase-money.[5] Under the Indian Law, therefore, cases such as that of *Taylor* v. *Caldwell*[6] would be decided somewhat differently. But where a material part of the subject-matter of a contract, supposed by both parties to exist, has, before the contract has been made, ceased to exist, the parties are discharged.[7] Thus, where A. contracts to pay an annuity to B. for the lives of C. and D., and it

[1] Illust. (*a*), section 56, *Indian Contract Act.*

[2] Section 56, *Ibid.*

[3] *Ibid.*

[4] Section 13. *Cf. Pain* v. *Mellor*, 6 Ves. 349.

[5] Illust. (*a*), *Ibid.* The Indian Legislature here adopts the principle of the Roman Law *periculum est emtoris*, which applied wherever there was a *completed* sale of a definite thing. Baron's *Pandekten*, section 269. *Res perit domino* is the ruling principle. See an application of this principle in *Elphick* v. *Barnes*, 5 C. P. D. 321; 49 L. J. C. P. 698.

[6] 3 B. & S. 826. See *ante*, para. 62, and *post*, para. 224.

[7] Section 21, *Clause* (*h*), *Specific Relief Act*, 1877; and section 20 of the *Indian Contract Act.*

turns out that, at the date of the contract, C., though supposed by A. and B. to be alive, was dead, the contract cannot be enforced.

Matter must also be legal.

211. The matter agreed upon must also be legal. Under the Indian Contract Act[1] the object of an agreement is lawful unless it is (*a*) forbidden by law;[2] or (*b*) is of such a nature that, if permitted, it would defeat the provisions of any law;[3] or (*c*) is fraudulent;[4] or (*d*) involves or implies injury to the person or property of another;[5] or (*e*) the Court regards it as immoral, or opposed to public policy.[6] Thus, where A. contracts to marry B., being already married to C., and being forbidden by the law to which he is subject to practise polygamy, the contract on A.'s part is illegal. But unless B. was also aware of A.'s existing marriage, in which case the contract would be wholly void, A. would be obliged to make B. compensation for the loss caused to her by the non-performance of his promise. Another illustration of the rule is afforded by the Indian Companies Act of 1882. Section 249 of that Act enacts that no Company shall have power to buy its own shares, and consequently any agreement in

[1] Section 23.

[2] For instance, agreements mentioned in sections 26, 27, 28, and 30 of the *Indian Contract Act*, or in sections 213—215 of the *Indian Penal Code*. *Cf.* also I. L. R. X. Allah. 577; I. L. R. XII. Bomb. 422; I. L. R. XVI. Cal. 436; No. 21, P. R. 1886.

[3] *Cf.* I. L. R. I. Allah. 751; II. *Ibid.* 902; III. *Ibid.* 852; I. L. R. IV. Cal. 929; I. L. R. I. Bomb. 550; VIII. *Ibid.* 398; No. 139, *Punjab Record*, 1883; 21 W. R. 381.

[4] Thus a contract by an agent for secret profits is a fraud on his principal, and therefore void. See Illust. (*g*), section 23, *Indian Contract Act;* and *Parker* v. *McKenna*, 1874, L. R. 10 Ch. 96; *Morison* v. *Thompson*, 1874, L. R. 9 Q. B. 480.

[5] *Cf.* 21 W. R. 381. *Cf.* also section 224, *Indian Contract Act.*

[6] "Public policy is an unruly horse and dangerous to ride," per Burrough, J., in *Richardson* v. *Mellish*, 2 Bing. at p. 252. See as to a combination of shipowners to keep up freights and to exclude rival traders from combination not being an actionable wrong, but justifiable as having the lawful object of protecting and extending their trade and increasing profits, *Mogul Steamship Co.* v. *McGregor, Gow & Co.*, (1892) A. C. 25.

CHAP. VIII.

violation of this provision would be illegal, and therefore void.[1]

So also a deed of sale executed in consideration of compounding a criminal offence not permitted by law to be compounded,[2] is void, both because it is forbidden by law and because it is opposed to public policy.[3] The common form of commercial Wagering Contracts called *Badni*, in which no deliveries are intended, and which are purely gambling transactions depending on the rise and fall of the market, are also held to be void as opposed to public policy.[4]

Aleatory or Wagering Contracts.

As to agreements by way of Wager (otherwise called Aleatory Contracts) the Indian Contract Act pronounces them generally to be void, and declares that no suit shall be brought for recovering anything alleged to be won on any wager, or entrusted to any person to abide the result of any game or other uncertain event on which any wager is made.[5] But an exception is allowed in favour of certain prizes for horse-racing. This law would not prevent one who repudiates the wager before the event is ascertained from recovering his

[1] Section 2, Cl. (*g*), *Indian Contract Act*, and section 23, *Ibid.*

[2] As to offences which are compoundable by Indian Law, see section 345, *Criminal Procedure Code of* 1898.

[3] No. 135, *Punjab Record*, 1882. *Cf. Windhill Local Board of Health* v. *Vint*, 45 L. J. Ch. D. 351. In a recent case Mr. Justice Vaughan Williams explained the law with regard to the illegality of a consideration for stifling a criminal prosecution in the following terms :—" When the friends of a man, who had been guilty of a criminal act, came forward and undertook to make good his default, in order to vitiate the transaction it was essential that the persons coming forward should be *actuated by a desire to prevent a prosecution* ; it was also essential the person to whom such undertaking was given should *intend or threaten a prosecution*, and should be *aware* that the persons giving the undertaking would not have come forward *but for the threat or the probability of the prosecution.*" *Jones* v. *Merionethshire Permanent Benefit Building Society*, (1891) 2 Ch. 587 ; see judgment on appeal, affirming the decision, (1892) 1 Ch. 173.

[4] No. 194, *Punjab Record*, 1882.

[5] Section 30, *Indian Contract Act*. *Cf.* No. 89, P. R. 1883 ; 12 Bomb. H. C. Reports, 51. As to the English Common Law, see 6 Moore, P. C. 300, 310.

deposit from the stake-holder.[1] Nor would it bar a suit for the amount of a bet paid by the plaintiff at the defendant's request.[2] As regards objections to Contracts based on grounds of public policy, it is as well to bear in mind the warning of an eminent English Judge (Jessel, M.R.): "You are not to extend arbitrarily those rules which say that a given contract is void as being against public policy; because, if there is one thing which more than another public policy requires, it is that men shall have the utmost liberty of contracting, and that their contracts, when entered into freely and voluntarily, shall be held sacred, and shall be enforced by Courts of Justice. Therefore you have this paramount public policy to consider, that you are not lightly to interfere with freedom of contract."[3] Another caution which it is necessary to state here in connection with void or illegal agreements is, that it does not follow that because an agreement may be open to an objection of this sort that a Court must necessarily and under all circumstances refuse to give any relief under it. On the contrary, any person who has received any advantage under such an agreement may be compelled to restore it, or to make compensation for it, to the person from whom he received it.[4]

Agreement must be one producing legal effects.

212. The agreement must also be such as produces a binding result upon the mutual relation of the parties. This is the objective element which gives to the subjective agreement of the Wills of the contracting parties its true legal character. Without a legal purpose or consequence in view, that is to say, the creation of some mutual relation which is a constituent element of common life, and consequently of legal order—such as marriage, sale, exchange, hiring, or some other

[1] *Varney* v. *Hickman*, 5 C. B. 271. *Cf. Hampden* v. *Walsh*, 1 Q. B. D. 196; *Hastelrow* v. *Jackson*, 8 B. & C. 225.

[2] I. L. R. V. Allah. 443.

[3] *Printing Company* v. *Sampson*, L. R. 19 Eq. 465.

[4] Section 65, *Indian Contract Act*.

of the numerous species of jural relations occurring in ordinary daily-life—the law takes no cognizance of what two persons may agree upon. I may agree with my friend to dine with him, or to take a walk with him, or to accompany him on a shooting excursion. But this agreement in no way creates any legal relation between him and me, and consequently produces no binding result. It is therefore no Contract. The object of the agreement is directed to no legal consequence but to an extra-legal one, which confers no right and imposes no corresponding duty. But if I promise to sell goods to another person and he accepts my promise, both he and I have a legal consequence in view, namely, that I shall relinquish my right in the goods for a given price, and that he shall thereby acquire my right and become my debtor for the price agreed upon.[1]

Formalities.

213. Lastly, in order to clothe an agreement with the legal character of a Contract, it must either be expressed in accordance with some prescribed formalities, or be the result of a lawful consideration, or it must combine both these qualifications. Thus, as late as the middle of the thirteenth century, an unsealed promise or agreement was not valid in England; and Bracton,[2] who wrote in the reign of Henry III., states the rule of law to be *ex nuda promissione non oritur actio:* no action arises from a naked promise. The Anglo-Normans adopted the rule of the later Roman Law[3] that a

[1] Stahl's *Die Philosophie des Rechts*, Vol. II., section 37, p. 323; Savigny's *System*, Vol. III., section 140, p. 309; Pollock's *Principles of Contract*, p. 2, 2nd ed.; Holland's *Jurisprudence*, p. 203.

[2] 1, 129, 298; Güterbock, Bracton, p. 139.

[3] Thus under the legislation of Justinian a written contract was so far conclusive evidence of liability, that the debtor could not raise the plea *exceptio non numeratæ pecuniæ*, by which he insisted that the money had not been counted out to him, beyond two years from the date of the contract. *Institutes*, III. 21. During this interval, if the debtor were really defrauded, he might protest in a public act against the writing which bound him, or bring an action against the creditor to compel him to give it up, or he could

promise made in due form and followed by assent constituted an obligation, which was valid without the aid of a consideration and precluded the obligor from denying that it was made. The requirement of a seal was of later growth, and was substituted in an illiterate age for the signature which few knew how to write.[1] According to the Indian Law[2] formalities such as writing, signature, attestation, registration, and delivery are required in the following (amongst other) cases:—

(*a*) An agreement without consideration made on account of natural affection between near relatives (requires to be in writing and registered).[3]

(*b*) A promise to pay a time-barred debt by the promisor or his agent (requires writing and signature).[4]

(*c*) A sale of tangible immoveable property worth Rs. 100 and upwards in provinces to which the transfer of Property Act, 1882, has been extended (requires a registered instrument).[5]

(*d*) A sale of such property worth less than Rs. 100 (requires either a registered instrument or delivery).[6]

(*e*) A mortgage securing Rs. 100 and upwards (requires a registered instrument signed and attested by at least two witnesses).[7]

(*f*) A mortgage securing less than Rs. 100 (requires an instrument signed and attested by at least two witnesses, or delivery).[8]

(*g*) Leases of immoveable property from year to year, or

make his exception perpetual by a formal announcement to the creditor of his intention to do so. *Sandars*, p. 449, 3rd ed.

[1] Clark-Hare's *Law of Contracts*, p. 121; Holmes's *Common Law*, p. 272.

[2] See Stokes's *Anglo-Indian Codes*, Vol. I., p. 496.

[3] Section 25, Cl. (1), *Indian Contract Act*.

[4] *Ibid*. Cl. (3).

[5] Section 55, *Transfer of Property Act*, 1882.

[6] *Ibid*.

[7] Section 59, *Ibid*.

[8] *Ibid*.

for any term exceeding a yearly rent (require a registered instrument).[1]

(*h*) Contracts on behalf of any Company under the Indian Companies Act (in certain cases must be in writing under the common seal of the Company, in others must be in writing signed by any person acting under the authority of the Company, and in others may be by parol on behalf of the Company by any person acting under the express or implied authority of the Company).[2]

(*i*) Negotiable instruments (must be in writing and stamped with stamps of a specified description).

But when formalities in the expression of Contracts are at the option of the parties, the mere fact that there may be an intention to put its terms into a more formal shape will not prevent there being a concluded binding contract, if the terms have been distinctly agreed upon.[3]

Consideration. 214. The modern English doctrine of Consideration answers in many respects to the Roman doctrine of *causa*, but it has a much wider signification than the latter. Cause in the sense of the Roman Jurists was that which gave validity to the Contract, and might consist in the form or nature of the Contract, or some fact on which it depended, or arising out of what was done or promised on either side. In the case of a Stipulation, the Cause was the formal question and reply; in the Contract *literis*, the entry in the books of the creditor with the debtor's consent; in the Consensual Contracts, the mutual agreement; in Contracts *re*, the delivery of the thing lent, pledged, or deposited. And turning to the Common Law, we find the Cause of a covenant in the sealing and

[1] Section 107, *Transfer of Property Act*, 1882.

[2] Section 67, Act VI. of 1882.

[3] *Fowle* v. *Freemans*, 9 Ves. 351; VIII. Mad. H. C. Reports, 57; I. L. R. III. Allah. 46.

delivery of the deed; of the obligation to pay a creditor, in the debt; and of a Parol Contract, in the thing given or promised in return. As thus viewed, Cause is a generic term which may coincide, but it is not synonymous with Consideration.[1] The Common Law of England recognises two types of Contracts—the Parol Contract, and the Agreement under Seal or Covenant; the latter deriving its validity from the sealing and delivery, which like the formal question and response of the Roman Law imply deliberation and assent, while the obligation depends in the former case on what is done or promised on the faith of the assurance held out by the promisor. But illustrative of the principle we have before adverted to, that complexity rather than simplicity is the characteristic of the early history of Law, we find that the parol contract was of later growth than the written and sealed covenant. The latter was the product of an age which looked chiefly to form, the former of a later period when men were inclined to disregard form and to look merely to the substance of the thing, in order that no wrong should be without an adequate remedy.[2] And precisely as in the Roman system the development of the law in the matter of Obligations generally was greatly facilitated by the prætorian simplification of procedure and introduction of new forms of actions,[3] so in England the strictness of the Common Law forms of writs was mitigated by the intervention of the Chancery Courts, presided over by men who were strongly imbued with the principles of the Roman Law. Thus the Prætor, after stating the cause of action, added in his instruction to a Judge—"Whatever in respect thereof the defendant ought to give to or do for the plaintiff, in that condemn him," a form of instruction which gave wide scope for the recognition of new sources of liability. In like manner under

[1] Clark-Hare's *Law of Contracts*, p. 187. [2] *Ibid*. p. 146.
[3] Muirhead's *Law of Rome*, p. 272.

CHAP. VIII. the operation of the Statute of Westminster II. c. 24, which provided in effect that where there was a wrong which, though analogous, did not fall within the scope of the writs in common use, the Clerks in Chancery were empowered to frame a like writ *in consimili casu*, adapted to the circumstances.[1]

Indian Law as to.

215. Under the Indian Contract Act an agreement "without Consideration" is void, except in certain specified cases; and "Consideration" is defined as follows:—"When, at the desire of the promisor, the promisee or any other person has done or abstained from doing, or does or abstains from doing, or promises to do or abstain from doing, something, such act or abstinence or promise is called a consideration for the promise."[2] It will be seen that this definition does not expressly require that the "something" should be of *some value*, as is the rule in English Law. "It is enough," said Tindal, C. J., in *Hitchcock* v. *Coker*, "that there is actually a consideration, that such consideration is legal, and *that it has some value*."[3] So, in *Thomas* v. *Thomas*,[4] Patteson, J., said: "Consideration means something which is *of some value in the eye of the law*, moving from the plaintiff." Mr. Whitley Stokes[5] is of opinion that strictly construed the Indian Act would appear to recognise a promise by A. to perform an already existing legal duty, *e.g.*, to give true evidence in a civil case, or not to evade process, or to pay a debt, as a sufficient Consideration to support a contract by B. if the promise be made at the desire of B. The language of the definition is undoubtedly defective, and possibly vague enough to give colour to such an argument. But the result which would follow from it was most probably never contemplated by the framers of the Act, and the Courts would probably

[1] Clark-Hare's *Law of Contracts*, p. 123.

[2] Section 2, clause (*d*).

[3] 6 A. & E. 438.

[4] 2 Q. B. 851, 859.

[5] *Anglo-Indian Codes*, Vol. I. 497.

construe the term "something" with reference to the English decisions already quoted, as intended to mean "something having some value in the eye of the law." Before the passing of the Contract Act it was held (in 1868) by the Madras High Court that an agreement by A. to pay money to B. in consideration of B.'s giving evidence on behalf of A., could not be enforced, for here the agreement is either for true evidence, and then there is no consideration, for every man is compellable to give such evidence, or for favourable evidence, either true or false, and then the consideration is vicious.[1] So also it was held by the Bombay High Court (in 1870) that a promissory note *payable on demand* given for interest due on a mortgage deed was void for want of Consideration.[2] No doubt if further time had been given for the payment of the due interest, the forbearance on the part of the creditor to press his claim immediately would have been a sufficient Consideration for a promissory note stipulating for payment at some future time.[3] But a promissory note *payable on demand* secured no advantage to the debtor, and did not necessarily involve any forbearance on the part of the creditor. It was therefore rightly held to be void for want of Consideration. The "act, abstinence or promise" which the Indian definition requires to form the basis of the Consideration must be lawful;[4] and we have already seen what Considerations and objects the Law regards as such.[5] But although the Consideration must be lawful and of some value, an agreement to which the consent of the promisor is freely given is not void merely because the Consideration is inadequate. Where, however, the promisor denies that his consent was freely given, as where a horse worth Rs. 1,000

Inadequacy of Consideration insufficient to set aside Contract.

[1] VIII. Mad. H. C. Reps. 7.
[2] VII. Bomb. H. C. Reps. 9 (o. c. i.).
[3] Clark-Hare's *Law of Contracts*, p. 202.
[4] Section 10, *Indian Contract Act*.
[5] See para. 211, *ante*.

CHAP. VIII. is alleged to have been sold for Rs. 10, the inadequacy of the Consideration is a fact which may be taken into account by the Court in determining whether the consent of the promisor was freely given.[1] Accordingly, where parties stand on equal ground, and deal with each other without any imposition or oppression, the mere inadequacy of Consideration, independent of other circumstances, is insufficient to set aside a Contract.[2] This is on the principle that parties who are of sufficient mental capacity for the transaction of business have a right to make their own bargains.[3] Thus, an agreement to pay interest at Rs. 10 per cent. per mensem, by a military officer to a native banker was held to be binding.[4] But where the parties stand on a different footing, as where one of the parties is practically in the power of the other, and there is reasonable ground for supposing that he has been overreached, or that imposition or oppression has been exercised upon him in obtaining his consent, Courts in India are not slow to interfere.[5] The gross inadequacy of the Consideration, or the unconscionable character of the bargain, may then be rightly considered in judging as to whether a free consent has been given. But, according to Chancellor Kent,[6] the inequality amounting to fraud, must be so strong and manifest as to shock the conscience and confound the

[1] Section 25, Expl. 2, *Indian Contract Act*. *Cf.* section 28 (*a*), *Specific Relief Act*, 1877.

[2] *Hind* v. *Holdship*, 2 Leading Cases in Equity, 4, American Ed. 1237.

[3] Clark-Hare's *Law of Contracts*, p. 201. As Hobbes puts it, "the value of all things contracted for is measured by the appetite of the contractors."

[4] No. 5, *Punjab Record*, 1887; No. 40, P. R. 1882. So in England an excessive rate of interest is not sufficient, standing alone, to invalidate a Contract in Equity. *Webster* v. *Cook*, 2 Chap. 342.

[5] The following cases may be referred to on this point:—I. L. R. I. Mad. 349; I. L. R. III. Cal. 192; 22 W. R. 341; No. 148, P. R. 1882. See also the *Dekkhan Agriculturists' Relief Acts* XVII. of 1879, XXII. of 1881, and XXII. of 1882.

[6] In *Osgood* v. *Franklin*, 2 Johns. Chan. 23. As to the Continental and Roman Law as to sales at under-value, see Pollock on *Contracts*, p. 703, 4th ed.

judgment of any man of common sense. In other words, it must be an unconscionable bargain, where one party takes an unfair advantage of the other.[1] As a rule of evidence under the Indian Law it is open to a person who is sued upon a written contract to deny the receipt of the Consideration, or to prove that it is different from what is described therein.[2] In the case of a negotiable instrument it is presumed until the contrary is shown that the Consideration duly passed.[3]

Exceptions to general rule that a Contract only affects parties to it.

216. It follows from the very conception of a Contract as previously defined, that a man cannot, as a general rule, incur liabilities from or acquire rights under a Contract to which he was not a party.[4] It would be contrary to common sense and the plain dictates of justice if the Law acted upon any other general rule. Accordingly, it has been frequently held that a man cannot by act of parties be compelled to accept performance of his contract from one who was not originally a party to it.[5] Thus, where goods are ordered of a particular manufacturer, another, who has succeeded to his business, cannot execute the order so as to bind the customer, who has not been made aware of the transfer of the business, to accept the goods. The latter is entitled to refuse to deal with any other than the manufacturer whose goods he intended to buy.[6] In like manner where the plaintiff sued upon a promise made by the defendant to X., that in consideration that X. would work for him he would pay the plaintiff a sum of money, it was held by the Court of Queen's Bench that the plaintiff could not recover, because he was not party to the contract.[7]

[1] Per Jessel, M. R., in *Middleton* v. *Brown*.

[2] Section 92, Cl. 1, *Evidence Act*, 1872; I. L. R. III. Bomb. 159; I. L. R. XI. Cal. 486.

[3] Section 118, clause (*a*), Act XXVI. of 1881.

[4] Anson's *Law of Contracts*, pp. 208, 212.

[5] *Robson* v. *Drummond*, 2 B. & Ad. 303; *Humble* v. *Hunter*, 12 Q. B. 310.

[6] *Boulton* v. *Jones*, 2 H. & N. 564.

[7] *Price* v. *Enston*, 4 B. & Ad. 433.

"But," as observed by Cockburn, C.J., in a later case,[1] "much work is contracted for which it is known can only be executed by means of sub-contracts; much is contracted for as to which it is indifferent to the party for whom it is to be done, whether it is done by the immediate party to the contract, or by some one on his behalf. In all these cases the maxim *qui facit per alium facit per se* applies."[2] Another exception to the general rule is in regard to obligations attached to land, which are said to run with the land. Of this character are covenants to repair, or to leave in good repair, or to deal with the land in any specified manner.[3] So, also, under the Indian Transfer of Property Act, where a house insured against damage by fire is transferred by A. to B., B., in case of such damage, may, in the absence of a contract to the contrary, require the money received under the policy to be applied in reinstating the house.[4] But covenants which are purely personal or collateral do not necessarily run with the land and pass to the transferee. Thus, where X., the lessee, covenanted to use his premises as a public house, and A., the lessor, covenanted not to build or keep any house for sale of beer or spirits within half a mile of the demised premises. Upon a transfer of the lease by X. to M. it was held that its covenants did not pass to M.[5]

Contractual rights and liabilities may be transferred—

(*a*) by assignment by party entitled;

217. But contractual rights and liabilities may be transferred by consent of the party entitled, or by operation of law. Neither the early Roman Law[6] nor the Common Law of England, apart from the customs of the Law Merchant, recognised the assignability of the benefit of a Contract so as to enable the assignee to sue upon it in his own name. It was necessary for the assignee to sue in the name of the assignor or his representatives.[7] But formerly in Equity,

[1] *British Waggon Co.* v. *Lea*, L. R. 5 Q. B. D. 149.

[2] *Ibid.* pp. 153, 154.

[3] Anson's *Law of Contracts*, p. 232.

[4] Section 49.

[5] *Thomas* v. *Hayward*, L. R. 4 Exch. 311.

[6] *Gaius*, XI. 38.

[7] *Ibid.* 39.

which in this respect followed the later Roman Law,[1] whenever the Contract was not for exclusively personal services, the assignee was entitled to enforce it in his own name, although his rights were affected by certain conditions.[2] Now, however, since the Judicature Act of 1873[3] the assignee of any debt or legal *chose in action* acquires all legal rights and remedies of the assignor.[4] But (1) the assignee takes subject to equities; (2) the assignment must be absolute; (3) must be in writing signed by the assignor; (4) express notice in writing must be given to the party charged, and the title of the assignee dates from the notice. In India prior to 1882 the doctrine of the Equity Courts had been frequently followed,[5] and the Civil Procedure Code also recognises the right of the transferee of a decree to have it executed on his own behalf, provided the transfer has been effected by an assignment in writing.[6] In Provinces other than the Punjab, Bombay, and British Burma the transfer of *choses in action* or "actionable claims" is now, however, governed by the provisions of the Transfer of Property Act of 1882.[7] No transfer of any actionable claim has any operation against the debtor until express notice of the transfer is given to him, unless he is a party to or otherwise aware of such transfer.[8] The notice must be in writing signed by the person making the transfer, or by his Agent duly authorised in this behalf.[9] On receiving such notice the

[1] Cod. IV. 39, 7.

[2] Anson's *Law of Contracts*, pp. 221, 222.

[3] 36 & 37 Vict. c. 66, s. 25, sub-s. 6.

[4] It is sufficient that there should be an "accruing debt" arising out of contracts, though it may not be due at the time of the assignment, or may only become due after a certain period after demand. *Walker* v. *Bradford Old Bank*, 12 Q. B. D. 11; and *Mercantile Bank of London* v. *Evans*, before Mr. Justice Bruce, reported in *Times*, Dec. 5th, 1898, p. 3.

[5] Mayne's *Hindu Law*, section 331.

[6] Section 232, Act XIV. of 1882.

[7] See Chapter VIII. *Cf.* as to meaning of "actionable claim," section 130; and I. L. R. XII. Cal. 470; XIII. *Ibid.* 297.

[8] Section 131, *Ibid.*

[9] Section 132, *Ibid.*

CHAP. VIII. debtor must give effect to the transfer.[1] Where an "actionable claim" is sold the debtor is discharged by paying the buyer the price and incidental expenses of the sale, with interest on the price from the day that the buyer paid it.[2] The transferee takes the debt subject to all the liabilities to which the transferor was subject in respect thereof at the date of the transfer.[3] It will be noticed that the statutory provisions of the Indian Law differ from those of the English Act in two main respects: first, in not requiring the transfer to be absolute; secondly, in not requiring the transfer to be in writing, except in the case of a decree. The Indian Act also imposes the restriction that no Officer connected with a Court of Justice can buy any "actionable claim" falling under the jurisdiction of the Court in which he exercises his functions.[4]

(*b*) by operation of law.

218. Rules of Law may also operate to transfer to one person the right or the liabilities of another. For instance, in the case of Death or Insolvency, or as the result of assignment of certain interests in land, *e.g.*, by way of Mortgage, Lease or Exchange. Marriage under the Roman Law left the property of the spouses on both sides untouched.[5] Under the older English Law Marriage had the effect of transferring to the husband conditionally the rights and liabilities of the wife, but under more recent legislation it has lost this effect since 1883.[6] In India it had ceased to do so since the

[1] Section 133, Act XIV. of 1882. [2] Section 135, *Ibid.*

[3] Section 137, *Ibid.* As to transfer of Marine or Fire Insurance Policies, see Act V. of 1866, section 15; as to transfer of Shares in Companies, section 29, and Acts VIII.—XI.; Table A. of Act VI. of 1882; and as to transfer of Debentures issued by the Secretary of State in Council and coupons for interest annexed thereto, 42 & 43 Vict. c. 60, s. 3; 43 Vict. c. 10, s. 3.

[4] Section 136, *Ibid.*

[5] Salkowski's *Roman Private Law*, section 146.

[6] *Vide* 45 & 46 Vict. c. 75, known as *The Married Women's Property Act*, 1882, which declares that "all property, real or personal, possessed by a woman before or acquired after marriage, is her separate property."

1st January, 1866. In the case of Death the rights and liabilities (except in the case of several joint contractors, which will be noticed presently) pass by representation to the executors or administrators of the deceased;[1] but they merely represent the original contracting party to the extent of his estate and no more.[2] The old Hindu Law contains a further limitation by restricting the power of a person in possession of ancestral property, and having a son or grandson alive, from alienating or charging such property except for a purpose which the law recognises as necessary. But this provision of the law has been held not to exempt a son or grandson from the discharge of the pious duty which is incumbent upon him by the same law of discharging all debts of his father or grandfather[3] which were not contracted for *immoral* purposes.[4] Assignment as the result of Insolvency is regulated in Presidency Towns by Act of Parliament,[5] and in other parts of British India by Chapter XX. of the Civil Procedure Code of 1882; and as the result of a transfer of certain interests in land by the Transfer of Property Act, 1882.[6]

Devolution of joint rights and liabilities.

219. Under the English Common Law on the death of one of several joint contractors his rights and liabilities pass, not to his personal representative, but to the surviving contractors.[7] But the Indian legislature has preferred to adopt the rule followed by Courts of Equity, according to which, unless a contrary intention appears by the Contract, joint rights and liabilities devolve on the surviving contractors and

[1] Sections 179, 188, and 191, Act X. of 1865.

[2] Section 282, Act X. of 1865. Mayne's *Hindu Law*, section 276; and section 234, *Civil Procedure Code of* 1882.

[3] Mayne's *Hindu Law*, section 274.

[4] L. R. 1 Ind. App. 321; I. L. R. XIII. Cal. 21. *Cf.* also I. L. R. XI. Bomb. 37; I. L. R. VIII. Allah. 204, 231, 279; I. L. R. IX. Mad. 424.

[5] 11 & 12 Vict. c. 21.

[6] Sections 40, 49, 55 (Cl. 2), 65, 108 (Cl. (*c*)), 109.

[7] *Richards* v. *Heather*, 1 B. & Ald. 29.

CHAP. VIII. the representatives of the deceased contractor jointly.[1] An exception, however, is made in the case of Government of India Securities. Thus, when a Government Security is payable to two or more jointly, and either or any of them dies, the security is payable to the survivor or survivors of those persons.[2] But it is expressly stated that this provision is not intended to affect any claim which the representative of the deceased person may have against the survivor or survivors in respect of such a security.[3]

Extinction the purpose of all contractual agreements.

220. It has been well observed by a foreign writer on the Roman Law that "every obligation carries with it the purpose (*Zweck*) of being again extinguished; dissolution of the obligation is the ultimate object and necessary result of the full exercise of that right to which the creditor can lay claim as arising from it."[4] This extinction or dissolution, which, if good by the law of the place where the Contract is to be performed will (subject to a few exceptions) be held good in

[1] Sections 42 and 45, *Indian Contract Act*. *Cf.* I. L. R. IV. Cal. 350; *Ibid.* 556; and I. L. R. V. Allah. 40.

[2] Section 5, Cl. (1), Act XIII. of 1886.

[3] Section 5, Cl. (2), Act XIII. of 1886.

[4] Dr. Salkowski's *Roman Private Law*, section 138, p. 696, Whitfield's *Translation*. This view is sharply criticised by Dr. Alois Brinz, who says that performance is not the purpose (*Zweck*) of obligation, however paradoxical this may seem. He argues that by performance the obligation becomes "purposeless" (*Zwecklos*), and that the true mission, aim, and purpose of an obligation lie in "non-performance" (*nicht-liestung*). *Lehrbuch der Pandekten*, Zweiterband, p. 8; Erlangen, 1879. But surely, when parties enter into a contractual obligation they contemplate not the *breach* but the rightful *fulfilment* of their respective promises? Their initial purpose or aim, therefore, is to *fulfil* and not to *break;* in other words, to reap the advantage of their engagement, though it is only when a breach occurs that the necessity of *enforcing* the obligation arises. (Dernburg, *Pandekten*, II. section 2, p. 4.) The "purpose" of the obligation is not, however, to be confounded with this necessity; on the contrary, the true purpose of clothing a transaction in a legal dress is to induce the parties to act righteously, under the known consequences of suffering (in the majority of cases) a severer pecuniary loss than would be involved in the fulfilment of the promise.

every other place where the question may come to be litigated,[1] may ensue in any of the following modes:— CHAP. VIII.

(a) *By agreement of parties.*

(a) By agreement of parties.

This agreement may either take the form of an absolute rescission of the original Contract (*contrarius consensus*)[2] or an alteration of its terms, or a substitution of a new contract for it, or a remission of performance wholly or in part, or the acceptance of partial, in satisfaction of complete, performance.[3] An agreement of this nature is subject to the rule which governs all Contracts under Indian Law[4] with regard to consideration. And the Consideration for the promise of each party is the abandonment by the other of his rights under the Contract.[5] But by English Law a promissory note or bill of exchange is said to stand on a different footing in this respect, and a discharge, though unsupported by consideration, is held to be valid.[6] How far the same distinction is applicable in India is doubtful.[7] By an alteration of the terms the performance of the original Contract may also be excused. Thus, to take an illustration from the Indian Specific Relief Act, 1877, where A. contracts in writing to let a house to B., for a certain term, at the rate of Rs. 100 per month, putting it first into tenantable repair. The house turns out to be not worth repairing, so, with B.'s consent, A. pulls it down and erects a new house in its place, B. contracting orally to pay rent at Rs. 120 per mensem. Here

(2) *Alteration of terms.*

[1] Story's *Conflict of Laws*, 8th ed., sections 331—337; Phillimore's *International Law*, Vol. IV. p. 604; Dicey, *Conflict of Laws*, p. 575.

[2] Just. *Inst.* 3, 29, 4.

[3] Sections 62 and 63, *Indian Contract Act*. As to Negotiable Instruments, see section 82, Act XXVI. of 1881.

[4] Section 25, *Contract Act*.

[5] Anson's *Law of Contract*, p. 258.

[6] *Foster* v. *Dawber*, 6 Exch. 839.

[7] See section 82, Act XXVI. of 1881, and compare section 25, *Indian Contract Act*.

the parties have agreed to an alteration in one of the terms of the agreement, namely, the amount of rent, and B. can only enforce the original Contract in writing subject to the variation made by the subsequent oral contract.[1] But in order to enforce a verbal alteration of a written contract it is not enough for the party who seeks to enforce it to show what he understood to be the new terms on which the parties were proceeding, but also that the other party had the same understanding.[2] An alteration of a term in a Contract may, however, be inferred from the conduct of the parties without an express agreement. Thus, where A. undertook certain building operations for X., which were to be completed by a certain date, or a sum to be paid as compensation for delay. While the building was in progress an agreement was made for additional work, by which it became impossible that the whole of the operations should be concluded within the stipulated time. It was held that the subsequent agreement was so far inconsistent with the first, as to amount to a waiver of the sum stipulated to be paid for delay.[3] The parties may also agree upon a complete substitution of a new Contract (*novatio*) by changing the nature of the obligation, or the parties to the Contract. Thus, where A. owes B. Rs. 10,000 and A. enters into an arrangement with B., and gives B. a mortgage of his (A.'s) estate for Rs. 5,000 in place of the debt of Rs. 10,000. This is a new contract which extinguishes the old one.[4] Or, suppose A. owes money to B. under a contract, and it is agreed between A., B., and C., that B. shall thenceforth accept C. as his debtor, instead of A. Here the effect of the substitution of parties

(3) *Substituted contract.*

[1] Illust. (*e*), section 26, Act I. of 1877.

[2] *Darnley* v. *London, Chatham and Dover Railway Co.*, L. R. 2 H. L. 60.

[3] *Thornhill* v. *Neats*, 8 C. B. N. S. 831; Anson's *Law of Contract*, p. 262.

[4] Illust. (*b*), section 62, *Indian Contract Act*. *Cf.* Salkowski's *Roman Private Law*, section 142, p. 714; Baron's *Pandekten*, section 266.

is to extinguish the old debt of A. to B., and to create a new debt from C. to B.[1]

Chap. VIII.

(b) *By condition subsequent.*

(b) By condition subsequent.

221. Thus the parties may stipulate that the Contract shall become void—(1) when a specified term is or is not fulfilled; (2) when a particular event occurs; (3) when one of them exercises an option to determine the Contract.[2] The most usual illustration of such a "condition subsequent," as it is called, is afforded by an ordinary English Bond, which is a promise defeasible upon a condition expressed in the Bond.[3] So, also, if A. agrees to sell and B. to buy a certain house subject to the approval of the title by B.'s attorneys, and the attorneys disapprove the title on reasonable grounds and *bonâ fide*, A. may rescind the contract.[4] And the rescission may be insisted upon even when the happening of the condition is at the will of the party making it.[5] A further illustration is afforded by the excepted risks in a charter party, or in a contract by a common carrier—"the act of God, the Queen's enemies, restraints of Princes and rulers, &c., *always excepted.*" The occurrence of the excepted risk releases the shipowner or the common carrier from the strict

[1] Illust. (*a*), section 62, *Indian Contract Act*. *Cf.* also *Commercial Bank of Tasmania* v. *Jones*, (1893) A. C. 313.

[2] Anson's *Law of Contracts*, p. 265; Stokes's *Anglo-Indian Code*, Vol. I. pp. 502, 503.

[3] See also the definition of a Bond in section 3, Clause 4 (*a*), of the *Indian Stamp Act*, 1879.

[4] I. L. R. VIII. Cal. 856, following the English cases of *Hudson* v. *Buck*, L. R. 7 Ch. D. 683, and *Hussey* v. *Horne-Payne*, L. R. 8 Ch. D. 670. See also *Head* v. *Tattersall*, L. R. 7 Exch. 7, as to a discharge optional on non-fulfilment of a term. But see remarks of Lord Cairns in case of *Hussey* v. *Horne-Payne*, when it came up on appeal to the House of Lords, L. R. 4 App. Cas. 321.

[5] I. L. R. V. Mad. 173, where the learned judge, *Muthusami Ayya*, lucidly explains the true principle on which this rule rests, and shows the benefit which may be derived even by an Indian Judge from the study of the works of German Jurists.

CHAP. VIII. performance of the contract.[1] Lastly, the determination of a Contract of domestic service by a month's notice supplies a good illustration of the third class of "conditions subsequent."[2]

(c) *By performance.*

(c) By performance.

222. Performance of the acts to which the person of incidence is obliged (*solutio ejus quod debetur*) is the natural and normal mode of extinction that substantially destroys every obligation.[3] For our present purpose it will be sufficient to refer to the two most ordinary forms in which such a performance may take place, *i.e.*, Payment (*solutio*) and Tender (*oblatio*). In Roman Law the term *solutio* included every kind of satisfaction, and related more to the contents of the obligation than to the payment of money.[4] But in our law Payment is deemed to consist in the performance either of an original or substituted Contract, by the delivery of money, or of negotiable instruments conferring the right to receive money. In this last event the payee may have taken the instrument in discharge of his right absolutely, or subject to a condition (which will be presumed in the absence of expressions to the contrary) that, if payment be not made when the instrument falls due, the parties revert to their original rights, whether those rights are, so far as the payee is concerned, rights to the performance of a Contract, or

(*solutio.*)

[1] Anson's *Law of Contracts*, p. 265. *Cf. Nobel's Explosives Co.* v. *Jenkins & Co.*, (1896) 2 Q. B. 326, where risk of goods being seized and confiscated if attempted to be carried further, amounted to a "restraint of Princes." It may be as well to quote here the most recent definition of what is meant by the act of God. In the case of *Nugent* v. *Smith*, L. R. 1 C. P. D. 423, it was laid down by Mellish, L. J., that to constitute the act of God "it is not necessary to prove that it was absolutely impossible for the carrier to prevent it, but that it is sufficient to prove that *by no reasonable precaution under the circumstances could it have been prevented*": p. 441.

[2] *Anglo-Indian Codes*, Vol. I. p. 503; Anson's *Law of Contracts*, p. 267.

[3] Salkowski's *Roman Private Law*, section 139, p. 698; Holland's *Jurisprudence*, p. 258.

[4] Dig. XLVI. 3, 54; L. 16, 176.

rights to satisfaction for the breach of one.[1] And in this connection it is well to remember that where the instrument happens to be inadmissible in evidence by reason of its not being duly stamped, the creditor is at liberty to fall back upon the original consideration. The law on this point has been very clearly laid down by the late Chief Justice of the High Court of Bengal (Sir Richard Garth). "When a cause of action for money is once complete in itself, whether for good sold, or for money lent, or for any other claim, and the debtor then gives a bill or note to the creditor for payment of the money at a future time, the creditor, if the bill or note is not paid at maturity, may always, as a rule, sue for the original consideration, provided that he has not endorsed or lost or parted with the bill or note under such circumstances as to make the debtor liable upon it to some third person. In such cases the bill or note is said to be taken by the creditor on *account of the debt*, and if it is not paid at maturity the creditor may disregard the bill or note and sue for the original consideration. *But when the original cause of action is the bill itself, and does not exist independently of it*,[2] * * * * here there is no cause of action for money lent otherwise than on the note itself. In such a case the note is the only contract between the parties, and if for want of a proper stamp or some other reason the note is not admissible in evidence, the creditor must lose his money."[3] A promisor may also, under certain conditions, be relieved from the responsibility of non-performance of his promise by a mere "offer" of performance. But to have this effect the offer must be (*a*) unconditional, (*b*) it must be made at a proper time and place, and under such circumstances that the person to whom it is made may have a reasonable opportunity of ascertaining that the

(2) Tender.

[1] Anson's *Law of Contracts*, pp. 273, 274.

[2] *E.g.*, where the money is lent upon the bill.

[3] I. L. R. VII. Cal. 259, 260; VIII. *Ibid.* 723, 724; No. 61, P. R. 1888.

person by whom it is made is able and willing *there and then* to do the whole of what he is bound by his promise to do. Thus, if the offer is an offer to deliver anything to the promisee, the promisee must have a reasonable opportunity of seeing that the thing offered is the thing which the promisor is bound by his promise to deliver. An offer to one of several joint promisees, or by one of several joint promisors to the promisee, has the same legal consequence as an offer to all of them or by all of them.[1] The technical English term for such an offer is "Tender," and according to English Law for a debtor to defend himself successfully by such a plea, he must continue always ready and willing to pay the debt, where performance consists in the payment of a sum of money; and when sued upon it, he can plead the tender, but must pay the money into Court.[2] This rule proceeds upon the principle that where the performance due consists in the payment of a sum of money, although a legal Tender may excuse non-performance on the part of a debtor, it does not constitute a discharge of the debt.[3] This seems only reasonable. But the Indian Contract Act does not draw any distinction between Tender by delivery and Tender by payment, and, therefore, a debtor whose tender of money is refused, need not, it is said, aver in a suit against him, that he is ready and willing to pay the debt, nor need he pay the money into Court.[4] But if money is paid into Court with a defence of tender, the plaintiff only recovers in the action the excess.[5] As to what

[1] Section 38, *Indian Contract Act*. *Cf.* also sections 46—50, as to what constitutes "a proper time and place"; and 16 W. R. 793; 3 C. L. R. 459 (following 22 W. R. 79); I. L. R. VI. Bomb. 692; and I. L. R. IX. Cal. 791. *Cf.* 22 Q. B. D. 537; and XI. Bomb. H. C. Rep. 106.

[2] *Smith* v. *Manners*, 28 L. J. C. P. 220; 5 C. B. (N. S.) 632; *Poole* v. *Compton*, 5 D. P. C. 468; S. C. 2 M. & W. 223; *Dixon* v. *Clark*, 5 C. B. 365; Anson's *Law of Contracts*, p. 274; 1 *Tidd's Practice*, 612.

[3] Anson's *Law of Contracts*, p. 274.

[4] Stokes's *Anglo-Indian Codes*, Vol. I., pp. 503, 504.

[5] *James* v. *Vane*, 2 El. & El. 883; 29 L. J. Q. B. 169.

constitutes a legal Tender as regards coinage and currency notes, reference must be made to the Indian Coinage[1] and the Indian Paper Currency Acts.[2] As to cases in which Government Promissory Notes are a legal tender, see Act III. of 1871, section 15. Amongst other substitutes for performance may also be mentioned "Compromise" (*transactio*)[3] and "Set-off." The former is the adjustment of any dispute in regard to which there is believed to be at the time a *bonâ fide* question between the parties,[4] either by a complete release, or by the acceptance of a part payment coupled with a promise not to claim the residue. It is immaterial whether the claim which the parties have compromised was one which would have been successfully asserted or not.[5] Provided there has been no misrepresentation or wilful suppression of facts.[6] According to English law the payment of a smaller sum in satisfaction of a larger is not a good discharge of a debt. Where, indeed, the right of the creditor itself is in dispute, but is *bonâ fide* believed in by him, the parties may compromise the subject of dispute in any manner they may agree upon; the forbearance of the creditor to enforce a right to which he honestly believes he is entitled, is a good consideration for the act or promise of the other party.[7] Where, again, the amount due is uncertain, the payment of a liquidated or certain sum would be a valid consideration for foregoing a claim for a larger though uncertain amount.[8] But where the right itself is undisputed and the amount due is also certain, there

(3) Compromises.

[1] Act XXIII. of 1870, sections 12, 13 and 14.

[2] Act XX. of 1882, section 16.

[3] For an explanation of the distinction between the *novatio* and *transactio* in the Roman sense, see Brinz, *Lehrbuch der Pandekten*, II. § 283, s. 389, 390. *Transactio* was independent of the means by which it was realised, whereas *novatio* was dependent on a *translatio* of the old into a new obligation.

[4] *Ex parte Lucy*, 22 L. J. Ch. 732; 4 De G. M. & G. 356.

[5] *Miles* v. *New Zealand Alford Estate Co.*, 32 Ch. D. 266; 55 L. J. Ch. 801.

[6] *Leonard* v. *Leonard*, 2 Ball & B. 171.

[7] Anson's *Law of Contracts*, pp. 74, 75.

[8] *Ibid.* p. 85.

CHAP. VIII. a promise to forego the claim or any portion can only be supported, according to English law, by the *giving of something different in kind*, or by a *payment at an earlier date.*[1] The Indian Law on the other hand, as we have seen, permits *every promisee to dispense with or remit, wholly or in part, the performance of the promise made to him*, or *to accept instead of it any satisfaction which he thinks fit.*[2] Thus, if A. owes B. Rs. 5,000 and A. pays to B. Rs. 1,000 and B. accepts them in satisfaction of his claim on A., this payment will be deemed to be a discharge of the whole claim.

(4) Set-off.

A "Set-off" (*compensatio*) is regarded in some systems as a mutual extinction of the creditor's claim and of the debtor's counterclaim upon the creditor so far as they cover one another in amount. This is the theory of the modern French Law, which prescribes that two debts cancel each other rateably from the moment that they co-exist (*ipso jure compensari*).[3] In the older Roman Law the right of *compensatio* was only admissible in the *bonæ fidei judicia*, and then only if the claims made available had arisen "*ex eadem causa*," that is, from the same obligatory relation. It was the great Marcus Aurelius who issued a rescript recognising the right of *compensatio* in all claims even *ex dispari causa*, that is to say, although they may have arisen from *different* obligatory relations. Still later the Emperor Justinian gave a further extension to the counterclaim by allowing it also in real actions (*in rem actiones*).[4] The counterclaim might also be one which was not actionable.[5] According to the Indian Law a counterclaim can only be set off if it is for an ascertained sum of money, and the parties with respect to it fill the same

[1] See *Pinnel's Case*, 5 Co. Rep. 117; Anson's *Law of Contracts*, pp. 83—85. *Cf. Foakes* v. *Beer*, 9 App. Cas. 605.

[2] Section 63, *Indian Contract Act*. See p. 241, *ante*.

[3] *Code Civil*, Act, 1290. *Cf. Cod. Just.* IV. 31, 4.

[4] Salkowski's *Roman Private Law*, section 140, pp. 702—707.

[5] Dig. XVI. 2, 6: *etiam quod natura debitur, venit in compensationem.*

character as they fill in the plaintiff's suit.[1] As the question whether a *set-off* is admissible is a question of procedure, it must be determined by the *lex Fori* or the law of the *forum* in which the action is pending.[2]

(d) By non-performance or breach.

(d) By non-performance.

223. The breach or non-performance of a contract always gives a right of action to the injured party, which will be more appropriately considered when we deal with Remedial Rights. But besides imposing a new obligation of this kind upon the promisor, there are circumstances under which a breach of Contract will also *discharge* the promisee from such performance as may be due from him. It is only from this aspect that the subject may be briefly noticed at present. Thus if the promisor has *refused* to perform, or *disabled* himself from performing his promise, the promisee may put an end to the Contract, unless he has signified by words or conduct his acquiescence in its continuance.[3] So when a Contract contains reciprocal promises, and one party *prevents* the other performing his promise, the Contract becomes voidable at the option of the party so prevented.[4] Or again when a contract consists of reciprocal promises, such that one of them cannot be performed, or that its performance cannot be claimed till the other has been performed, and the promisor of the latter promise fails to perform it, the maker of the former promise may rescind the Contract.[5] Lastly, where time is the essence of the contract, failure to perform it at the fixed time renders the Contract voidable at the option of the promisee.[6]

[1] Act XIV. of 1882, section 111. But confer I. L. R. XI. Cal. 557, where it was held that a right to a set-off may exist independently of the Civil Procedure Code. See also I. L. R. XVI. Cal. 711. As to the meaning of "ascertained," *Cf.* I. L. R. VII. Allah. 284.

[2] *Meyer* v. *Dresser* (1864), 16 C. B. (N. S.) 646; Dicey, *Conflict of Laws*, p. 716 (12).

[3] Section 39, *Indian Contract Act*.

[4] Section 53, *Ibid.*

[5] Section 54, *Ibid.*

[6] Section 55, *Ibid.* *Cf.* I. L. R. VI. Cal. 64; *Ibid.* 681; 49 L. J. Ch. 166.

Chap. VIII.

(e) *By impossibility of performance.*

(e) By impossibility of performance.

224. It has been stated above that the subject-matter of a contractual agreement must be *possible*, for an agreement to do that which is *impossible in itself*, *e.g.*, to discover treasure by magic, is not one which the law will recognise.[1] But as effecting the *discharge* of a *valid* Contract, the impossibility must be one of a physical or legal character arising *after* the formation of the contract. In such cases relief is afforded not upon any exception to the general rule, but upon the construction of the Contract. For instance, in the case of an absolute promise to marry, the death of either party discharges the Contract, because it is inferred or presumed that the Contract was made upon the condition that both parties should live.[2] So, also, where A. agreed with B. to give him the use of a music-hall on specified days, for the purpose of holding concerts, and before the time arrived the building was accidentally burned, it was held in England that both parties were discharged from the Contract. In this case Blackburn, J., laid down the rule as follows:—

"The principle seems to us to be that in Contracts in which the performance depends on the continued existence of a given person or thing, a condition is implied that the impossibility of performance, arising from the perishing of the person or thing, shall excuse the performance." And the reason of the rule is, "because from the nature of the Contract, it is apparent that the parties contracted on the basis of the continued existence of the particular person or thing."[3] As, for instance, in the case quoted above,[4] of a

[1] *Vide* para. 210, and section 56, *Indian Contract Act*.

[2] See the admirable judgment of the American Court in *Dexter* v. *Norton*, quoted in Clark-Hare's *Law of Contracts*, p. 645.

[3] *Taylor* v. *Caldwell*, 3 B. & S. 826. *Cf.* also *Hall* v. *Wright*, 3 E. B. & E. 746; *Boast* v. *Frith*, L. R. 4 C. P. 1; *Anglo-Egyptian N. Co.* v. *Rennie*, L. R. 10 C. P. 271; *Howell* v. *Coapland*, 46 L. J. Q. B. 147; 1 Q. B. D. 258. But see p. 224, *ante*.

[4] Page 64. But here the agreement was impossible in itself. And *cf.* *Clifford* v. *Watts* (1871), L. R. 5 C. P. 577.

promise to sell a horse already dead. So, again, if the performance of a Contract has been prevented by an Act of Parliament the breach is excused on the broad ground *lex non cogit ad impossibilia.* Thus where the defendant demised certain premises to the plaintiff for a long term of years, and the defendant covenanted that "neither he nor his assigns would, during the term, permit any messuage to be built on a paddock fronting the demised premises," and subsequently a railway company under powers given them by an Act of Parliament compulsorily purchased the paddock and built a railway station upon it, it was held, in an action brought against the defendant for breach of covenant, that he was discharged from his covenant by the subsequent Act of Parliament which compelled him to assign to the railway company, and so put it out of his power to perform his covenant.[1] Again, in regard to Contingent Contracts to do or not to do anything if an uncertain future event *happens*, the rule of the Indian Law is, that they cannot be enforced by law unless and until that event *has happened.*[2] Thus, if A. contracts to pay B. a sum of money when B. marries C., but C. dies without being married to B. Here the event upon the *happening* of which A.'s contract was made conditional becomes impossible, and therefore A. is discharged from the performance of his promise.[3] It may be, however, that the enforcement of a Contract is expressly made contingent on the *non*-happening of a particular event. In such a case so far from a *subsequent* impossibility of the event occurring intervening to effect a *discharge*, it is the very circumstance

[1] *Bailey* v. *De Crespigny*, L. R. 4 Q. B. 180; 38 L. J. Q. B. 98.

[2] Section 32, *Indian Contract Act*. See *ante*, § 60. Under the Roman Law an exception was made to the principle that the impossibility of performance related to the time when it could be claimed, when the contract referred to anything *extra commercium*. In such a case the contract was treated as *nefas* or immoral, and could not be validated by any subsequent change of circumstance. *Dig.* 45, 1, 83, § 5; and 137, § 6; 18, 1, 34, § 2.

[3] Section 32, Illust. (*e*), *Ibid.*

 which immediately entitles the promisee to *enforce* the promise made to him. Thus, if A. agrees to pay B. a sum of money if a certain ship does *not* return, and it happens that the ship is sunk on the voyage, B. can enforce his Contract when the impossibility of the event occurring is established.[1] Suppose, however, that A.'s promise was contingent *on the return* of the ship within a fixed time, and within that time the ship was sunk or burnt. Here the impossibility of the event occurring within the stipulated period, upon the *happening* of which the enforcement of A.'s promise was contingent, would cause the Contract to become void, in accordance with the rule first mentioned, and the parties would be immediately discharged from all further liability.[2] It is only necessary to repeat the caution that a party to a Contract cannot claim to be discharged by reason of impossibility of performance resulting from his own voluntary act. If, for instance, he disables himself from performing his promise before the time for performance arrives, he becomes immediately liable for all the consequences of a breach of Contract. But the other party is absolved from the performance of *his* promise.[3]

(*f*) *By operation of law.*

(*f*) By operation of law.

225. Lastly, there are certain involuntary grounds of extinction which destroy an obligation without co-operation of the persons interested.[4] These result from rules of law which, operating upon certain sets of circumstances, cause the discharge of a Contract.[5] These rules may be considered under the heads of (1) *Merger*, (2) *Alteration*, and (3) *Insolvency*.

[1] Section 33, Illust., *Indian Contract Act*.

[2] Section 35, Illust. (*a*), *Ibid*.

[3] Section 39, *Ibid*. *Cf*. *Planché* v. *Colburn*, 8 Bing. 14.

[4] Salkowski's *Roman Private Law*, section 103, p. 719.

[5] See Anson's *Law of Contracts*, Chap. V., p. 326.

(1) The Roman term for "Merger" was "*Confusio*," and implied the union of claim and debt in the same person. It sometimes (*nonnunquam*) extinguished the obligation and at other times only suspended it. In like manner there might be a coalescence in the same person of a lesser and superior right, as, for instance, the title to the Servitude and the Ownership in the servient property, or the Pledge-right and the Ownership. Ordinarily such a coalescence by merging the lesser in the superior right caused the former to be extinguished. But under certain circumstances this result was not permitted to prejudice the person who had succeeded to the superior right. Thus where the Pledge-right gave him a better security as regards the thing, in relation to other pawnees, than the proprietary right, he could avail himself of the former by way of action and *exceptio*.[1] So also under the Indian Law, when the owner of a charge on immoveable property becomes absolutely entitled to that property, the charge or incumbrance is extinguished, unless he declares by express words or necessary implication, that it is to continue to subsist, or such continuance would be for his benefit.[2] In English Law the term Merger, as applied to the Law of Contracts, means the acceptance of a security which in the eye of the law is a *higher* for one of a *lower* operative power. Thus a judgment recovered extinguishes by Merger the right of action arising from breach of Contract. And in like manner if two parties to a simple contract embody its contents in a deed which they both execute, the simple contract is thereby discharged.[3]

[1] Salkowski's *Roman Private Law*, section 103, p. 501.

[2] Section 101, *Indian Transfer of Property Act*, 1882. *Cf.* L. R. 10 Ind. App. 62; I. L. R. II. Allah. 826; III. *Ibid.* 682; IV. *Ibid.* 525; VII. *Ibid.* 571; I. L. R. VI. Bomb. 404, 561; No. 173, *Punjab Record*, 1882; I. L. R. III. Cal. 307. Amongst English cases consult *Toulmin* v. *Steere*, 3 Mar. 210; *Watts* v. *Symes*, 1 De G. M. & G. 240.

[3] Anson's *Law of Contracts*, p. 326.

CHAP. VIII. The rules governing this process are thus summarised by Sir William Anson:—[1]

(*a*) The two securities must be different in their legal operation, the one of a higher efficacy than the other. A second security taken in addition to one similar in character will not affect its validity unless there be a discharge by substituted agreement.

(*b*) The subject-matter of the two securities must be identical.

(*c*) The parties must be the same.

In India a deed has ordinarily no higher efficacy than a simple Contract, and it has been more than once doubted whether the doctrine of Merger applies here at all.[2] So also it has been held that the fact that a money decree has been obtained on a mortgage-bond, does not destroy the lien on that property. It is open to a plaintiff to establish his right on the bond as well as on the decree.[3] On the other hand, the term has been loosely applied to every substitution of a new for an old Contract, the liability under the latter *merging* it is said in that of the former.[4] And even to the substitution of a subsequent arrangement between a judgment debtor and his creditor, which it was said constituted an *obligation* which *merged* the *decree* in itself.[5] A true instance of "Merger," in the Roman sense of "*Confusio*," occurs in the Indian Negotiable Instruments Act, 1881, wherein it is provided that if a bill of exchange which has been negotiated is, at or after maturity, held by the acceptor *in his own right*, all rights of action thereon are extinguished.[6]

[1] Anson's *Law of Contracts*, p. 326.
[2] 10 W. R. 15; 11 W. R. 487.
[3] XIV. Beng. L. R. 408 (F. B.); I. L. R. IV. Cal. 29; No. 69, *Punjab Record*, 1876.
[4] No. 17, *Punjab Record*, 1881; No. 30, *Punjab Record*, 1884.
[5] No. 51, *Punjab Record*, 1885.
[6] Section 90, Act XXVI. of 1881. *Cf. Freakley* v. *Fox*, 9 B. & C. 130.

(2) *Alteration.*—If after a contract has been reduced to writing one of the parties to it alters the instrument intentionally, without the consent of the other party, in a material part, whether by erasure or addition, the Contract is discharged.[1] The Indian Contract Act contains no provision on the point, but the Indian Courts have generally acted upon the principles recognized by Courts in England.[2] The Indian Negotiable Instruments Act, 1881, also contains a provision that "any material alteration" of a negotiable instrument renders the same void as against any one who is a party thereto at the time of making such alteration, and does not consent thereto, unless it was made in order to carry out the common intention of the original parties.[3] But the rule as to the discharge of agreements by reason of a material alteration is only strictly applicable where it is sought to *enforce* the obligation otherwise arising from the instrument, or of which the instrument furnishes the only legal proof. It has no application where the instrument is produced merely as *proof* of some right or title created by, or resulting from, its *having been executed*, or to prove any collateral fact.[4] As to what amounts to a material alteration depends largely upon the character of the instrument. Under 45 & 46 Vict. c. 64, the following alterations are material: any alteration of the date, the sum payable, the time of payment, the place of payment, and when a bill has been accepted generally, the addition of a place of payment without the acceptor's consent. In India it has been held that the alteration of a marginal entry on a promissory note, which did not form an

[1] Anson's *Law of Contracts*, p. 327.

[2] III. Mad. H. C. Repts. 247; XI. Bomb. H. C. Repts. 303; VIII. Beng. L. R. 305; No. 22, *Punjab Record*, 1883; No. 103, *Ibid.*; No. 118, *Punjab Record*, 1885; I. L. R. VII. Cal. 616; I. L. R. VII. Bomb. 418. *Cf.* I. L. R. VII. Mad. 302.

[3] Section 87, Act XXVI. of 1881.

[4] *Davidson* v. *Cooper*, 11 M. & W. 800. *Cf.* also I. L. R. VII. Mad. 302; and III. Mad. H. C. Repts. 347; I. L. R. IX. Mad. 399; and XII. *Ibid.* 239.

integral part of the note, did not affect its validity.[1] And so where the addition serves only to state explicitly what was already clearly implied in the document, and what the law would infer from it, the addition is regarded as immaterial, and does not vitiate the document.[2] But where the obligee of a bond executed by one person forges the names of two other persons as obligors, he cannot recover on the bond even as against the obligor who really did execute the bond.[3]

(3) *Insolvency.*—The statutory release of a person in insolvent circumstances from liability in respect of debts is regulated in the Presidency Towns of India by Act of Parliament.[4] and in other parts by the Code of Civil Procedure.[5]

Rules for construction of Contracts.

226. A few brief rules have been stated in a previous paragraph[6] for the interpretation of Laws generally, many of which will also be found useful in the construction of Contractual Agreements. But there are two broad rules which may be said to supply generally the true guide for the construction of Contracts in Writing. The first is that *words are to be construed in their plain and literal meaning.* The reason for this is, that as language was given to man to express his thoughts, he will be taken to mean precisely what he has said; and as it is not the duty of Courts to make new Contracts for parties, but simply to give effect to those entered into by them, whether foolish or wise, the parties will be held bound by the language employed by them if it is plain and unambiguous. But it may happen that the parties have given a broader meaning to certain words or

[1] No. 118, *Punjab Record*, 1885.

[2] XI. Bomb. H. C. Repts. 203; follg. *Aldous* v. *Cornwell*, L. R. 3 Q. B. 573.

[3] I. L. R. VII. Cal. 616; follg. *Davidson* v. *Cooper*, 13 M. & W. 352; and *Gardner* v. *Walsh*, 24 L. J. Q. B. 285.

[4] 11 & 12 Vict. c. 21, sections 59—61.

[5] Sections 357, 358, Act XIV. of 1882. But a Bankruptcy Bill is now before the Indian Legislature, and may become law at no distant date.

[6] Para. 79, p. 84, *ante*.

expressions than can be attributed to them by a strictly literal interpretation, and if this intention can be fairly collected from the *context* effect may rightly be given to it. Hence arises the *second* rule of construction, which is that *an agreement ought to receive that construction which will best effectuate the intention of the parties to be collected from the whole of the agreement.* The reason for this rule is, that greater regard is to be had to the clear intention of the parties than to any particular words which they may have used in the expression of their intent.[1] Other subsidiary rules have also been devised, which are based on the same general principle of giving effect to the intention of the parties so far as it can be discerned from the instrument executed by them. Thus, Courts will correct obvious mistakes in writing and grammar (*falsa orthographia, sive falsa grammatica non vitiat chartam*); they will restrain the meaning of general words by more specific and particular descriptions of the subject-matter to which they are to apply; they will assign to words susceptible of two meanings that which will make the instrument valid (*nam verba debent intelligi cum effectu ut res magis valeat quam pereat*); and they will construe words most strongly against the party who used them (*verba fortius accipiuntur contra proferentem*).[2] The last-mentioned rule requires some explanation.[3] The object at which it aims is to prevent men from affecting ambiguous expressions, which they would be inclined to do if they were afterwards at liberty to put their own construction on them.[4] But the rule is only to be applied as a last resort and where all other rules of exposition fail to elucidate the real meaning of the language used in the instrument.[5] And it is also properly

[1] Anson's *Law of Contracts*, p. 252.

[2] *Ibid.* p. 253; Sheppard's *Touchstone*, Chap. V. p. 88, 7th edition.

[3] As to this maxim, *cf. Birrell* v. *Dryer*, 9 App. Cas. 345; *Burton* v. *English*, 12 Q. B. D. 218; 53 L. J. Q. B. 133.

[4] Cruise, *Dig.* Tit. 32, Ch. 20, s. 13; Sheppard's *Touchstone*, Chap. V., p. 88.

[5] Bacon's *Elements*, *Reg.* 3, p. 14.

CHAP. VIII. applicable only to instruments executed by the grantor alone. Thus, where the instrument is of the nature of an Indenture, inasmuch as it is executed by both parties, the language is to be understood as that of both parties, for which one alone is not responsible.[1]

Classification of Contracts. 227. We have hitherto discussed the principal rules which regulate the formation, extinction, and construction of Contracts in general. But something remains to be said in regard to the particular features and characteristics which distinguish certain Contracts from others. To do this some sort of preliminary classification is necessary. Kant has adopted a triple classification of *Gratuitous*, *Onerous*, and *Cautionary* Contracts.[2] Others again that of *Onerous* or *Bilateral* and *Liberal*, *Lucrative* or *Unilateral* Contracts.[3] English writers follow a more technical and arbitrary division, and distinguish between *Formal* and *Simple* Contracts; the former including (1) Contracts of Record, and (2) Contracts under seal; the latter (1) Contracts required by law to be in some form other than under seal, and (2) Contracts for which no form is required.[4] Such a classification would obviously be unsuitable in systems where the distinction between Contracts under seal and Simple Contracts is not recognised, and for purposes of general Jurisprudence it is, therefore, of little use. Perhaps the simplest mode of classification and the least technical has reference more to the *object* of performance than to the *form* of the Contract. Either the contract is intended directly to accomplish the *principal* object of performance, or it is merely intended to be *ancillary* to that object. In the former case the contract may be fitly described as belonging to the class

[1] Sheppard's *Touchstone*, Chap. V., p. 88, note (81).

[2] *Philosophy of Law*, p. 122.

[3] Ihering, *Der Zweck im Recht*, Vol. I., 121.

[4] Anson's *Law of Contracts*, p. 43.

of "Principal Contracts," in the latter of "Accessory Contracts."[1] This is the classification which Professor Holland has adopted,[2] and it has the advantage of being both intelligible and simple. The following table which Mr. Whitley Stokes has constructed upon the basis of this classification shows at a glance what kinds of Contracts would fall under each head :—

A.—*Principal Contracts* are those whose object is—

1. Alienation.
   - (*a*) Gift.
   - (*b*) Exchange.
   - (*c*) Sale.
   - (*d*) Assignment of Contractual Right.
2. Permissive Use.
   - (*a*) Loan for consumption.
   - (*b*) Loan for use.
   - (*c*) Letting for hire.
3. Marriage.
4. The Creation of a Trust.
5. Service.
   - (*a*) Deposit.
   - (*b*) Work on materials.
   - (*c*) Carriage.
     - (i) by land.
     - (ii) by water.
   - (*d*) Professional Service.
     - (i) legal.
     - (ii) medical.
   - (*e*) Master and servant.
   - (*f*) Master and apprentice.
   - (*g*) Agency.
   - (*h*) Partnership.
6. Negative Service.
7. Aleatory gain.
   - (*a*) Wagers.
   - (*b*) Lotteries.
   - (*c*) Annuities.
   - (*d*) Bottomry.
   - (*e*) Respondentia.
   - (*f*) Insurance.
     - (i) Fire.
     - (ii) Life, Illness or Accident.
     - (iii) Marine.

[1] Salkowski's *Roman Private Law*, section 106, p. 509.

[2] *Jurisprudence*, p. 211.

CHAP. VIII. B.—*Accessory Contracts* are the following—

1. Guarantee.
2. Indemnity.
3. Security. { (*a*) Mortgage. (*b*) Pawn. (*c*) Lien. (*d*) Hypothec. }
4. Warranty.
5. Ratification.
6. Account stated, and Promissory Notes.
7. For further Assurance.

Some of these Contracts have already been incidentally considered in dealing with the general Law of Contract. But a few words may now be added in explanation of the remainder.

Alienation.

228. The power of dealing with things which belong to one in proprietary right is inseparable from the notion of individual or separate Ownership. So long as property belongs to the Tribe or Family, the power of any individual member of the community to dispose of it, in whole or in part, must necessarily be restricted. And the restriction must be more or less rigid according as the constitution of the Tribe or Family itself is rigorously exclusive or is more heterogeneous in character, and has elements of expansion within it, or according as the enjoyment of property is strictly communal or regulated according to more lax principles. Thus Tribes that are endogamous, that is to say, which forbid intermarriages outside their own circle,[1] and recognise no other artificial means of extension, are naturally more conservative than those whose tribesmen are dependent on other Tribes for their wives, and whose composition admits of artificial extension by the admission of strangers. A village community, for instance, composed of the descendants

[1] McLennan's *Studies in Ancient History*, pp. 24—27.

of a single stock of pure Rajput ancestors would, if no partition had taken place amongst its members, be found to recognise far less powers of alienation than perhaps a neighbouring community, which was composed of various Tribes or Clans, originally located together under the leadership of some powerful Chief, but having little inter-cohesion or interests in common.[1] Thus, again, the Joint-Family of the *Mitacshara* system is very different to the Joint-Family of the *Dayabhaga*. In the one case the personality of the individual members is sunk in that of the corporate body represented by the Family, and it is impossible for any one of them to predicate that any particular portion of the joint estate belongs to him. In the other system each member has defined interests which he can dispose of without reference to his co-owners. The general term to express the various forms in which this power of disposition may be exercised is *Alienation*, and as applied to tangible property it may assume one of three distinct forms: *Exchange*, *Gift*, or *Sale*. Of these Exchange is undoubtedly the oldest, and its history takes us back to primitive times when the use of money was still unknown, and when the rude commerce of the period was carried on by one thing being given or exchanged for another. It has been described as "one of the precocious manifestations of the human mind."[2] The subject is now regulated in India by the Transfer of Property Act, 1882, or at least in those Provinces to which the Act has been extended.[3] By that Act Exchange is defined as "the transfer of Ownership of one thing for the Ownership of another, *neither thing or both things being money only.*"[4] Such a transfer can only be made in the manner provided for the transfer of similar property by sale;[5] and the rights

Exchange.

[1] *Cf.* No. 107, P. R. 1887.

[2] "*Man as a Member of Society,*" in the July, 1897, No. of the *Monist*, p. 545.

[3] Chap. VI., Act IV. of 1882.

[4] Section 118, *Ibid.*

[5] Chap. VI., Act IV. of 1882. *Cf.* section 54, *Ibid.*

CHAP. VIII. and liabilities of the parties are similar to those resulting from a sale.[1] A Gift is a transfer made voluntarily and without consideration by one person, called the donor, to another, called the donee, and accepted by or on behalf of the donee.[2] The concurrence of the donor and the donee must take place in order to render the donation perfect; and consequently the acceptance by or on behalf of the donee must be made during the life-time of the donor and while he is still capable of giving. Thus, if the donor dies or becomes insane before acceptance is made, the Gift is void. The same result follows if the donee dies before acceptance.[3] In the case of immoveable property the Indian Law requires that the transfer must be effected by a registered instrument signed by or on behalf of the donor, and attested by at least two witnesses. And in the case of moveable property, either by a registered instrument similarly signed, or by delivery, which may be effected in the same way as goods sold may be delivered.[4] The power of disposition may be restrained with reference to the claims of the Family, or the Creditors of the donor. Thus, according to the Customary Law of the Punjab, Gifts to daughters of ancestral immoveable property can only be made with the consent of the donor's male collaterals.[5] So sons at times

[1] Section 120, *Ibid.* *Cf.* section 55, *Ibid.*; and as regards moveables, sections 37—55, 73—75, 93, 94, 97—107, *Indian Contract Act.*

[2] But a gift to a person not in existence, and therefore not capable of accepting gift at the time it takes effect, is void. *Tagore* v. *Tagore*, IX. B. L. Reps. 377, 397, 400, 404; I. L. R. II. Cal. 265; X. Cal. Law Reps. 207. But a fœtus in the mother's womb, or a person adopted under Hindu Law by a widow after her husband's death, is supposed by a fiction to have been in existence at the time of the father's or husband's death. *Tagore* v. *Tagore*, IX. B. L. R. 377.

[3] Section 122, Act IV. of 1882.

[4] Section 123, *Ibid.* *Cf.* section 90, *Indian Contract Act*, as to delivery of goods. In Provinces to which the *Transfer of Property Act*, 1882, has not been extended, a written instrument of gift is not required.

[5] See the Authorities quoted in para. 57 of my *Digest of Civil Law.* But gifts to a *Khana-damad*, or son-in-law who lives with his father-in-law as in a *Beenah* marriage common in Ceylon, are frequently permitted.

possess a customary power to restrain a Gift of even acquired immoveable property.[1] In the case of ancestral immoveables the Hindu Law according to the *Mitacshara* also recognizes the power of sons or grandsons to object to any alienation unless effected for some pressing necessity.[2] And both the English[3] and Indian Law[4] refuses to permit "fraudulent transfers" (*i.e.*, a transfer made with intent to defraud prior or subsequent transferees, or to defeat or delay creditors). Thus, a Gift by a Muhammadan not *bonâ fide* nor on any good consideration, but made with the intention of thereby protecting the property from those who were at the time his creditors was held void by the Privy Council.[5] Nor does the Law permit any private alienation of property which has once been attached by process of Judicial procedure.[6] A Gift which is otherwise valid may be accompanied with conditions, such as that the donor should be maintained by the donee during his lifetime, and that his funeral ceremonies should be performed after his death; that the donee should forego claims against the donor, and should defray expenses of the worship of an idol: or that the property should pass to another in a particular event.[7] But a gift will be invalid which creates an estate unknown to or forbidden by the Law, or which contains provisions which are repugnant to the nature of the grant, such as a restraint upon alienation or partition.[8] Lastly, a transfer of Ownership in exchange

[1] No. 2, P. R. 1877.

[2] Mayne's *Hindu Law*, sections 226, 227, 292. See also para. 141, *ante*.

[3] 13 Eliz. c. 5; Hunt's *Fraudulent Conveyances*, 2—8.

[4] Section 53, *Indian Transfer of Property Act*, 1882. *Cf*. also I. L. R. II. Allah. 891; 6 Moore's Ind. App. 27.

[5] I. L. R. X. Cal. 616 (P. C.). In this case the Privy Council laid down that the principles of the English Statute of Elizabeth for avoiding transactions intended to defraud creditors have properly guided Indian Courts in administering law according to justice, equity, and good conscience.

[6] Section 276, Act XIV. of 1882.

[7] Mayne's *Hindu Law*, section 328.

[8] *Tagore* v. *Tagore*, IX. Beng. L. R. 377; *Aushotosh Dutt* v. *Durga Churn*

CHAP. VIII.

Sale.

for a price paid or promised, or part-paid and part-promised, is commonly called a sale.[1] The Law may or may not, as we have just seen,[2] impose certain formalities for effecting such a transfer. Subject to these formalities when prescribed a Sale is complete, in the case of immoveables, when the price is agreed upon, and from that moment the ownership of the property is transferred to the vendee.[3] This rule is similar to that which prevailed in the Roman Law.[4] But in the case of goods the question depends on whether they are (a) ascertained, or (b) unascertained, unmade or unfinished, or (c) are sold with immoveable property, or (d) by auction.[5] The transfer of Ownership ensuing upon a completed contract does not, however, necessarily deprive the vendor of his right to look to the property which is the subject of sale as a security for the payment of the agreed price. This right may be asserted in the case of goods, and in the absence of any contrary agreement between the parties, in one of two ways: (a) by refusing to deliver them so long as the price or any part of it remains unpaid,[6] or (b) where he has already parted with goods, by stopping them in transit if the buyer becomes insolvent (*i.e.*, has ceased to pay his debts in the usual course of business, or is incapable of paying them) before the goods reach him.[7] Stoppage in transit entitles the seller to hold the goods stopped until the price is fully paid,[8] and also after the lapse of a reasonable time, and after giving

Stoppage in transit.

Chatterjee, L. R. 6 Ind. App. 182; I. L. R. VII. Cal. 279; Mayne's *Hindu Law*, sections 328, 355; X. Cal. Law Reps. 207.

[1] *Transfer of Property Act*, 1882, section 54. *Cf.* section 77, *Indian Contract Act*, 1872.

[2] Page 262.

[3] No. 27, *Punjab Record*, 1879.

[4] Salkowski's *Roman Private Law*, section 122, pp. 592—594.

[5] *Vide* sections 78, 79, 85, 87, 122, *Indian Contract Act*. *Cf.* the case of *Gilmour* v. *Supple*, 11 Moore, P. C. 566.

[6] Section 95, *Indian Contract Act*, 1872.

[7] Section 99, *Indian Contract Act*. *Cf.* Explanation to section 96, *Ibid.*

[8] Section 106, *Ibid.*

notice to the buyer of his intention to do so, to re-sell them.[1] Where a valid re-sale takes place the buyer must bear any loss, but is not entitled to any profit, which may occur on such resale.[2] This remedy is, however, only an optional one, and in accordance with the maxim previously considered (*quilibet potest renunciare juri pro se introducto*),[3] need not be asserted. The vendor may, if he prefers to do so, rescind the contract.[4] Special provisions exist in the Indian Law as to sales in execution of decrees,[5] or for arrears of land revenue,[6] or of property of proclaimed accused persons who have absconded.[7]

Rights and liabilities of buyer and seller.

228*a*. The rights and duties of buyer and seller upon a sale are regulated in the absence of any Contract to the contrary by certain general rules. These rules so far as they relate to sales of immoveable property in India are embodied in the Transfer of Property Act,[8] and so far as they affect goods are to be found in the Contract Act.[9] By the Roman Law every vendor was deemed to covenant for quiet enjoyment of the object sold (*habere licere*), and also to warrant the qualities of the thing of which assurance was given (*dicta promissa*). But according to the strict Jus Civile he was only responsible for latent defects in the case of fraudulent silence. Under the Ædilian Edict the vendor was liable absolutely, and the purchaser had the option of an action for rescission of the purchase (*actio redhibitoria*), or for proportionate reduction of the purchase-money (*actio æstimatoria* or *quanti minoris*).[10] By the older English Law the use of the words "grant" or

[1] Section 107, *Indian Contract Act*.

[2] *Ibid.*

[3] Para. 88, *ante*.

[4] I. L. R. VI. Cal. 64.

[5] Sections 286 *et seq.*, Act XIV. of 1882.

[6] Sections 75—96, *Punjab Land Revenue Act*, 1887.

[7] Section 88, *Criminal Procedure Code*, 1898.

[8] Section 55, *Indian Contract Act*. Exchanges are governed by the same rules.

[9] Sections 109—116, Act IX. of 1872.

[10] Salkowski's *Roman Private Law*, section 122, pp. 599 and 602.

 "give" in a conveyance was held equivalent to a covenant for quiet enjoyment, but more recent legislation has not maintained this construction.[1] In the case of a contract for the sale of goods of a specified description which the buyer has *no opportunity to inspect*, the goods according to English Law must not only in fact answer the specified description, but must also be saleable or merchantable under that description.[2] So also on the sale of an article the better opinion appears to be that the vendor undertakes that he has a right to sell it; in other words, "that he sells a chattel, and not a law suit."[3] But where the buyer has *had* an opportunity of examining the article, there is no engagement implied in the contract of sale that the seller warrants against latent defects unknown alike to himself and to the purchaser.[4] In such cases the law refuses to assist a careless purchaser, and acts upon the maxim *caveat emptor* (let the purchaser beware), which it has been well said[5] still forms a corner stone of the contract of sale as interpreted in England and the United States. This maxim implies that it is for the buyer to inform himself, and not for the seller to inform the buyer, and by requiring the latter to take care of his own interests has been found best adapted to the wants of trade in the business transactions of life.[6] The actual presence of the object of the sale is sufficient to do away with any inaccurate description of it by the seller (*præsentia corporis tollit errorem nominis*), who not unnaturally is expected to recommend his own wares. Thus it is that Courts act upon the maxim

[1] 8 & 9 Vict. c. 106, section 4.

[2] *Jones* v. *Just*, L. R. 3 Q. B. 197. In the recent case of *Drummond* v. *Van Ingen*, L. R. 12 App. Cas. 284, the House of Lords laid down the rule that goods must be fit for use in the manner in which goods of the same quality and general character ordinarily would be used.

[3] *Eichholz* v. *Bannister*, 17 C. B. (N. S.) 708.

[4] See the American case of *Eagan* v. *Call*, 10 Casey, 237, where the whole doctrine is most perspicuously stated. Clark-Hare's *Law of Contract*, p. 459.

[5] Clark-Hare's *Law of Contract*, p. 458.

[6] See Davis, J., in *Hyatt* v. *Boyle*, quoted in Clark-Hare's *Law of Contracts*, p. 505.

simplex commendatio non obligat (a simple commendation [of goods] does not bind), a maxim which is borrowed, like so many others recognised in modern law from the Jurisprudence of Rome.[1] The English in common with the Indian Law also recognises the principle that a seller can give to the buyer of goods no better title than he himself possesses. But both systems of law admit certain exceptions to the rule based mainly on the apparent Ownership which the *de facto* and unqualified possession of goods is generally deemed to evidence.[2] The English Law[3] and some other systems[4] admit also an exception in favour of purchasers who buy goods in "open market" (*market overt*), in regard to which the Indian Law has no distinct provision.

Contracts for permissive use.

229. Contracts for permissive use may be classed under three heads, according as they refer to (*a*) a loan for consumption (*mutuum*); (*b*) a loan for use (*commodatum*); or (*c*) a letting for hire (*locatio conductio*). Here again we have to go to Roman Law for an explanation of these terms. The classification which is based upon them is perhaps as convenient a one as can be devised, and it serves to mark the distinction between the different classes of contracts which are embraced within it in a manner which is at once simple and intelligible, and which, if not properly observed, might lead to confusion. Thus in the Roman sense, a *mutuum* was the grant (*datio*) of such things as are weighed, numbered, or measured, with the object of their becoming the property of the receiver, and with the intention of afterwards receiving others of the same kind and character.[5] The contract does

(a) Mutuum.

[1] "That which," says Ulpian, "a vendor alleges in order to recommend his wares, is to be regarded as neither alleged nor promised." Dig. IV. 3, 37.

[2] Section 108 and Exception, *Indian Contract Act*.

[3] Pollock's *Law of Contracts*, 397; Leake's *Digest of the Law of Contracts*, 95.

[4] Notably the German, which extends the doctrine to all sales made by a lender in the course of his business. *Cf.* § 935 of the German Civil Code, and Art. 2280 French C. C.

[5] Dig. XLIV. 7, 1, section 2. In the old Hindu Law such loans might

CHAP. VIII. not contemplate the return of the specific thing which was originally given, for that is the distinguishing feature of a *commodatum*, but of a thing of the same genus (*sed idem genus*).[1] Hence it was also called *mutui datio*, because from being mine it becomes yours, and so, if it do not become yours, an obligation does not arise.[2] From the very nature of the contract it is necessary that the grantor should be the owner.[3] The sole responsibility of the borrower is to return the equivalent in kind, *e.g.*, things of the same quantity and genus. The obligation to pay interest does not necessarily result from such a transaction, which, in the absence of a contrary stipulation, is essentially a gratuitous one[4] like the old Hindu *Uddhara*.[5] But interest might always be stipulated for, as to which it may be noted that, while in India at the present day it is not uncommon to meet with agreements for the payment of 75 per cent., the maximum rate fixed by the law of the Twelve Tables was 10 per cent. which was eventually reduced by Justinian to 6 per cent. The avarice of money-lenders was moreover checked by the provision that compound interest (*anatocismus*) which the Hindu lawgivers

take place with respect to corn, fruit, wool, and draught-animals lent to be paid in the same kind of equal value. *Manu*, Ch. VIII., section 151.

[1] Dig. XII. 1, 2, pr.

[2] *Ibid.* section 2. The derivation from *ex meo tuum* is, however, erroneous. Sandars's *Justinian*, lib. III. 14, p. 414, 2nd ed. Varro (*De Lingua Latina*, lib. IV.) derives the term *mutuum* from the Greek word μοῖτον. In its proper acceptation *mutuum* did not designate the contract, but the object lent. *Ortolan, Explic. Historique des Instituts*, tome III. section 1209, p. 139. The *mutuum*, or "exchange" (from *mutare*), was a form of loan which was not based, like the *nexum*, upon a binding declaration of the debtor expressly emitted before witnesses, but upon the mere transit of the money from one hand to another, and which is supposed to have originated in dealings with foreigners as the *nexum* did in business dealings at home. Mommsen's *Hist. of Rome*, Vol. I. Bk. I. Ch. XI. p. 201, *Eng. trans.*

[3] Dig. XII. 1, 2. pr. section 4.

[4] Salkowski's *Roman Private Law*, section 106.

[5] See the text of *Katyayana*, quoted in the *Vyavhara Mayukha*, Chap. V., sections 1, 2—4.

significantly called "wheel-interest,"[1] was not claimable; and the student of Hindu Law will find in the rule that in no case shall the interest be accumulated *ultra duplum*, *i.e*, beyond the amount of Capital lent,[2] a provision which will remind him of the Hindu doctrine of *damdupat*.[3] The most ordinary example of a loan for consumption is where money is placed with a banker to be drawn out as the creditor may demand. Such a transaction establishes the relation of debtor and creditor between the banker and the person who leaves the money with him, and, like the Roman *mutuum* or the *deposit* of the old Hindu Law,[4] it usually carries no interest. Following the course of English Legislation[5] the Usury Laws were repealed in India in 1855, and by an enactment passed in that year the objections advanced by Bentham to the principle of those laws was triumphantly vindicated, the parties being left for the future to settle their

[1] Burnell's *Manu*, Ch. VIII. section 153.

[2] Salkowski's *Roman Private Law*, pp. 510, 511.

[3] 5 Bomb. H. C. Reps. 157, 195 (o. c. j.); Burnell's *Manu*, Chap. VIII. section 151; I. L. R. IX. Bomb. 233. A law of Bocchoris, King of Egypt, similarly prescribed that interest was to cease as soon as the original debt was doubled; and this was probably the source from which the Greeks, and still later the Romans, borrowed their laws on the same subject. Vide *Les Obligations en Droit Égyptien*, p. 68, par Eugène Revillout, Paris, 1886. It is also curious and interesting to remark that the old Hindu Law regulated the maximum interest in proportion to the risk incurred by the creditor. Thus, *Yajnyawalkya* ordains that "borrowers who travel through vast forests" may pay ten per cent., while such as "traverse the ocean" may pay as much as twenty per cent. *Vyavhara Mayukha*, Chap. V. sections 1, 3. The Brahminical author of Manu's *Institutes*, regulates the rate of interest in the order of the four castes, ranging from two to five per cent., the Brahmin, of course, receiving the most considerate treatment. Chap. VIII. section 142, pp. 200, 201, Burnell's translation. But in the case of corn, fruit, wool, or draught-animals lent to be paid in the same kind of equal value, the sum of principal and interest should not exceed *five times the principal! Ibid.* section 151.

[4] Narada enumerates a *deposit* amongst the transactions which carry no interest in the absence of a special agreement. *Vyavastha Chandrika*, Vol. II. p. 623.

[5] 17 & 18 Vict. c. 90.

CHAP. VIII.

own terms as to payment of interest.[1] But the circumstance that the Indian Legislature has been compelled to depart from this principle in the Sonthal Purganas[2] and in the Dekkhan,[3] proves that, however sound the principle may be in the abstract, it cannot be universally applied in a state of society where the parties do not contract on an equal footing. On the Bombay side it has been held that the Act of 1855 does not affect the Hindu or Muhammadan Law as to interest,[4] and in a still later decision it has been also held that the rule of *damdupat* is not affected by the law of limitation, so as to enable a creditor to recover more interest than the rule in question permits.[5] On the Calcutta side a curious question has been raised in connection with this rule in regard to a son's liability to pay his father's debts. The obligation to do so, it is contended, is a moral one, although enforced by our Courts, and the nature of this obligation must be determined by reference to the sacred Codes of Hindu Law, and not by the laws imposed by a foreign Government. The repeal of the Usury Laws may have extended the legal obligation of the debtor, but it cannot extend the moral or religious obligation of his son. The son is required by special texts to pay the debts of his father; but the liability being primarily a moral one, its extent ought to be determined by Hindu Law, and no higher rate of interest ought to be allowed than is permitted by that law.[6]

(b) Loan for use.

(*b*) A loan for use (*commodatum*) consists in the entrusting of a thing (chiefly moveable) for gratuitous use, which is of determinate character and compass, and for a period fixed beforehand, or resulting from the object of the loan.[7] Since

[1] Section 2, Act XXVIII. of 1855. [2] Reg. III. of 1872, section 6.

[3] *Vide* Dekkhan Agriculturalists' Relief Act, 1879, sections 13, 14.

[4] 3 Bomb. H. C. Reps. 130 (o. c. j.); 7 *Ibid.* (o. c. g.); 10 *Ibid.* 385. But see 5 Beng. L. Reps. 500.

[5] I. L. R. IX. Bomb. 235, following III. *Ibid.* 312.

[6] I. L. R. II. Cal. 213; Siromani's *Commentary on the Hindu Law*, p. 183.

[7] Salkowski's *Roman Private Law*, section 121, p. 587.

the contract contemplates the advantage merely of him to whom the loan is made, the better opinion at Rome appears to have been that the borrower (*commodatarius*) must answer for both negligence and diligence.[1] He has to safeguard the thing with all the diligence which the most careful father of a family would exercise in his own affairs,[2] and to treat it conformably to its nature and the contract. Thus if I lend you a horse, to be used by you as far as a certain place, you are not liable upon the loan, if, without any neglect occurring on your part, the horse has been injured upon that very journey.[3] But suppose I lend a man my silver spoons to enable him to invite his friends to supper, and he afterwards takes them abroad with him. Here the use has not been conformably to the contract, and the borrower is rendered liable for any mishap by shipwreck and the like.[4] On the other hand the duties of the borrower and lender are in some degree correlative. The lender (*commodator*) must be taken to lend for the purpose of a beneficial use by the borrower. In the Language of the Roman Law he is expected to confer a benefit and not to deceive the borrower. Thus if he knowingly (*sciens*) lends faulty vessels for the storage of wine or oil, and the wine or oil poured in is spoilt or runs out, he is liable for the damage by a "contrary action" (*contrario judicio*).[5] This principle, which was said by Coleridge, J., to be "so consonant to reason and justice that it cannot but be part of our law," was applied by the English Court of Queen's Bench in the case of *Blackmore* v. *The Bristol and Exeter Rail. Co.*[6] The Indian Legislature has also incorparated it in the Indian Contract Act, which enacts that the bailor is bound to disclose to the bailee faults in the goods bailed, *of which the bailor is aware*, and which materially interfere with the use of them, or expose the bailee to extra-

[1] Dig. XIII. 6, 5, section 2.
[2] Dig. XIII. 6, 18, pr.
[3] Dig. XIII. 6, 5, section 2.
[4] Dig. XIII. 6, 18, pr.
[5] Dig. XIII. 6, 18, section 3.
[6] 27 L. J. Q. B. 167.

ordinary risks; and if he does not make such disclosure, he is responsible for damage arising to the bailee *directly* from such faults.[1] As regards the degree of care required from the borrower (or "bailee" as the Indian Law calls him), the Indian Act fixes the standard as that of an ordinary prudent man, having regard to the bulk, quality, and value of the goods bailed.[2] He is consequently not liable in the absence of any special contract, for the loss, destruction, or deterioration of the thing bailed, when he has taken the requisite amount of care of it.[3]

(c) Letting for hire.

(*c*) A letting for hire (*locatio et conductio*) is a form of contract by which is promised the transfer of the use of a thing (*locatio conductio rei*) for a certain time in consideration of an equivalent in money (*merces, pensio*).[4] The hirer (called *conductor*) acquires the mere detention of the thing, which he has to treat conformably to the contract; upon the termination of which he has to return it to the lessor in the same condition as he received it, and to discharge the amount of the hire. Thus the Roman agricultural tenant was expected to do all work in the field at the proper time, so as not to deteriorate the land by unseasonable cultivation, and he was also expected to give an eye to the buildings so as to avoid dilapidation.[5] Similarly, under the Punjab Tenancy Act, 1887, a tenant having a right of occupancy is liable to be ejected, (*a*) if he has used the land in a manner which renders it unfit for the purpose for which it was intended; or, (*b*) if he has without sufficient cause failed to cultivate the land in the manner and to the extent customary in the locality.[6] The lessor (*locator*) was bound to secure to the hirer the peaceable enjoyment of the thing and its produce

[1] Section 150, Act IX. of 1872. [2] Section 151, *Ibid.*

[3] Section 152, *Ibid.*

[4] Salkowski's *Roman Private Law*, section 123, p. 604; Windscheid, Vol. II., section 399, p. 498.

[5] Dig. XIX. 2, 25, section 3. [6] Section 39.

(*uti frui licere*), and to compensate the hirer for any injury that he may have sustained from undisclosed defects of the thing.[1] According to the Indian Contract Act, the locator (or bailor) would be responsible in the last-mentioned case, whether he was or was not aware of the existence of such defects.[2] The hirer, on the other hand, is expected, in the absence of any special contract, to take the same care as a borrower,[3] and if he does this he is not responsible for the destruction or deterioration of the thing.[4] In letting moveables no formalities are required, but a lease of immoveable property from year to year, or for any term exceeding one year, or reserving a yearly rent, can be made only, as previously stated, by a registered instrument. All other leases of immoveable property may be made either by an instrument or oral agreement. The rights and liabilities of the lessor and lessee of immoveable property, except in the Bombay Presidency, the Punjab, and British Burma, are now regulated throughout British India by the Transfer of Property Act, 1882:[5] in the excepted provinces, in the absence of any special contract, by local usage, the principles of English Law, or by such rules as may be consonant to justice, equity, and good conscience.

CHAP. VIII.

Marriage.

230. It is only as creating personal obligations between the parties that we need consider Marriage as a branch of the Law of Contract. And from this aspect we may distinguish the rights and obligations which (*a*) arise from a mere *promise to marry*, from (*b*) those which follow upon a *completed* marriage.

(*a*.) It is a very disputed question whether a mere promise of Marriage should lay the foundation for an action

[1] Salkowski's *Roman Private Law*, section 123, p. 606; Windscheid, Vol. I. section 400, p. 502.

[2] Section 150.

[3] Section 151.

[4] Section 152.

[5] *Vide* section 108, Act IV. of 1882.

CHAP. VIII.

for damages in the event of one of the parties subsequently repudiating the promise. But in England,[1] America,[2] and Prussia,[3] the right of the injured party to bring such an action is firmly established, and it has also been repeatedly recognised by the British Courts in India.[4] It is denied on the other hand in Italy,[5] and only permitted in France[6] and Austria[7] upon proof of "real injury" having occurred in consequence of the breach. In order to sustain such an action (which does not appear to have been known in England prior to 1674) it must be shown that the parties entered into it with free consent, and thus anything amounting to fraud or deceit in an essential of Marriage, or to duress, will discharge the opposite party.[8] So will a mistake as to *person* avoid the contract, as where a woman agrees to marry a man believing him to be someone else;[9] or the discovery of bodily or mental infirmity, either of the promisor or promisee,[10] or of dissolute or unchaste conduct of the party complaining of the breach.[11] Damages in an action for breach of promise are not governed by precisely the same rules as are applicable to actions upon ordinary contracts, in

[1] Macqueen's *Law of Husband and Wife*, 3rd ed. 199.

[2] *Law of Marriage and Divorce*, by David Stewart, San Francisco, 1884, sections 25, 26, pp. 13, 14.

[3] *Landrecht*, II. T. N. 1, 33, 75, 82.

[4] 24 W. R. 380.

[5] *Codice Civile del Regno d' Italia*, Art. 53.

[6] There is no express provision in the French Civil Code on the point, but on proof of "real injury" an action has been held to be sustainable under Art. 1382, which enacts that everyone is bound to repair the injury caused by his act. *Cf.* §§ 823—825, German Civil Code.

[7] *Civil Code of the Austrian Monarchy*, Part I., Art. 46, p. 13, Joseph M. Chevalier De Winiwarter's English translation.

[8] *Law of Marriage and Divorce*, by David Stewart, sections 80—83, pp. 70—84.

[9] *Reg.* v. *Millis*, 10 C. & F. 534.

[10] *Aitchison* v. *Baker*, Peake Ad. Cases, 103. But see *Hall* v. *Wright*, El. B. & E. 746.

[11] *Irving* v. *Greenwood*, 1 Car. & P. 360; *Foulkes* v. *Sellway*, 3 Esp. 236; *Young* v. *Murphy*, 3 Bing. N. C. 34.

which they are given by way of compensation and not of punishment.[1] The plaintiff is entitled to recover not only an indemnity for pecuniary loss, and for disappointment of reasonable expectations of material and worldly advantage resulting from the intended Marriage, but also compensation for wounded feelings, and the mortification and pain the plaintiff has been wrongfully made to undergo.[2] In aggravation of damages the plaintiff may prove that by means of his promise the defendant seduced her; or the Court may take into consideration the mode in which the engagement was broken off, or any circumstances showing cruel, indecent, or insulting conduct on the part of the defendant. In mitigation of damages the defendant may plead the fact of the plaintiff's unchastity, though known at the time of the promise or condoned, her general bad character, and, it appears, the fact of his being afflicted with an incurable disease, or the plaintiff having married elsewhere.[3] In India, where infant marriages amongst both Hindus and Muhammadans are the rule, the consent of parents and guardians is substituted for that of the actual parties. It frequently happens that a sum of money is paid to the girl's father as a consideration for the Marriage; and Sir Henry Maine sees in this practice a trace of the widely diffused ancient institution of Bride Price, which he believes was the earliest form of Stridhan, or woman's separate property.[4] But in modern times when the father takes any money, he takes it for his own use, and with no thought of settling it on the daughter.[5] If the marriage is subsequently broken off by the girl's parents, the money so paid, as well as the price of all ornaments given to the girl, may be recovered by the disappointed

[1] *Hamlin* v. *Great Northern Rail. Co.*, 1 H. & N. 408, 410, 411.

[2] *Law of Marriage and Divorce*, by D. Stewart, section 26, p. 14; 24 W. R. 380.

[3] *Ibid.* No. 59, *Punjab Record*, 1876.

[4] *Early History of Institutions*, pp. 321—324.

[5] Siromani's *Comment. on the Hindu Law*, p. 372.

CHAP. VIII. bridegroom.[1] But a suit for specific performance of a Marriage-Contract will not lie.[2]

(*b.*) The rights and obligations which result upon a completed Marriage may next be briefly stated. The husband in the first place acquires the right to connubial cohabitation with his wife, and a refusal on her part to cohabit with him is not justified by any conduct short of a cause for divorce, or judicial separation.[3] Where, however, the parties are living apart by consent, and *à fortiori* where it has been agreed between them that no suit for the restitution of conjugal rights shall be instituted, the parties to the agreement will be held bound, and a petition by either party will be dismissed.[4] If the wife declines without a justifiable cause to cohabit with her husband, the latter by the English and Indian Laws may enforce the matrimonial duty by petition or suit. But it is the boast of American writers that suits of this character for restitution of conjugal rights have never been known in the United States, where no court can compel discordant husbands and wives to live together.[5] How far wives in America may be congratulated on the absence of such a power we need not stay to inquire. But in a country where infant Marriages are mostly met with, and with the experience of *Rukmabhai's Case* before us,[6] the policy of

[1] I. L. R. X. Cal. 1054; No. 86, *Punjab Record*, 1875; No. 106, *Punjab Record*, 1879. In England a transaction of this kind would be regarded as partaking of the nature of a marriage brocage contract, and consequently void. *Kent* v. *Allen*, 2 Verne, Part II. 588. *Cf.* No. 116, *Punjab Record*, 1880.

[2] Section 21, Cl. B., *Specific Relief Act*, 1877; I. L. R. VII. Bomb. 122 (O. J.).

[3] Section 33, *Indian Divorce Act*, 1869; *Weldon* v. *Weldon*, L. R. 9 P. D. 52. As to Hindu Law, I. L. R. X. Bomb. 301; 23 W. R. 178. As to Muhammadan Law, see Amir Ali's *Personal Law*, pp. 252, 253, and Macnaghten's *Principles*, Chap. VII. para. 8; also I. L. R. VIII. Allah. 149, F. B.; and No. 164, P. R. 1889.

[4] Macqueen's *Law of Husband and Wife*, pp. 188, 189.

[5] *Law of Marriage and Divorce*, by David Stewart, section 175, p. 142.

[6] I. L. R. X. Bomb. 301. *Cf.* No. 79, *Punjab Record*, 1880.

attempting to enforce cohabitation between discordant husbands and wives may well be doubted. A similar right to connubial cohabitation is vested in and may be exercised by the wife against her husband subject to the same conditions. In the next place, the husband, by virtue of his right to the society of his wife, can claim damages against another person who has so beaten or maltreated his wife as to deprive him for any time of her company and assistance.[1] Against an adulterer the husband (as we have seen) can also claim damages.[2] On the other hand, although by recent legislation[3] a wife may be sued separately for her torts, the husband is not thereby relieved from liability for general wrongs committed by her during Marriage, and may still be joined as a defendant at need.[4] Both the married parties acquire by the Marriage certain rights of succession in the other's estate in the event of his or her dying intestate; and by the present Law of England they are mutually liable for each other's support.[5] Both the Hindu[6] and Muhammadan[7]

[1] Blackstone's *Comment.* III. 14; Pollock's *Law of Torts*, pp. 196, 197.

[2] As to Hindus being competent to bring such an action, see Siromani's *Commentary on the Hindu Law*, p. 101, paras. 24, 25.

[3] *The Married Women's Property Act*, 1882.

[4] Macqueen's *Law of Husband and Wife*, pp. 90—92; *Pollock on Torts*, p. 50.

[5] Macqueen's *Law of Husband and Wife*, p. 80. Even where the husband has turned the wife out of doors for misconduct, he will still be responsible for necessaries supplied to her while living apart if she had no means of support. *Wilson* v. *Glossop*, L. R. 19 Q. B. D. 379. He sends her forth, it is said, with an implied credit for necessaries. Per Best, C. J., in *Hunt* v. *De Blaquiere*, 5 Bing. 557.

[6] Mayne's *Hindu Law*, section 379; Siromani's *Comment. on the Hindu Law*, p. 258, para. 80; I. L. R. II. Bomb. 634. The principle that a man's first duty is to support his wife and family is beautifully expressed by Manu: "He who bestows gifts on strangers with a view to worldly fame, while he suffers his family to live in distress, though he has power to support them, touches his lips with honey, but swallows poison: such virtue is counterfeit." XI. 9 (as translated by Sir W. Jones). Burnell's translation (p. 325) is slightly different.

[7] Amir Ali's *Personal Law of the Mahomedans*, Chap. IX. pp. 279—285;

CHAP. VIII. Laws impose upon the husband the duty of maintaining the wife, and the obligation attaches from the moment of Marriage, and continues in force, subject to chaste conduct, during the existence of the relation. But there is apparently no express provision imposing the correlative duty on the wife of supporting an infirm or indigent husband. By Hindu Law, however, the husband is at liberty to appropriate his wife's separate property in case of extreme distress, or during illness, or while a creditor keeps him in prison.[1]

Creation of a Trust.

231. It is not our purpose here to consider the various obligations which are merely incidental to a Trust. Those obligations are remote from the main purpose of the Trust itself, which is defined as an obligation annexed to the Ownership of property and arising out of a confidence reposed in and accepted by the owner or declared and accepted by him, for the benefit of another, or of another and the owner.[2] They come into existence, no doubt, as the consequence of the consent of parties creating a Trust, but they are independent of their control, and may often be enforced by persons who were not parties to the transaction, nor even in existence at the time the Trust was created. In this sense these incidental Obligations are therefore distinguishable from those which properly spring from Contract, with which we are now alone concerned.[3] But when a person for a valuable consideration agrees to settle specific property for the benefit of another, be becomes a trustee of the property for the intended object, and his obligation arises as the direct result of a true contractual agreement. Thus a promise to make a payment of money or a settlement of property in

Macnaghten's *Precedents*, Chap. VI., Case XXXI. R. 2; Baillie's *Digest*, p. 441.

[1] Mayne's *Hindu Law*, section 569; *Tagore Law Lectures for* 1878, pp. 325—327.

[2] Section 3, *Indian Trusts Act*, 1882.

[3] Anson's *Law of Contracts*, p. 8; Markby's *Elements of Law*, section 617.

consideration of, or upon a marriage actually taking place, is an agreement of this kind which the law will enforce, provided, according to English Law, it is in writing and signed by the promisor or some person duly authorised by him.[1] In such a case the trusts upon which it is so agreed that the property shall be settled will fasten upon it; and if it happens to be money, and the money had been laid out in purchase of land, it may be followed into such land. But if a person contract to settle such property as he shall die possessed of, he may dispose of his property as he pleases during his lifetime, and the covenant will affect only such property as he may leave after payment of his just debts; and if a person contract to secure an annuity either by a charge on land, or by investment in Government Securities, or by the best means in his power, this does not create a charge on his property generally.[2] Chap. VIII.

232. In the table above given the more important Contracts which relate to the performance of "Service" are specified. Of these the first is "Deposit," which was understood by Roman Jurists to be a Contract by which some person (called a *depositor*) entrusts to another (*depositarius*) a moveable thing for gratuitous custody. The depositary was merely under obligation to take charge of the thing and to restore it when desired, and was only responsible for non-restitution in case of fraud (*dolus*) or gross negligence (*culpa lata*).[3] But the modern Civilian writers also include under the general term of "Deposit" two other species, to which they have given the names "irregular Deposit" (*depositum irregulare*) and "Sequestration." The former is an obligation which arises when things of a consumable nature are Deposit.

[1] Statute of Frauds (29 Car. II. c. 3), section 4. *Cf. Shadwell* v. *Shadwell*, 9 C. B. (N. S.) 159.

[2] Lewin on *Trusts*, 8th ed. 141; Stokes's *Anglo-Indian Codes*, Vol. I. p. 514.

[3] Salkowski's *Roman Private Law*, section 121, p. 584.

CHAP. VIII. deposited with another on the understanding that the depositary returns a like quantity of the same thing. It is very akin to a loan for use, from which it is only distinguishable by reference to the intention of the parties. A loan is given in the interest of the borrower; an "irregular Deposit" in the interest of the depositor. Thus money left with a banker to be returned in specie on demand would, as some continental Jurists contend, fall under the latter denomination.[1] "Sequestration"[2] takes place when several persons lay claim to a thing, which is placed in the custody of a third person pending a settlement of the dispute.[3] The person to whom the property is thus entrusted would be called in English Law a "stake-holder"; and under the English and Indian systems of Civil Procedure he could institute an interpleader suit against all the claimants for the purpose of obtaining a decision as to whom the payment or property should be made or delivered to, and of obtaining indemnity for himself.[4] The stake-holder is primarily the agent of the depositors, and he can deal with the money deposited so long only as his authority subsists.[5] Thus where money is paid or goods delivered for an illegal purpose, the person who has so paid the money or delivered the goods may recover them back before the illegal purpose is carried out; but if he waits till the illegal purpose is carried out, or if he seeks to enforce the illegal transaction, in neither case can he maintain an action.[6] In English Law a Deposit for reward takes place when property is left with warehousemen, wharfingers, livery-stable keepers, and innkeepers, or in "cloak-rooms" of Railway Companies.

[1] Windscheid's *Pandekten*, Vol. II., section 379, pp. 432—434 (note 7).

[2] The term is said to be derived from *secus*, and signifies that the *sequester* stands aside and holds the property impartially. *Ibid.* p. 435, note 2.

[3] Dig. XVI. 3, 6.

[4] Section 470, Act XIV. of 1882.

[5] *Hampden* v. *Walsh*, L. R. 1 Q. B. D. 194, 195.

[6] Per Mellish, L. J., *Taylor* v. *Bowers*, *Ibid.* at p. 300. *Cf.* para. 211, *ante*.

In the case of innkeepers their liability is now regulated in England by Statute Law.[1] This Statute does not apply to India, where the Common Law of England has been held to govern the relation of innkeeper and guest in a case between a European and a Parsi.[2]

Work on materials.

233. The Hiring of Services may assume one of two forms. The contract may either contemplate the performance of a definite piece of work or working upon materials supplied by the *locator* (or hirer); or it may have in view the performance of certain personal services. In the former case the contract was called by Roman Jurists *locatio operis*, in the latter *locatio operarum*.[3] But it was not easy in practice to maintain this distinction, or to say at times whether a given contract partook more of the nature of one kind than of the other. So, also, a question not unfrequently arose whether the contract was really one of buying and selling, or of letting and hiring. Thus, if I agreed with a goldsmith that he should make rings for me *out of his own gold* for a certain remuneration, Cassius was of opinion that this was a contract of buying and selling of the material, but of letting and hiring of the labour. The more approved opinion was that the entire contract was one of buying and selling. But if I had agreed to give the goldsmith my gold, and to pay him a certain remuneration for his labour, it was admitted without dissent that this was a contract of letting and hiring.[4] In both cases of hiring of services the responsibility of the person that is to do the work or to let his services, is extended to making good the consequences of his *imperitia* or unskilfulness.[5] In the case of certain Professional Services the old Jurists, as Ulpian tells us, regarded the labour given as a kindness, and not as laying the foundation of an action for

Professional Services.

[1] 26 & 27 Vict. c. 41. [2] III. Bomb. H. C. Reps. 137 (o. c. j.).

[3] Salkowski's *Roman Private Law*, section 123, p. 609.

[4] Gaius, iii. 147. [5] Dig. XIX. 2, 9, § 5.

letting and hiring.[1] In this category were included Services rendered by advocates, grammarians, land surveyors, philosophers, geometricians, and others who practised "liberal professions" (*liberalia studia*), who might indeed accept a fee (called an "*honorarium*"), but could not sue to enforce it. The Prætor in the exercise of his equitable Jurisdiction partly remedied this hardship.[2] But, as it has already been stated,[3] we have a survival of the old law in the existing rule which prevails in England and India, under which a barrister is precluded from validly contracting for the payment of his services. Other classes of legal practitioners in India can only enforce contracts of this nature if they are made in writing signed by the person retaining or employing them, and are filed, within fifteen days from the day on which they are executed, in the District Court, or in some Court in which some portion of the business in respect of which they have been executed has been or is to be done.[4] And the Legislature has imposed a further restriction by enacting that in any suit brought to enforce any such agreement, the Court may, if the agreement is not proved to be fair and reasonable, reduce the amount payable thereunder and award such other sum for the costs, fees, charges, and disbursements in respect of the business done in the same manner as if no such agreement had been made.[5] The Indian Courts also look with disfavour on agreements to pay for a pleader's services out of the property in litigation. But it has long been the practice to stipulate at the time of engagement for a portion of the fee being paid only on success, and such stipulations have been judicially recognized.[6] It is different of course if the promise is made subsequently. In such a case the pleader having contracted to give his services for a stated fee, the promise to pay an additional fee would ordinarily be regarded

[1] Dig. XI. 6, 1, pr.

[2] *Ibid.*

[3] Para. 122, *ante*.

[4] Section 28, Act XVIII. of 1879.

[5] Section 29, *Ibid.*

[6] I. L. R. VIII. Bomb. 413.

as a *nudum pactum*, unless the services subsequently rendered were such as were not originally contemplated and were only performed in consideration of the client's promise to pay an additional fee.[1] Domestic service is generally held to imply a monthly engagement involving a month's notice on either side.[2] Thus, if a servant leaves his employ during the month, he is not entitled to any wages for the fractional period of a month during which he may have rendered service.[3] On the other hand, the mere fact of his having been prevented by sickness from doing work would not debar him from claiming wages. The rule of a month's notice or a month's wages in lieu of notice only applies to domestic menial servants. Where the servant is employed to render skilled service a longer notice is generally required, which is regulated, in the absence of any special contract, with reference to custom and the nature of the particular service.[4] Thus, where a band-master was engaged in India without any fixed term of service, but on the understanding that his engagement would be for a long period, it was held that under the circumstances he was entitled to six months' wages in lieu of notice.[5] So the housekeeper of a large hotel has

Domestic Services.

[1] I. L. R. II. Bomb. 362.

[2] Leake's *Digest of the Law of Contracts*, pp. 203, 673. The question whether the engagement may not be determined at the end of the first month, by notice given by either party at the end of the first fortnight, or even without such notice, was raised in *Moult* v. *Halliday*, (1898) 1 Q. B. 125, but was not determined. In a more recent case before the Lambeth County Court, Judge Emden held that it was proved to his satisfaction that there was a custom that the usual engagement between domestic servants and employers might be terminated at the end of the first month by notice given by either party at or before the end of the first fortnight of service: *Maud Edmunds* v. *Alice Thornton*, reported in *Times*, 2nd Dec. 1898, p. 14.

[3] 1 Hay's *Reports*, 297; X. Bomb. H. C. Reps. 57. But see 16 W. R. 60.

[4] Each case of this kind must depend on its own circumstances. Leake's *Digest of the Law of Contracts*, 673; *Christophridis* v. *Gooljar*, reported in Sconce's *Master and his Domestic Servant*.

[5] No. 43, *Punjab Record*, 1876.

CHAP. VIII. been held not to be a menial servant,[1] and the same has been held in regard to a governess.[2] To justify the summary dismissal of a servant without notice his misconduct must be of a marked character, rendering it impossible that the relation of master and servant could continue, as, for instance, disobedience of a lawful order, absence without leave, dishonesty, or other gross misconduct.[3] If a servant is wrongfully discharged, he is bound, if possible, to obtain fresh employment, and the wages which have been, or might have been, gained by such employment are deducted from the compensation to which he is entitled.[4] A master is not bound to give a menial servant a character, and no action will lie against him for refusing to give it.[5] The death of the master puts an end to the contract of service;[6] and as a winding-up order generally has the effect of putting an end to the company as a going concern, except for the purposes of winding-up, it operates as a notice of discharge to its servants.[7] The liability of a master for injuries sustained by the servant in the course of his employment depends on whether the injury is the actual consequence of neglect or want of skill of the master.[8] If it is the consequence of want of skill or neglect of the servant himself, or of some third person, the master would not be

[1] *Lawler* v. *Linden*, Ir. Rep. 10 C. L. 188.

[2] *Todd* v. *Kerrich*, 8 Ex. 151; 22 L. J. Ex. 1.

[3] No. 43, *Punjab Record*, 1876. Accepting a bribe justifies dismissal. *Boston Fishing Co.* v. *Ansell*, 39 Ch. D. 339. The fact that an agreement states certain grounds justifying a dismissal will not prevent a master from dismissing the servant for incompetence. I. L. R. II. Cal. 33.

[4] *Hochster* v. *De la Tour*, 22 L. J. Q. B. 458; *Hartland* v. *General Exchange Bank*, 14 L. T. 863. *Cf.* explanation to section 73, *Indian Contract Act*. *Cf.* also *Beckham* v. *Drake*, 2 H. L. Cas. 606.

[5] *Carrol* v. *Bird*, 3 Esp. 201; 6 Rev. Rep. 824; *Handley* v. *Moffat*, Ir. Rep. 7 C. L. 104; 21 W. R. 231.

[6] Section 201, *Indian Contract Act*. See also Anson's *Law of Contracts*, p. 324, as to incapacitating illness of the servant.

[7] Section 137, Act VI. of 1882.

[8] Section 225, *Indian Contract Act*. A master is bound to take all reasonable precautions to secure the safety of his workmen. *Brydon* v. *Stewart*, 2 Macq. H. L. 30.

responsible.[1] Another important principle to be borne in mind in connection with the law of Master and Servant is, that the servant is not permitted to make secret profits at the expense of his master. Thus, if a master sends his servant to pay a bill, and gives him money for the payment, then if the tradesman makes the servant a present, the master is entitled to the benefit of it, because it amounts to a reduction of the price of the goods.[2] This rule was fully considered in a recent Indian case where the learned Chief Justice of the High Court, North-West Provinces, made the following observations:—"Now, if the account is an *open* one, that is, an account of which the items have never been checked or settled, and if the transaction amounts to a taxation of the bill and a reduction of the price by the servant, it is obvious that the servant obtains the reduction for his master; that the money in his hands always remains the master's property, and that if he appropriates it he steals it. But if the master himself has *settled* the account with the tradesman for a specific sum, and he sends the servant with the money, and the servant, after making the payment asks the tradesman for a present, then if the servant takes the present and keeps it, he is not guilty of stealing, because he has no intention to steal: the money is given to him by a person whom he believes to have a right to give it. It may be that according to the strict equitable doctrines of the Court of Chancery, the servant is bound to account to his master for the money. But, however this may be, his act is a very different matter from a criminal offence, and I do not think he can be convicted of criminal breach of trust merely because, by a mere

[1] As to injuries sustained from negligence of a fellow-servant in the course of their common employment, the law is now regulated in England by 43 & 44 Vict. c. 42. *Cf. The Duty and Liability of Employers*, by W. H. Roberts and George Wallace, 3rd ed., Chap. X. p. 234. In cases arising out of a statutory duty, the maxim *volenti non fit injuria* is not applicable. *Baddeley* v. *Earl Granville*, L. R. 19 Q. B. D. 423.

[2] *Hay's Case, In re Canadian Oil Works Co.*, 1875, L. R. 10 Ch. App. 593; *Mayor of Salford* v. *Lever*, (1891) 1 Q. B. 168.

CHAP. VIII. equitable doctrine of the Court of Chancery, it was obligatory upon him to render an account."[1] Special laws at times regulate the rights and liabilities of particular classes of servants. Thus, in the case of Shipmasters and Seamen the governing Statute in England is 57 & 58 Vict. c. 60,[2] and in India Act I. of 1859, sections 47 to 58.[3] The relation of Master and Apprentice is likewise regulated by Statute law.[4]

Agency. 234. The extent to which the rights and liabilities of contracting parties may be effected by the contract being made through the intervention of an agent has already been dealt with.[5] But it remains to consider the principles which govern the relation of Principal and Agent *inter se*. This relation arises out of the Contract of Agency, and is primarily regulated by that Contract. The acceptance of the employment by the Agent, and the Principal's consent (express or implied) to his acting for him, are sufficient to constitute the relation, and no *express* consideration is necessary to create it.[6] Thus, a gratuitous agent is not bound to undertake the agency, but having undertaken it, he becomes liable for any loss resulting directly from his own neglect, want of skill, or misconduct.[7] Indeed the original conception of Agency was that of a *gratuitous* management of a lawful business, whether it consisted in the performance of work or service, administration, or legal transaction, based on kindness and friendship. Thus, Paulus declares that "a Mandate (the

[1] I. L. R. VIII. Allah. 120, at pp. 138, 139. See as to "secret profits" made by a promoter of a company, L. R. 33 Ch. D. 85.

[2] VI. Bomb. H. C. Reps. 42 (o. c. j.) refers to the old repealed Act of 17 & 18 Vict. c. 104.

[3] VI. Bomb. H. C. Reps. 138.

[4] Act XIX. of 1850. Apprentices to sea-service are governed by Act I. of 1859 (section 4), and in England by 57 & 58 Vict. c. 60.

[5] *Vide* para. 205, *ante*.

[6] Section 185, *Indian Contract Act*. *Cf.* Dig. XVII. 1, 1, pr.

[7] II. Mad. H. C. Reps. 449; and section 212, *Indian Contract Act*. As the Roman jurist Paulus well expressed it: "It is a matter of good will to undertake a mandate, and of necessity to carry it out." Dig. XIII. 6, 17, section 3.

Roman term for a commission of agency) is nothing save as gratuitous (*mandatum, nisi gratuitum, nullum est*)."[1] The addition of a reward transmuted the transaction into one of letting and hiring.[2] According to the Indian Law the Agent's duty to his Principal is, (*a*) to render proper accounts on demand, (*b*) to communicate with him in all cases of difficulty, and to seek to obtain his instructions, (*c*) not to deal on his own account in the business of the Agency without first obtaining his Principal's consent and acquainting him with all material circumstances which have come to his own knowledge on the subject, (*d*) to conduct his Principal's business according to his directions, or, in the absence of any such directions, according to the custom which prevails in doing business of the same kind at the place where the Agent conducts such business, (*e*) to act with reasonable diligence and to use such skill as he possesses,[3] and, subject to his right of lien to be presently mentioned, to pay to his Principal all sums received on his account. The Agent is also liable to account to his Principal for all benefits gained by him in dealing on his account in the business of the Agency.[4] As against his Principal the agent possesses the following rights:—

(*a*) to retain out of monies belonging to his Principal in his hands all sums due to himself in respect of advances made or expenses incurred by him in conducting the business of the Agency;

[1] Dig. XVII. 1, 1, § 4.

[2] *Ibid.* section ult. 1.

[3] Sections 211—215, 218, *Indian Contract Act.*

[4] Section 216, *Ibid.* *Cf.* I. L. R. VIII. Allah. 128. On the subject of commissions and bribes paid to agents, see *Harrington* v. *Victoria Graving Dock Co.*, L. R. 3 Q. B. D. 549. In this last case the Lord Chief Justice said: "I am of opinion that when a bribe or promise of a bribe is given to a person employed by another, and is given by some one who has contracted with the employer, in order to induce the agent to do something in contravention or derogation of his duty of loyalty and fidelity to his employer, that is a corrupt bargain." See also No. 531 of 1883 (by Chief Court of the Punjab), and the case of *Shipway* v. *Broadwood*, reported in the *Times* of the 18th January, 1899, in which the Appeal Court refused to enforce a contract for the purchase of a pair of horses on the ground that the veterinary surgeon employed by the purchaser had also agreed to accept a commission from the seller.

CHAP. VIII.

(*b*) to exercise a lien on his Principal's goods and papers;

(*c*) to be indemnified against the consequences of all lawful acts done by him in the conduct of the Agency;

(*d*) to be compensated for personal injury caused by his Principal's neglect.[1]

Partnership.

235. The definition of a contract of Partnership which the Indian Legislature has adopted is taken from Kent's Commentaries,[2] and runs as follows:—"'Partnership' is the relation which subsists between persons who have agreed to *combine* their property, labour, or skill in some business, and to *share* the profits thereof between them."[3] This definition, while it is sufficiently clear to exclude such an agreement as that known to the Roman Law as a *societas leonina*—where one party is to have *all* the *profit* and the other to have *all* the *loss*[4]—is open on the other hand to the criticism passed upon it by the late Master of the Rolls (*Sir George Jessel*), that it excludes dormant partners who put nothing in—neither capital, nor skill, nor anything else, as when a share is given to the widow of a former partner.[5] Indeed the futility of

[1] Sections 217, 221—223, 225, *Indian Contract Act*.

[2] Vol. III. 23.

[3] Section 239. The English Partnership Act of 1890, adopting, apparently, a suggestion of the Privy Council (*see* p. 289, note [1]), defines Partnership as "the relation which subsists between persons carrying on a business in common with a view to profit," and seems to avoid the criticism noticed in the text.

[4] Ulpian agreed with Cassius that such a partnership agreement is void. Dig. XVII. 2, 29, section 2. Indeed, so essential is the expectation of profit deemed to be that it is to be implied in every partnership, and if the business of the latter cannot be carried on except at a loss, it may be dissolved, although entered into for life. I. L. R. Bomb. 468, 474.

[5] *Pooley* v. *Driver*, L. R. 5 Ch. D. at p. 473. But the *Indian Contract Act* enacts that no widow or child of a deceased partner of a trader receiving, by way of annuity, a proportion of the profits of the business, shall by reason only of such receipt be deemed to be a partner of such trader, or subject to any liabilities incurred by him. Section 243. The Roman law seems to have been opposed to the notion of a person being admitted into partnership as the result of a mere gift. Thus Ulpian expressly says: *donationis causa societas recte non contrahitur*: a partnership is not properly contracted upon the ground of a gift. Dig. XVII. 2, 5, section 2.

all attempts to give an exhaustive definition of a contract such as we are now dealing with may be judged from the circumstance that Mr. Justice Lindley quotes no less than fifteen such attempts, and no two of these definitions exactly agree.[1] With such an example before us we can admire the wisdom of the Roman Jurist (Javolenus) who said *omnis definitio in jure civili periculosa est:* every definition in the Civil Law is dangerous.[2] Leaving therefore to others the task of suggesting a more exhaustive definition of a Partnership, it will be sufficient here to mention that it is a contract which, under the Indian Law, requires no formalities to complete it, and it may be entered into for life or for a limited period. But no matter for what period a Partnership may have been entered into, it may be dissolved at any time upon proof that (*a*) the business cannot be carried on except at a loss, or (*b*) that a partner has become of unsound mind, or (*c*) has been adjudicated an insolvent, or (*d*) has done some act by which his whole interest in the partnership property or profits is legally transferred to some third person, or (*e*) has become incapable of performing his part of the partnership contract, or (*f*) has been guilty of gross misconduct in the affairs of the partnership or towards his partners.[3] In the case of (*c*), (*d*), and (*f*) the insolvency, act, or misconduct must be that of a partner other than the partner seeking the dissolution. A Partnership, moreover, is dissolved in all cases by its business being (or becoming) prohibited by law.[4] Thus, if A. is a partner with ten others in a certain business, and an Act is passed which makes it unlawful from the date of the Act for more than ten persons

[1] *Law of Partnership*, pp. 2, 3, 3rd ed. In *Mollwo, March, and others* v. *Court of Wards*, X. Beng. L. Reps. at p. 312, the Privy Council alluded to these numerous definitions, and contented itself by saying that to constitute a partnership, the parties must have agreed to carry on business, and to share profits in some way in common. *Vide* p. 320.

[2] Dig. L. 17, 202.

[3] Section 254, *Indian Contract Act*.

[4] Section 255, *Ibid.*

CHAP. VIII. to carry on that business in Partnership, the Partnership of which A. was a member is dissolved upon the passing of the Act.[1] It may also be terminated by expiration of the term for which it was originally formed, or, if entered into for a particular undertaking, by the termination of that undertaking, or by the death of any partner, or lastly, at any time with the consent of all the partners, who may also agree amongst themselves as to the division of profits and losses. But in the absence of any contract to the contrary, the Indian Legislature has enacted that the relations of partners to each other are to be determined according to fixed rules.[2] If a Partnership entered into for a fixed term be continued after such term has expired, the rights and obligations will, in the absence of any agreement to the contrary, remain the same as they were at the expiration of the term, so far as such rights and obligations can be applied to a Partnership at will.[3] Partners are bound to carry on the business of the partnership for the greatest common advantage, to be just and faithful to each other, and to render true accounts and full information of all things affecting the Partnership to any partner or his legal representative.[4] In regard to the distribution of assets upon a dissolution, the rule is that Partnership property must be applied in the first instance in payment of the debts of the firm, and if there is any surplus then the share of each partner must be applied in payment of his separate debts or paid to him. The separate property of any partner on the other hand must be applied first in the payment of his separate debts, and the surplus (if any) in the payment of the debts of the firm.[5] But until the business of the Partnership is completely wound up, the rights and obligations of the partners continue in all things

[1] Pollock on *Partnership*, p. 75.

[2] Section 253, *Indian Contract Act*.

[3] Section 256, *Indian Contract Act*.

[4] Section 257, *Ibid*.

[5] Section 262, *Ibid*. *Cf*. L. R. 12 App. Cas. 160.

necessary for that purpose.[1] Thus, notwithstanding dissolution, a partner has implied authority to bind the firm so far as may be necessary to settle and liquidate existing demands, and to complete transactions begun, but unfinished, at time of dissolution.[2] Besides the ordinary Partnership above mentioned there is a special form of trading association which deserves a brief notice. It is now known in France[3] as *la société en commandite*, in Germany as *Kommandit Gesellschaft auf Aktien*,[4] and in America as a Limited Partnership, for the origin of which one has to go to the Mediæval History of Italy. Its leading feature is, that the liability of some of its members to bear losses is restricted to a defined amount, namely, the capital contributed by them to the concern. It derives its name from the Latin verb *commendare*, "to trust," and was probably at first more in the nature of a Trust than a Partnership. In Louisiana in the United States a limited Partner is still called "the partner *in commendam*." It was only under an Ordinance of Louis XIV., published in 1673, that it was apparently first distinctly recognised in France as a contract of Partnership, but its present form dates from the enactment of the *Code de Commerce*. Its origin is ascribed to the practice in mediæval times of nobles in Italy and France embarking their capital with traders for purposes of commercial speculation without disclosing their names to the outside world. The relation thus created between the capitalist and the trader was called *accomandita*, whence the term *société en commandite;* and by means of such associations the nobles were able to evade the restrictions of the Canonical Law, which regarded the business of money-

[1] Section 263, *Indian Contract Act*.

[2] Lindley on *Partnership*, Bk. ii. Chap. 2, section 3.

[3] The *Code de Commerce* (Arts. 23—28) recognises two forms of *commandite* partnerships, *simple* and *par actions*, which do not differ in principle, but only as regards the form of their constitution.

[4] *Das allgemeine deutsche Handelgesetzbuch*, Von Makower, p. 150, Arts. 174—206, Berlin, 1871.

CHAP. VIII. lending—chiefly carried on in those days by despised Jews and barbarian Lombards or Langobards—as degrading and abhorrent. These societies thus gave an outlet to a large amount of accumulated and unremunerative capital, which would otherwise have lain by unutilised, and it was chiefly through them that the prosperous trade of the Mediterranean was sustained and extended.[1] It is remarkable that England—the most commercial country in Europe—should alone have excluded this form of Limited Partnership from its commercial system, although Mill and other writers have strongly recommended it on economical grounds. The only attempt to legislate on the subject, by introducing the system of making loans on condition of receiving a share of the profits[2]—which the Indian Legislature has also followed[3]—is said to have proved more mischievous than otherwise, by luring people into the very danger it was intended to protect them from.[4] In all cases where such loans are made the question whether, as regards third persons, the relation of Partnership does or does not exist is made to depend on the real intention and contract of the parties. "The Law," as was observed by the Privy Council, "in cases of this kind, will look at the body and substance of the arrangements, and fasten responsibility on the parties according to their true and real character."[5] It only remains to add that a contract to enter into Partnership, no period being specified for the duration of the proposed Partnership, cannot be specifically enforced.[6] This is on the principle that a Court will not lend itself to do a vain thing, for if it enforced such a contract either of the parties might at once dissolve the Partnership,

[1] *The Law of Limited Partnership*, by Clement Bates, pp. 18—21, Boston, 1886; Pollock's *Essays in Jurisprudence*, p. 100.

[2] 28 & 29 Vict. c. 86. [3] Sections 240, 241, *Indian Contract Act.*

[4] Pollock's *Essays in Jurisprudence*, pp. 103, 104.

[5] *Mollwo, March, and others* v. *Court of Wards*, X. Bengal Law Reps. 312, at p. 323. *Cf.* I. L. R. IV. Allah. 74.

[6] Section 21, Illust. (*d*), *Specific Act*, 1877.

in accordance with the rule that a Partnership at will is dissolvable at pleasure.[1] As to the principle on which damages are to be assessed for breach of contract to admit to a Partnership, reference may be made to the case of *Lewin* v. *Morrison*.[2]

Contracts for negative Service.

236. Where one of the parties to a Contract promises to abstain from doing a particular act, it is said to be a "Contract for negative service." The Law looks with jealousy and disfavour on such restrictions upon natural freedom, and in India the Legislature has gone even further than in England in limiting the power of individuals to bind themselves by such agreements. Thus, subject to three exceptions, *every* agreement by which any one is restrained, either partially or absolutely, from exercising a lawful profession, trade, or business of any kind, is to that extent void.[3] This provision if much more comprehensive than the corresponding rule of the English law, and the reason for the Indian Legislature adopting a more extended rule is probably that stated by Kindersley, J., in *Oakes* v. *Jackson*.[4] "Trade in India," the learned judge observed, "is in its infancy; and the Legislature may have wished to make the smallest number of exceptions to the rule against contracts whereby trade may be restrained." The consequence of this difference in the law of the two countries is, that an agreement in restraint of trade executed in England, to be performed in India, though valid according to the *lex loci contractus* (or law of the place of contract), may be void in India, which it would be unless it fell within any of the exceptions to the rule recognised by

[1] Section 253, clause (8), *Indian Contract Act*.

[2] 3 Agra (High Court, N. W. P.) Reps. 151.

[3] Section 27, *Indian Contract Act*. *Cf.* I. L. R. VIII. Cal. 809; and No. 29, *Punjab Record*, 1874.

[4] I. L. R. I. Mad. at p. 145. This decision was followed by Mattusami Ayyar, J., in *Ragavayya* v. *Subbayya* (1889), I. L. R. XIII. Mad. 475. See also I. L. R. XI. Cal. 545.

the law of India.[1] This is upon the general principle to be noticed hereafter, that although, as regards its formation, the validity of a contract is determined by the law of the place where it is entered into, yet if it is to be performed in another country, the *lex fori* (or law of the forum) would govern so far as to prevent a violation of a prohibitory law of its own State.[2] The exceptions to the above rule are (*a*) a saving of agreements not to carry on business of which the good-will is sold, (*b*) of similar agreements between partners prior to dissolution, or (*c*) during continuance of Partnership.[3] But it is important to bear in mind that the scope of the Section (27) of the Indian Act is not to be extended beyond its legitimate object; and thus contracts by which in the exercise of his profession, trade, or business, a man enters into ordinary agreements with persons dealing with him which are really necessary for the carrying on of his business, are not to be deemed invalid. So where a person having a licence for the manufacture of salt entered into a contract with a firm of merchants, whereby it was provided that he should not manufacture salt in excess of the quantity which the firm at the commencement of each manufacturing season should require him to manufacture, and that all salt manufactured by him should be sold to the firm for a fixed price for a term of five years, it was held by Mr. Justice Handley, of the Madras High Court, that whether or not the first of these clauses was invalid under Section 27 of the Indian Contract Act, it was

[1] I. L. R. I. Mad. 134; No. 85, P. R. 1874.

[2] Pollock's *Principles of Contract*, p. 339, 4th edition; No. 88, *Punjab Record*, 1867.

[3] Section 27, *Indian Contract Act*. As to a vendor of a goodwill of business subsequently soliciting customers of old house to deal with him, see *Pearson* v. *Pearson*, 27 Ch. D. 145; *Vernon* v. *Hallam*, L. R. 34 Ch. D. 748; and *Baines* v. *Geary*, L. R. 35 Ch. D. 154. But even where agreements not to carry on similar trade are enforceable, the obligation is a purely personal one, and not a mere incident to the transfer of property. Thus a purchaser from a trustee in bankruptcy or liquidation acquires no right to enforce it. *Walker* v. *Mottram*, L. R. 19 Ch. D. 355.

Chap. VIII.

separable from the second clause which was not bad as being in restraint of trade.[1] Again, agreements in restraint of legal proceedings are void, subject to a saving of a contract to refer questions that have already arisen or that may arise.[2] Thus, where a contract stipulated that "all disputes regarding cost and maintenance of party walls were to be decided by the Government Surveyor, whose decision should be final," it was held that there was no right of action independently of the valuation and award of the Government Surveyor.[3] So, also, where by a written agreement a tenant of a furnished house agreed to make good or pay for loss or damage to house and furniture, the amount, if disputed, to be settled by two valuers, it was held that the settlement of the amount by the valuers was a condition precedent to the right of the landlord to bring an action in respect of alleged dilapidations.[4]

Wagers.

237. "Aleatory Contracts" are Contracts by way of Wager, and a Wager may be best defined as "a contract by which two or more parties agree that a certain sum of money or other thing shall be paid or delivered to one of them on the happening or not happening of an uncertain event."[5] It is something hazarded on the issue of an uncertain event, and to constitute it there must be a risk on both sides. Thus, if one of the parties has "the event in his own hands," the transaction lacks an essential ingredient of a Wager.[6] It has otherwise all the requisites of a legal contract, namely, parties, consideration, subject-matter, and the meeting of minds. But it has this peculiarity, that its performance is in the alternative, that is, by one party or the other according

[1] *Mackenzie* v. *Striramiah* (1890), I. L. R. XIII. Mad. 472. *Cf.* also I. L. R. 17 Cal. 320.

[2] Section 28, *Indian Contract Act*, and section 21, *Specific Relief Act*, 1877. *Cf.* No. 120, P. R. 1879.

[3] I. L. R. VI. Bomb. 528.

[4] *Babbage* v. *Coulburn*, L. R. 9 Q. B. D. 235.

[5] 2 Bouvier's Dict. 647; *Cf.* Anson's *Law of Contracts*, 173, 174.

[6] I. L. R. IX. Bomb. 358.

CHAP. VIII. as one or the other loses. Hence in an American case (known as *Shumate's case*) a Wager was said to be a contract upon a contingency by which one may lose, although he cannot gain, or the other gain, but cannot lose. It is, in short, all loss to one party and all gain to the other.[1] By the Common Law of England Wagers as a general rule are valid and enforceable in the Courts. But the Courts only grudgingly recognised the rule, and succeeded in hedging it round with so many exceptions that at last it became the settled practice to require that "the subject-matter of a Wager must be at least perfectly innocent in itself, and must not tend to immorality or impolicy."[2] Finally, in the present reign, a Statute was passed which declared "all contracts or agreements, whether by parol or in writing, by way of gaming or wagering" to be null and void, and prohibited any suit to be brought in any Court of law or equity "for recovering any sum of money or valuable thing alleged to be won upon any wager."[3] But in deference to the national spirit for games and sports the Statute expressly excludes from its application any subscription or contribution for any plate, prize, or sum of money to be awarded "to the winner of any lawful game, sport, pastime, or exercise." This Statute furnished the model for Indian legislation on the same subject, and Acts XVI. of 1848 and VIII. of 1867 closely followed its provisions. These enactments have more recently been repealed, but the prohibition against all actions founded on Wagers has been repeated in the Contract Act, which declares that "agreements by way of wager are void."[4] The Indian Law, however, differs from the English in recognising only a single exception in favour of certain prizes for "horse-racing." But the mere circum-

[1] *Contracts for Future Delivery and Commercial Wagers*, by T. Henry Dewey, pp. 9, 10, New York, 1886.

[2] Per Le Blanc, J., in *Gilbert* v. *Sykes*, 16 East, 159.

[3] 8 & 9 Vict. c. 109, section 18.

[4] Section 30, Act IX. of 1872.

stance that a wagering Contract is "void" does not make it "illegal," and therefore there is nothing to prevent the agent of a party to such a contract from suing for fees and brokerage in respect of it, or for money paid by him to other persons on the loss of a Wager.[1] So in England it has been held that a loan of money intended to pay lost bets is recoverable, and Jessel, M. R., based this decision on the ground that "the mischief had been completed before the money was lent." "The money," he observed, "was advanced to enable the borrower to pay the bets which he had already made and lost, which seems to me an entirely different thing from a loan of money to enable a man to make a bet."[2] By a mere extension of the same principle it has also been held that one who is employed to make bets for another is liable, *if the bets are paid*, to pay over the money to his employer.[3] Again, some recent decisions in England appear to have established the somewhat dangerous doctrine that if A. employs X., who belongs to a society which enforces, upon pain of expulsion, invalid or illegal contracts, to make a void or even illegal contract, and X. having made it would be subject by the rules of the society to which he belongs to loss if he did not fulfil its terms, A. is bound to enable X. to fulfil those terms or to indemnify him for having fulfilled them.[4] It is probable that in the construction of the Indian Law on the subject of Wagers the Indian Courts would be obliged to follow the English decisions, in accordance with the principle recently laid down by the Privy Council that where the provisions of a Colonial Statute are identical with those of an Imperial Statute, Colonial Courts should follow

[1] XII. Bomb. H. C. Reps. 51. *Cf. Beeston* v. *Beeston*, L. R. 1 Ex. D. 13.

[2] *Pyke's case*, L. R. 8 Ch. D. 756.

[3] *Bridges* v. *Savage*, L. R. 15 Q. B. D. 363.

[4] *Read* v. *Anderson*, L. R. 13 Q. B. D. 779; *Seymour* v. *Bridge*, L. R. 14 Q. B. D. 460: see the remarks of Sir William Anson on these cases, *Law of Contracts*, pp. 202, 203.

CHAP. VIII.

Lotteries.

the decisions of the Courts of Appeal on the Imperial Statute.[1] Lotteries are illegal both in England[2] and in India.[3] But it is not every transaction which is agreed to be decided by lot that is a Lottery. Thus it has been held that where twenty persons agreed that each should subscribe Rs. 200 by monthly instalments of Rs. 10, and that each in his turn as determined by lot should take the whole of the subscriptions for one month, this agreement was not illegal.[4] To constitute a lottery the solution of the question in each case must depend upon mere chance. Where any element involving skill or inquiry is introduced, the competition ceases to be illegal. Thus, where a prize of £1,000 was offered as a prize for a correct prediction of the numbers of male and female births and the number of deaths in London, during the week ending December 11th, 1897, and the plaintiff, who had given a correct prediction, claimed the prize, it was held by the Court of Appeal that although the prediction depended very largely upon chance, there was an element of statistical inquiry brought into it, which prevented the competition from being treated as one of a lottery.[5] As falling within the general definition of an Aleatory or Wagering contract but yet enforceable by the Courts, may be mentioned (*a*) Life Annuities, (*b*) Bottomry, which is a loan to a shipowner secured on the hull, to be repaid only in case a voyage ends successfully, (*c*) Respondentia, a similar loan to a shipowner but secured on the cargo, and (*d*) Insurance, which is a contract to indemnify against a contingent loss in consideration of a premium, and which may assume one of three forms: Life, Fire, and Marine Insurance, all having the same general features in common. In all these contracts the payment of money to one of the parties is made to depend upon the happening or non-happening of a particular event; and

Life Annuities and certain other contracts exceptionally treated.

1 *Trimble* v. *Hill*, 49 L. J. P. C. 49.

2 23 Vict. c. 28.

3 Section 294, *Indian Penal Code*.

4 I. Mad. H. C. Reps. 448.

5 *Hall* v. *Cox*, reported in *Times* of the 3rd December, 1898, p. 4.

viewed from this aspect it is difficult to distinguish between a bet against a particular horse winning a specified race and a bet against a particular ship reaching with her cargo a specified port.[1] Yet the one transaction would not be recognised by a Court of Law, while the other would be perfectly valid in the form of a contract of Marine Insurance, provided the party effecting the Insurance were *interested* in the thing *insured*. He must have in fact what is called an "insurable interest."[2] But there is one important difference between a policy of Life Insurance and a policy of Marine or Fire Insurance which deserves to be noticed. The former is simply a contract that in consideration of a certain annual payment, the Insurance Company will pay at a future time a fixed sum, calculated by it with reference to the value of the premia which are to be paid, in order to purchase the postponed payment. *The policy in such a case never refers to the reason for effecting it.* Policies of Insurance against Fire or Marine risk on the other hand are contracts to recoup the loss which parties may sustain from *particular causes*.[3] They are thus essentially contracts of indemnity,[4] and if the

[1] Anson's *Law of Contracts*, p. 174.

[2] 19 Geo. II. c. 37 (as to Marine Insurance), and 14 Geo. III. c. 48 (as to Insurance generally). This phrase was explained by Lawrence, J., as follows:—"To be interested in the preservation of a thing is to be circumstanced with respect to it *as to have benefit from its existence, prejudice from its destruction.* The property of a thing and the interest derivable from it may be different: of the first, the price is generally the measure; but by interest in the thing every benefit or advantage arising out of or depending on such thing may be considered as being comprehended." *Lucena* v. *Crauford*, 2 B. & P. N. R. 269. This definition was approved in *Wilson* v. *Jones*, in which Blackburn, J., observed: "I know no better definition of an interest in an event than that indicated by Lawrence, J., in *Barclay* v. *Cousins*, and more fully stated by him in *Lucena* v. *Crauford*, *that if the event happens the party will gain an advantage, if it is frustrated he will suffer a loss.*" L. R. 2 Exch. at p. 153.

[3] *Law* v. *London Indisputable Life Policy Co.*, 24 L. J. Ch. 199.

[4] They have been so treated by writers of all countries. *Lucena* v. *Crauford*, 2 B. & P. N. R. 269; I. L. R. IV. Bomb. at p. 308. As to the French Law, see Goirand's *French Code of Commerce*, pp. 304, 305.

insured recovers the amount from any other source the insurer may recover from him *pro tanto*.[1] Such contracts are now well known in India,[2] and on the Bombay side where a brisk trade is carried on with ports on the coast of Africa and in Madagascar, traders borrow money on what is termed *avung*,—that is, money borrowed on the condition that it is not to be repaid, except in case of the safe arrival of the goods in the home ports, on the return voyage, in which event the loan becomes repayable, with interest at a high rate. It is also the well established practice for the lender of an *avung* loan to insure the goods as a means of indemnifying himself against the loss which he must necessarily sustain if the goods do not arrive safely. But an *avung* loan does not apparently give the lender a charge on the goods.[3] In the absence of any native law on the subject of Marine Insurance, the Courts in India generally follow the principles recognized by English Courts.[4] And thus Sir C. Sargent, late C. J. of the Bombay High Court, in the *avung* loan case held that plaintiff suing upon a policy of Marine Insurance was bound to show that he had an interest in the goods.[5]

Accessory Contracts.

238. We next have to consider the class of agreements which fall under the head of Accessory Contracts, the object of which is to create a Right which is merely "ancillary" to another Right. One of the most frequently occurring forms of such agreements is that known to the Indian Law as a

Guarantee.

Contract of Guarantee, which is defined as "a contract to perform the promise or discharge the liability of a third

[1] *Darrell* v. *Tibbitts*, L. R. 5 Q. B. 560.

[2] VI. Beng. L. Reps. 218; VII. *Ibid.* 347; XV. *Ibid.* 3, Appendix; I. Bomb. H. C. Reps. 6, 229; III. *Ibid.* 1 (a. c. j.); VII. *Ibid.* 39 (o. c. j.); II. Mad. H. C. Reps. 355; VI. N. W. P. H. C. Reps. 311.

[3] I. L. R. IV. Bomb. 305, at pp. 309, 310.

[4] XII. Bomb. H. C. Reps. 23; III. *Ibid.* 1 (a. c. j.); I. L. R. II. Bomb. 550; I. L. R. IV. Bomb. 314.

[5] I. L. R. IV. Bomb. at p. 309.

person in case of his default."[1] The person who gives the Guarantee is called the "surety," the person in respect of whose default the Guarantee is given is called the "principal-debtor," and the person to whom the Guarantee is given is called the "creditor."[2] This terminology seems to indicate that the obligation to which the Guarantee is subsidiary must be one which is legally enforceable *at the time*. Thus, as a minor cannot legally contract,[3] a Guarantee of his promise would impose no liability against the surety. But as a creditor may sue the surety alone,[4] it is possible that the liability of the latter may continue to be enforceable, as having been kept alive by acknowledgments, although that of the principal-debtor may have become barred by lapse of time.[5] Unlike the Roman and English systems, under which a Guarantee is a formal contract, the Indian Law permits a Guarantee to be either oral or written.[6] The consideration for such an undertaking may be anything done, or any promise made, for the benefit of the principal-debtor;[7] and the liability of the surety is co-extensive with that of the principal-debtor, in the absence of any agreement to the contrary.[8] It may, therefore, be less than that of the principal-debtor but cannot be greater. A Guarantee may also be limited to a single transaction or it may be extended to a series of transactions. In the latter case it is called a "Continuing Guarantee."[9] Thus, where B. became surety under a bond to Government for the treasurer of a Collectorate, and the Collector yearly examined the accounts and struck a balance which he certified to be correct, but upon his subsequently discovering that the treasurer had embezzled moneys

Continuing Guarantee.

[1] Section 126, *Indian Contract Act.* [2] *Ibid.*

[3] Section 10, *Indian Contract Act. Cf.* contra the *French Civil Code*, Art. 2012.

[4] IV. Mad. H. C. Reps. 190; VII. *Ibid.* 368; No. 8, P. R. 1866.

[5] No. 2, *Punjab Record*, 1878; I. L. R. XII. Cal. 330.

[6] Section 126, *Indian Contract Act.* [8] Section 128, *Ibid.*

[7] Section 127, *Ibid.* [9] Section 129, *Ibid.*

CHAP. VIII. during each year it was held that B.'s liability continued.[1] It is open to the surety, however, to revoke his Guarantee with respect to future transactions at any time by giving notice to the creditor;[2] and, in the absence of any contract to the contrary, the death of the surety operates as a revocation of a "Continuing Guarantee," so far as regards future transactions.[3] Two persons who are primarily liable to a third person may agree amongst themselves that one of them shall only be liable on the default of the other. But where the creditor is not a party to this arrangement he is not affected by it, although he may have been aware of its existence.[4] Here the Indian Law departs from the rule recognized by English Courts that the creditor, having notice that the relation of principal and surety exists between his co-debtors, is affected by the consequences of that relation.[5] But the provision of the Contract Act does not prevent a person who accepts bills of exchange for the accommodation of another from pleading that he was only an "accommodation acceptor." This was so held in a suit brought by the Bank of Bengal, and the decision proceeded on the ground that the liability which is undertaken by the acceptor and the drawer of a bill is in no sense a joint liability. No doubt each of them contracts to pay the same sum of money, but they contract severally in different ways, and subject to different conditions.[6] The rights and obligations which arise out of a Contract of Guarantee may be considered from a three-fold aspect, as affecting the creditor, the principal-debtor, and, where there are two or more sureties, the sureties themselves. Thus, in his relation to the surety, while, as we have seen, the creditor can proceed against him alone without joining the principal-debtor as a co-defendant, he cannot, without the consent of the surety, vary the terms of the contract between

[1] IX. Beng. L. R. 364.

[2] Section 130, *Indian Contract Act.*

[3] Section 131, *Ibid.*

[4] Section 132, *Ibid.*

[5] *Wythes* v. *Labouchere*, 3 De G. & J. 593.

[6] I. L. R. III. Cal. at p. 184.

CHAP. VIII.

Discharge of surety.

himself and the principal-debtor. Any such variance made without the consent of the surety has the effect of discharging the latter as to all transactions subsequent to the variance.[1] Thus a lessee agreeing to pay rent at a higher rate without consent of his surety, is a "variance" discharging the latter.[2] So also it has been held, following a long current of authorities in England, that the acceptance of interest in advance by the creditor has the effect of giving time to the principal-debtor, and consequently operates as a discharge to the surety.[3] But of course, if the surety consents to such an arrangement he is not discharged.[4] Mere forbearance, however, on the part of the creditor to sue the principal-debtor or to enforce any other remedy against him does not, in the absence of any provision in the guarantee to the contrary, discharge the surety.[5] Again the variance must be in the terms of the contract *between the principal and the creditor*. Thus a contract made with a third person to give time to the principal-debtor does not operate as a discharge of the surety.[6] Nor will a release of one surety discharge the others, nor even free the surety so released from his responsibility to the other sureties.[7] Under the Negotiable Instruments Act, 1881, it is also competent to the holder of an accepted bill, when giving time or otherwise dealing with the acceptor in a manner which would discharge the other parties, to expressly reserve his right to charge the other parties, and in such case they would not be discharged.[8] As between the surety and the principal-debtor, the latter is under an implied promise to indemnify the surety, who is entitled on his part to recover from the principal-debtor whatever sum he has *rightfully* paid under the

Relation between surety and principal-debtor.

[1] Section 133, *Indian Contract Act; Polak* v. *Everett*, 1 Q. B. D. 673, 674, approved in *Greenwood and another* v. *Francis*, Times, 20th Dec., 1898, p. 12.

[2] I. L. R. III. Allah. 9.

[3] I. L. R. IV. Cal. 134.

[4] Section 135, *Indian Contract Act;* I. L. R. VI. Cal. 241 (P. C.).

[5] Section 137, *Indian Contract Act;* I. L. R. V. Bomb. 651.

[6] Section 136, *Ibid.*

[7] Section 138, *Ibid.*

[8] Section 39, Act XXVI. of 1881.

CHAP. VIII. Guarantee, but no sums which he has paid *wrongfully*.[1] Thus it has been held that where a surety by signing a balance of account and acknowledging the balance to be due deprived himself of the benefit of a plea of limitation which was successfully raised by the principal-debtor, he could not recover from the latter the amount which he had been compelled to pay under the decree against him. In other words the decision proceeded upon the ground that a moral obligation to pay a debt barred by limitation is no sufficient reason why a surety should, by discharging it to satisfy his own conscience, impose a legal liability on a third person.[2] Where the surety pays rightfully he is invested with all the rights which the creditor had against the principal debtor.[3] Thus under the Indian Contract Act he is entitled to the benefit of every security which the creditor has against the principal-debtor *at the time when the contract of suretyship is entered into*, whether he knew of its existence or not; and if the creditor loses, or, without the consent of the surety, parts with such security, the surety is discharged to the extent of the value of the security.[4] But the weight of authority in England appears to be in favour of extending the benefit even to securities acquired by the creditor subsequently.[5] As between several sureties each is liable, in the absence of any contract to the contrary, to pay an equal share of the whole debt, or of that part of it which remains unpaid by the principal-debtor.[6] And if one of them is compelled to pay the whole

[1] Section 145, *Indian Contract Act*. He is also entitled to interest on monies paid on the principal's account. No. 98, *Punjab Record*, 1881.

[2] No. 30, *Punjab Record*, 1878. *Cf.* No. 7, *Punjab Record*, 1882 (Privy Council), as to right of surety to compel principal to indemnify him for sums which he had been compelled to pay as security in a Foreign State, where contract was to be performed.

[3] Section 140, *Indian Contract Act*. *Cf.* 50 L. J. Ch. 355.

[4] Section 141, *Ibid*.

[5] *Forbes* v. *Jackson*, L. R. 19 Ch. D. 615; S. C. 51 Ch. D. 690.

[6] Section 146, *Indian Contract Act*. As between several sureties, in a suit by one for contribution, only such defences are available as one principal may have against another principal. Per Lord Justice Smith in *Greenwood and another* v. *Francis*, Times, 20 Dec. 1898, p. 12.

debt he can compel the others to contribute.[1] But the co-sureties may bind themselves to the creditor in different sums, and in such a case they are all liable to pay equally as far as the limits of their respective obligations permit. Thus, suppose A., B., and C., as sureties for D., enter into three several bonds, each in a different penalty, namely, A. in the penalty of Rs. 10,000, B. in that of Rs. 20,000, C. in that of Rs. 40,000, conditioned for D.'s duly accounting to E., D. makes default to the extent of Rs. 30,000, A., B., and C., are each liable to pay Rs. 10,000 ?[2]

Indemnity.

239. A contract by which one party promises to save the other from loss caused to him by the conduct of the promisor himself, or by the conduct of any other person, is called a "Contract of Indemnity."[3] The Indian Law defines the rights and liabilities of an indemnity-holder or promisee, but says nothing of those of the promisor. The former is entitled to recover from the promisor all damages, costs and sums which he may be compelled to pay in any suit in respect of any matter to which the promise to indemnify applies. It may be express or implied.[4] Thus where the plaintiff offered to give up certain trucks on being indemnified, and the defendants without saying anything took the trucks, it was held that there was an implied promise to indemnify.[5] It is

[1] No. 86, *Punjab Record*, 1868. A surety against whom judgment has been obtained by the principal creditor for the full amount of the guarantee, but who has paid nothing in respect thereof, can maintain an action against a co-surety to compel him to contribute towards the common liability; and for this purpose the allowance of a claim by the principal creditor against the estate of a deceased surety is equivalent to a judgment; and where the principal creditor is a party to the action, the surety may obtain an order upon the co-surety to pay his proportion to the principal creditor. Where the principal creditor is not a party, he may obtain a prospective order directing the co-surety, upon payment by the surety of his own share, to indemnify him against further liability. *Wolmerhausen* v. *Gullick*, (1893) Ch. 514.

[2] Section 147, *Indian Contract Act*.

[3] Section 124, *Ibid*.

[4] Section 125, *Ibid*. *Cf.* I. L. R. V. Cal. 811.

[5] *Dugdale* v. *Lovering*, L. R. 10 C. P. 196.

CHAP. VIII.

also implied in every Contract of Agency with respect to all acts done by the agent in good faith.[1] But if the act which the agent is employed to perform is criminal, the promise on the part of the principal to indemnify him is illegal and therefore void.[2] This is upon the principal that "there is no contribution between wrong-doers."[3] The promisor like a surety is probably entitled to the benefit of every remedy by which the person indemnified could have protected himself against, or reimbursed himself for the loss.[4]

240. Contracts by way of Security, such as Mortgage, Pledge, Lien, and Hypothec have already been dealt with, and need no further explanation.[5] The same may be said of Warranty [6] and Ratification.[7]

Rights *quasi ex contractu*.

241. We have now concluded our examination of those Rights "in personam" which arise directly from Contracts. But there are other personal Rights which arise out of certain relations resembling those created by contract and which are said to create Obligations *quasi ex contractu*. These must now be considered. The Roman Jurists included all such cases in a residuary class under the general denomination *obligationes ex variis causarum figuris*.[8] Obligations of this kind are similar in their subject-matter to Contractual Obligations, but whereas these latter arise from agreements which are *intended* to produce an actionable obligation between the contracting parties, the primary object of the former is *not* the creation of an Obligation. Hence they are really not contracts at all, but are said to arise *quasi ex contractu*: "as it were from Contract," to show that the conception to which they serve as an index is connected with the conception with

Obligations arising from various kinds of causes.

[1] Section 223, *Indian Contract Act*. [2] Section 224, *Ibid.*
[3] See Pollock's *Law of Torts*, pp. 170, 171.
[4] Per Lord Cairns, L. C., in *Simpson* v. *Thomson*, 3 App. Cas. 284.
[5] *Vide* paras. 166—173, 180, 181, *ante*.
[6] Para. 228a, *ante*, p. 266.
[7] Para. 205, *ante*. [8] Dig. XLIV. 7, 1 pr.

which the comparison is instituted by a strong superficial analogy or resemblance.[1] They are also said to arise *ex lege*, because "although the person of incidence has not undertaken a special duty to the person of inherence, yet the law casts that duty upon him, as if he had so undertaken it."[2] They aim at the restoration of a benefit, or the equivalent thereof, conferred by the claimant but unjustly retained by the defendant.[3]

Chap. VIII.

Examples of.

242. Amongst Obligations of this class may be included the following :—

(*a*) A claim for necessaries suitable to his condition of life, supplied to a person incapable of contracting, or on his account.[4] Such a claim must be satisfied from the property of the person to whom or on whose account the necessaries are supplied. By English law the incapable person would also be personally liable, but the Indian Act in refusing to recognise his capacity to contract, would appear to exclude such a personal liability.[5] On the other hand, by English Civil Law "a father who gives no authority, and enters into no contract, is no more liable for goods supplied to his son, than a brother or an uncle, or a mere stranger would be."[6] But the Indian Act in entire accordance with the humane spirit of the Hindu Law assumes that a parent *is* civilly liable to support his children,[7] just as it

[1] Maine, *Ancient Law*, 7th ed. 344.

[2] Holland's *Jurisprudence*, pp. 182, 183.

[3] Keener, *Selection of Cases on the Law of Quasi-Contract*, cited by Holland, p. 215, 6th ed.

[4] Section 68, *Indian Contract Act*.

[5] Section 11, *Ibid.* *Cf.* para. 200, *ad fin.*

[6] *Mortimore* v. *Wright*, 6 M. & W. 482. But 31 & 32 Vict. c. 122, section 37, makes it an offence, punishable summarily, wilfully to neglect to provide adequate food, clothing, medical aid, or lodging for his child, being in his custody, under the age of fourteen years. *R.* v. *Downes*, L. R. 1 Q. B. D. 25.

[7] Section 68, Illust: (*b*).

CHAP. VIII.

recognises in another direction the motives of gratitude and natural affection (subject to certain forms) as furnishing a sufficient consideration for a promise.[1] Thus Manu ordains that a mother and a father in their old age, a virtuous wife, and an infant son must be maintained even though by doing a hundred times that which ought not to be done.[2] The person who refuses to support his parents, his wife, and his children ought to be punished by the king.[3] The pre-Islamic law recognised no obligation on the part of either of the parents to maintain their children, nor was any relation bound to maintain any other. But the Muhammadan law introduced a change in this respect, and we now find it expressly stated in the Hedaya not only that "the maintenance of minor children rests on their father," but it would seem that "no person can be his associate or partner in furnishing it."[4]

Reimbursement of person paying money due.

(b) The right of a person who is *interested* in the payment of money, which another is bound by law to pay, or, as the English Law expresses the rule, who *is compellable by law to pay it*, and who therefore pays it, to be reimbursed by the other.[5] Thus, where a sub-lessee pays rent to a superior landlord, for which the intermediate lessee is liable under a covenant he is entitled to be reimbursed.[6] So is the amount paid for costs in defending a suit brought against a minor, which if successful would have

[1] Section 25, cl. 1 and 2, *Indian Contract Act*. *Cf.* Anson's *Law of Contracts*, p. 80.

[2] Siromani's *Commentary on the Hindu Law*, Chap. VIII. p. 252.

[3] *Manu*, Chap. VIII. 389.

[4] Amir Ali's *Personal Law*, pp. 288—296.

[5] Section 69, *Indian Contract Act*. *Cf.* I. L. R. IV. Bomb. 643; VI. *Ibid.* 244.

[6] I. L. R. IV. Cal. 369.

deprived him of property;[1] and so is also money paid by the mortgagee of a *patni* tenure to save the same from sale under Regulation VIII. of 1819.[2] Thus also, under English Law, where the mortgagees of a ship, who had taken possession, paid off the wages due to the crew from the owners for the purpose of liberating her from proceedings in the Court of Admiralty.[3] Where, however, a husband paid the premia on a life policy belonging to his wife, not being under any contract with his wife so to do, and not being under any mistake as to his title to the policy, it was held that he had no lien on the policy as against her.[4] Nor is it in every case in which a person has been benefited by the money of another, that an obligation to repay that money arises. The question is not to be determined by nice considerations of what may be fair or proper according to the highest morality. To support such a suit, there must be an obligation, express or implied, to repay.[5]

Of person enjoying benefit of non-gratuitous act.

(*c*) That of a person who lawfully does[6] anything for another person, or delivers anything to him, *not intending to do so gratuitously*, and such other person

[1] I. L. R. VII. Cal. 140.

[2] I. L. R. (1897), 25 Cal. 305.

[3] *Johnson* v. *Royal Mail Steam Packet Co.*, L. R. 3 C. P. 38.

[4] *Leslie* v. *French*, 23 Ch. D. 552.

[5] L. R. 2 Ind. App. at p. 143. The general rule of English Law is that no man can make himself the creditor of another by paying that other's debt against his will or without his consent. *Per* Willes, J., in *Johnson* v. *Royal Mail Steam Packet Co.*, L. R. 3 C. P. 43. So in the case cited in the text, the Privy Council say (at p. 143) it is well settled that there is no obligation in the case of a voluntary payment by A. of B.'s debt. See, however, what is said below as to the liability of a person accepting the benefit of an act not *intended* to be gratuitous.

[6] This term includes the payment of money for another. I. L. R. XII. Cal. 213. And a payment may be *lawfully* made, although the payer has no actual interest in making it. It is enough that it is made in good faith in the belief that he has an interest. I. L. R. VII. Cal. 573.

enjoys the benefit thereof, to receive compensation from the latter in respect of, or to compel him to restore, the thing so done or delivered.[1] In the Roman Law a person who rendered a voluntary service of this kind was called a "negotiorum gestor;" and both he and the person for whom the service was rendered were under a mutual liability which was said neither to arise from contract nor from tort, but for convenience sake (*neque ex contractu neque ex maleficio sed utilitatis causa*).[2] Thus he who meddled in another man's affairs in his absence was bound to use the most perfect care (*ad exactissimam diligentiam compellitur reddere*), and to render an account of his management.[3] On the other hand he was entitled to be reimbursed for whatever he had expended to the other's advantage, and to be indemnified for any personal liability incurred by him in the interest of the other party.[4] The English law requires that the benefit should be conferred on the defendant at his request under circumstances which raise an implied promise of payment. But it is not necessary that the "request" should be expressly made: it may be implied.[5]

[1] Section 70, *Indian Contract Act*. *Cf.* I. L. R. V. Allah. 400. But it has been recently held by the majority of a full Bench of the Calcutta High Court that there is no general rule of equity to the effect that whoever, having an interest in an estate, makes a payment in order to save the estate, obtains a charge on the estate; and therefore, in the absence of a statutory enactment, a co-sharer who has paid the whole revenue, and thus saved the estate, does not, by reason of such payment, acquire a charge on the share of his defaulting co-sharer. I. L. R. XIV. Cal. 809.

[2] Dig. XLIV. 7, 5 pr.; Just. *Inst.* 3, 27, 1.

[3] Just. *Inst.* 3, 27, 1.

[4] Dig. III. 5, 2.

[5] "Whether the request be direct, as where the party is expressly desired by the defendant to pay; or indirect, as where he is placed by him under a liability to pay, and *does pay*, makes no difference." *Brittain* v. *Lloyd*, 14 M. & W. 762.

The person benefited must, however, be in a position to exercise a free option to accept or refuse the tendered service, otherwise no promise to pay for it will be implied. Thus, in the case of *Boulton* v. *Jones*,[1] already mentioned,[2] where goods were ordered from one tradesman and supplied by his successor in business, without any notification of the change to the defendant, and the defendant received the goods and consumed them, it was held that as defendant had not contracted with the plaintiff, and had no option of refusing the goods, but was allowed to act upon the supposition that they were sent by the tradesman from whom they were ordered, the defendant was not liable for their price. Under the Indian Contract Act the result must have been different. For under that Act, if a tradesman leave goods at B.'s house by mistake, and B. treats them as his own, he is bound to pay A. for them.[3] It is important to notice that under the Indian Act compensation is not payable unless the defendant actually derives *benefit* from the Act or service rendered. Thus if a person in endeavouring to rescue another's property from imminent danger incurs outlay, but notwithstanding his efforts the property is wholly destroyed, the owner of the property would not apparently be legally bound to pay him for his services, or even to reimburse him for actual expenses.[4] So a person who is employed to sell on the terms of receiving remuneration on

CHAP. VIII.

[1] 2 H. & A. 564; S. C., 27 L. J. Exch. 117. *Cf.* also *Taylor* v. *Laird*, 25 L. J. Exch, 329.

[2] Para. 216, *ante*.

[3] Illust. (*a*), section 70, *Indian Contract Act*. *Cf.* also section 72, *Ibid.*

[4] Cunningham and Shepherd's *Indian Contract Act*, p. 204, 6th Ed.; Stokes's *Anglo-Indian Codes*, Vol. I. p. 533.

CHAP. VIII.

the sale is not entitled to be remunerated for work done in the mere attempt to sell.[1]

Of finder of goods.

(*d*) The responsibility of a finder of goods to take such care of the goods as a man of ordinary prudence would, under similar circumstances, take of his own goods.[2] If such care is taken the finder is not responsible for the loss or deterioration of the goods in his custody.[3] The right of the finder of a lost article to retain possession of it against all parties but the real owner, has already been considered.[4]

Of person receiving money paid under mistake or coercion.

(*e*) To return money paid by mistake or under coercion.[5]

The form in which this obligation is enforced in the English law is by an action "for money had and received." But according to that law there is this limitation to the rule, that the mistake must be one of fact and not of law.[6] The English Courts have recently, however, engrafted an exception upon this general principle, which is said to have been adopted for the purpose of putting an end to litigation, by laying down that although a private person may take advantage of it to retain money which has been paid to him under a mistake of law, a Court of Justice will not do so itself, and it will not allow its own officer to act so. On the contrary, it will direct its officer to do that which any high-minded man would do, *viz.*, not to take advantage of such a mistake. Thus, if money is paid under a mistake of law to the trustee

[1] Cunningham and Shepherd's *Indian Contract Act*, p. 204, 6th ed.; Stokes's *Anglo-Indian Codes*, Vol. I. p. 533.

[2] Sections 71 and 151, *Indian Contract Act*.

[3] Section 152, *Ibid.*

[4] Para. 139, *ante*.

[5] Section 72, *Indian Contract Act*. *Cf.* I. L. R. I. Allah. 79; II. *Ibid.* 674; IV. *Ibid.* 6, 19; I. L. R. XV. Cal. 665; L. R. 11 App. Cas. 84. *Cf.* also amongst English authorities, *Green* v. *Duckett*, 11 Q. B. D. 275; and *Atkinson* v. *Denby*, 30 L. J. Exch. 361. *Cf.* also section 86 of the *Indian Trusts Act*.

[6] *Bilbie* v. *Lumley*, 2 East, 469; *Stevens* v. *Lynch*, 12 East, 38; *Brisbane* v. *Dacres*, 5 Taunt. 143.

in a bankruptcy, or to an officer of a Court of Common Law, the Court will order him to repay it as soon as the mistake is discovered.[1] In India it would seem that the legislature has drawn no distinction between the right to receive money paid under a mistake of fact and under a mistake of law: in either case the action would apparently be maintainable. But both in England and in India a money payment, not really recoverable, made under compulsion of law, *i.e.*, under pressure of execution proceedings, may be recovered back.[2] So again money paid in discharge of a decree which is subsequently reversed by a superior court may be recovered back.[3] It is also the prevailing view that a suit will lie to recover money which a judgment-debtor pays out of Court to his creditor, but which the latter fails to certify to the Court.[4]

Compensation for failure to discharge obligations arising out of *quasi-contracts*.

243. It only remains to be added that where the Obligation resulting from a *quasi-contract* has not been discharged, any person injured by the failure is entitled to receive the same compensation from the party in default, as if such person had contracted to discharge the Obligation and had broken his contract.[5]

Rights against Official persons or Corporate Bodies.

244. Private persons may also at times have the right to compel Public Officers or Corporate Bodies to exercise their functions, if the non-exercise thereof would injuriously affect their property, franchise, or other personal Right. Actions to enforce Rights of this kind are regulated in India by express rules, and can only be asserted in certain of the High Courts.[6] But in this connection it is important to observe

[1] *Ex parte Simmonds*, L. R. 14 Q. B. D. 308.

[2] I. L. R. VII. Cal. 648 (P. C.). *Cf.* also 12 Moore, Ind. App. 65.

[3] 10 Moore, Ind. App. 203; I. L. R. III. Cal. 30.

[4] I. L. R. III. Allah. 533, 538; I. L. R. VIII. Mad. 277 (F. B.); I. L. R. IX. Cal. 788; and No. 83, *Punjab Record*, 1884 (F. B.). But see *contra*, I. L. R. XI. Bomb. 6 (F. B.).

[5] Section 73, para. 3, *Indian Contract Act*.

[6] Chap. VIII., *Indian Specific Relief Act*, 1877.

CHAP. VIII. that public corporations to which an obligation to keep public roads and bridges in repair has been transferred are not liable to an action in respect of mere non-feasance, unless the legislature has shown an intention to impose such liability upon them. Thus in an action for damages for injuries caused by the neglect of the appellant municipality to repair a bridge, it was held, following *Sanitary Commissioners of Gibraltar* v. *Orfila*,[1] that by the County Incorporations Act, 1879, under which it was incorporated, that there was no indication of an intention to impose the liability sought to be enforced.[2]

[1] 15 App. Cas. 411.

[2] *Municipality of Pictou* v. *Geldert*, (1893) A. C. 524 (P. C.).

CHAPTER IX.

PRIVATE LAW.—THE PROTECTION OF RIGHTS.

245. "RIGHT is not mere theory, but living force" is the thesis upon which a late eminent German Jurist constructed his now famous doctrine of the "Battle for Right."[1] In a well-regulated state of society the Scales and the Sword personify Justice, the former typifying that they are intended to weigh out and adjudge to each of the contending parties his fair share of Right, the latter that it is meant to defend, if need be, the administration of Justice from all external interference. But in more primitive and unsettled times the Scales are wanting and the Sword is wielded by brute force. As observed by Carlyle in his scathing criticism of the charge of the Lord Chief Justice (Cockburn) to the grand jury in the celebrated Governor Eyre's case, "Unwritten if you will, but real and fundamental, anterior to all written laws and first making written laws possible, there must have been, and is and will be, coeval with human society from its beginnings to its ultimate end, an actual martial law of more validity than any other law whatever." In a rudely-constituted society, in which the elements of a State are still in the concrete, each individual in the community is left to work out his own remedy for any wrong he may have suffered at the hands of another.[2] The measure of his right to redress is regulated by no other standard than his own

CHAP. IX.

Self-help.

[1] *Der Kampf um's Recht.* Von Rudolph von Ihering.

[2] *Geist des römischen Rechts*, Vol. I., pp. 120—122, Leipzig, 1878.

sense of the wrong inflicted, and his power to obtain redress depends on the physical power he is able to command. The only controlling voice is that of popular Justice, which, no doubt, to a certain extent, may be presumed to exercise a moral and physical influence to prevent a tyrannical use of Self-help. But the spirit of the Ancient Law is a spirit of Revenge, which is best expressed in the Jewish canon of "an eye for an eye, a tooth for a tooth."[1] It is a spirit completely in harmony with the social conditions of a time, characterized by a hot blooded and vindictive desire of retaliation on the part of the injured party. Such a spirit, at once violent and revengeful, refuses to submit to wrong, and evolves for itself the maxim: "Do not allow your right to be trampled with impunity under another's feet."[2] But under the humanizing influence of advancing civilization the omnipotence of Self-help, which is at least a rude substitute for redress at the hands of the constituted organs in a well-regulated State, gradually submits to one limitation after another until it is for the most part superseded by judicial remedies. The need of some agency to determine disputes as to Rights is soon felt, and the good offices of some mutual friend or respected grey-beard are perhaps invoked to settle the contest, or recourse is had to the altar of some prescient Deity, whose priest announces the decision with all the authority of inspired wisdom, or the parties may agree to abide by the oath of one of them. A further development brings us to a point of time when the State has itself undertaken the task of deciding such disputes, and we then have the Judge, representing the sovereignty of the state, substituted for the private arbitrator, and the extra judicial oath is transformed into the solemn oath administered to witnesses in the course of a legal trial. The personal energy which

[1] *Geist des römischen Rechts*, Vol. I., p. 126; Dauz's *Der Sacrale*, section 2, p. 7.

[2] Kant, *Metaphysische Anfangsgrunde der Tugendlehre*, 2nd ed. p. 185.

gave birth to the theory of Self-help is now superseded by the higher energy of the Supreme Power of the State, and the ancient formula of what may be called the survival of the Fist Law, "*ego tibi manum iniicio*" (I lay my hand upon thee) is substituted by that of the later law: *si quidem habeat rem, manu* MILITARI OFFICIO JUDICIS *ab eo possessio transfertur*, when possession can only be forcibly taken from another through the intervention of the constituted Judicial Authority, and by the compulsory means at the disposal of the judge: if need be, by the hand of the soldier.[1] It is now recognized that Self-help, as an expression of individual caprice which in its effect is unreliable and indefinite, is contrary to the nature of legal order.[2] Accordingly the rule is established that "that which can come about publicly through the magistrate must not be committed to individuals, that opportunity may not be afforded of making greater disturbance."[3] Thus it is that the place of Self-help is at last taken by Procedure, to make good before a Court the right which has been violated, by investigation and establishment of what is in dispute, and by judicial relief.[4] And with the introduction of Procedure the Club-law and Fist-law (the *manum conserere*) recede into a barbarous Past.[5] But the old notion of Self-help is still not completely eradicated, and even the modern law permits its exercise in certain exceptional circumstances. Thus every person is declared to have a right, subject to certain restrictions, which the Indian Law is careful to specify with great precision,[6] to defend—

First—His own body, and the body of any other person against any offence affecting the human body.

Secondly—The property, whether moveable or immove-

[1] Dig. VI. 1, 28, and 68; Cod. 7, 53, 7.

[2] Salkowski's *Roman Private Law*, section 23, p. 48.

[3] Dig. L. 17, 176 pr.

[4] Salkowski's *Roman Private Law*, p. 119.

[5] *Geist des römischen Rechts*, Vol. I., p. 150.

[6] See sections 99—106, *Indian Penal Code*.

CHAP. IX.

able, of himself or of any other person, against any act which is an offence falling under the definition of theft, robbery, mischief, or criminal trespass, or which is an attempt to commit any of these offences.[1]

246. Now the regular and ordinary protection of a Right consists in the judicial recognition of an actually existing Right, which is vindicated against some violation that has either (*a*) already occurred, or (*b*) that is threatened. In the latter case the law interferes with the view of "prevention," in the former with that of "redress." The remedy in the one case assumes the form of an Injunction, which is granted to *prevent* the breach of an obligation existing in favour of the applicant; in the other of an "Action," which is granted to enable the person of inherence from losing, or the person of incidence from gaining, from a *breach* of an obligation which has already *occurred*.

Perpetual and Temporary Injunctions.

247. Injunctions may be either Perpetual or Temporary, according as they are unlimited or limited as to time, and they may be granted either for the purpose of restraining a breach of contract or the commission of a tort. In India the former class of Injunctions is regulated by the Specific Relief Act,[2] and the latter by the provisions of the Code of Civil Procedure.[3] As a general rule a Perpetual Injunction is only granted where damages would not be an adequate remedy, and a Temporary Injunction only where delay would make it impossible or highly difficult to do complete justice at a later stage.[4]

Right of Action.

248. In a formal or processual sense "Actio" means simply the act of proceeding, and is the term applied to the judicial prosecution of a Right. But in a material sense it is the Right to the institution of a judicial process, *jus judicio*

[1] Section 97, *Indian Penal Code*.
[2] Chap. X., Act I. of 1877.
[3] Sections 492 and 493, I. P. C.
[4] Pollock's *Law of Torts*, pp. 166, 167.

persequendi,[1] which is generally known as a "Right of Action" (*Das Klagerecht*), and for the foundation of which a Private Right must exist, or, at least, be asserted to exist.[2] The "Right of Action" is thus, on the one hand, not to be confounded with the antecedent Right upon which it is based, of which it is merely an adjunct or "immanent quality" (*immanente eigenschaft der Rechte*). But, on the other hand, it is impossible to disconnect it from the Right from a violation of which it arises.[3] The right and the action, in fact, are linked to each other by the closest ties: the former is the creator, while the action is the creature.[4] In other words, the Antecedent Right is converted by the violation of it by another into a "Right of Action," which is explained by the Roman Jurist Celsus to be "nothing else than the Right to sue in Court for that which is due to one."[5] The decision of the Judge only serves to make manifest either the pre-existence or non-existence of the Right.

Real and Personal Actions.

249. In the Roman Law Actions were divided into impersonal or real (*in rem*) and personal (*in personam*), the latter arising out of Obligations, and directed originally against a certain (*i.e.*, the obliged) person, the former arising out of legal relations by which a right of the person entitled is vindicated against every third person. The *actio in personam* contemplates the giving, doing, or performing something, while the *actio in rem* is directed against the possessor of the thing, and is that by which we either claim that a corporal thing is ours, or that some right belongs to us, *e.g.*, of *usus*, or usufruct.[6] This classification has to a certain extent been preserved in modern systems of law, and thus in England and the United States of America a suit to enforce a

[1] Dig. XLIV. 7, 51.

[2] *Cf.* Dig. L. 17, 15.

[3] *Beitrage zur Theorie des Klagerechts*, von Dr. Alexander Plosz, Leipzig, 1880, p. 32.

[4] *The Pandects*, by J. E. Goudsmit, § III. 87, p. 245, Eng. trans.

[5] Dig. XLIV. 7, 51; Just. *Inst.* 4, 6, pr.

[6] *Gaius*, IV. 2, 3.

CHAP. IX. Maritime Lien or to obtain a Divorce is regarded as a proceeding *in rem*. The object of the process in the Admiralty Court is to obtain the thing itself, or a satisfaction out of it, for some claim resting on a real or *quasi* proprietary right in it.[1] So in an action for Divorce the object of the proceeding is to change the *status* (the *res*) of the parties established by the relation of marriage, and so far the proceeding is one *in rem*. When the decree relates to the custody of the children it is also *in rem*, but so far as it relates to property-rights, alimony, and the like, it is properly a proceeding *in personam*.[2] The attachment of property as a process of execution bears some analogy to, but is not strictly, a proceeding *in rem*.[3] In India judgments, orders, or decrees of a competent Court in the exercise of Probate, Matrimonial, or Insolvency jurisdiction, which confer upon or take away from any person any legal character, or which declare any person to be entitled to any such character, or to be entitled to any specific thing, not as against any specified person but absolutely, are regarded as Judgments *in rem*, which operate as conclusive proof against the whole world of the existence or non-existence of the legal character or title which they confer, declare, or take away.[4]

Cause of Action.

250. In our modern system the antecedent Private Right is the Title (*klagerechtstitel*) by virtue of which we claim redress for the infringement or violation, which is the ground or subject-matter of the Action.[5] Hence modern Jurists consider the term "*Actio*" from a two-fold aspect, that is to say, from a material and a processual aspect. In the former

[1] Hawes's *Jurisdiction of Courts*, section 92, San Francisco, 1886.

[2] *Ibid.* section 95.

[3] *Ibid.* section 245.

[4] Section 41, *Indian Evidence Act* (I. of 1872). *Cf.* II. Mad. H. C. Repts. 276, and 7 Sutherland's *Weekly Reporter*, 338, where the subject of judgments *in rem* is exhaustively considered. See also I. L. R. IV. Cal. 171 (F. B.).

[5] Plosz's *Beitrage zur Theorie des Klagerechts*, pp. 37, 38.

it is held to denote the Right of the plaintiff, in the latter the Act of the person resorting to judicial aid for the enforcement of his Right.[1] Accordingly, when we speak of a *causa actionis* (Ger. *Klagerecht*), we mean not only the immediate Fact which occasions an appeal to the "established organs of legal protection,"[2] but also the Right which has been violated thereby, which is regarded as the *causa proxima actionis.*[3] Now a Cause of Action in a processual aspect may, speaking very generally, be said to arise (*actio nascitur*) either in consequence of the infringement of a Right *ex contractu* or *ex delicto*, that is to say, either in consequence of wrongful acts which are breaches of Contract, or of Wrongs which are "independent of Contract."

Object of the Action.

Compensation.

251. In the case of a wrongful act which constitutes a breach of Contract, the object of the Action may be either Compensation or Specific Performance. In the former case the Compensation must be limited to the loss and damage which arose in the usual course of things from the breach of Contract, or which the parties knew, when they made the Contract, to be likely to result from the breach of it.[4] But in estimating the loss or damage arising from a breach of Contract the means which existed of remedying the inconvenience caused by the non-performance of the Contract must be taken into consideration.[5] In the English Law a distinction is drawn between *liquidated damages* and what is called a *penalty*, but the Indian Legislature has not preserved this distinction.[6] Thus, the Indian Contract Act enacts that "when a Contract has been broken, if a sum is named in the Contract as the amount to be paid in case of such breach, the party complaining of the breach is entitled, whether or not

Distinction between *liquidated damages* and *penalty* abolished in India.

[1] Savigny's *System*, Vol. V., section 4, pr. pp. 5, 6; Arndt's *Pandekten*, 196, p. 134. [2] Lenz *Recht des Besitzes*, pp. 40, 41.

[3] *Cf.* No. 71, *Punjab Record*, 1883.

[4] Section 73, *Indian Contract Act*. [5] *Ibid.* explanation.

[6] I. L. R. I. Mad. 349; III. *Ibid.* 228.

CHAP. IX. actual damage or loss is proved to have been caused thereby, to receive from the party who has broken the Contract *reasonable compensation not exceeding the amount so named.*"[1] The effect of this provision is to give the Courts a discretion in every case—except where a bond is given for the performance of a public duty or act in which the public are interested, and for which a special rule exists[2]—to award less but not more than the sum named in the Contract as the amount to be paid in case of breach.[3] But the discretion ought to be exercised with care, caution, and on sound principles, and not arbitrarily. As a general principle the damages decreed ought to be commensurate with the injury sustained, with the view of restoring to the party who has suffered from the breach of Contract such advantage as might reasonably have been in contemplation of the parties had the breach never occurred. And where *ex necessitate rei* it is impossible to fix the amount of damages actually resulting from a breach of Contract, the rule generally adopted by Courts of Equity is not to interfere with the Contract of the parties, who, in anticipation of the breach of Contract, have stipulated that a fixed sum shall be regarded as the measure of compensation to be paid by the person who violates the Contract.[4] But the party who suffers from the breach may also, according to the English and Indian law, in certain

[1] Section 74, *Indian Contract Act.* [2] See exception, *Ibid.*

[3] I. L. R. VIII. Cal. 286; IX. *Ibid.* 692.

[4] I. L. R. V. Allah. 258. As to agreements to pay an enhanced rate of interest if principal and interest are not paid on due date, see I. L. R. VI. Allah. 63, 64, 197; I. L. R. IX. Cal. 615, 689; I. L. R. X. Mad. 203; I. L. R. X. Mad. 294; I. L. R. XII. Mad. 161; I. L. R. XIV. Bomb. 200; I. L. R. XV. Allah. 232. *Cf.* with these another class of cases where the enhanced interest is to be calculated from the date of the bond, and not to be payable in the future only. In the latter only a reasonable interest is claimable. I. L. R. III. Allah. 260, 441; I. L. R. VI. Mad. 167; I. L. R. XIII. Cal. 165; I. L. R. XVII. Mad. 62. The distinction is well discussed in Cunningham and Shepherd's *Contract Act*, pp. 224—226, 6th ed. *Cf.* also No. 135, P. R. 1889.

CHAP. IX.

Specific Relief.

cases, claim what is called "Specific Relief" either in conjunction with, or in substitution for, Compensation.[1] But in other systems this special remedy is not permitted upon the principle *nemo potest præcise cogi ad factum;* no one can be compelled to perform a thing.[2] In England and in India the remedy can be enforced by imprisonment of the defaulter, or by attachment of his property, or by both.[3]

How given.

Specific Relief is given in one of three ways: (*a*) by taking possession of certain property and delivering it to the claimant; (*b*) by ordering a party to do the very act which he is under an obligation to do; or (*c*) by preventing a party from doing what he is under an obligation not to do.[4]

In what cases.

Contracts which may be specifically enforced in India are the following:—[5]

(*a*) When the act agreed to be done is in the performance, wholly or partly, of a trust;

(*b*) When there exists no standard for ascertaining the actual damage caused by the non-performance of the act agreed to be done;

(*c*) When the act agreed to be done is such that pecuniary compensation for its non-performance would not afford adequate relief; or

(*d*) When it is probable that pecuniary compensation cannot be got for the non-performance of the act agreed to be done.

And by way of explanation the Indian Act lays down the further rule for the guidance of Courts, that unless and until the contrary is proved, the Court shall presume that the breach of a Contract to transfer immoveable property cannot be adequately relieved by compensation in money, and that the breach of a Contract to transfer moveable property can be thus relieved.

[1] Sections 12 and 19, Act I. of 1877; 21 & 22 Vict. c. 27.
[2] Holland's *Jurisprudence*, p. 267, n. (4).
[3] Section 260, Act XIV. of 1882.
[4] Section 5, Act I. of 1877.
[5] Section 12, *ibid.*

CHAP. IX.

Wrongs independent of Contract.

252. "Wrongs independent of Contract" are those which arise out of an act or omission (not being merely the breach of a duty arising out of a personal relation, such as that of a trustee or of husband and wife, or undertaken by Contract), which is related to harm suffered by a determinate person in the following ways:—[1]

(a) It may be an act which, without lawful justification or excuse, is intended by the agent to cause harm and does the harm complained of;

(b) By an act in itself contrary to law, or an omission of specific legal duty, which causes harm not intended by the persons acting or omitting;

(c) By an act or omission causing harm which the person so acting or omitting did not intend to cause, but might and should with due diligence have foreseen and prevented;

(d) In special cases, by not avoiding or preventing harm which the party was bound, absolutely or within limits, to avoid or prevent.

Torts.

Such wrongs in English Law are called Torts, a term derived from the French language, and are to be distinguished from Crimes as being "infringements or privations of the private or civil Rights belonging to individuals, considered as individuals, whereas Crimes are a breach of public Rights and Duties which affect the whole community, considered as a community."[2] A Tort may, therefore, be said to be a Civil Wrong, the liability for which is the result either of wilful injury to others, or wanton disregard of what is due to them (*dolus*), or of a failure to observe due care and caution which has similar, though not intended or expected, consequences (*culpa*).[3] And as observed by Sir Frederick Pollock,[4] the

Definition of.

[1] Pollock's *Law of Torts*, p. 19; *Cf. Draft Civil Wrongs Bill for India*, Part I., sections 8 and 9.

[2] Blackstone's *Commentaries*, Vol. IV. p. 4, ed. of 1876.

[3] Pollock's *Law of Torts*, p. 17.

[4] *Ibid.* p. 12.

whole law on the subject is but a development of the second of the three famous precepts borrowed by Justinian from a lost work of Ulpian,[1] which is said to constitute the fundamental principles of law, namely, *alterum non laedere:* to hurt no one. This precept indicates the moral standard which is inseparable from any civilized system of Jurisprudence, the non-recognition of which would reduce Society to a state little short of anarchy, where life would be unsafe, and property insecure. But this precept must not be so understood as to justify every sort of interference with the independent exercise of a right of property, simply because the intended exercise might hurt somebody. Thus the mere fact that a person has suffered some damage from the act of another will not necessarily make that act unlawful or actionable as a civil wrong. For in the lawful exercise of his right the person entitled is not compellable to consider the injurious consequences which may nevertheless result to another person, as, for instance, by setting up a rival trade. Nor could he be held answerable for such consequences. In cases of this nature the rule of law to be applied is, *qui, jure suo utitur, nemini facit injuriam* (*he who uses what is his own by law is deemed to injure no one*); and if any damage has resulted, it is treated as *damnum absque injuriâ:* damage without (legal) injury.[2]

Motive not considered.

252a. Again, it is equally important to bear in mind that, speaking generally, the law of England does not take into account *motive* as constituting an element of civil wrong. As lucidly explained by Lord Watson in the now celebrated case of *Allen* v. *Flood*,[3] "Any invasion of the civil rights of another person is in itself a legal wrong, carrying with it liability to repair its necessary consequences, in so far as they are injurious to the person whose right is infringed, whether the

[1] Dig. I. 1, 10, s. 1; Just. *Inst.* I. 1, 3.

[2] Weiske's *Rechtslexicon*, Bd. IX. tit. *Recht*, s. 147.

[3] (1898) A. C. at p. 92. *Cf.* also *Bradford Corporation* v. *Pickles*, (1895) A. C. 587.

motive which prompted it be good, bad, or indifferent. But the existence of a bad motive, in the case of an act which is not in itself illegal, will not convert that act into a civil wrong for which reparation is due. A wrongful act, done knowingly and with a view to its injurious consequences, may, in the sense of the law, be malicious; but such malice derives its essential character from the circumstance that the act done constitutes a violation of the law."

Classification of Wrongs.

253. To attempt to give an exhaustive list of such Wrongs for which the law allows a civil redress is beyond the scope of the present work, even if it were possible to do so with any degree of success. But the following grouping exhibits the more familiar and typical species of Torts under three well marked and easily intelligible divisions, which is perhaps the best classification that can be suggested.[1]

GROUP A.

Personal Wrongs.

1. Wrongs affecting safety and freedom of the person (*e.g.*, assault, false imprisonment).
2. Wrongs affecting personal relations in the family (*e.g.*, seduction, enticing away of servants).
3. Wrongs affecting reputation (*e.g.*, defamation).
4. Wrongs affecting a man in his estate, condition, and convenience of life generally (*e.g.*, deceit, slander of title, malicious prosecution, conspiracy).

GROUP B.

Wrongs to Property.

1. Trespass: (*a*) to land (*e.g.*, disturbance of easements, &c.).
   (*b*) to goods (*e.g.*, conversion, &c.).
2. Interference with Rights analogous to property (*e.g.*, patents, copyrights, &c.).

[1] Pollock's *Law of Torts*, p. 7. *Cf.* Mr. Justice Cave's classification of "personal rights" in *Allen* v. *Flood*, (1898) A. C. at p. 29.

GROUP C.

Wrongs to Person, Estate, and Property.

1. Nuisance.
2. Negligence.
3. Breach of absolute dealings specially attached to the occupation of fixed property, to the ownership and custody of dangerous things, and to the exercise of certain public callings.

254. Whenever an actionable Wrong has been done, the party wronged is entitled to recover damages, the measure of which is regulated in England by the Judge, while the amount is fixed by the Jury. In India where the Court exercises the functions of both Judge and Jury, it is the Judge who determines as well the principle upon which the damages are to be assessed, as the amount the plaintiff is entitled to recover. Damages may assume the form of *nominal*, *ordinary*, or *exemplary* damages, and a few words of explanation may here be offered as to each. Nominal damages are so called because they bear no relation even to the cost and trouble of suing, and the sum awarded is so small that it may be said to have "no existence in point of quantity." Such damages are only possible when an absolute Right is infringed, without any sensible harm being caused which may be estimable in a money compensation.[1] This is said to be an instance of *injuria sine damno*, which is nevertheless sufficient to found an action.[2] The object of the action in such cases is simply to vindicate the Right, and as every injury imports damage,[3] so the law meets the requirements of the case by allowing nominal damages for the invasion of the Right. Thus, a man may have an action

Measure of damages.

Nominal.

[1] Pollock's *Law of Torts*, p. 158.

[2] *Kali Kishen Tagore* v. *Judoo Lal Mullick* (1879), *Privy Council Judgments*, compiled by Baldeva Ram Dave, p. 289.

[3] Per Lord Holt, C. J., in *Ashby* v. *White*, 2 Lord Raym. at p. 955.

CHAP. IX.

against another for riding over his ground, though it do him no damage. But no action can be maintained where there is neither *damnum* nor *injuria*.[1] Thus where there is not an absolute duty to forbear from doing a certain thing, but only not to do it so as to cause actual damage, in all such cases the proof of real appreciable damage is the foundation of the

Ordinary.

plaintiff's right, and there is no question of nominal damages. Again, the proof of damage must be such as can be shown by a plain witness to a plain common juryman, and not merely such as the microscope of the naturalist, or the tests of the chemist, may possiby disclose. The law accordingly disregards results which are not made palpable to the ordinary senses of mankind. So if it were made out (in a case of alleged nuisance caused by smoke and deleterious vapours) that every minute a millionth of a grain of poison were absorbed by a tree, or a millionth of a grain of dust deposited upon a tree, that would not afford a ground for interference by injunction, although after the lapse of a million minutes the grains of poison or the grains of dust could be easily detected.[2] Hence it follows that whatever sum is awarded, whether large or small, it must afford a fair measure of compensation to the plaintiff with reference to the actual harm sustained by him. But the test of what is a fair sum under the circumstances is not necessarily that which it would cost to restore the plaintiff to his former condition. The law does not aim at restitution but compensation, and the true test is, what sum would afford under the circumstances of each particular case, a fair and reasonable compensation to the party wronged for the injury done him, the plaintiff's own estimate being regarded as the maximum limit. Damages

Exemplary.

awarded on this principle are called *ordinary*. It may happen, however, that a wrong is done to a man which is not only an

[1] *Kali Kishen Tagore* v. *Judoo Lal Mullick*, *supra*.

[2] Per James L. J., in *Galvin* v. *North Brancepeth Coal Co.* (1874), L. R. 9 Ch. at p. 709.

injury in the ordinary sense, but is in itself of so grave and reprehensible a character, or is done under such circumstances as aggravate the injury and import insult or outrage, that it is next to impossible to measure damages by any strict numerical rule. Thus, gross defamation, seduction of a man's daughter with deliberate fraud, a wanton trespass of land, persisted in with violent and intemperate behaviour, are instances where damages are covered by a well deserved disapproval of the defendant's conduct, and are said to be *exemplary* as expressing indignation at the character of the defendant's wrong rather than the value of the plaintiff's actual loss.[1]

Damages can only be claimed once for same cause of action.

255. It is a rule of procedure, founded on the obvious principle that it is the interest of the State that there should be an end of law suits (*interest reipublicæ ut sit finis litium*),[2] that every suit shall include the whole of the claim which the plaintiff is entitled to make in respect of the same Cause of Action.[3] As applied to Torts, this rule requires that damages resulting from one and the same cause of action must be claimed and assessed once for all. "When the whole thing," as Best, J., expressed it,[4] "has but one neck, and that neck has been cut off by the act of the defendant, there is but one right of action, and that is satisfied by one recovery." Thus a man who has had a verdict for personal injuries cannot bring a fresh action if he afterwards finds that his hurt was graver than he supposed.[5] So a man who has been beaten or wounded must sue for all his damage, past, present, and future, certain and contingent. He cannot maintain an action first for a broken arm, subsequently for a broken rib, even though he did not know of the latter injury when he

[1] Pollock's *Law of Torts*, pp. 162, 163.

[2] See an application of this maxim in *Ex parte March*, 67 L. T. 594; 9 Morrell, 286.

[3] Section 43, Act XIV. of 1882.

[4] *Richardson* v. *Mellish*, 2 Bing. 240.

[5] Pollock's *Law of Torts*, p. 165.

commenced his first action.[1] So an action for damages by a lessee of a farm by reason of fraudulent representations that the farm was thoroughly drained was held to exhaust the cause of action, and to prevent a second action for subsequent damages arising from the same fraudulent representation.[2] But unless the immediate cause of action is the same the rule will not of course apply. Thus, the recovery of damages for a previous injury will not prevent a second action from being maintained for damages for a *subsequent* injury arising from the same act, *if that act is not in itself unlawful.* In such a case it is the occurrence of damage and not the act itself which gives rise to a cause of action. This is well illustrated by the recent decision of the House of Lords in *Darley Main Colliery Co.* v. *Mitchell.*[3] There lessees of coal under the respondent's land worked the coal so as to cause a subsidence of the land and injury to houses thereon in 1868. For the injuries thus caused the lessees made compensation. They worked no more, but in 1882 a further subsidence took place causing further injury. It was held by the House of Lords that the cause of action in respect of the further subsidence did not arise till that subsidence occurred, and that an action could be maintained for the injury thereby caused.[4] Again, the right to personal security is distinct in kind from the right to safe enjoyment of one's goods.[5] Thus, trespass to goods is not the same cause of action as trespass to the person, and it is immaterial whether the injury is caused by voluntary trespass or is the result of negligence. Thus, where the plaintiff, driving a cab, was run down by a van negligently driven by the defendant's servant, and the cab was damaged and plaintiff suffered bodily harm, it was held

1 Per Lord Bramwell in *Darley Main Colliery Co.* v. *Mitchell*, L. R. 11 App. Cas. p. 144.

2 *Clarke* v. *York*, 52 L. J. Ch. 32.

3 L. R. 11 App. Cas. 144.

4 See particularly the instructive judgment of Lord Bramwell at pp. 144—147.

5 Dig. IX. 2, 13, pr.

that after suing and recovering for the damage to the cab, the plaintiff was free to bring a separate action for the personal injury.[1]

Special damage by breach of statutory duty.

256. Where private persons suffer special damage by the breach or non-performance of a public duty, the possibility or otherwise of a private right of action depends on the scope and language of the statute taken as a whole. If the Legislature, at the same time that it creates a duty, points out a special course of private remedy for the person aggrieved, then it is generally presumed that the remedy so provided was intended to be, and is, the only remedy.[2] But the harm in respect of which an action is brought must be within the mischief aimed at by the statute.[3]

Rule of trespass being merged in felony not applicable to India.

257. Where the same facts amount to a Felony,[4] and are such as in themselves would constitute a Civil Wrong, the English Courts formerly adopted the rule that the civil remedy is not available for a person who might have prosecuted the wrong-doer for the Felony, and has failed to do so. The principle upon which this rule was founded seems to have been that the interest of the public required that the law should be vindicated before the individual who is

[1] *Brunsden* v. *Humphrey*, L. R. 14 Q. B. D. 141.

[2] Pollock's *Law of Torts*, p. 168.

[3] *Atkinson* v. *Newcastle Water Works Co.*, L. R. 2 Ex. D. 441.

[4] Various definitions of this term have been given. Low Latin *felo* or *fello*, and old French, *felon*, a traitor, a rebel. Spelman would derive it from two words (*fee-lon*), the one signifying a fief or feud, the other price or value. But this derivation is fanciful. Mr. Skeat thinks it is clearly of Celtic origin, and he refers to the Gael. *feallon*, a traitor, from the Irish and Gael. verb *feall*, to betray. *Ety. Dict.* p. 206, *voe felen*. Blackstone defines Felony as "an offence which occasions a total forfeiture of either lands or goods, or both, at the common law; and to which capital or other punishment, *may* be superadded according to the degree of guilt." IV. 95. *In les Termes de la Ley*, felonies are said to be serious crimes, so called "from the ancient English word '*fell*' or '*fierce*,' because that they are intended to be done with a cruel, bitter, fell, fierce, or mischievous minde." The term is not known in the existing criminal law of India.

CHAP. IX.

wronged was permitted to have recourse to a civil remedy.[1] But recent cases have considerably restricted the operation of this rule, if they have not virtually abrogated it, and it is now difficult to say what is the extent of the rule or how it is to be applied.[2] In India it has long since been settled that the rule is wholly inapplicable.[3]

Locality of wrongful act affects remedy.

258. The locality of a wrongful act may also affect the remedy. Thus, if it was committed in a place outside the territorial jurisdiction of the Court, and within the jurisdiction of a foreign Court, the question whether the person wronged had or had not a remedy would depend, in England, on the application of the following rules.[4] Four distinct cases may be supposed:

(1.) Where the act is justified or excused according to the law of the forum, where the action is brought, as well as the local law, or *lex loci delicti commissi.*

In such a case there is no conflict of law and there is obviously no remedy.

(2.) Where the act, although wrongful by the local law, would not constitute a wrong if done in England.

In such a case it is said the Court will not "give a remedy in the shape of damages in respect of an act which, according to its own principles, imposes no liability on the person from whom the damages are claimed."[5]

[1] *Per* Huddleston, B., in *Appleby* v. *Franklin* (1885), 17 Q. B. D. at p. 94.

[2] *Cf. Midland Insurance Co.* v. *Smith* (1881), 6 Q. B. D. at p. 568; *Ex parte Ball, In re Shepherd* (1879), 10 Ch. D. 667; Pollock's *Law of Torts*, p. 173; Pollock's *Civil Wrongs Bill for India*, p. 5, note to section 12.

[3] 6 W. R. 9, Civil Ref.; I. L. R. III. Mad. 6; IV. Mad. 410; IX. Mad. 463. See also the observations of Lord Macaulay in his *Introductory Report upon the Indian Penal Code*, note A, at pp. 440, 441, Vol. VII.; *The Works of Lord Macaulay*, edited by his sister, Lady Trevelyan.

[4] Summarised by Professor Pollock, *Law of Torts*, p. 175. See also Dicey, *Conflict of Laws*, p. 659.

[5] *The Halley*, L. R. 2 P. C. 193, 204; *The M. Moxham*, L. R. 1 P. D. 107.

Chap. IX.

(3.) The act, although wrongful by the law of England, may be justified or excused by the local law.

Here also the English Courts will not allow an action, and it is immaterial whether the act was from the first justifiable by the local law, or, not being at the time justifiable, was afterwards ratified or excused by a declaration of indemnity proceeding from the local sovereign power.[1] But an exception to the rule would probably be recognised where the local law permitted no remedy for a manifest wrong, such as an assault committed by one British subject upon another British subject, without any special justification or excuse.[2]

(4.) The act may be wrongful by both laws.

In such a case an action lies in England without regard to the nationality of the parties, provided the cause of action is not of a purely local kind, such as trespass to land.[3]

Joint wrongdoers may be sued jointly or severally.

259. When more than one person is concerned in the commission of a wrong, the person wronged has his remedy against all or any one or more of them at his choice. This rule rests upon the broad principle that amongst joint wrongdoers each is answerable for the act of all, that is to say, for the whole damage resulting from the wrongful act.[4] It is no excuse to say that he was acting, as an agent or servant, on behalf and for the benefit of another, although that other may well also be liable. The civil law refuses to recognise degrees of responsibility amongst wrongdoers. But when the plaintiff once makes his election he is concluded by it, upon the principle that where a man has an option to choose one or other of two inconsistent things, when once he has

[1] *Blad* v. *Bamfield*, 4 Swanst. 603, 604; *The M. Moxham*, L. R. 1 P. D. 107. *Cf.* also *Phillips* v. *Eyre*, L. R. 6 Q. B. 1.

[2] *Scott* v. *Lord Seymour*, 32 L. J. Exch. 61.

[3] *The Halley*, L. R. 2 P. C. 202. *Cf. The M. Moxham*, L. R. 1 P. D. at p. 109; *British South Africa Co.* v. *Companhia de Mocambique*, (1893) A. C. 602.

[4] *Livingstone* v. *Bishop*, 1 Johns. U. S. 290; Pollock's *Law of Torts*, pp. 63, 170.

made his election it is final and cannot be altered (*quod semel placuit in electionibus, amplius displicere non potest*).[1] After recovering judgment against some or one of the joint authors of a wrong, he cannot according to English Law, although the American Courts act upon a somewhat different rule,[2] sue the other or others for the same matter, even if the judgment in the first action remains unsatisfied. This is on the ground that by recovery of judgment the cause of action for the wrong is merged in the judgment (*transit in rem judicatam*), and to permit a multiplicity of actions in respect of the same wrong would be against the principle of convenience which is expressed in the maxim *interest reipublicæ ut sit finis litium*.[3]

Rule as to contribution amongst wrongdoers.

260. As between wrongdoers themselves one who has been sued alone and compelled to pay the whole damages has no right to indemnity or contribution from the others. But the scope of this rule is properly restricted to those cases where the act is clearly illegal, for in such cases each wrongdoer must be presumed to know that he was doing an unlawful act.[4] It is otherwise where the matter is indifferent in itself, and where the act is done in honest ignorance, or in good faith. Here the rule against contribution does not apply. Or the rule itself may be thus expressed :—A wrongdoer by misadventure is entitled to indemnity from any person under whose apparent authority he acted in good faith; a wilful or negligent wrongdoer has no claim to contribution or indemnity.[5]

Transferability of rights in action.

261. We have seen that a right or *chose in action* is generally transferable by the person of inherence, and the trans-

[1] *Cf. Scarf* v. *Jardine*, 7 App. Cas. 360; 51 L. J. Q. B. 612.
[2] *Livingstone* v. *Johnstone*, 1 Johns. U. S. 290.
[3] *Per* Lord Blackburn in *Brinsmead* v. *Harrison*, L. R. 7 C. P. at p. 553.
[4] *Adamson* v. *Jarvis*, 4 Bing. at p. 73; Pollock's *Law of Torts*, pp. 170, 171.
[5] Pollock's *Law of Torts*, pp. 171, 172.

feree may sue to enforce the right in his own name.[1] But a right of this kind which arises from an act which causes harm of a purely personal nature short of death to a determinate person is supposed to be so intimately connected with his individuality that the right dies with his person: *actio personalis moritur cum persona.* The estate of the wronged person has consequently no claim, and, on the other hand, that of the wrongdoer is not liable.[2] Certain statutory exceptions to this rule have previously been noticed, and it is here only necessary to add that even an action commenced in the lifetime of the wronged person for a tort will be put an end to by his death.[3]

Extinction of rights in action.

262. The remedial right in action may also be extinguished in several other ways. For instance, by (1) a formal release on the part of the person of inherence, (2) waiver, (3) set-off, (4) bankruptcy, (5) merger, (6) estoppel by judgment, and (7) limitation, or expiry of the time within which the law allows the remedy to be enforced, and which varies very considerably according to the nature of the right violated. But if an action has been commenced the Bankruptcy or Insolvency of the plaintiff will not necessarily bar the suit unless the assignee or receiver appointed by the Court declines to continue the suit and to give security for the costs thereof within such time as the Court may order.[4] So, for a plea to Estoppel by Judgment to be effectual as a bar, the fact or

[1] Para. 217, *ante.*

[2] Thus where a plaintiff brought an action for damages and an injunction against the firm of *T. & Co.* for torts committed by the firm. The firm consisted of T. alone, who died more than six months after the commencement of action, and the action was continued against his executors; it was held that T. having died more than six months after the commission of the acts complained of, no action, either for damages or injunction, could be maintained against his executors: *Kirk* v. *Todd,* 21 Ch. D. 484; 52 L. J. Ch. 224. See also *Blyth* v. *Flodgate,* (1891) 1 Ch. 337; 60 L. J. Ch. 66.

[3] Section 361, illust. (*c*), Act XIV. of 1882.

[4] Section 370, Act XIV. of 1882.

issue must have been directly and substantially in issue in a former suit between the same parties, or between parties under whom they or any of them claim, litigating under the same title, in a Court of competent jurisdiction.[1] Where a fact or issue has been so raised and decided the matter is held to be concluded between the parties and cannot again be litigated, upon the principle of the maxim *res judicata pro veritate accipitur.*[2] And as regards limitation it may be prevented from running by reason of the legal disability of the person of inherence, arising from his minority, insanity, or other mental incapacity.[3] Or it may be interrupted by the absence in foreign territory of the person against whom the action lies,[4] or by the death of the person of inherence before the right to sue accrues,[5] or by an injunction or order of a Court staying the institution of a suit.[6] Or, again, a new period of Limitation may arise in consequence of an acknowledgment in writing signed by the person against whom the property or right is claimed,[7] or of payment of interest, or part payment of principal, or of receipt of produce of mortgaged land.[8] Lastly, it is a principle that a Court will not try a suit in which the matter in issue is also directly and substantially in issue in a previously instituted suit for the same relief between the same parties or their legal representatives (*lis alibi pendens*) in a Court other than a foreign Court.[9] This is on the broad ground of the rule *nemo bis*

[1] Section 13, *Ibid.; Boileau* v. *Rutlin*, 2 Exch. 665; Dig. XLIV. 2, 7, 4; XLIV. 2, 14, pr.

[2] Dig. L. 17, 207. *Cf.* section 41, Act I. of 1872, as to certain judgments being conclusive proof of matters decided by them, even when not *inter partes*.

[3] Section 7, *Indian Limitation Act* (XV. of 1877).

[4] Section 13, *Ibid.*

[5] Section 17, *Ibid.*

[6] Section 15, *Ibid.*

[7] Section 19, *Ibid.*

[8] Section 20, *Ibid.*

[9] Section 12, Act XIV. of 1882; *McHenry* v. *Lewis* (1882), 22 Ch. D. 397.

vexari debet in eadem causa : no man ought to be vexed twice in the same cause.[1]

Rule of *lis pendens.*

262*a*. Another effect of the rule of *lis pendens*, which has been held to be applicable to India,[2] and to have even a wider operation in this country than in England, where the Statute of 2 Vict. c. 11, s. 7, requires *lis pendens* to be registered,[3] is, that a purchaser *pendente lite* is bound by the decree made against the person from whom he purchases. It is a rule founded on a great public policy, for otherwise alienations made during a suit might defeat its whole purpose, and there would be no end to litigation.[4] Hence arises the maxim *pendente lite nihil innovetur* (nothing is changed during the suit), the effect of which is not to annul the conveyance, but only to render it subservient to the rights of the parties in the litigation.[5]

What constitutes a *litis pendentia.*

262*b*. To constitute a *litis pendentia* (a pending suit) there must be a *litis contestatio*,[6] and this expression has had a very interesting history which requires to be studied before one can thoroughly comprehend the modern doctrine on the subject. In the ancient Roman system of *legis actiones*, the stage at which the judicial contest was deemed to have begun was

[1] For the English case law on the subject, see *Ewing* v. *Orr-Ewing* (1882), 22 Ch. D. 456; (1883), 9 App. Cas. 34; (1885), 10 App. Cas. 453; *Thornton* v. *Thornton* (1886), 11 P. D. 176.

[2] See section 52, *Transfer of Property Act*, 1882. The doctrine is confined to interests in land and does not apply to chattels, that is to say, to personal property, except leaseholds and possibly money in Court: *Wigram* v. *Buckley*, (1894) 3 Ch. 483; 63 L. J. Ch. 689.

[3] Dan. *Ch. Forms*, p. 136; Order 61, r. 22, of the Rules framed under the Judicature Act. The registration holds good for five years. See also *Kasim Shah* v. *Unnadapershad Chattergee*, 1 Hyde, Cal. Rep. 160.

[4] *Bellamy* v. *Sabine*, 1 De G. & J. 566. See the explanation of the rule in *Metcalfe* v. *Pulvertoft*, 13 Rev. Reps. 63.

[5] *Metcalfe* v. *Pulvertoft*, 2 Ves. & B. 200. For the history of this doctrine reference may be made to Vangerow, *Lehrbuch der Pandekten*, 1, § 160 (5), pp. 255—261, 7th ed. of 1876.

[6] *Per* Lord Lyndhurst, in *Kinsman* v. *Kinsman*, 1 R. & M. 622.

CHAP. IX. when the parties appeared before the Prætor, and invoked the witnesses present to hear the subject of their dispute. Passing on to the formulary system which succeeded that of the *legis actiones*, the *litis contestatio* was then reached, when the parties having appeared before the Prætor, and made their statements, the Prætor reduced the same into a formula, which was then handed over to the *judex*, or judge, for trial. Still later, when the functions of magistrate and judge (or, as we would say, judge and jury) were combined in the person of the appointed magistrate, the *litis contestatio* was complete when the plaintiff had made his oral declaration and the defendant had replied to it. Here, however, it is important to notice that an exceptional rule appears to have been introduced in regard to a particular form of action known as the *hereditatis petitio*, which had reference to the peculiar doctrine of the Roman Law permitting anyone to enter upon an inheritance and acquire a title thereto by means of usucapion if the proper heir did not show due diligence in asserting his rights. It was accordingly held, in the class of case referred to, that the possessor was attributed with *mala fides*, and all the consequences of a *litis contestatio* applied, from the date of his receiving notice of the action. The misconception that this rule, which, as just explained, was purely exceptional and introduced with reference to the peculiarities of the Roman law in regard to vacant inheritances, was really intended to operate as a general rule applicable to all actions alike, gave rise to the modern doctrine of *insinuation* or notice which is favoured by most civilian writers.[1] It is this doctrine also which has been followed by the American Courts,[2] and also in India,[3] where it has been

[1] *Cf.* Savigny, *System*, Vol. V. pp. 242, 243; Sintenis *Civil Recht*, Vol. I. p. 320 (note 1), Leipzig, 1868.

[2] *Murray* v. *Ballow*, 1 Johns. Ch. 576; *Union Trust Co.* v. *South. Nav. Co.*, 130 U. S. Reps. 571.

[3] I. L. R. XV. Cal. 647, at p. 651; I. L. R. XII. Mad. 180; No. 30, P. R. 1891. See also section 52, *Transfer of Property Act*, 1882.

held that the *litis contestatio* is reckoned from the date when the summons has been served upon the opposite party. The *lis*, of course, ceases to be *pendens* when a final decree has been passed in the cause, or when the suit has been otherwise adjusted or withdrawn.[1] But where an appeal is allowed, any dealing with the property, the subject-matter of the suit, during the pendency of the original suit, or during the pendency of the appeal after notice of the appeal by delivery of summons has reached the respondent in appeal, must be determined with reference to the general doctrine of *lis pendens*.[2] So also in proceedings on review, it has been held that a new *lis pendens* is only created by citation served upon the opposite party. Thus, in *Pierce* v. *Stinde*, their Lordships of the Privy Council laid it down as clear "that when a sale of land is made *between* the date of final judgment affecting the land *and the date when the proceeding in error is commenced to reverse this judgment*, it is *not* subject to a *lis pendens*, and the purchaser will get a good title by the purchase, notwithstanding the circumstance that the judgment is afterwards reversed in the proceeding under the writ of error."[3] As explained by an American Court, "a decree which puts an end to the suit has not heretofore been considered less final, because it was subject within a limited time to be reviewed upon a bill of review."[4]

[1] Holtzendorff's *Rechts Lexikon*, Vol. III. p. 277, tit. *Rechtshängigkeit; Kinsman* v. *Kinsman*, 1 R. & M. 622; I. L. R. XII. Bomb. 217; No. 144, P. R. 1889; Bennett, *Lis Pend.* 120.

[2] I. L. R. VII. Mad. 98; No. 30, P. R. 1891. *Cf.* 20 S. W. R. 204.

[3] 11 Moor. App. 364. *Cf.* No. 56, P. R. 1896, where the allusion to proceedings on review and on error seems to overlook the Privy Council decision referred to in the text, which recognises that a NEW *lis pendens* may arise after citation of the opposite party.

[4] *Ludlow's Heirs* v. *Kidd's Executors*, 3 Ohio, 541.

CHAPTER X.

PROCEDURE.

Chap. X.

Procedure defined.

263. Procedure is the term used to express "the mode of proceeding by which a legal right is enforced, as distinguished from the law which gives or defines the right, and which by means of the proceeding the Court is to administer; the machinery as distinguished from the product."[1] It constitutes that branch of Law which is called "Adjective," as distinguished from that other branch which is called "Substantive." The one branch instructs us as to what steps are to be taken for the realisation of those Rights and the enforcement of those Duties which are explained and defined in the other. The Adjective is thus the complement of the Substantive, without which the latter would be valueless, a body without legs, a set of principles without life, or, to use the expressive language of a German Jurist, "a fire which did not burn, a light which gave no light."[2] It is part also of the function of the Adjective law to point out the limits within which, in the exceptional cases where a sufferer is allowed to redress his own wrong, self-help is permissible. Forms of procedure are amongst the earliest institutes in the History of Law, and the further we recede back into that History, the larger the influence we find attributed to the observance of such forms. It is often objected that the introduction of a law of Procedure piles up and increases the difficulties of a just administration of the Laws, harasses and

[1] *Per* Lush, J., in *Poyser* v. *Minors*, L. R. 7 Q. B. D. at p. 333.

[2] Von Ihering, *Der Zweck im Recht*, Vol. I. p. 322.

impedes a Judge in his discovery of truth, and often compels him to pass a judgment which is in direct opposition to his own convictions. And yet, when we remember that the experience of centuries has confirmed the necessity of rules of Procedure, we may be assured that the advantages to be derived from such a system far outbalance the hardships resulting from it. Freedom in the choice of Procedure means generally Freedom of judicial Arbitrariness and Partiality, freedom of Chicanery, and an abuse of the process of a Court of Justice.[1] But as a clock requires a hand to indicate the hour, so the machinery of Procedure needs a guiding and controlling hand to work it efficiently. This hand is the Supreme Executive Authority in a State, which generally delegates its function of administering the Law to other appointed Organs, which are called Courts of Justice.

Classes of Courts of Justice.

264. These Courts of Justice may be established either to redress Wrongs or to punish Crimes. In the former case they are called Civil Courts, in the latter Criminal Courts. Each class may, again, consist of either Original or Appellate Courts, according as they are intended to exercise an original or merely an appellate jurisdiction. The former, again, may be invested with an exclusive Jurisdiction for the trial of particular classes of Civil suits or of Crimes of a particular kind, or with a jurisdiction which they may possess concurrently with some other Court of equal or superior standing. Thus, in England, County Courts have exclusive jurisdiction for the trial of Small Causes, and the Divorce Division of the High Court of Justice for the trial of all causes in which the object of the suit is the annulment of the Marriage relation. So in India we have Courts of Small Causes, which have the exclusive cognizance of all suits of a civil nature, of which the value does not exceed five hundred

[1] *Geist des römischen Rechts*, Part III., section 50, pp. 15—22: Leipzig, 1877.

rupees, other than those which are expressly declared by the Constituting Act to be beyond their jurisdiction.[1]

Choice of Court.

265. This classification of Courts into Courts of Original, Appellate, Concurrent, or Exclusive Jurisdiction, renders it necessary that proceedings should be commenced in the appropriate Court, and any defect in this respect will vitiate the entire proceedings. The Legislature is therefore particular when constituting different classes of Courts to specify the powers and jurisdiction of each, and the conditions under which they may exercise their respective jurisdictions. The limitation may also have reference to territorial or pecuniary jurisdiction, or to both. Thus, in India, a civil suit other than a suit relating to immoveable property or for the recovery of moveable property under distraint must be instituted in a Court within the local limits of whose jurisdiction—

(*a*) the cause of action arises; or

(*b*) all the defendants, at the time of the commencement of the suit, actually and voluntarily reside, or carry on business, or personally work for gain; or

(*c*) any of the defendants, at the time of the commencement of the suit, actually and voluntarily resides or carries on business, or personally works for gain; provided that either the leave of the Court is given, or the defendants who do not reside, or carry on business, or personally work for gain, acquiesce in such institution.

And in respect of suits arising out of contract, the cause of action is deemed to arise either—

(*a*) where the contract was made; or

(*b*) where it was to be performed, or performance thereof completed; or

(*c*) where in performance of the contract any money to

[1] Section 15, Act IX. of 1887.

which the suit relates was expressly or impliedly payable.[1]

Suits relating to immoveable property, or to moveable property actually under distraint or attachment, must be instituted where the subject-matter is situate.[2] Suits for compensation for wrongs to person or moveables may be instituted either in the Court within whose jurisdiction the wrong was committed or the defendant resides.[3]

Matters of procedure are governed by the local or territorial law (*lex fori*).

266. All matters of procedure are exclusively governed by the law of the forum whose aid is sought for remedial purposes. This is a principle of universal recognition, and admits of no exception. As was said by a great English judge (Lord Tenterden), "a person suing in this country must take the law as he finds it; he cannot, by virtue of any regulation in his own country, enjoy greater advantages than any other suitors here, and he ought not, therefore, to be deprived of any superior advantage which the law of this country may confer. He is to have the same rights which all the subjects of this kingdom are entitled to."[4] Everything connected with the enforcement of a right is included under the head of "procedure." It embraces, therefore, the rules of evidence, the rules which govern the limitation of actions,[5] the rules which regulate all legal remedies, and the methods by which decrees of civil Courts may be enforced.

Commencement of judicial proceedings.

266*a*. To enforce a judicial remedy, the party who seeks the intervention of the Court, and who in Civil suits is called

[1] Section 17, Act XIV. of 1882, as amended by Act VII. of 1888.

[2] Section 16, Act XIV. of 1882.

[3] Section 18, *Ibid.*

[4] *De la Vega* v. *Vianna* (1830), 1 B. & Ad. 284, 288. See also *Don* v. *Lippmann* (1837), 5 Cl. & F. 1, 13, *per* Lord Brougham.

[5] Thus an obligation may be enforced in England, although barred by its own proper law (*lex loci contractus* or *solutionis*, or *lex delicti commissi*), if action is brought within the period prescribed by English law: Westlake, §§ 238, 239.

a plaintiff and in Criminal proceedings a complainant, begins by making a statement of facts upon which the claim to redress, or the demand for the punishment of the wrong-doer, is founded. This statement in India is embodied in civil suits in what is termed a plaint (the *libellus conventionis* of the Justinian Law), which must be written, verified, and signed, and must bear a Court Fee Stamp of the prescribed value;[1] and in criminal proceedings in a complaint, which, if it refers to an offence not cognizable by the Police, must be in writing and bear a Court Fee Stamp of eight annas,[2] or in other cases may be made orally or in writing.[3]

Issue of Summons or Citation.

267. The next step is to issue the summons or citation for the appearance of the defendant. It may be interesting to glance for a moment at the gradual development of this process. Thus in the early Roman law the plaintiff had to produce the defendant, and until he appeared no judicial redress could be obtained. To secure this end the plaintiff possessed, under the Law of the Twelve Tables, the *in jus vocatio*, the right of compelling the defendant to appear before a Magistrate. If the defendant refused to comply with this summons the plaintiff called upon the bystanders to witness the fact, and he was then authorised, if the defendant still refused, to lay hands upon him (*manus injectio*), and to employ force to compel his attendance. The defendant might, however, avoid compliance by furnishing a *vindex*, or security, who took the action upon himself. At a subsequent period, the *promissio*, with or without security, took the place of the *in jus vocatio*, and consisted in a penal promise by the defendant, or by another for him, to present himself upon a certain day *in jure*. In the Provinces a single noti-

[1] Sections 4, 6, 7, Act VII. of 1870.

[2] Schedule II. 1 (*b*), Act VII. of 1870.

[3] Section 4, Act V. of 1898.

fication of the suit by the plaintiff to the defendant (*litis denuntio*), with a summons to appear at the next *conventus*, was all that was necessary. And finally, in the Law of Justinian, the issue of a summons against the defendant followed upon the delivery of a bill of plaint (*libellus conventionis*) before the competent judge.[1] In the old English system the theory that nothing could be done until the party complained against was brought into Court was preserved, and when the rigour of the rule was afterwards relaxed the fiction of an appearance was still recognised. Various indirect modes for securing this appearance were at one time resorted to, suggesting the inference that the submission of the defendant was in theory if not in fact regarded as voluntary.[2] The old Hindu lawyers struck out from the beginning a far simpler and more sensible course. Legal investigation was regarded by them as the necessary condition for a proper administration of justice, which was the primary duty of all kings and governors.[3] The aggrieved person had to represent his case to the king, and if after interrogation his representation appeared to be just, the defendant, unless exempted by infirmity, was summoned by an order under seal. If infirm, a carriage had to be provided,[4] precisely as the Twelve Tables ordained.[5] Narada also permits the claimant to detain his adversary, if he is trying to evade payment, until the summons arrives; and amongst those who are declared exempt from arrest or summons it is curious to notice that the bridegroom, a person engaged before the Magistrate, or about to perform a sacrifice (or conducting the funeral obsequies of a member of his family), or engaged in the affairs of Government (or trying a cause), are mentioned in

[1] Salkowski's *Roman Private Law*, section 191, pp. 942—944.

[2] Markby's *Elements of Law*, section 836, p. 420.

[3] *Mitacshara*, Chap. I., section 1, para. 1.

[4] *Ibid.*, section 3, para. 6.

[5] Salkowski's *Roman Private Law*, section 191, p. 942.

CHAP. X.

the Roman Digest[1] as well as by Narada.[2] Under the existing Civil Procedure Code for India a summons, or, if the defendant's rank entitles him to such a mark of consideration, a letter[3] is issued under the signature of the Judge or of such Officer as he appoints, and sealed with the seal of the Court, directing the defendant to appear in person or by pleader.[4] It ought whenever it may be practicable to be served on the defendant in person or on his agent,[5] but in certain cases substituted service is permitted.[6]

Appearance in Court and Pleadings.

268. The parties having appeared in Court, the plaintiff proceeds to make a declaration which is an amplification of his written plaint, to which the defendant then gives his answer, and a substance of the examination of the parties is reduced to writing by the Judge.[7] It is remarkable that the rules on this subject contained in the Hindu Law books are worthy of an advanced system of Jurisprudence, and closely agree with those now incorporated in the Civil Procedure Code of 1882. Thus the declaration is required to be technically precise, comprehensive and yet concise, conformable to the original complaint, and comprising the dimensions and quantity of the property in dispute, the names of the complainant and of his adversary, and the names of their respective ancestors.[8] If there is any variation between the declaration and the complaint it may prove fatal to the cause.[9] A declaration which is absurd, unmeaning, frivolous, at variance with possibility, and unsusceptible of proof must be rejected.[10] But an amendment is allowed until the answer is given, "being stopped by the answer, the corrections must cease."[11]

[1] II. 4, 2.

[2] *Mitacshara*, Chap. I., section 3, para. 10.

[3] Section 91, Act XIV. of 1882.

[4] Section 64, *Ibid.*

[5] Section 75, *Ibid.*

[6] Section 82, Act XIV. of 1882.

[7] Sections 117—119, *Ibid.*

[8] *Mitacshara*, Chap. I., section 4, para. 5.

[9] *Ibid.*, para. 2.

[10] *Ibid.*, paras. 10 and 11.

[11] *Ibid.*, para. 15. *Cf.* section 53, Act XIV. of 1882; 2 Mad. H. C. Reps. 51; and 24 W. R. 147.

The answer must likewise embrace the declaration (*e.g.*, be capable of refuting it), be solid (*e.g.*, not inconsistent with reason), clear (not ambiguous), consistent (agreeing in all its parts), and obvious (not needing any further explanation). It is only when the answer fulfils these conditions that it is regarded as a true answer.[1] The answer may be a confession, a denial, a special plea (equivalent to the English plea of confession and avoidance), and a plea of former judgment (the English *res judicata*).[2] Narada, to whom most of these rules are ascribed, declares that not to amount to an answer "which is dubious, not to the point, too confined, too extensive, or not embracing all the parts of the declaration." That again which "is relative to other matter, incomplete, obscure, confused, not obvious, or absurd," is a faulty answer.[3] Under the existing system of pleading the answer may either raise a defence affecting Procedure, as, for instance, that another suit is pending between the same parties and concerning the same subject-matter, *res judicata*, want of capacity to sue, limitation, non-joinder or misjoinder, and the like ; or affecting the Contract or Wrong sued upon, as, for instance, accord and satisfaction, credit unexpired, denial of agreement or facts alleged, coercion, fraud, or undue influence, infancy of defendant, payment, release, want of consideration, contributory negligence, and the like. If the defendant does not

[1] *Mitacshara*, Chap. I., section 5, paras. 3 and 4.

[2] *Ibid.*, paras. 5—10. It has been recently held that a former decision is no less *res judicata* because it may have been founded on an erroneous view of the law, or a view of the law which a Full Bench has subsequently disapproved. I. L. R. X. Cal. 1087. *Cf.* No. 20, P. R. 1891, as to the competency of Courts. But it is very doubtful if the proposition laid down in this judgment of the Chief Court of the Punjab, that the competency of one Court as compared with another is affected by the circumstance that in the one case an appeal lies in the first instance to, say, the District Courts and in the other directly to the High Court, is correct. The Madras High Court has pronounced that there is "no authority" for any such general proposition: I. L. R. XVII. Mad. 273.

[3] *Ibid.*, para. 1.

CHAP. X. appear and answer on the day fixed he is accounted *indefensus*, and the Court may proceed to hear the case *ex parte*. But if the plaintiff fails to appear in person or by duly authorized agent or pleader, and the defendant, if present, denies the claim, the suit must be dismissed. But if the defendant admits any portion of the claim the Court must pass a decree in terms of such admission.[1] After the parties have made their respective statements, it is the duty of the Judge, according to the Indian Law, to settle the questions of law and fact upon which the parties are at issue, and a date is then fixed for the hearing of the cause.

The trial. 269. On the date fixed for the hearing of the cause the parties are bound to produce their respective proofs, documentary or oral, and in order to facilitate the proper investigation of a claim, in every well-considered system of Procedure, certain general rules exist regulating the burden of proof. In the old Hindu Law the general rule that he who has anything to prove (*i.e.*, asserts the existence of facts) is to do so and not any other person, is as strictly laid down as in modern Laws of Evidence;[2] and a text of Harita explains the general rule by adding that "when a special exception and former judgment are pleaded, the defendant shall adduce the proof; in a total denial, the plaintiff."[3] Here we have merely a statement in a different form of two well-known rules of Evidence, (*a*) that "the burden of proof in a suit or other judicial proceeding lies on that person who would fail if no evidence at all were given on either side,"[4] and (*b*) that "the burden of proof as to any particular fact lies on that person who wishes the Court to believe in its existence, unless it is provided by any law that the proof of

[1] Sections 98, 101, Act XIV. of 1882.

[2] *Mitacshara*, Chap. I., section 6, paras. 2 and 3. *Cf.* section 101, Act I. of 1872 (*The Indian Evidence Act*).

[3] *Mitacshara*, Chap. I., section 6, para. 4.

[4] Section 102, Act I. of 1872.

that fact shall lie on any particular person."[1] This last proviso refers to the doctrine that in certain classes of facts the Courts will draw a "presumption" by which certain propositions are to be assumed to be sufficiently proved when certain other propositions have been established.[2] Thus the burden of proving that a person is alive who has not been heard of for seven years is cast by the Indian Law on the person who affirms it;[3] and so also the burden of proving that a person in possession of anything is not the owner, is on the person who asserts the negative.[4] In like manner a Court may presume the existence of any fact which it thinks likely to have happened, regard being had to the common course of natural events, human conduct, and public and private business, in their relation to the facts of the particular case.[5] Thus, that judicial and official acts have been regularly performed; that evidence which could be and is not produced would, if produced, be unfavourable to the person who withholds it. The Law also prescribes certain rules for the *admissibility* of evidence, the two main ones being, that oral evidence must be direct and not hearsay,[6] and that secondary evidence of the contents of documents can only be adduced when primary evidence is not forthcoming or is beyond the reach of the Court.[7] It is open to the Court to bring persons on to the record and to make them parties whose presence may be necessary in order to enable the Court effectually and completely to adjudicate upon and settle all the questions involved in the suit.[8]

Judgment.

270. When such evidence as the parties desire to produce has been taken and the parties have been heard either in person or by their respective pleaders or recognised agents,

[1] Section 103, Act I. of 1872.
[2] Holland's *Jurisprudence*, p. 270.
[3] Section 108, Act I. of 1872.
[4] Section 110, *Ibid.*
[5] Section 114, Act I. of 1872.
[6] Section 60, *Ibid.*
[7] Sections 61, 65, *Ibid.*
[8] Section 32, Act XIV. of 1882.

CHAP. X.

the Court proceeds to record its opinion on the various issues which have been previously framed for determination. This record of the Court's decision is called a judgment, which may be purely declaratory of the existence or non-existence of an "antecedent right," whether affecting property or status, or it may assume the form of an order for the payment of money by way of compensation or restitution, or for the specific performance of or abstention from a certain act. The judgment should also direct by whom the costs of each party in the course of the litigation are to be paid, and in this matter the Court has generally a wide discretion.[1] But the ordinary rule is that the losing party pays his adversary's costs, and since the time of Justinian this is the only check upon vexatious or frivolous litigation. Under the earlier Roman Law a *calumniæ judicium*, or action for vexatious litigation, was allowed to the defendant for a tenth part of the thing against one who knew that his proceedings were wrongful, and brought his action with the view of annoying his opponent.[2] Such actions are now discouraged as tending to the mere multiplicity of suits.[3]

How far binding on parties.

May be set aside on appeal within certain limits.

271. A judgment once passed is binding upon the parties unless it is set aside (*a*) on appeal, or (*b*) by review, or (*c*) is void in itself. The necessity for an appeal is undeniable, with the object of repairing the unfairness or unskilfulness of Judges, although sometimes, as a Roman Jurist (Ulpian) shrewdly observes, "it probably results in altering for the worse judgments well pronounced."[4] The limits and interval within which an appeal is allowable are fixed by the legislature. But the mere fact of an appeal having been lodged does not produce any suspensive effect on the judgment of the lower Court (*medio tempore nihil novari oportet*),[5] which

[1] Section 220, Act XIV. of 1882.

[2] Gaius, IV. 175, 178.

[3] I. L. R. I. Bomb. 467.

[4] Dig. XLIX. 1, 1 pr.

[5] Dig. XLIX., 7, 1 pr.; *Cf.* section 545, Act XIV. of 1882.

may be executed in the ordinary way. But the Appellate Court may for sufficient reason order the execution to be stayed.[1] Execution can only take place on the application of the successful party, or of a party to whom relief in some form or another has been granted by the decretal order.[2] With the delivery of the "*judicium*" or judgment the official function of the judge is ended.[3] He is then, so far as the particular suit is concerned, *functus officio*. But a party considering himself aggrieved by a judicial order may also in certain cases and under prescribed conditions obtain a rehearing of the cause in the same Court by means of what is called a Review of Judgment.[4] Lastly, a Judgment may be inoperative (*a*) by reason of incapacity of the Judge to take cognizance of the case,[5] or (*b*) by reason of defective capacity for proceedings of a party.[6] In either case the Judgment is regarded as void, and is not an actual sentence (*pro nulla hoc habetur nec est ulla sententia*). Thus, if a Judge decides a case which is beyond his jurisdiction (whether territorial or pecuniary is immaterial), or in which he is personally interested (thereby transgressing the fundamental principle

CHAP. X.

Review of Judgment.

Void Judgment.

[1] Section 545, Act XIV. of 1882. [2] Section 223, *Ibid.*

[3] A curious question arose in *Queen Empress* v. *Salig Ram*, No. 16 P. R. 1897, Cr., where an accused person used insulting language to a magistrate upon the latter reading out his final order. The magistrate thereupon fined the accused under section 228, Indian Penal Code. On appeal the Sessions Judge reversed this latter order on the ground that, the magistrate having delivered his judgment before the insulting words had been used, it could not be held that he was insulted during a stage of a judicial proceeding. But the Chief Court, on the revision side, differed from the Sessions Judge and restored the order of the magistrate—the Chief Judge holding that the original proceeding against the accused must be held to have continued until the accused was allowed to leave the Court, or was removed in custody. Mr. Justice Frizella concurred in reversing the order on the ground that "a magistrate cannot be considered to have concluded a case the very moment he has announced his order, while his judgment is still in his hands and before he could possibly have turned to any other occupation."

[4] Section 623, Act XIV. of 1882.

[5] Dig. II. 2, 1, section 2. [6] Dig. XLII. 1, 45, section 2.

CHAP. X.

nemo debet esse judex in propria causa),[1] it is not the judgment of a competent Court, and will not be binding upon the parties. So also a judgment pronounced against undefended minors, or who were not legally represented, is invalid.[2] The Roman Law went further, and declared invalid a decision which was passed in express opposition to statutes, or a decree of the Senate, or an Imperial Constitution.[3] But a mere error in the application of a rule of law did not of itself vitiate a Judgment so as to make it void.[4] The nullity of a Judgment may be established—

(*a*) defensively, on the part of the defendant, when it is sought to be enforced, against him; or

(*b*) aggressively, on the part of the party condemned, by his suing to have the judgment declared void.[5]

Exceptional Rules of Procedure.

272. As the Law of Procedure is a general law, it is applicable to all persons alike,[6] unless the Legislature makes any modification in favour of particular individuals or certain

[1] Even the slightest pecuniary interest is sufficient to disqualify a judge from adjudicating upon a case. So if there is reasonable suspicion of bias on his part, though there might not have been bias in fact, he is disqualified. *Reg.* v. *Milledge* (1879), 4 Q. B. D. 332; and *Reg.* v. *Gaisford*, (1892) 1 Q. B. 381. *Cf.* also I. L. R. XV. Mad. 83. But where the tribunal is an administrative, rather than a judicial, body, a less strict rule applies. Thus where a person was prosecuted for falsely representing himself as a solicitor by the Incorporated Law Society before a magistrate who was himself a member of that Society, it was held that, as the circumstances did not show any probability of bias on the part of the magistrate, he was not disqualified by the mere fact of his membership from adjudicating. *Reg.* v. *Burton, Ex parte Young*, (1897) 2 Q. B. 468. *Cf.* also *Allinson* v. *General Council of Medical Education*, (1894) 1 Q. B. 750; and *Leeson* v. *Medical Council*, 43 Ch. D. 366; 59 L. J. Ch. 233.

[2] See Chap. XXXI., Act XIV. of 1882; XI. Cal. L. R. 15, 210; I. L. R. XII. Cal. 542; No. 100, *Punjab Record*, 1882.

[3] Dig. XLIX., 1, 19.

[4] Dig. XLII., 1, 32. *Cf.* to same effect, I. L. R. XV. Allah. 327.

[5] 20 W. R. 86; I. L. R. VI. Bomb. 148; I. L. R. IX. Cal. 358, 363, 367; IX. *Ibid.* 810; 14 Moore's Ind. App. 393; and Civil Appeal (M.S.) No. 110 of 1886 of the Chief Court, Punjab; *Flower* v. *Lloyd*, L. R. 6 Ch. D. 297.

[6] The general rule is thus stated in section 10 of Act XIV. of 1882: "No person shall by reason of his descent or place of birth be in any Civil proceeding exempted from the jurisdiction of any of the Courts."

classes of persons. Thus, no Judge, Magistrate, or other Judicial Officer is liable to arrest under civil process while going to, presiding in, or returning from his Court;[1] the same privilege extends to the parties, their pleaders, recognised agents, and witnesses, while going to, attending at, or returning from, a tribunal having jurisdiction in the matter pending before it, or believing in good faith that it has jurisdiction.[2] The State may also exempt certain persons from personal appearance by reason of rank[3] or sex.[4] On the other hand, it may place certain other persons under special disabilities. Thus alien enemies in British India can only sue with the permission of the Governor-General in Council.[5] And a Foreign State is only allowed to do so when (*a*) it has been recognised by Her Majesty or the Governor-General in Council, and (*b*) the object of the suit is to enforce the private rights of the head or of the subjects of the Foreign State.[6]

CHAP. X.

[1] Section 642, Act XIV. of 1882.

[2] *Ibid.*, Clause 2.

[3] Section 641, Act XIV. of 1882.

[4] Section 640, *Ibid.*

[5] Section 430, *Ibid.* A British subject resident and carrying on trade in an enemy's country is, equally with an alien enemy, incapable of suing in a British Court; and the reason of the rule was explained to be that the fruits of the action may not be remitted to a hostile country, and so furnish resources against this country: *McConnell* v. *Hector* (1802), 3 Bos. & P. 113; 6 Rev. Reps. 724; *Brandon* v. *Nesbitt*, 3 R. R. 109; and *Marryat* v. *Wilson*, 1 Bos. & P. 430.

[6] Section 431, Act XIV. of 1882.

CHAPTER XI.

INTERNATIONAL PRIVATE LAW.

CHAP. XI.

Object and scope of International Private Law.

273. OWING to the large intercourse which in modern times exists between persons resident in different countries, brought about partly by the great strides which commerce has made and partly by the increasing facilities for travel, it often happens that Courts are called upon to adjudicate with respect to matters arising between persons of different nationalities, and based upon contractual agreements entered into in one place to be performed in another. In such cases questions arise not only as to what Courts have jurisdiction, but as to what Law is to be applied to the particular case. It is the object of International Private Law, which deals with the application of the Laws of different States to the international relations of private citizens, to indicate the principles by which questions of this kind are to be solved. In antiquity we find very few traces of such a theory of Law, for the simple reason that a capacity for Rights was generally denied to foreigners, and in theory a Roman, like an Englishman, carried his personal law with him wherever he went.[1] By the old Roman Law a foreigner was regarded as outside the pale of law, a mere waif and a stray (*wildfang oder biesterfrei*).[2] Thus the Roman Civil Law was not applicable to any one who was not a Roman citizen, and although with the spread of commerce a *jus gentium*—characterised as

[1] Wachter, *Ueber die Collision der Privatrechts-gesetze, im Archiv für die civilistische Praxis*, XXIV., section 242.

[2] Savigny, *Hist. of Roman Law in the Middle Ages*, 1, p. 118.

a law *quod apud omnes gentes peræque custoditur* (that which prevails equally among all nations),[1] governing foreigners in their relations with one another or with citizens,[2] was gradually developed under the equitable jurisdiction of the Prætors, a collision or conflict between the foreign and the Roman Law was from the nature of the thing impossible. At a later period, when Roman Citizenship was extended by Caracalla to every free inhabitant of the Empire, uniformity and not diversity of laws was the prevailing principle; and thus in the Justinianian compilations there are no rules for the application of local laws, but only for the interpretation of the declarations of the private will according to the peculiarities of local phraseology. It is in the later Middle Ages that we first hear of the doctrine of Personal and Real Statutes, the one conferring on the person the quality that adheres to him everywhere, the other based on the theory of territorialism. The former took no account of actual domicile, and the inconvenience resulting from its application, when persons belonged to different nationalities, was sought at times to be overcome by the device of the parties to written contracts declaring beforehand by what law they wished to be bound *quâ* obligations arising out of such contracts. Declarations of this kind were called *professiones juris*. But this "free choice" of fixing the law according to which an individual wished to be bound, it seems probable, only applied to matters of secondary importance, such as obligations by contract, in regard to which the State had no immediate interest. In regard to all other matters affecting the *jus publicum* the true and general principle, subject only to a few exceptions in favour of married women, freedmen, ecclesiastics, and the monarch, perhaps was, as Savigny[3] following Lupi contends, *that birth determined the law.* Thus in the

Personal and Real Statutes.

[1] Just. *Inst.* 1, 2, 1. [2] Voigt, *Jus nat.* ii. 661.

[3] *Hist. of Roman Law in the Middle Ages*, translated by Cathcart, Vol. I., p. 135.

same country, and often in the same city, the Lombard lived under the Lombardic, and the Roman under the Roman Law, and the same distinction of laws was also applicable to the different Germanic races—Franks, Burgundians, and Goths, each having their own laws though residing in the one place. It was this system of Personal laws that Bishop Agobardus so forcibly illustrated when he observed in his epistle to Louis le Debonnaire, "It often happens that five men, each under a different law, may be found walking or sitting together."[1] The origin of the other principle has been traced back by Eichhorn and others to the notion of a voluntary submission of the individual, both as to his person and property, to the Law of some Free-burghal Community,[2] or of some great Feudal Lord. The voluntary association of the individual in the Burghal Community, or his submission to some powerful Landowner, whose vassal and bondsman he became, was equally subversive of the former system of personal laws. Under this new theory Descent no longer exercised any influence, but only Domicile; and the Free Community or the Feudal Lord regulated the Law by which property situated within the territorial limits of its or his autonomy was to be governed. Thus at the close of the Middle Ages three distinct sets of rules were applicable according as they affected the person, immoveable property, or an act. Domicile (*lex domicilii*) furnished the key to the appropriate Law in the first case, the site or situation (*lex rei sitæ*) in the second, and the locality of the action (*locus regit actum*) in the third. In the case of moveables their easy

[1] *Hist. of Roman Law in the Middle Ages*, Vol. I., p. 100. *Cf.* also Laghi, *Il Diritto Internazionale Privato*, Vol. I., sections 26 and 27, pp. 26—28.

[2] The free Italian Burghal-Communities (*borghi franchi*) had various privileges, amongst which was the important one that a stranger who sought an asylum within them became at once free and a citizen. "Thus," says Laghi (*Il Diritto Internazionale Privato*, section 32, p. 33), "in contradistinction to the old feudal maxim that the 'air makes a slave,' we have the new principle 'the air makes a freeman.'" See note [1], p. 358, *post*.

transport from place to place served to identify them with the person of the owner, and thus the maxim came to be recognised *mobilia personam sequuntur* (moveables follow the person). The nomenclature adopted by writers of this period for the three sets of rules just mentioned was *statuta personalia*, *realia*, and *mixta*. A rule of law whose operation may extend outside the territory of the law-giver, or extraterritorially, is a *statutum personale;* one whose operation is confined strictly to the territory of the law-giver is called a *statutum reale*, while *statuta mixta* are those which regulate the form of acts, or persons and acts together.[1]

Statuta personalia, realia, and mixta.

Courts bound to observe the *lex fori* in the first instance.

273*a*. But it follows from the notion of complete Sovereignty which must be yielded to each independent State, that the lawgiver may, if he chooses, absolutely prohibit the recognition of any foreign Law, in which case the Courts, as the organs of the Legislature, can only administer the *lex fori*, or that Law which is exclusively and naturally their own. It is merely out of friendly respect to the *comitas nationum*, and as an act of courtesy, that one State recognises the Law of another State, and it may do so subject to any restrictions and rules it chooses to prescribe. A Court of Justice is bound therefore, in the first instance, to look to the Law of its own State, and it is only when that Law fails to speak on the point, that it may seek a rule of decision in the principles of International Private Law. But there is this general limitation to be observed, that no Judge ought to recognise a foreign Law which, according to the fundamental principles of the Law of his own State, would be considered immoral or opposed to public policy.[2] Thus no action would lie in

[1] Holtzendorff's *Encyklopädie der Rechtswissenschaft*, Vol. II., pp. 673—676; Von Bar's *International Law*, translated by Gillespie, section 5, p. 28.

[2] *Hamlyn & Co.* v. *Talisker Distillery*, App. Cas. 261; Burge, I., 199. It is on this broad principle that Guido Fusinato criticises a decision of the Court of Appeal of Ancona of the 22nd March, 1884, pronouncing a divorce between a German subject (Von Bremen) and an Italian lady (Guilia Salvini), in his interesting monograph *Questioni di Diritto Internazionale Privato*. By

CHAP. XI.

England for the recovery of a slave, since by the *lex fori* the moment a slave touches the soil of England he becomes free.[1] So also an action for damages for breach of promise of marriage could not be sustained in the Courts of a country, the law of which prohibited such actions.[2]

Provincial or Local Laws.

274. The same principles are to be observed in the application of Provincial or Local Laws of the same State. So far as those Laws are either expressly recognised by the State or do not contravene the fundamental principles of the general Law of the State, they are entitled to recognition by all Courts (*fora*) within the State. Thus in India the British Legislature has recognised the Hindu and Muhammadan Laws in all matters relating to Succession, Adoption, Marriage, Divorce, Gift, Dower, Caste and Religious Institutions;[3] and all Courts in British India are thus bound to give effect to those personal Laws within the limits prescribed by the Legislature.

Choice of *Forum*.

275. In the older phase of Roman Law there existed but one *forum* for all suits in which Roman citizens were defendants and that was Rome itself. At a later period, when Roman citizens might be sued in the Provinces and were permitted to acquire landed property there, the *forum rei sitæ* came to be introduced, but even then the unity of the Empire

Art. 12 of the Preliminary dispositions of the Italian Civil Code no laws or judgments of a foreign country can be allowed to operate in derogation of the prohibitive laws of the Italian Kingdom concerning persons, &c.; and as § 148 only recognises death as dissolving a valid marriage, an Italian Court was bound to respect this provision and refuse to enforce a foreign law which was opposed in principle to that of its own country.

[1] As it was resolved in *Cartwright's Case*, "the air of England is too pure for a slave to live in." Broom's *Const. Hist.* 93. See also *Somersett's Case*, *Ibid.* 65; and *Forbes* v. *Cochrane*, 2 L. J. K. B. (O. S.) 67; 26 Rev. Rep. 402. But *query*, if a contract relating to the sale and purchase of slaves would not be enforceable if valid by the law of the domicile of the contracting parties? *The Opinions of Grotius*, by D. P. De Bruyn, p. 75.

[2] Holtzendorff, *Encyklopädie der Rechtswissenschaft*, Vol. II., pp. 681—684.

[3] Section 15, Reg. IV., 1793; section 16, Reg. III., 1803; section 5, Act IV. of 1872.

was so generally recognised that it was a matter of little moment whether the real action was brought in the *forum domicilii* or *forum rei sitæ.*[1] The only persons, however, whom a Magistrate could compel to answer in a suit by requiring caution (or security), were persons who either were themselves actually present in his jurisdiction or possessed property there, by means of which a *missio in possessionem*[2] of the creditor could be carried out.[3] This principle was first reached in *actiones stricti juris* with a definite place of performance. But with other Obligations the Magistrate did not compel the debtor to answer unless *bona fides* required it; and this was always assumed where money was agreed to be paid at a particular place. Within these limits the *forum contractus* exercised a concurrent jurisdiction with the *forum domicilii.*[4] In modern times the test whether the Special Law of this or that State is applicable depends upon what Local Law (or *lex generalis*) is generally regulative of the legal relation in dispute. Thus, in questions of Status and Family Law, the *judex domicilii* will decide; in questions as to Things, the *judex rei sitæ.* Suits as to Succession will fall partly to the one and partly to the other; questions as to Obligatory Contracts will belong partly to the *judex domicilii*, partly to the Court of the place of the Contract (*forum contractus*) or Delict (*forum delicti commissi*). But these general principles undergo two modifications—an extension in so far as the defendant may consent to subject himself to the jurisdiction of another Court, and a limitation in so far as the plaintiff may renounce some particular jurisdiction. From

[1] Von Bar's *International Law*, section 120, p. 521.

[2] That is to say an installation (*missio*) in the possession of the whole property or specific things belonging to another, as has resulted from a Magisterial decree—especially as a compulsory measure against contumacious persons. The person installed (*missus*) acquired by securing possession bare, yet legally protected, detention with the view of care-taking and supervision, and a right of pledge. Salkowski's *Roman Private Law*, section 31, p. 159.

[3] Von Bar's *International Law*, p. 523.

[4] *Ibid.* pp. 523—526.

CHAP. XI.

this option must, however, be excluded all legal relations over which the parties have not a full power of disposal.[1] Thus, in questions as to the validity of a Marriage, or its dissolution, that Court only is competent in whose territory the parties, between whom that relation exists, have their legal domicile.[2] So an English Court will not ordinarily entertain a petition for Divorce, unless the husband be domiciled in the country.[3] This is upon the principle that parties in marrying make the Law of the place where they marry or where they intend to have their matrimonial home part of their contract, the husband's domicile being that of the wife,[4] and that they can be divorced only for causes and by Courts recognised by such Law.[5] But the more correct theory recognised by English Courts since 1858, is that Marriage is a Status created by Law which differs in different States, and that as the Laws of each State are made for and apply to whatever is permanently in such State, a party may be divorced only in and according to the Law of the place where he or she is domiciled.[6] A foreign divorce, therefore, if pronounced by a Divorce Court of the country where the parties to an English marriage are domiciled, will, under the present state of the law, dissolve an English marriage and be held valid in England.[7] In regard to Delicts considerations of a different

[1] *Cf. Birt* v. *Bontinez*, L. R. 1 P. & D. at pp. 485—489.

[2] Von Bar's *International Law*, pp. 516, 517; *Wilson* v. *Wilson*, L. R. 2 P. & D. 442. But a judicial separation may be obtained from a Court in whose jurisdiction the parties are merely residing, if the necessities of the case demand that one of them should be protected against a matrimonial wrong done by the other. *Armytage* v. *Armytage*, TIMES, 22nd June, 1898, p. 17.

[3] *Brodie* v. *Brodie*, 30 L. J. P. D. & A. 185. *Cf. Gillis* v. *Gillis*, 8 Ir. Rep. 597, Equity.

[4] *Dalhousie* v. *McDonall*, 7 Cl. & Fin. 817.

[5] *Lolley's Case*, 2 Clark & F. 567, n.; *McCarthy* v. *De Coix*, 2 Clark & F. 558, n.

[6] *Law of Marriage and Divorce*, by David Stewart, San Francisco, 1884, pp. 182, 183, section 213; *Shaw* v. *Gould* (1868), L. R. 3 H. L. 55, at p. 85; *Wilson* v. *Wilson* (1872), L. R. 2 P. & D. at p. 442; *Niboyet* v. *Niboyet* (1878), 4 P. D. 1, 19, C. A.

[7] Dicey, *Conflict of Laws*, App. 757.

character affect the question of jurisdiction than in the case of Obligations arising out of Contract. In the case of Obligations *ex contractu* the primary rule is that all jurisdiction is territorial and *extra territorium jus dicenti impune non paretur.*[1] But the acquisition of an actual domicile counts as a voluntary submission to the Courts of that country, which operates also as a withdrawal of submission to the Courts of the former domicile. In the case of Obligations *ex delicto*, the person who has received damage ought to be allowed some more efficient protection than the creditor enjoys in other Obligations which rest upon freewill, and is all the more entitled to adhere to that jurisdiction which has once been established, irrespective of whether the person who has committed the Delict lives at the place where it was committed, or has property there, as in many cases it is not known till afterwards who it was who did commit the Delict. In cases of this kind the injured person is absolutely entitled to choose between the *forum delicti commissi* and the *forum domicilii.*[2] But if an act done in a foreign country is made the foundation of an action in England, it must be shown that the act is wrongful as well by the law of England as by the law of the country where it was done.[3]

The *forum* for trial of Criminal Offences.

276. Von Bar, the great German writer on International Law, from whose celebrated work the above principles have been mainly deduced, mentions four different theories, which appear in different legislations and in the works of different authors, in regard to International Criminal Law.[4] These theories rest on the divergent principles of territoriality, per-

[1] *Sirdar Gurdyal Singh* v. *The Raja of Faridkot*, (1894) A. C. 670.

[2] Von Bar's *International Law*, pp. 517, 518. See this principle recognised by the Indian Legislature in section 18, Act XIV. of 1882.

[3] Rattigan's *Private International Law*, 152; Dicey, rule 175, p. 659; No. 4, P. R. 1897.

[4] *International Law*, sections 132—135, pp. 626—639. What follows in the text is mostly taken from this work.

CHAP. XI. sonality, protection of person and property, and of prevention, and may be briefly noticed.

Territoriality. 277. The first theory is that a Criminal Statute is limited to the territory for which it was enacted,[1] and that any act committed in another country is beyond its influence. The principle upon which this theory is based is the broad and undeniable one, that every State has the right of punishing criminal acts which have taken place within its own territory, from which it follows directly that each must recognise the authority of its neighbour, which rests upon the same foundation, and not attempt, therefore, to extend its own authority to acts done in another country. This proposition which all recognise is, nevertheless, open to the serious objection that it fails to secure the proper punishment of Crimes against public order. The greatest Crimes may go unpunished in a criminal's native country, if after the deed, committed perhaps a few miles beyond the frontier, he can escape from the Officers of that State and make his way to the State to which he belongs. The objection may be to a certain extent removed by the adoption of treaties of Extradition, which are now frequently entered into between independent States, under which the State in whose territory an offender takes refuge surrenders him to the State in whose territory the act was committed. But in the first place most States refuse to give up their own subjects, and even if a State were prepared to do so, the difficulty in the application of the general principle would not in all cases be completely removed. Thus it may be that a Crime would be committed by a subject of one State against that State, or against fellow-subjects, in some place where there is either no magisterial authority at all, or one that exercises its jurisdiction on uncivilised principles,

[1] It is a general principle "that the penal laws of our country cannot affect the laws and rights of citizens of another," per Grose, J., in the celebrated case of *Ogden* v. *Folliott*, 2 Revised Reports, at p. 745; and see per Buller, J., S. C., at p. 743.

which we cannot in any way recognise. To adhere rigidly to the principle of Territoriality in such a case would be either to exclude all punishment or to subject the offender possibly to some cruel and barbarous punishment, which would shock our sense of humanity. The advocates of this theory have therefore been obliged to make certain exceptions upon grounds of expediency, and have attempted to justify them by maintaining that the State has an interest in inflicting punishment in these cases. But to arrogate a jurisdiction solely on the ground of interest, where no right to it exists, is merely a justification of judicial murder.

Personal theory.

278. The second theory extends the Criminal Law of any State not merely to Offences committed there, but also to Offences committed by its citizens abroad. This view is founded upon the assumption that Criminal Laws are Personal Statutes, which impose obligations upon the subjects of a State which can never be permitted to be transgressed even in the Territory of another State. But the most remarkable consequences follow from an unconditional claim of the *forum ligeantiæ* to exercise jurisdiction over citizens of a State for offences against its laws when committed by them abroad. Is a person, it is asked, to be liable to punishment for an act which was sanctioned, or perhaps required by the Law or Custom of the country in which he was temporarily resident? How can our State ask its subjects to observe all the provisions of our Laws which are in conformity with our legal theories, our fashions, and our institutions, in a foreign land, where it may be that every one observes different rules of conduct? Suppose, as Schwarze remarks, that to take the Law into one's own hands is criminal in this country, but can only be visited with civil disabilities in another. Is the Judge of this country to punish one who returns home after the lapse of years with the criminal consequences of such an act? These and many other difficulties, it is said, must arise

if the Law of the Domicile is to be tied round the necks of its subjects like a rope. The principle of Personality is nevertheless applied, though only to a limited extent, in most European States, and notably in France, where it is made the foundation of Articles 5—7 of the Code d'Instruction Criminelle. In England it finds expression in a Statute which enacts that a British subject may be indicted for murder, manslaughter, or bigamy, whether committed within the Queen's dominions or without, and may be tried in any place in England or Ireland in which he shall be apprehended or be in custody.[1] The Indian Legislature has also recognised it to a certain extent by rendering British subjects liable for offences committed out of British India if the Political Agent, if there be one, for the territory in which the offence is alleged to have been committed, certifies that, in his opinion, the charge ought to be inquired into in British India.[2]

Protection theory.

279. Recognising that all Crimes committed in the country and all Crimes committed by natives abroad, must be punished, the third theory proceeds to lay down the rule that the State has a right to protect itself and its subjects from injury, and is therefore privileged to visit any injury with punishment. But the right to punish for Crime is not a necessary corollary from the right of the State to protect its subjects; and even if it could be deduced from the latter it would only be subsidiary to the primary right of the State in which the injured persons are to punish the wrong-doers. It is now thought that the principle ought to be confined to cases

[1] 24 & 25 Vict. c. 100, sections 9, 57. It was under this Statute (section 4) that Johann Most was convicted of inciting to murder the Emperor of Russia by the publication of a newspaper called the *Freiheit*. L. R. 7 Q. B. D. 244.

[2] Section 188, Criminal Procedure Code of 1898; and section 4, Indian Penal Code, as to Offences committed abroad by "Servants of the Queen," *i.e.*, officers or servants appointed or employed in India by or under authority of 21 & 22 Vict. c. 106.

where the offence, committed beyond its territory, compromises the security of the State, and is not sufficiently prevented by the Criminal Law of the State where it is committed.[1]

Prevention theory.

280. The fourth and last theory depends on a cosmopolitan conception of Criminal Law, which assumes that a penal offence has the same character wherever it is committed, and that therefore the development of the Law applicable to it is not limited by the local limits of the State. It is supported in some quarters by appealing to the *forum deprehensionis*, or jurisdiction within which the offender is apprehended, a doctrine much favoured by German Criminal Lawyers of the sixteenth and seventeenth centuries, but which had been rejected by the Italians, and is now only recognised in a few individual States, and there only under important limitations. By others it is supported upon a theory of Prevention, according to which the State has no other object in inflicting punishment than to protect itself from future injury that may be wrought by the wicked will of the criminal manifested in his act. But the falsity of this theory of Prevention is now generally acknowledged; while the extension of Criminal Law to all Offences wherever and by whomsoever committed is calculated to render the administration of justice continually open to the inconvenience of diplomatic intervention. Neither the German Criminal Code of 1871 nor the English Law lends any support to this fourth theory.

Territorial theory most generally adopted.

281. Of the above theories the one based on Territoriality is stringently adopted by English Jurists, and is also most generally recognised by Continental States. It is certainly the least open to objection, though, as we have seen, it may need to be supplemented by the application in certain excep-

[1] A resolution to this effect was adopted by the "Institut de Droit International" at its Brussels Session in 1879.

CHAP. XI. tional cases of other principles. It is at all events not a matter of dispute that all persons present in a country are subject to the Criminal Law there recognised. Thus the Indian Penal Code provides that "*every* person" shall be liable to punishment under that Code and not otherwise, for every act or omission contrary to the provisions thereof, of which he shall be guilty within the territories vested or which may become vested in Her Majesty by 21 & 22 Vict. c. 106, from and after the 1st May, 1861.[1] But, on the other hand, the penal authority of the State can never properly extend to any acts committed abroad other than those which are committed by its own subjects.[2] By a fiction of Law, however, crimes committed on board of ships upon the high seas are considered as having been committed in the territory, of which they are deemed to be a roving part, of the State whose flag the ship is entitled to carry.[3] And this extra-territoriality is retained by ships even when lying in a foreign port, though in this case there might be a concurrent jurisdiction in the Courts of the State to which the port belongs. By a recent Statute, resulting from the decision of the majority of the Judges in *Reg.* v. *Keyne* (known as the *Franconia case*), the Law of England visits with punishment Offences committed by a foreigner in a British port or anywhere within one marine league of the British shore upon the open sea.[4]

What Criminal Law is to be applied.

282. It is conceded that in regard to offences committed within a State the Law of that State alone can be adminis-

[1] Section 2, Act XLV. of 1860.

[2] *Cf.* 35 Hen. VIII. c. 2; section 188, Act V. of 1898; I. L. R. X. Bomb. 186; No. 20, *Punjab Record,* 1878, Criminal.

[3] *The Merchant Shipping Act,* 1894; *Reg.* v. *Anderson,* 1 C. C. 161; *Attorney-General for Hong Kong* v. *Kwok-a-Sing,* 5 P. C. 179; *Reg.* v. *Keyne,* L. R. 2 Exch. D. 63.

[4] 41 & 42 Vict. c. 73, section 2. *Cf.* as regards India, VIII. Bomb. H. C. Reps. 63, Cr. Cas.; and as to Offences on the high seas beyond the limit of three miles, VII. Bomb. H. C. Reps. 89, Cr. Cas.

tered by a native Court.[1] So also in regard to Crimes committed by a subject abroad, the Law of his own country, if he is tried there, can alone determine the penalty to be imposed, except that in awarding punishment the Law of the place where the act was done may be considered as serving to mitigate the character of the act. It is argued that the application of the subject's own Law cannot result in any real injustice, for he is (or ought to be) acquainted with the principles of the Law which lie at the root of the legislation of his own country, and carries that knowledge with him, or is at least deemed to do so. So, on the other hand, the rule that where an act is not criminal abroad it must go unpunished everywhere, cannot be accepted without certain modifications. It would never be tolerated, for instance, that a murder committed by a subject in a barbarian territory, where the Law provided no punishment for such a Crime, should go unpunished in his own country. It is to avoid being bound by barbarian rules of this kind that England and France in their dealings with heathen nations reserve the right of punishing Crimes committed in those countries by their subjects according to their own Law.[2] Subject, however, to this necessary restriction, the general principle of Criminal Jurisprudence is, "the quality of the Act done depends on the Law of the place where it is done."[3]

[1] Von Bar's *International Law*, section 131, p. 625.

[2] 6 & 7 Vict. c. 94; 38 & 39 Vict. c. 85; 41 & 42 Vict. c. 67. So in India, section 188, Act V. of 1898. Thus if a Native British Subject in any place outside British India, or a European British Subject in any State in alliance with us, commits an act, which is an offence under the Indian Penal Code, he is liable even though it is not an offence according to the law of the place in which it was committed. VIII. Bomb. H. C. Reps. 92, Cr. Cas.; II. Mad. H. C. Reps. 444.

[3] Per Mellish, L. J., in *Attorney-General of Hong-Kong* v. *Kwok-a-Sing*, 5 P. C. 179.

CHAPTER XII.

PUBLIC LAW.

CHAP. XII.

Definition.

283. THE branch of Law which we now propose to consider is that which embraces those institutions which concern the position and the relations of individuals to one another as members of a State, as well as the legal relations of the State as a body politic. In order to distinguish this branch from that which more particularly deals with the legal relations of individuals as such, to which the name Private Law is given, we call it Public Law. This division has been sharply criticised by Austin as unscientific, inconvenient, detestable, and as resting upon no intelligible basis.[1] But from the age of Ulpian down to the present time it has been recognised as affording a convenient treatment of topics which are best considered by themselves, as more directly affecting the constitution and well-being of the State as a unit, than the individuals who compose the State in their relations with one another, and who in the department of Private Law are regarded as so many distinct and independent units. Now, in order that men may participate in what is right, and on account of their mutual influence on one another, a Juridical Constitution uniting them under one Will is requisite. This relation of the individuals of a nation to each other constitutes THE CIVIL UNION in the Social State; and viewed as a whole in relation to its constituent members, it forms THE POLITICAL STATE.[2] The system of Law which is requisite

[1] *Jurisprudence*, Vol. II., Lect. XLIV., pp. 770–786.

[2] Kant's *Philosophy of Law*, p. 161.

for a People constituting a Political State is that which is more especially the sphere of the department of Law with which we are now concerned. CHAP. XII.

Scope of Public Law.

284. The Roman Jurists understood by the term Public Law *quod ad statum rei Romanæ spectat:* that which relates to the institutions of the Roman Empire, as contrasted with that which concerns the convenience of individuals (*quod ad singulorum utilitatem*). The proper sphere of the former was said to be "religion, the priests, and magistrates (*publicum Jus in sacris, in sacerdotibus, in magistratibus consistit*)."[1] Remembering that every State contains in itself three Powers, the Legislative, the Executive, and the Judicial,[2] Public Law may be also considered under the same triple classification.

Legislative Power united.

285. The Legislative Power can only belong to the united Will of the People, for it is only as the expression of that Will that Laws can do no wrong, agreeably to the maxim, *volenti non fit injuria.*[3] The mode in which the united and consenting Will of the People is to be declared, is regulated in each State by the Constitution of that State, which determines the structure of the given Supreme Government, and the character of the Person, or the respective characters of the Persons, in whom, for the time being, the Sovereignty shall reside.[4] In the Middle Ages the fundamental character of all States was dynastical and aristocratical, and the ruling Prince identified himself with the State, while the People were looked upon as bound merely to pay taxes, to render military service when called upon, and to obey the Officers of the State. This was the Patrimonial Theory, according to

View of the State in the Middle Ages.

[1] Dig. I. 1, 1, section 2; Just. *Inst.* 1, 1, 4.

[2] Kant's *Philosophy of Law*, p. 165. *Cf.* Aristotle, *Polit.* IV. 11, 1; Montesquieu, *Esprit des Lois*, XI., Ch. 6.

[3] *Cf.* Hobbes, *Leviathan*, Ch. XVIII., p. 135; Ch. XXVI., pp. 205—207, Oxford, 1881. Austin's *Jurisprudence*, Vol. I., 275.

[4] Austin, *Jurisprudence*, 1, 274.

 which the Prince, like a private person, exercised certain rights over his Land and People by right of Ownership, precisely as a private owner exercises over his goods and chattels. It was thus in a thoroughly realistic sense that Louis XIV. of France used the celebrated phrase, *l'état c'est moi* ("I am the State"), and the same idea was fully shared by other Kings and Sovereign Princes of that age, and even by the presiding Magistrates of so-called Free States.[1] The Philosophers of the Eighteenth Century, on the other hand, built their notion

Contrat social.

of a State upon a Social Contract (*contrat social*),[2] which the individual members composing the State were presumed to have entered into by their voluntary association in the one Community. No theory has been more vigorously discussed, none has ever been heralded with such outbursts of extravagant praise, or subjected to such violent criticism and abuse, as this concept of a Social Contract, originally propounded by Hobbes, adopted by Locke, and made famous by Jean Jacques Rousseau, a citizen of Geneva. Regarded by some as the triumphal assertion of the rights of man, by others as the direct incentive for revolt and the parent of the doctrines preached by Nihilists and Anarchists, the *Contrat Social* is talked of by everyone and understood by few. It is not within the province of this treatise to examine the arguments by which Rousseau, with all the fascination of a masterly style, endeavoured to base the origin of a State on an original voluntary pact. It will be sufficient to direct attention to two weak points of this doctrine. In the first place, by attempting to solve the great problem of sovereignty, by the resolution of an original convention, Rousseau anticipates the achievements of centuries. He presupposes as a starting point a degree of political sagacity and a disposition to submit to the supremacy of law which could never have

[1] Bluntschli, *Gesammelte kleine Schriften*, Vol. II., p. 71.

[2] Much as Plato makes Glaucon propound a theory of Justice as "a contract neither to do nor to suffer wrong." *Repub.* bk. II.

characterised a people in a primitive condition of nature. A popular convention may be conceived in changing the form of the State, or in planting the State upon new territory by a population already politically educated, but not as the basis of a primal creation.[1] Again, by teaching that we are only members of a State by reason of an original voluntary pact, Rousseau gives the incentive to every ill-disposed or wrong-headed person, on attaining his manhood, of asserting that he has not given his consent to such laws as he disapproves of, and is consequently not bound by them, or even of attempting to overthrow all civil society as no longer desired by him. It is the dreaded consequences of this teaching, rather than the direct teaching itself, which have caused Rousseau to be so violently assailed; and a recent learned French writer does not hesitate to call him the "*aïeul*" (or grand-parent) of Anarchists and Nihilists.[2] It may be conceded that Rousseau never himself intended to propound any such revolutionary doctrine. Indeed, Apostle of Liberty though he is called, it is remarkable that in no system is the individual so completely bound hand and foot and subordinated to the collective will of the community as in Rousseau's *Contrat Social.* Having once expressly or tacitly consented to the contract which has admitted him into membership, the individual thenceforward delivers himself up as a living slave for the community to do as it likes with his body and his worldly possessions.[3] "There is and can be," he says, "no kind of fundamental law which is obligatory upon the body of a people, not even the *Contrat Social.*"[4] From this perpetual submission the individual can only be released by all his fellow citizens agreeing in solemn assembly to break the common contract.[5] The power of political majorities could

[1] Burgess, *Political Science and Constitutional Law*, Vol. I., p. 62.

[2] *Le Compte de Vareilles-Sommières* in his *Principes Fondamentaux du Droit*, p. 96.

[3] Lib. I. Ch. VI., p. 248.

[4] Lib. I. Ch. VII., p. 249.

[5] Lib. II. Ch. XVII.

Chap. XII.

hardly have been more exaggerated or placed on a loftier basis, and it is not altogether undeservedly that the *Contrat Social* has been called "the breviary of despotism."[1] Indeed, by denouncing all those restrictions which tend to mitigate the despotism of majorities, he has paved the way for worse tyrannies than those he assailed.[2] So that whether we regard the Social Contract theory from a historical or from a purely social stand-point, it is undoubtedly open to serious objections; and as a learned Italian writer eloquently observes, having commenced with the apotheosis of pure reason, it ended in the bloodshed of a civil war: the calm of dialectical logic was succeeded by the frantic movements it gave to the guillotine.[3] "Thus it always happens," continues the same writer: "a flake of snow that is detached from the crest of a mountain is scarcely even observed, but rolling down the side of the mountain it becomes an impetuous avalanche."[4] Descending into the next century this view of a Social Contract, which had penetrated everywhere, and paved the way for the French Revolution, was succeeded by another which represented the State as a natural growth independent of the human Will. The only element of truth in either of these theories lies, says Puchta with cutting sarcasm, in its negation of the other.[5] The true theory is rather that States are the product of a gradual and continuous development of human society,[6] and owe their origin to the human Will, not indeed the Will of Individuals as such, but as members of one Community; in other words to the Will of the Totality, or the

True theory of origin of States.

[1] *Les Principes Fondamentaux du Droit*, p. 97.

[2] Lecky, *Democracy and Liberty*, Vol. II., p. 193.

[3] *Proudhon* says: "*La vogue de Rousseau a coûté à la France plus d'or, plus de sang, plus de honte que le règne detesté des trois fameuses courtisanes ne lui en avait fait répondre.*" Idée Générale de la Revolution au XIXe. Siècle, p. 135.

[4] *Filosofia del Diritto Privato*, per Pietro Cogliolo, Firenze, 1888, p. 17.

[5] *Cursus der Institutionen*, Vol. I., section 12, pp. 25, 26.

[6] Burgess, *Political Science and Constitutional Law*, Ch. II., p. 59.

People as a Whole. This Popular Will (*Volksgeist*) is the natural source of the State and of its Constitution. It produces the State as it produces Law, by uniting the People in the expression of a common Will to subject themselves to this Authority as the Organ of Law. But this product is only reached after centuries of slow internal growth. By nature, Man, as Aristotle long ago taught us, is essentially a Political Being (πολιτικον ζωον), and his inclinations and his fears led him early in his history to seek the co-operation and association of his fellow men. Ethnical homogeneity, there is reason to believe, constituted the original basis of all political society, and it was only by very slow degrees that this primitive notion was gradually widened to embrace the geographical organization which underlies the constitution of modern nationalities. Indeed, Aristotle himself, in the passage we have quoted from, is considering man as a member of a city State, which, from his ideal stand-point, was the highest social organization attainable. In this ideal or perfected State, man, says Aristotle, "is the best of animals." But "when separated from law and justice he is the worst of all."[1] Arts, laws, and governments are, in fact, necessary for peoples "as crutches are for old men."[2] Viewed at the present day from a scientist's point of view, the State, as now developed into an organised political unit, is but the Man in image. The Organism of the State is a mere reflexion or type of the human Organism.[3] In this Organism the Individual is sunk in the Whole. The Whole is everything, the Individual nothing.[4] For the State, as Schelling maintains, is as little constituted for the individual man, as the latter is for the State, but both share an undivided joint-existence, which Adam Müller likens to a snail inseparable

[1] *Pol.* I., 2, sections 15, 16 (Jowett's Translation).

[2] By Rousseau, in his letter to *M. Philopolis.*

[3] Bluntschli, *Gesammelte kleine Schriften*, Vol. I., p. 278; "*Der Stat is der Man.*"

[4] *Ibid.* p. 289.

CHAP. XII.

from its shell. This apotheosis of the State, as Ahrens calls it,[1] is nothing else than the climax of the ancient notion of a State, with its roots extending far into the soil of Oriental Pantheism, which knew no intellectual principle substantially distinct and separable from that of the all-pervading Divine Intelligence. In more modern times the Social State has succeeded the Patrimonial, and the participation of the subjects of a State in the transaction of its affairs is now regarded as a part of their Private Right. The three leading forms of existing Governments are Monarchical, Democratical, and Despotic; but whatever may be the form of Government, the actual Sovereign Authority of a State, whether it be vested in a Monarch, a President, or a Representative Body, must in theory be absolutely omnipotent. For whoever would restrict the Supreme Power of the State must have more, or at least equal power as compared with the Power that is so restricted, and if he is to be considered capable of judging what is right in every case, he may also publicly order Resistance. But such a one, and not the Actual Authority, would then be the Supreme Power, which is contradictory. For the same reason, as Kant well observes, resistance of the highest Legislative Authority can never but be contrary to the Law, and must even be regarded as tending to destroy the whole legal Constitution. In order to be entitled to offer such resistance, a Public Law would be required to permit it. But the Supreme Legislature would by such a Law cease to be Supreme, and the People as Subjects would be made Sovereign over that to which they are subject; which is also a contradiction.[2] To regulate how the various Organs of the Sovereign Power are to exercise their respective functions; what rule of succession is to govern the devolution of the Supreme Executive Authority;

Leading forms of Government.

Province of Constitutional Law.

[1] *Philosophie des Rechts*, Vol. II., p. 285.

[2] *Philosophy of Law*, pp. 175, 177.

what are the privileges, powers, and responsibilities of Ministers, of Judges, Magistrates, and Inferior Officers of Government; under what conditions large Corporate Bodies like Municipalities and Local Boards are to be allowed to govern themselves in all matters of internal administration; how the people are to be represented in Parliament or some other Constitutional Assembly; how Laws are to be passed or repealed; what relations shall subsist between the Mother Country and her Colonies; or between the Church and State; who shall control the Army, and exercise the prerogative of declaring War or Peace; these and other like matters are included in the province of Constitutional Law.

Executive or Administrative Law.

286. Precisely as in Nature every Life requires Organs for its expression, so also the State is animated from within by the living breath of its various Official Organs. The more powerful and active the State is, in its external relations, the more distinct and vigorous will be the character of its Organs. Thus the spirit of the Roman Consulate so inspired even weak men like Cicero that it raised and strengthened them to conquer their weakness, and to appear dauntless in the discharge of their duty. And thus, too, the consciousness of the dignity of his Kingly Office transformed an irresolute Louis XVI. in his last moments into a man of courage, who in the calm spirit of resignation and fearlessness with which he met his sad fate became a hero, and thus threw a halo of martyrdom round his death, which has served to transmit his name to posterity as one who at least died as became a King, if in life he was only distinguished for his weakness, dullness, and vacillation. It may also be safely asserted that the more Powers that are brought into play in a State, the more rules will be needed to regulate their functions. As civilization becomes more highly organized and complex, as machinery increases and population and industries agglomerate, new wants, interests, and dangers arise which imperiously require

increased regulation. It is impossible to leave a great metropolis or a vast fluctuating industrial population with as little regulation as a country village or a pastoral people.[1] But it is not in the least true that every extension of the State's activity in the sphere of Administration produces a corresponding diminution in the freedom of the Individual. The State and Private Freedom do not stand in any natural opposition, and the gain of the one is not necessarily measured by a loss of the other. In fact there is no modern State which on the one hand can suffer all Progress to be left entirely in the hands of Individuals, or on the other hand can alone undertake to initiate and guide it. But it is precisely in the proper relation of the State's Activity to Private Activity that views so largely differ, and which distinguishes one System of Administration from another. Thus, in France the State often interferes in matters which in England are left to the care of Individuals. In the former all great progress has been due to Statesmen like Richelieu, Sully, and Colbert, or to absolute Monarchs like Louis XI., Louis XIV., or Napoleon, or, lastly, has been the outcome of the Laws of the Great Revolution. In England, on the contrary, Self-Administration and Local-Government have produced the greatest results. The ambition of the Frenchman is to secure Official employment rather than an independent and rich private existence.[2] He applies all his zeal and industry in the performance of Official functions, and is skilled in all the mechanism of Official business. The Englishman loves his personal freedom above everything else, and, at least in the opinion of foreigners, shows more skill in the conduct of his own affairs than in matters of Statecraft.[3] The inclinations and capacities of the

[1] Lecky, *Democracy and Liberty*, Vol. I., p. 272.

[2] See Demolin's *A quoi tient la supériorité des Anglo-Saxons*, Ch. I., p. 3 *et seq.*

[3] Bluntschli, *Gesammelte kleine Schriften*, Vol. I., p. 310. In 1861 an English Minister declared in Parliament "that numbers of employés in the various departments of the Civil Service were utterly incompetent to dis-

People of each State must in short be left to work out the problem of how far the interference of the State is justifiable or otherwise; and in what departments of Administration it is to exercise a larger or a more limited influence.[1] Experience has shown that the sudden introduction of institutions of exotic growth into a country which was unsuited by the character, idiosyncrasies, or state of culture of its inhabitants to receive them, has only ended in disastrous failure. In illustration of this remark one may be excused for referring to the fact that the concession of Local Self-Government to Municipalities and Local Boards in India was followed almost immediately afterwards by a withdrawal of the privilege from many of the Local Bodies upon whom it had been conferred.[2] But subject to the above consideration the topics which may be said to fall fairly within the sphere of an intelligent and wise Administration may be enumerated as follows:—(*a*) the promulgation of Laws; (*b*) the administration of Justice; (*c*) the detection and prevention of Crime; (*d*) the control of the Coinage and Paper Currency; (*e*) the collection of Taxes; (*f*) the control and regulation of the Army and Navy; (*g*) the government of Colonies and Dependencies; (*h*) the working of a system of Poor Laws; (*i*) the regulation and management of Lunatic

Topics within scope of Administrative Law.

charge the services of their posts, that they were often grossly ignorant, sometimes absolutely stupid, occasionally thoroughly worthless." Such a description is no longer true, as the Civil Service has been greatly improved in recent years, and now attracts some of the best men that our Universities produce.

[1] *Cf.* Ahrens, *Philosophie des Rechts*, Vol. II., pp. 290—292.

[2] Only recently (in November, 1898) the Government of the North-Western Province was compelled to point out that the Municipal Board of Agra had failed to rise to the level of the duties imposed on it—that it had parted with control over its subordinates, had allowed arrangements to continue which facilitated—even encouraged—malversation of public funds, and that the state of affairs left the Government no option but to formally consider the question whether the Board should not be superseded under section 63 of Act XV. of 1883: *Pioneer Mail* of the 18th November, 1898. *Cf.* the remarks of Professor Dr. Ernst Meier, apud Holtzendorff, *Encyklopädie*, p. 1097, on the danger of an undue extension of Local Self-Government.

Asylums; (*j*) the supervision of Trades and Professions; (*k*) the maintenance of proper means of Communication, by land and water; (*l*) the carriage of Letters and Parcels through the Post and the transmission of Telegraphic Messages; (*m*) the introduction of Sanitary Reforms which are calculated to raise the health of the community, or alleviate or prevent human suffering;[1] and all other matters calculated to promote the Material and Moral Welfare of the people composing the State.[2] The responsibility of persons entrusted with Administrative or Executive functions may be considered either with reference to their Official or Private responsibility. In the former aspect they are answerable to the State for the proper discharge of their duties, neglect of which may entail dismissal from Office, or, in the case of a more serious dereliction, may involve, in a Constitution like that of England, impeachment before Parliament, as in the celebrated case of Warren Hastings. But, on the other hand, over-zeal for the public service or individual interest may at times, despite all precautions and the general efficient character of an Administration, lead a Public Officer in the discharge of what he conceives to be his duty, to commit a private Wrong. For such a Wrong he is, like everybody else, accountable in a Court of Law. The principle which underlies this private responsibility is, that obedience to administrative orders is no defence to an action or prosecution for acts done in excess of legal authority.[3] But it must not be forgotten

Responsibility of Executive Officers.

[1] Here again the measures adopted should aim simply at the necessary protection of the community, avoiding as far as is compatible with that supreme duty any undue meddling or inquisitorial interference with the right of an adult man to regulate his own private household, otherwise scientific protectionism becomes hygienic tyranny.

[2] Compare the excellent observations of Paul Leroy Boileau on the proper functions of a State in his interesting monograph on *The Modern State*, Chap. V., p. 63, and in Part II. of the same book (*Social Science Series*).

[3] Dicey's *Constitutional Law*, pp. 23, 203.

that the protection of the Rights of Individuals is not the only purpose of a State, or interference with a Private Right the only evil it has to guard against. The State has also to fulfil certain other important tasks in the various departments of intellectual and economical existence, and it has above all to guard against a possible destruction of the Administration as a Whole. The welfare of the State, the supreme end of all Law and Order (*salus reipublicæ suprema lex*), is not simply the well-being and happiness of the Citizens of the State, but its own Highest Good. It signifies that condition in which the greatest harmony is attained between its Constitution and the Principles of Right.[1] No people were ever more sensible of this than the Romans. They were zealous in the protection of Private Rights, and no people before or since has shown a greater aptitude than they displayed in the organisation of a Judicial System. But this practical people were equally sensible of the danger of pushing the principle too far, that in the exercise of its Sovereign Rights the State must stand on the same footing as the Individual in the assertion of his Subjective Rights. They accordingly distinguished between a *jurisdictio inter privatos* and a *jurisdictio inter populum et privatos*: the one dealing with legal disputes between Private Persons, and the other with those between the Community (*populum*) and a Private Person. For the latter the jurisdiction of the Censor was substituted for that of the Prætor, and he decided without the aid of *judices* (the jury), and not according to strict Civil Law, but the *Jus Æquum*.[2] In our own modern System the absence of amenability of the Civil Servants of the Crown to Special Tribunals is admitted even by English writers to be "not wholly beneficial."[3] And some traces of a special pro-

[1] Kant's *Philosophy of Law*, p. 173.

[2] Mommsen, *Römisches Staatsrecht*, I., pp. 162—169, Leipzig, 1876; *Das Verwaltungsrecht*, apud Holtzendorff, 1157-58.

[3] Dicey's *Law of the Constitution*, p. 203.

CHAP. XII. tection to the interests of Government and the acts of its Agents are not wanting in the English and Indian Statute Books. Thus various Statutes exist in England regulating the responsibilities of different classes of Executive Officers, such as Sheriffs, Bailiffs, Customs, Excise, and Police Officers, and providing for the protection of such persons that all actions against them for anything done or purporting to be done by them as Public Servants shall be commenced within a short period after the act complained of and not afterwards.[1] These provisions are merely limited applications of the continental doctrine that in matters of high policy the Administration has a discretionary authority which cannot be controlled by any Court. Thus, in France the ordinary Civil Tribunals cannot pronounce on the validity of any administrative act (*acte administratif*), nor entertain an action brought by a private individual against an Official for a wrong done in discharge of his Official duties. Redress in such cases must be sought from the Administrative Tribunals (*tribunaux administratifs*).[2] In Germany, according to the *Gerichtverfassungsgesetz* of the 27th January, 1877,[3] which came into force on the 1st October, 1879, all claims against Imperial Officials (*Reichs-beamte*) for illegal acts or omissions in the discharge of their Official functions must be instituted in the *Landgerichte*, and the same rule prevails (under the operation of Special Ordinances) in several of the Independent States, such as Prussia, Bavaria, Saxony, Wurtemburg, Baden, with respect to actions against Officials of those

[1] Chester's *Powers, Duties, and Liabilities of Executive Officers*, pp. 9, 54—56, 98, 109—113, 235—291. In India *cf.* Act 2, Schedule II., *Limitation Act of* 1877; I. L. R. VI. Cal. 9; I. L. R. I. Allah. 269; *Ibid.* 4, 102; I. L. R. VIII. Bomb. 421. As to non-responsibility of a public body for non-performance of a duty, such as the repair of a public highway, see *Cowley* v. *Newmarket Local Board*, House of Lords, 9th August, 1892, *Times* of 10th August, p. 13; and *cf.* also *Municipality of Picton* v. *Geldert*, (1893) App. Cas. 524.

[2] Dicey's *Law of the Constitution*, 189—191.

[3] Section 70.

Chap. XII.

Act of State not examinable in Courts of Justice.

States.[1] But an act done by the authority, previous or subsequent, of the Government of a Sovereign State in the exercise of *de facto* Sovereignty is not examinable at all in the Courts of Justice of any other State. Thus, where the Chief of an Independent State exercising the Sovereign power of that State within its territories, confiscates property within those territories, the confiscation must be respected by British Courts of Justice. And if the fact of such confiscation is disputed, it must be ascertained by the Court before which the question is raised in the same manner as all other facts which are in issue between the parties.[2] An exception would seem, however, to be allowed to the operation of this general rule where the confiscation was clearly opposed to the Law of Nations, and where, in a suit between two private persons, the act of confiscation was set up as a defence by one party to the claim of the other. Thus where a contract was made in England between two Danish subjects, one of whom was domiciled in England, and afterwards, during a war between England and Denmark, the Danish Government confiscated the debt and required it to be paid by the debtor, who was then in Denmark, and he paid it accordingly; the English Court of King's Bench (Lord Ellenborough, C.J.), on a suit brought in England, after the peace, by the creditor against the debtor, held that the payment to the Danish Government was no discharge, although it would have been so by the Laws of Denmark, upon the ground that such a confiscation was not justified by the Law of Nations.[3] And of course it is open to a British Municipal Court, when a defendant sets up as justification something which is alleged to be an act of State, to inquire whether the Act relied upon is one of that

[1] *Civil Processordnung mit Gerichtsverfassungsgesetz*, Text-Ausgabe mit Anmerkungen und Sachregister von R. Sydow, p. 48, n. (7), Berlin, 1881.

[2] Vol. XIV. Suth. W. R. 218; No. 7, P. R. 1882; No. 21, P. R. 1894; I. L. R. V. Mad. 273.

[3] *Wolff* v. *Oxholm*, VI. M. & S. 92.

Chap. XII. character.[1] With the above qualification the general rule is, that so far as such an act affects persons not subject to the Government in question, it is not examinable in the ordinary Courts of that State. If and so far as it affects a subject of the same State, it may be, and in England it is, examinable by the local Courts in their ordinary jurisdiction. But in most Continental countries the remedy for such acts must be sought before a Special Tribunal.[2] In India the question of the powers of Municipal Courts to adjudicate upon transactions which are of the nature of Acts of State has frequently formed the subject of judicial decision. Thus it has been held that the seizure or confiscation of the property of the late King of Delhi was an Act of State or War, in respect of which the Municipal Courts had no jurisdiction.[3] So a grant made in pursuance of the Right of Conquest is a similar Act of State outside the cognizance of a Municipal Court.[4]

Judicial. 287. The last head under which the Activity of a State displays itself in the domain of Public Law is the Judicial. In the co-operation of these three Activities the State realises its true Autonomy, which consists in its organising, forming, and maintaining itself in accordance with the Laws of Freedom.[5] But although the last to be considered, the Judicial function of a State is very far from being the least important. Indeed the real character of a State is best reflected in this Department of its Activity, which shows how it discharges its duty as the Guardian of Order, in punishing any transgression of the Public Law. But Judicial Punishment (*pœna forensis*) can never be rightly administered merely as a

[1] *Bombay, Burmah Trading Co.* v. *Mirza Muhdi Ali Sheragee*, X. Beng. Law Reps. 345.

[2] Pollock's *Law of Torts*, p. 98.

[3] No. 2, *Punjab Record*, 1872, *Privy Council.*

[4] No. 1, *Ibid.*, *Privy Council.*

[5] Kant's *Philosophy of Law*, p. 173.

means for promoting another Good either with regard to the Criminal himself or to Civil Society, but ought in all cases to be imposed only because the individual on whom it is inflicted has committed a Crime.[1] The pharisaical principle, "It is better that one man should die than that the whole people should perish," is quite inadmissible in any civilised System for the administration of Justice, for it confounds Justice with Expediency, which can never be tolerated. But Crimes understood as transgressions of Public Law may be divided into two broad classes, according as the transgression is calculated to affect the general welfare or simply individuals as such. In the Roman Law the latter were regarded as mere Civil Delicts giving rise to a liability for damages as compensation to the person injured, while Public Crimes were left at different periods to the cognizance of the King, the Senate, or the Magistrate, but without any very distinct rules of procedure in accordance with which such offences were to be tried. In Modern Systems the classification of liability is based not so much upon any distinction in the nature of the liability as upon the difference in the tribunal in which the party liable is proceeded against, that is to say, whether it happens to be a Criminal or a Civil Tribunal. In the French and Indian Law only those Offences are Criminal which are dealt with in the Penal Code.[2] The State may accordingly put itself in motion either to correct a particular Offence *per se*, without regard to the condition of Will that induced the offender to commit it, or it may take that condition of the Will into account. Hence the distinction fully recognised in the Indian Law, between Acts which are Offences *per se*, and other Acts which are only Criminal if done with a particular intention. Thus, Waging War against the Queen, Kidnapping from British India or from lawful

[1] Kant's *Philosophy of Law*, p. 195.

[2] See the definition of an "Offence" in section 40, Ind. P. C.

CHAP. XII. Guardianship, Adultery with a married woman, and the several instances of Negligence constituting an Offence without a positively mischievous purpose, are cases in which the Offence consists only of an Act. If the Act, as viewed by the Legislature, is done, the Offence is committed, and the penalty incurred irrespective of the intention. But in cases of Theft, Breach of Trust, Personal Violence, Threats, and Defamation, the physical Act must spring from a dishonest or malicious intent in order to constitute an offence.[1] The Criminal Law in fact is founded upon the moral end of the State, in virtue of which the State is constrained to resist the law-defying Will. But in resisting particular manifestations of the Will in individuals, the State does not undertake the impossible task of regulating whole chapters of their lives, as if it were an Academy proposing to itself the task of reforming all its individual citizens. Unless the Moral Freedom of the Individual is to be abrogated altogether, the State must leave the Individual free to infringe the principles of Morality to a certain extent, by abstaining from insisting by Force upon the observance of these principles after a certain limit. What that limit shall be must vary at different periods in different countries, but it ought to be fixed in correspondence with the manners, customs, and requirements of the people, and the condition of the country.[2]

Procedure. 288. In every well-ordered State its Judicial Activity must be regulated by fixed Rules of Procedure, according to which the machinery of the Courts is set in motion either with the view of punishing Offenders or redressing Private Wrongs. These Rules fix the jurisdiction of the Courts and the mode in which the trial is to be conducted, and they may vary according as the parties happen to be private individuals or

[1] *Reg.* v. *Rahimat*, I. L. R. I. Bomb. 147, 152.

[2] Von Bar's *International Law*, pp. 643—645.

as one of the parties happens to be the State itself and the other a Private Person. In England the State may obtain redress either by the ordinary forms of action or by simpler prerogative modes of process, while redress against the State for the violation of any legal right can only be had by means of a "Petition of Right,"[1] which is said to owe its origin to Edward I. The remedy cannot be capriciously refused by the Crown or its responsible advisers, and is obtainable *ex debito justitiæ*, though the form and application be to the grace and favour of the Crown.[2] In India, as we have seen, the State is liable to be sued in the ordinary way, but only after notice, in the name of the Secretary of State for India in Council.[3] But suits against foreign Sovereign Princes, Ruling Chiefs, and States can only be instituted with the previous consent of the British Government certified by the signature of one of its Secretaries, and such consent can only be given under certain specified conditions.[4] In the case of Criminal Offences the Indian Law distinguishes between "cognisable" and "non-cognisable" Offences: the former being Offences for which the Police may arrest without a warrant of a Magistrate, the latter being those in which a warrant is necessary. There are also certain Offences for which the Offender cannot be tried except upon complaint by the injured person, and others again except

[1] It is settled law that a Petition of Right will lie for damage resulting from a breach of contract by the Crown, whether the breach is occasioned by acts or omissions of Crown officials. L. R. 11 App. Cas. 607. But no engagement made by the Crown with any of its military or naval officers in respect of services either present, past, or future can be enforced in any Court of Law. *Mitchell* v. *The Queen*, (1896) 1 Q. B. 121, n. Nor does a Petition of Right lie in respect of a claim founded upon *tort*, because the Crown can do no wrong. *Tobin* v. *R.* (1864), 16 C. B. (N. S.) 310.

[2] Per Lord Langdale, M. R., in *Ryves* v. *The Duke of Wellington* (1846), 9 Beav. at p. 600.

[3] Ch. XXVII., Act XIV. of 1882. See p. 31, *ante*.

[4] Section 433, Act XIV. of 1882.

CHAP. XII. with the previous sanction of some Government Authority or Court.[1]

Civil responsibility of Judges.

289. The necessity of maintaining the independence of Judges and protecting them from actions on the part of malignant or dissatisfied suitors, has given rise to the rule that "no action will lie against a Judge for any acts done or words spoken in his judicial capacity in a Court of Justice."[2] But the immunity only extends to some act of a kind which the Judge had power to do, or at least which he *bonâ fide* believed himself to have power to do, in a matter within his jurisdiction. If the matter lies outside his jurisdiction, and this defect was brought to his notice, or ought to have been known by him, and was intentionally ignored, he will not be exempt from liability.[3] But the onus of proving these facts lies on the plaintiff in every such case, since there is a presumption in Law that judicial acts are regularly and rightly done: *omnia præsumuntur rite et solenniter esse acta.*[4] The rule of immunity extends to acts done by persons exercising *quasi*-Judicial functions such as Members of Naval and Military Courts-Martial or Courts of Inquiry, constituted in accordance with Military Law and Usage.[5] It is also applied to a limited extent to Arbitrators, and to any person in a similar position. Such a person is only liable for a corrupt or partisan exercise of his office, but not for errors of judgment.[6] The Indian Law as to the responsibility of Judges or other persons acting judicially is regulated by Statute,

[1] Sections 195—199, Act X. of 1882.

[2] *Scott* v. *Stansfield*, L. R. 3 Exch. 220.

[3] *Calder* v. *Halket*, 3 Moor. P. C. Cas. 28, 78.

[4] Broom's *Legal Maxims*, 4th ed., 908; Taylor's *Law of Evidence*, section 126. For the Indian Law, see section 115, Illust. (*c*), Act I. of 1872.

[5] *Dawkins* v. *Lord Rokeby*, L. R. 7 H. L. 744; *Dawkins* v. *Prince Edward of Saxe Weimar*, L. R. 1 Q. B. D. 499.

[6] *Tharsis Sulphur Co.* v. *Loftus*, L. R. 8 C. P. 1; *Stevenson* v. *Watson*, L. R. 4 C. P. D. 148.

which enacts that no such Judge or person shall be liable to be sued for any act done in discharge of his judicial duties, whether or not within the limits of his jurisdiction, *if in good faith he believed he had jurisdiction.*[1] If the matter is within his jurisdiction the question of good faith will not arise.[2]

[1] Act XVIII. of 1850. *Cf.* as to the proper interpretation of this Act, I. L. R. I. Mad. 89; I. L. R. IX. Cal. 341; No. 57, *Punjab Record*, 1870; No. 58, *Punjab Record*, 1871.

[2] See I. L. R. I. Allah. 280.

CHAPTER XIII.

INTERNATIONAL LAW.

CHAP. XIII.

General statement.

290. The subject of the present Chapter consists of those Rules which regulate the inter-relation of States. In a legal sense a State has the same capacity for Rights as a Natural Person, and in its external transactions with other States it exhibits that side of its character which is called its International Personality. Each State as a member of the general Family of States possesses the same legal Nature as every other member of that Family, and to respect this common Nature based upon a common Humanity, is the foundation of all International Comity.

History.

291. In its present highly developed form International Law may be said to be of modern growth, and to have been the outcome of the partition of Europe into Free and Independent States. So long as Rome continued to exercise a sway which was almost Universal, the conditions necessary for the establishment of an International Code were wanting. For without perfect Equality in Autonomy there can be no Equality of Rights, and where this Equality is wanting the existence of International Law, in its true elements, is impossible. Thus the absolute World Empire of one Nation involves in principle the negation of the very foundation of International Law.[1] But the germs of this Law may be traced back to a remote antiquity. The privileges of Ambassadors, the sanctity of Treaties, the respect due to Neutral

[1] Bluntschli's *Das Moderne Völkerrecht*, p. 13, Nördlingen, 1878. *Cf.* Laghi, *Il Diritto Internazionale Privato*, sections 40, 41, pp. 43, 44.

States in time of War, rough rules regarding Extradition, Clemency to Prisoners, and Contraband of War, were recognised by the Nations of Antiquity no less than by those of modern Europe. It must nevertheless be added that these Rules, sanctioned by the "usages of all mankind,"[1] were only respected so long as they did not clash with personal pride, ambition, and self-interest. The Ambassadors of Darius to Athens and Sparta were ignominiously put to death, and an act of perfidy on the part of a Roman Envoy (Ambustus), "who came as an Ambassador but acted as an enemy," brought destruction on Rome at the hands of Brennus, the Gaulish King.[2] The treaty of Caudium, ratified by the oath of two Roman Consuls, by means of which four legions were saved from certain death, was indignantly repudiated at Rome.[3] Agesilaus respected Neutrality by asking the Asiatic States through which he passed whether they wished him to "pass as a friend or as an enemy."[4] The prisoners at Platæa, whose lives were guaranteed on condition of surrender, were judicially murdered by Spartan Commissioners. Marius put to death the unresisting inhabitants of a Numidian town. Sylla commanded a wholesale slaughter of the Samnites; and the Athenians committed gross atrocities at Melos, which is but a single instance out of several that could be cited of the cruel and treacherous transactions of the most enlightened people of antiquity, which are familiar to every reader of Thucydides. But most of these acts of violence were done under the cloak of political necessity,[5] and were regarded at the time as not even justifiable upon that ground. The historian who recounts them betrays his own opinion by either simply recording the dry

[1] Herodotus, VIII., 136.

[2] Plutarch, *in vit. Camill.*, p. 102, Langhorne's translation.

[3] Livy, *Hist.* IX., 7—12; Arnold, *Hist. of Rome*, II., 216.

[4] Plutarch, *in vit. Ages.*, p. 422, Langhorne's translation. *Cf.* Vattel's *Law of Nations*, bk. iii., Ch. 7, p. 341.

[5] Hosack's *Law of Nations*, p. 15.

CHAP. XIII. fact without a word of extenuation or comment, or else, like Sallust, he does not hesitate to denounce them as *contra jus belli*.[1] Thus, as Bluntschli well observes,[2] the ambition, pride, selfishness, and love of power of individual Nations, hindered in Antiquity the growth of an International Law, and destroyed the still weak germs of that Law, to which we have alluded, before they had been properly consolidated and strengthened by the sanction of a long and uniform usage. So in the Middle Ages the Christianity of the period recognised no Law except for Believers. Those who were Unbelievers were Barbarians, and enjoyed no Rights. Ideally Law and Justice were indeed supposed to prevail everywhere, and the writings of the renowned scholastic Jurists, Bartolus ("the star and luminary of lawyers and the lantern of Equity"), Baldus and Accurtius, still survive to prove that the study of Law was by no means neglected in this age. But while there was no dearth of Ideas of Right, there was wanting the political machinery to convert those ideas into practical Rules of Conduct, and the taunt is not without truth that Bartolus, Baldus, and Accurtius are now chiefly remembered as having been targets for the wit of Rabelais. We may not indeed be justified to go the length of saying with Laurent that "The Middle Ages neither comprehended Sovereignty nor the general interests of Society" (*le moyen âge ne comprenait pas la Souveraincté, ni les intérêts généraux de la société*)—a statement which Italian writers[3] stoutly controvert. But it must at least be admitted that the State as then understood was very different to the modern State. Besides in this age Theory, imperfect as it was, ill-harmonised with Practice. In reality rude Force governed instead of Law. It was pre-eminently the Period when Club Law was more especially respected, and where this is the case

[1] *Jugurth.*, Ch. 91. [2] *Das Moderne Völkerrecht*, p. 13, Nördlingen, 1878.

[3] Laghi, *Il Diritto Internazionale Privato*, section 55, pp. 61, 62.

there is obviously no room for the application of the principles of International Law.[1] Indeed the establishment of the modern International Law is the work of Science, which has awakened the slumbering legal consciousness of the Civilized World. She has taught Mankind to transmute Ideas of Right into Principles of Law, and she has finally triumphantly vindicated the great moral truth that *Religious Faith neither establishes nor hinders the obligation of Law.* But Science is simply an Instructress. She *teaches* but cannot *enforce* her precepts, for which she needs the aid of Practice, backed by Political Power. Thus, Science without Practice is as useless as the most perfect Code of Laws without Courts of Justice to administer it. It is only when Practice follows in the track of Science, when States in their dealings with each other observe, under the sanction of a General Comity, definite International Rights and Duties, that the growth of International Law becomes visible. But it is with the empirical principles of this Law, deduced from existing Practice, and not with the transcendental principles based upon Scientific Theories of Law, that the student of General Jurisprudence is concerned. With the extreme purists of the Analytical School it is incorrect to speak of a Law of Nations, because a Law implies a Command from a Political Superior to a Political Inferior, whereas every State is the Political Equal of every other State, however greatly the Power and Resources of the one may differ from those of another. Now, it may be conceded, as the late Count von Moltke observed in his famous letter to Professor Bluntschli, that the want of any central authority to enforce its rules is without doubt the weak point in International Law.[2] But just as we have seen the above narrow conception of Law fails to take into account the Customary Law of archaic Commu-

[1] *Das Moderne Völkerrecht*, pp. 16, 17.

[2] *Times*, Feb. 1st. 1881; Tome XIII., No. I., p. 79, *Revue de Droit International*, 1881.

CHAP. XIII. nities, so it pays no regard to the force of Public Opinion and Custom as supplying the sanction by which the Law of Nations is enforced. In the one case as in the other the Law is based on past Practice and Usage, and just as in the Practice and Usage of individual men the distinction between Law and Morality is recognised, though it may be relatively undefined, so in the Practice of Nations some Duties are conceived of as positive, and others as only honourable.[1] International Law is thus said to consist "in certain rules of conduct which modern civilized States regard as being binding on them in their relations with one another with a force comparable in nature and degree to that binding the conscientious person to obey the laws of his country, and which they also regard as being enforceable by appropriate means in case of infringement."[2] But the ultimate compulsory *motive* for obedience to such rules is the fear of provoking *general* hostility;[3] while the *object* of all such rules is to secure and not to endanger the existence of States, to protect their freedom and not to oppress them.[4] For this reason one of the fundamental principles of International Law is, that *no State has the right to interfere in the internal administration of another State.* But this rule, though universally acknowledged, is nevertheless subject to exceptions, founded on one of the two following grounds: (1) that interference is demanded by self-preservation; or (2) by the existence of an extraordinary state of things brought about by the crime of a Government against its subjects.[5] Subject then to this very limited right of interference, justifiable only as an extreme and imperative measure, International Law seeks to regulate in Peace the friendly intercourse of Nations

[1] Pollock's *Essays in Jurisprudence and Ethics*, p. 35.

[2] Hall's *International Law*, 1880.

[3] Pollock's *Essays in Jurisprudence and Ethics*, p. 38.

[4] Bluntschli's *Das Moderne Völkerrecht*, p. 20.

[5] Woolsey's *Introduction to the Study of International Law*, section 42 (*d*) to the rules of Neutrality, p. 57.

with one another, and in War the conduct of all operations in accordance with the principles of Humanity, treating all States alike—the Great and the Small, the Giant and the Pigmy standing on the same level.[1]

Topics falling within scope of International Law.

292. The topics which fall within the natural scope of the Science of International Law may be briefly considered for the purposes of the present Chapter with reference—

(*a*) to those Qualities or Rights (*völkerrechtliche Eigenschaften der Staaten*) which are involved in the existence of States, and which are vested in them as International Persons, including those of Sovereignty, Independence, and Equality;

(*b*) to those rights which the State has in common with Individuals or with Artificial Persons;

(*c*) to the right of redress for violations of International Rights;

(*d*) to the rules of Neutrality.

Essential qualities of a State.

293. Viewed as an International Person no particular form of Constitution is requisite for a State; it may be Representative or Absolute, Monarchical or Republican. All that is requisite is that the People as a Whole, within any given territory, should be permanently organised as a constituted Government. The actual fact of an independent existence, and not the manner of its origin, constitutes the right to International recognition as a State. But in the case of a newly-formed State, so long as its independent existence is openly contested and the issue of the contest is doubtful, no other State is bound to recognise it as a member of the general Family of States. This recognition—which is the necessary evidence that the State has acquired the right to be treated as independent—only follows when the new State has been firmly established, and its position, as such,

Sovereignty and Independence.

[1] Bluntschli's *Das Moderne Völkerrecht*, p. 10.

CHAP. XIII.

secured; and then it is due even by a State from which the new State has separated, or whose rights of Sovereignty have been violated in the formation of the latter. Thus Spain was obliged to recognise the Independence of the Netherlands, and the German Empire that of the Swiss Cantons, by the Peace of Westphalia;[1] and England in like manner was reluctantly compelled to acknowledge that of her rebellious subjects across the Atlantic who had formed themselves into the United States of America.

Union of States under one Sovereign.

293a. On the other hand the union of two or more separate States under the one Sovereign, by choice or right of succession, does not necessarily involve the extinction of the International Status of the States so united. Modern examples of this kind of personal union are afforded by that of Sweden and Norway, of the Dukedom of Schleswig-Holstein with the Crown of Denmark, of the Kingdom of Hanover with the Crown of England, and of the Principality of Neuenburg with the Crown of Prussia.[2]

Sovereignty, what it implies.

The Sovereignty of a State implies its independence of any Foreign State, and the uncontrolled exercise of its political Will. Its attributes are the right to determine its own constitution, to legislate for its own people and territory, to appoint representatives to conduct its relations with other States, and lastly, Self-Government and Self-Administration.

Semi-Sovereignty.

But a State may by its free act surrender a part of these rights, and accept a

Vassal States.

subordinate position under a more powerful State. In such a case the former is regarded as the Vassal of the latter, and

Protected States.

its International Status is restricted accordingly. So also a State which merely submits itself to the protection of another loses thereby its claim to be regarded for International purposes as entitled to complete rights of Sovereignty.

[1] Bluntschli's *Das Moderne Völkerrecht*, sections 37, 38, pp. 76, 77. *Cf.* Hall's *International Law*, section 26, pp. 82—87.

[2] *Ibid.*, section 51, p. 82. The Kingdom of Hanover ceased to belong to the British Crown from the death of Will. IV. in 1837, when it descended by the Salic law to the Duke of Cumberland.

Such was the Republic of Cracow, while it remained under the protection of Austria, Russia, and Prussia, and before its union with Austria (in 1846) ; such was the condition of the Ionian Islands while they remained under the protection of England prior to their union with Greece (in 1864) ;[1] and such may also be described as the condition of the Chiroki Nation under the political control of the United States. In India we have numerous examples of Semi-Sovereign States answering to both Vassal and Protected States: The principalities of Kashmir, Baroda, Mysore, and Hyderabad[2] belong to the former category, and Cabul to the latter. The former, like the Indian Nations under the political control of the United States, are regarded as having a semi-independent position: not as States, not as Nations, not as possessed of the full attributes of Sovereignty, but as a separate people, with the power of regulating their internal and social relations. They are in fact "dependent political communities," or suzerainties,[3] holding such relations to the British Indian Government that they are considered as being so completely under the sovereignty and dominion of the latter that any attempt to acquire their lands, or to form a political connection with them, would be considered as an invasion of our territory, and an act of hostility towards the British Government.[4] Their subjects are also, for international purposes, in the same position as British subjects.[5] Nipal, amongst native States in the East, stands, however, on a somewhat exceptional footing. It is regarded as an Independent Kingdom and cannot be classed with any of the other Native States of

In India numerous examples of both.

[1] Bluntschli's *Das Moderne Völkerrecht*, section 78, p. 95.

[2] In Lord William Bentinck's time the term "sovereignty" was only used in corresponding with the Nizam among all the princes of India. He was treated more as an ally than a feudatory. D. C. Boulger's *Lord William Bentinck* (*Rulers of India Series*), p. 133.

[3] Interpretation Act of 1889 (52 & 53 Vict. c. 63). See Ilbert's *Government of India*, pp. 268, 269.

[4] *Cf. The Chiroki Nation* v. *Kansas Rail. Co.*, 135 *United States Reports*, p. 641. See pp. 653, 655.

[5] Ilbert's *Government of India*, p. 269.

CHAP. XIII.

India proper. So long as a State retains its full Independence and Sovereignty, its International rights are not affected by its size or power. As an organization clothed with a Jural-Personality every State stands on an equality with every other State, and has the same claim to the recognition of its International Status. In all essential relations, in the right to send and receive Ambassadors, in ceremonials, in signing treaties, each State is treated on the same footing as another.[1] It has already been pointed out that interference by one State in the Internal Administration of another State is only justifiable upon grounds of self-preservation.[2] Now this principle of self-preservation lies also at the bottom of what is popularly called the Balance of Power (*Europäisches Gleichgewicht*). This phrase does not mean that each State must remain exactly on the same level with another in point of territorial power or extent of population. Nor does it contemplate that existing States must remain stationary for all time, which would be to ignore the laws of internal growth and development.[3] But what it means is simply the peaceful co-existence of different neighbouring States, or, in other words, the guarantee of national existence against the designs of States of the first rank. The maintenance of this Balance of Power has become an established part of the International Law of Europe, and affords the only reliable guarantee for the peace of Europe. The most memorable instances of its application in recent times have been the interposition of the four Powers in 1840, which forced Mehemet Ali to renounce the Provinces of the Turkish Empire, of which he held possession, that of France and England in 1854, to preserve the integrity of the same Empire against the designs of Russia,[4] and that of the Six Great European Powers in 1897 to prevent the Turks from reaping the full

Rights of Equality.

Balance of Power.

[1] Bluntschli's *Das Moderne Völkerrecht*, section 89, p. 100.

[2] Para 291, *ante*.

[3] Bluntschli's *Das Moderne Völkerrecht*, sections 95—98, pp. 102, 103.

[4] Woolsey's *International Law*, section 44, p. 61.

fruit of their victories over the Greeks, and to compel them to be content with a mere strategic reconstruction of the Greek frontier and the payment by Greece of a moderate war indemnity.

CHAP. XIII.

Change in form of Government does not affect International Status.

293b. The International Personality of a State suffers no change, although the form of Government in that State may undergo alterations. But diplomatic usage requires that any such alteration in the form of Government should be announced to the other States with which the State in question has international relations.[1] As a necessary corollary from the Right of Independence to which each State is entitled, it follows that the Head or Representative of that State must be free from all foreign jurisdiction.[2] His person and the effects he brought with him are inviolate from the Laws of the land where he happens to be sojourning for the time. This exemption is based on the fiction of "Extra-territoriality," in accordance with which Sovereigns travelling abroad with their trains, Ambassadors with their suite, families, and servants, and Ships of War, though actually within a foreign territory, are treated as if they were outside of it.[3] The Extra-territorial Person is accordingly free from all liability to be sued in the domestic tribunals of a foreign State, or to be taxed. But he is bound, on the other hand, to abstain from all acts which are hazardous to the safety of the Community, or the Sovereignty of the State where he is so sojourning. Thus, if the Extra-territorial Person had target-practice in his garden, which endangered the safety of the people outside, or if he kindled a fire which threatened to spread beyond his own limits and to damage the property of others, the privileges of Extra-territoriality would cease to be operative, and this upon the broad ground that the respect which a State owes to the dignity and independence of a

Extra-territoriality.

Its limits.

[1] Bluntschli's *Das Moderne Völkerrecht*, sections 123, 125, pp. 117, 118.
[2] *Ibid.*, pp. 121—124.
[3] Woolsey's *International Law*, p. 101; Holland's *Jurisprudence*, p. 329.

 Foreign State must be conditioned by a necessary care for its own safety.[1]

A State may have private Ownership.

294. The State as an organised Community clothed with an Artificial Personality has certain rights in common with other Artificial Persons. Thus, it may possess land and other property in Private ownership, and it may become the creditor of a Foreign State or of private individuals. In relation to other States, such property has the same character of exclusiveness and free disposal as private property. But this Right of Property is a Public Right attaching to the State as such, and is not vested in the Head of the State as a Personal Right, which he can sell and barter at pleasure, as was not unfrequently done in the Middle Ages.[2] The State itself may acquire territory by purchase or gift, by conquest accepted as a fact and at length ending in prescriptive right, or by occupation of land not previously included within the territory of any other State. But a claim founded on mere discovery, which was the basis upon which Pope Alexander the VI. partitioned the new World between Spain and Portugal in 1493, when unaccompanied by any actual exercise of political rights, is held at the present day to be too vague to receive general recognition.[3] The high Sea is incapable by nature of separate appropriation, and is therefore regarded as free to all.[4] The rights of all Nations to the use of the high Sea being therefore the same, each Nation has equal rights of fishery upon it with another.[5] But Bays of the Sea, like Delaware Bay—declared to belong exclusively to the United States in 1793—and called in England the "Kings' Chambers," are deemed to be within the jurisdiction

Acquisitions, how made.

Right over Bays and narrow Seas.

1 Bluntschli, *Das Moderne Völkerrecht*, section 137, p. 122.

2 *Ibid.*, sections 284, 292, pp. 172—177, 178.

3 *Ibid.*, section 278, note, pp. 168, 169; Vattel 1, § 208; Rivier 1, p. 194.

4 *Ibid.*, section 304, p. 183.

5 *Ibid.*, section 307, p. 184; Rivier 1, pp. 243, 361. Numerous Fishery Conventions exist between Great Britain and other nations. See 59 Geo. III. c. 38; 35 & 36 Vict. c. 45; 54 & 55 Vict. c. 37; 56 Vict. c. 17.

of the States to whose territory the Promontories embracing them belong.[1] Great Britain has also long claimed supremacy in the narrow Seas adjoining her Islands. Thus, her supremacy between the Isle of Wight and England is undisputed. So is also that of Turkey over the Dardanelles and the Bosphorus, although entrance through the Straits into the Black Sea, except for all foreign vessels of War interdicted by the Treaty of London in 1841, is open to the Mercantile Marine of all Nations under the Treaty of Paris of 30th March, 1836.[2] Where a Navigable River forms the boundary between two States, both are presumed to have the free use of it, and the dividing line will run into the middle of the channel, unless the contrary is shown by long occupancy or agreement of parties.[3] In the case of a River which rises within the bounds of one State and empties itself into the Sea in another, modern international usage generally allows, in the case of most such Rivers flowing through the territory of Christian Nations, a right of free navigation to those who dwell on the upper waters.[4]

Over Navigable Rivers.

295. A Nation no less than a private Individual has an indisputable right to preserve its Good Name or Reputation in its external relations wlth its neighbours. The influence of a Good Name upon its intercourse with other Nations cannot in fact be exaggerated, and it naturally increases with refinement and civilization. To a barbarian Ruler like a Theebaw it may seem an indifferent thing what his neighbours think about his actions, and the violation of the rights and privileges appertaining to diplomatic persons, and of all laws of humanity, may appear to him to be matters with which he alone is concerned. But a civilized Nation cannot afford, even if it had the inclination, which is unlikely, to

Right of Reputation.

[1] Bluntschli's *Das Moderne Völkerrecht*, section 309, pp. 185, 186; Woolsey's *International Law*, section 56, pp. 84, 85.

[2] *Ibid.*, section 309, pp. 185, 186; Woolsey, section 57, pp. 87, 88. See also Arts. 2 & 3 of the Treaty of London, 1871.

[3] Woolsey, section 58, p. 88.

[4] *Ibid.*

CHAP. XIII.

disregard the good opinion of the rest of the civilized world. It is this distinction which excludes the one from the pale of international intercourse, and makes the other respectable and worthy of friendship in the eyes of its neighbours. As Vattel observes: "A Nation, the reputation of which is well established, and especially one the glory of which is striking, finds itself sought by all Sovereigns. They desire its friendship and fear to offend it. Its friends and those who wish to become such favour its enterprises, and its detractors do not venture to show their ill-will."[1] It is a right therefore which is highly prized, and the greater the value set upon it the more sensitive is the nation to the avoidance of all causes which might detract from its reputation or incur the censure of other civilized Nations. This sense of Honour is thus one of the great bulwarks of International Law, the violation of which can never be lightly disregarded.

Remedial Rights between States.

296. The Remedial Rights to which a State is entitled for a violation of any of the rights above mentioned vary according to the nature and extent of the right actually violated. If the latter consists in an insult to its dignity a suitable apology may be a sufficient reparation; while the unjust deprivation of property may not only call for the restoration of that property, but for an additional satisfaction.

Means of forcible redress for International Wrongs.

297. Where Remedial Rights are not peacefully (*viâ amicabili*) conceded by the State committing a violation of them, the injured State is obliged to resort to other means of redress. Unlike in this respect to individuals, who can appeal to a higher tribunal to protect them in the exercise of their rights, Independent States have no natural superior, and in the absence of an International Tribunal for the adjustment of international disputes, they are obliged to redress themselves, and thus to assume the position of judges in their own cause. The means of redress which are therefore open to States are multiform in character, but are all

[1] Bk. I., Ch. XV., p. 91.

founded on Force and the application of Political Power. They may consist in measures which, although partaking of a hostile character, fall short of War, or they may finally assume the form of Actual War as the only possible means of obtaining Justice.

Means of Redress short of War.

298. Measures for redress of International Wrongs falling short of Actual War may be described under three heads, namely, *Embargo*, *Retorsion*, and *Reprisal*.

(*a*.) An Embargo (from the Spanish and Portuguese *embargar*, to *hinder* or *detain*), in its special international sense, is a detention of foreign Ships in a port in anticipation of War breaking out with the Nation to which they belong. If the measure is followed by Actual War the Ships are regarded as captured, but if by Peace they are restored, and in this event compensation has also to be awarded for the hostile seizure. It is a species of Reprisal which is too akin to robbery, occurring as it does in the midst of Peace, to receive any general assent, and it is sometimes stipulated in Treaties that it shall not be exercised between the contracting parties, as in the case of the Treaty between Prussia and the United States of North America of the 11th July, 1799, article 16. Distinguished from such a hostile seizure is a *Civil Embargo*, which is enforced for the purpose of national welfare or safety, as for the protection of commercial vessels against the rules of belligerent powers which would expose them to capture.[1] It is called by the French *le droit d'Angarie*, a term which is derived from old Persian, and in Mediæval Latin (in the form *angaria*) denoted any compulsion or vexation.[2] "As an interference with the paramount principle of national independence it can only be justified," says

[1] Bluntschli's *Das Moderne Völkerrecht*, section 509, p. 285; Woolsey's *International Law*, section 114, pp. 191, 192.

[2] Woolsey's *International Law*, App. III., note 6, p. 441. *Cf.* Hall's *International Law*, section 278, p. 693.

CHAP. XIII. Phillimore, "by that clear and overwhelming necessity, which would compel an individual to seize his neighbour's horse or weapon to defend his own life."[1]

Retorsion. (*b.*) *Retorsion* (from Latin *retorquere*, French *retordre*, retort), or Retaliation, is an application between Independent States of the old principle of *lex talionis*,[2] by the one State treating another or its subjects in like circumstances according to the rule it has itself set. It is not so much directed to resent a positive act of wrong, as the inequitable administration of a foreign Law. Thus, if State A. gives a preference in its Legislation to Natives as compared with Creditors of another State, or the Customs Tariff of State A. is differential and specially disadvantageous to subjects of State B., in such and like cases, State A. is well within the exercise of its strict rights. But the aggrieved Power may adopt the same or analogous measures to bring the State giving provocation back to a sense of propriety and justice.[3]

Reprisals. (*c.*) Reprisals (from the Latin *reprehendere* not *reprimere*) are measures of Self-help directed to bring home to an offending State a consciousness of some specific wrong-doing, and by this means to compel it to recognize the violated right of another State, and to give satisfaction for the wrong committed. It may consist in the seizure and confiscation of property belonging to the offending State or its subjects, but preferably the former; the suspension of commercial intercourse with it; the expulsion of its subjects; or, lastly, the deprivation of their personal liberty. But modern usage amongst civilized Nations is not in favour of directing Reprisals against the property or persons of innocent subjects of an offending State, and measures of this kind can only be excused on the ground of extreme necessity, or as justified by the special circumstances of the particular case, as where a State has seized and

[1] *International Law*, Vol. III., 42.

[2] *Cf. Dig.* II., 2, 1.

[3] Bluntschli's *Das Moderne Völkerrecht*, section 505, pp. 283, 284; Woolsey's *International Law*, p. 192; Hall's *International Law*, p. 335, 2nd ed; Rivier, II., 189—191.

detained the Envoy of another State charged with a mission to it.[1] Reprisals are thus merely a means of putting pressure, by something short of War, upon a wrong-doing State, from which redress cannot be obtained by purely amicable means. Reprisal differs from Retorsion in this, that the essence of the former consists in the hostile seizure of the property or subjects of another Nation by way of security until it should have listened to the just reclamation of the offending party; while Retorsion includes all measures which do an injury to another, similar and equivalent to that which we have experienced from him.[2]

Pacific Blockade.

(*d.*) Pacific Blockade is another means of constraint short of War of which the present century affords several examples, one of the most memorable being that of La Plata in 1845-48 by France and England, which was pronounced by Lord Palmerston "as from first to last illegal." It has the effect of closing ingress and egress to Ships of the offending State, and, according to Bluntschli,[3] Neutral States are not to be affected by it. But, as Mr. Hall observes, a Blockade so limited would be illusory, and if the practice is to be maintained at all, the power of forbidding communication, and of, at least, detaining Ships in case of disobedience, is absolutely necessary. Blockade is thus essentially an incident of War, and from the nature of the thing cannot be so conducted as to affect blockaded States alone.[4]

Actual War.

299. Actual War,[5] that highest trial of right according to

[1] Bluntschli, sections 500 and 501, pp. 281, 282; Hall's *International Law*, p. 335; Woolsey, p. 192; Rivier, II., pp. 191—198.

[2] Woolsey, p. 193.

[3] Page 285, section 507. Rivier refers to a case which occurred in 1886 where the blockade was so restricted, II., p. 199.

[4] Hall's *International Law*, p. 340; Rivier, II., p. 198.

[5] The old German word for war *Urlog* (still preserved in the Netherlands as *oorlog*), points to the ancient belief that God gives the victory, and that war is a judgment of God, which Lord Bacon also introduces in his definition of war—"when princes and states, that acknowledge no superior on earth, shall put themselves upon the justice of God for the deciding of their con-

CHAP. XIII.

Bacon, has been felicitously described as "the litigation of Nations."[1] Regarded in this light most continental Writers of the present century (such as Hautefeuille, Clavo, Riquelme, and Bluntschli) consider that the issue of a declaration or manifesto before the commencement of hostilities is necessary, just as a notice is necessary for an action in Private Law. This is the equivalent of the *clarigatio* which distinguished a *Justum bellum* in the time of Cicero,[2] and of the solemn *diffidatio*[3] of the Middle Ages, one of the last examples of which occurs in the reign of Louis XIII of France in 1635.[4] But neither English Jurists (Phillimore and Twiss) nor American (Wheaton) share this opinion, and Mr. Hall sums up the general conclusion with reference to theoretical opinions and recent practice in the following words:—

Is a previous declaration necessary?

General conclusion.

"Looking at the foregoing facts, as a whole, it is evident that it is not necessary to adopt the artificial doctrine that notice must be given to an enemy before entering upon War. The doctrine was never so consistently acted upon as to render obedience to it at any time obligatory. Since the middle of last century it has had no sensible influence upon practice."[5] In England a formal announcement is made by a proclamation issued by Her Majesty and posted in the City of London.

troversies by such success as it shall please Him to give to either side." The high German *werra*, French *guerre*, and English *war* on the other hand significantly refer to the muddle, confusion, and pell-mell consequences ordinarily resulting from war. Rivier, *Principes du Droit des Gens*, II. 202.

[1] Holland's *Jurisprudence*, p. 332.

[2] *De Officiis*, I., II.; *De Republica*, 2, 17. The *clarigatio* was a solemn demand for redress, a religious solemnity with which the *Fetialis* declared war upon an enemy, in case he should refuse to give satisfaction within thirty-three days for injuries sustained.

[3] From *diffio*, "to disperse by blowing," with reference to the arrival of the herald being announced by blowing a trumpet (?).

[4] Rivier, *Principes du Droit des Gens*, II., pp. 223, 224.

[5] Hall's *International Law*, p. 348. See also the Manual prepared by Lord Thring for English officers, quoted by the late Sir H. S. Maine, *International Law*, pp. 131, 132.

War only possible between Sovereign States.

299*a*. Sovereign States alone have the right of waging war (*Jus belli*) against each other; and there can be no such condition as a war between a State on the one hand and mere individuals on the other.[1] If a State is placed in the circumstance of having to proceed to violent or repressive measures against individuals, such as pirates or filibusters, it treats them as public enemies (or, as the Roman law regarded them, as *latrones aut praedones*—robbers and plunderers),[2] and punishes them accordingly. But in such cases it does not wage war, and the rules which regulate modern warfare between States have no sort of application. The most recent instance of this sort of armed hostility on the part of individuals is that known as the Jamieson Raid against the South African Republic, for which the principal offenders were tried, convicted and sentenced to various terms of imprisonment by the High Court of Justice in England, as persons owing allegiance to Her Majesty. But a State may authorise and invest a body of its own citizens with the powers of government to exercise the same in distant parts of its possessions or spheres of political activity, and with the power to wage war, as in the case of the East Indian Company.[3] The delegated power thus conferred would enable the recipients to wage war in the proper sense of the term against a common enemy within the restricted limits of their activity, for which the history of British India, prior to the direct assumption of sovereignty by the Crown in 1858, affords numerous examples.

Negative effects of commencement of War.

300. The outbreak of War produces certain negative effects which involve, in the first place, the abrogation and suspension of Treaties of certain kinds, such as Treaties of

[1] Rivier, *Principes du Droit des Gens*, Vol. II., p. 207; Maine quoting Lord Thring's *Manual*, p. 131, *International Law*.

[2] Dig. L. 16, 118.

[3] Charter of Charles II. of 1661, and Charter of 1683.

CHAP. XIII.

Alliance, Commercial Treaties, Postal Conventions, and the like between the belligerent-States, and, in the next place, the cessation of all non-hostile relations between subjects of the belligerent-States. With regard to the latter the general rule is that the subjects of enemy-States are themselves enemies, and it follows logically that they may be expelled or otherwise treated as enemies if found within the territories of a belligerent-State after the outbreak of War. But a modern and humane usage has grown up of allowing the subjects of an enemy-State to remain, either for a specified time after the commencement of War, or during good behaviour.[1]

Fundamental rules of modern warfare.

301. Colonel Napier, in his history of the Peninsular War, observes that "there is as much difference between the modern and the ancient soldier, as between the sportsman and the butcher." The humanizing influence of advancing civilisation has also in no less degree changed the usages of warfare, and the limits as to the right of violence against the person or property of enemies are now understood in a far narrower sense than in the period preceding the present century. But what those precise limits are cannot be more accurately stated than by appealing to the general principle, that "the measure of permissible violence is furnished by the reasonable necessities of War," which, theoretically speaking, is said to be absolute.[2] Within this limit a belligerent must be left free to attain the immediate object of War, which consists in crushing the enemy as best he can, and as promptly as possible. In view of this supreme object, said Von Moltke, "all means are permissible except those which are positively condemned (*verwerflich*)," amongst which may be included assassination, use of poison, and useless butchery or cruelty. But as in warfare the exigences of the moment

[1] Hall's *International Law*, p. 359.

[2] As Vattel observes: "Right goes hand in hand with necessity and the exigency of the case, but never exceeds them." Bk. III., ch. 8, p. 346.

may override all considerations except those which concern the preservation of the State, even the dictates of humanity may have to give way to such supreme necessity.[1] Nevertheless, as Grotius observes, *in publico autem periculo, quae modum excedit securitas immisericordia est:* "in a public danger, a disregard of the danger which goes beyond the just limit is want of compassion."[2] It is therefore impossible to prescribe hard and fast rules which shall be observed in all cases, no matter what the exceptional circumstances may be. Thus, the determination of "reasonable necessity," in the theoretical rule above mentioned, lies in practice so much in the hands of belligerents that it becomes not infrequently indistinguishable from convenience.[3] So, also, since the duties implied in the improved usages of War, so far as they are not of positive obligation, are reciprocal, they do not continue to bind the one belligerent if they are violated by the other. Hence measures of Retaliation, the only actual limit to which in practice must be left to the guiding sentiment of a brave and honorable people, who will naturally shrink from the perpetration of cruelty to non-combatants, or the commission of any other act which would be unworthy of their reputation. But subject to these general considerations it may be laid down that there are three fundamental rules of War, which all Christian Nations now recognise, namely:—

(*a*) that redress of injuries and not conquest or plunder is the lawful motive of War;

[1] It was on the score of urgent necessity that Prince (then Count) Bismarck justified the sinking of some English vessels in the Seine at Duclair during the Franco-German War of 1870—71.. "The report shows," said the German Chancellor, "that a pressing danger was at hand, and every other means of meeting it was wanting: the case was therefore one of necessity, which even in time of peace may render the employment or destruction of foreign property admissible under the reservation of indemnification." Hall's *International Law*, section 278, p. 695.

[2] *De Jure Belli et Pacis*, III. 15, 1.

[3] Hall's *International Law*, p. 362; Vattel, bk. III., ch. 8, p. 346.

CHAP. XIII.

(b) that War is waged between opposing States by combatants, and is not waged against non-combatants;

(c) that the smallest amount of injury consistent with the necessity of War, is to be inflicted.[1]

Treatment of non-combatants.

302. In regard to the treatment of non-combatants the general usage of modern warfare rests on the principle enunciated by Portalis[2] and so well expressed by Talleyrand, that War is not a relation between a man with another, but between State and State, in which private persons are only accidental enemies, not such as men, nor even as members or subjects of the State, but simply as its defenders.[3] It follows from this principle that non-combatants, that is to say, private persons taking no part in the conflict, ought to be unmolested, and their property, moveable as well as immoveable, allowed to remain uninjured.[4] As Aurelian said: "Let soldiers live on the spoil of the enemy, not on the tears of the provincials" (*annona sua contentus sit, de præda hostis non de lachrymis provincialium vivat*). But as an invader is often necessarily dependent for supplies on the productions of the enemy's country, he is permitted to make "Requisitions," a term which it is generally believed was first invented by Washington, for such articles as are needed by his army for consumption or temporary use, such as food for men and animals, and clothes, waggons, horses, railway material, boats and other means of transport, and of the compulsory labour, whether gratuitous or otherwise, of workmen to make roads, to drive carts and for such other services.[5]

Contributions permitted.

[1] Woolsey's *International Law*, section 125, p. 214. *Cf.* Vattel, bk. III., ch. 8.

[2] See Heffter, section 119.

[3] Despatch to Napoleon of 20th November, 1806.

[4] Bluntschli, section 573, p. 323; Hall's *International Law*, pp. 388—390; Woolsey's *International Law*, section 130, p. 224.

[5] Bluntschli, section 653, p. 367; Hall's *International Law*, section 140, p. 391; Rivier, II., pp. 321 *et seq.*

Legal effect of capture of private moveables by enemy.

302*a*. Although in theory, as pointed out in the preceding paragraph, private property ought to be inviolable in War, circumstances may arise which might render it justifiable to depart from the general rule. The custom of abstaining from exercising the extreme right conferred by War of seizing private property obtains only so long as not only the owners but also the community to which they belong, abstain from all acts of hostility.[1] Again, however rigorous military discipline may be, it is found in practice that a commander cannot always prevent a soldier or a body of soldiers from seizing valuable moveables belonging to private persons. Private property may also be seized as forming the cargo on an enemy's ship. The question may therefore arise, What is the effect of capture on the prior rights of ownership?[2] To solve this question we have, as in so many other cases, to go back to Roman Jurisprudence for a guiding principle. As the result of War the Roman Law treated the property of an enemy as *res nullius*, or no man's property, which was therefore as open to seizure as any wild bird or wild beast. But to give the captor a legal title to his booty it was necessary to take it within the fortified precincts of a Roman camp (*intra præsidia*).[3] So in modern times, in the case of a maritime capture, to ensure a good title to the captor the ship and its cargo, or the cargo belonging to the enemy found on a neutral ship, must be produced before a Prize Court and formally condemned as prize.[4] Until this or some analogous procedure is adopted, the person into whose possession the captured property comes cannot confidently rely on his title by capture so as to satisfy the principles of International Law. And as we have seen, if a wild bird or wild animal escapes from the possession of its captor, the title of the latter ceases to

[1] Maine, *International Law*, p. 194.

[2] *Ibid.* pp. 94, 95; Rivier, II., 319, 320.

[3] D. 49, 15, 5, section 1.

[4] Maine, *International Law*, 96; Rivier, II., 319, 320. But see *The Gauntlet*, L. R. 4 P. C. 184; 40 L. J. Adm. 34.

CHAP. XIII. exist,[1] so in the case of a capture of private moveable property which has not been completed in the manner recognized by International Comity, the captor's title is not so completely established that it may not be subsequently defeated by the original owner. A curious instance of this is supplied by an English Case. There a British ship was captured by the French and subsequently purchased by a British subject under a French bill of sale, and it was held in an action brought in England that the ship was still the property of the person from whom she was captured.[2] Lord Eldon held it to be clear law that it was not competent to a British subject to purchase a captured British ship, for this disability was founded on his allegiance not to aid the enemy, and consequently, despite the French condemnation of the ship in question, the property still remained in the original owner. Apart from this special doctrine, the sentence of a foreign Prize Court is conclusive upon every matter within the jurisdiction of such Court which has formed the ground of condemnation and is clearly stated so in the judgment.[3] In England the jurisdiction over all matters of prize, and everything consequential to a capture, belongs exclusively to the Admiralty Division of the High Court of Justice,[4] and an appeal lies to the Judicial Committee of the Privy Council.[5] The Jurisdiction includes the power to condemn as lawful prize captures properly made; to order the restoration of property wrongfully captured, and award damages against the captor; and to inflict punishment in the special cases provided for by the Naval Prize Act, 1864 (27 & 28 Vict. c. 25).

[1] *Ante*, section 132.

[2] *Woodward* v. *Larking* (1801), 3 Esp. 286.

[3] *Bolton* v. *Gladstone*, 5 East, 155; 11 Rev. Rep. 532; *Hobbs* v. *Henning*, 34 L. J. C. P. 117; 13 W. R. 431.

[4] *Lindo* v. *Rodney*, 2 Dougl. 613, n.; *Mitchell* v. *Rodney*, 2 Bro. P. C. 423; Williams and Bruce, Adm. Prac., 2nd ed., Chaps. I.—IX. inclusive. Since 1864 the jurisdiction is regulated by the *Naval Prize Act*, 1864 (27 & 28 Vict. c. 25).

[5] Section 5 of the Naval Prize Act.

Chap. XIII.

303. The right to kill and wound armed enemies, which is incident to all War, is nevertheless subordinated to the humane condition that those enemies are able and willing to continue the struggle. Thus, as a general rule, a belligerent is bound not to refuse quarter, and not only not to take the lives of those who are incapacitated by their wounds or disease from acting as combatants, but to render them such medical and other relief as is possible under the circumstances. A belligerent may make all persons who form part of the enemy's combatant force Prisoners of War on their being captured or on their surrender, and may subject them to such personal restraint as may be necessary for their safe custody. He is bound, on the other hand, to supply them with necessary food and clothing, and in return he may exact from them such services as are suitable to their rank and condition, other than participation in the actual contest with the enemy. A Prisoner of War who escapes may be lawfully killed in the effort to recapture him, but as it is only a misfortune to become a prisoner, so it is no crime in him to try and regain his freedom, and such an attempt ought not to involve punishment, although it might necessitate a more rigorous confinement. By mutual agreement an exchange of prisoners may take place between belligerents, and this practice has in modern times almost superseded the ancient right of exacting ransom. Lastly, among the special rules connected with actual warfare, may be mentioned the right of a belligerent to punish all persons, when they happen to fall into his hands, who have been guilty of any distinct violation of the recognised Rules of War, such as those who are convicted of marauding, using a flag of truce to obtain information, assassination, or poisoning wells.[1] The foundation of all

Special rules of War.

Quarter not to be refused.

Treatment of sick and wounded.

What persons can be made prisoners.

A prisoner of War attempting to escape may be killed.

But not subjected to punishment on recapture.

Exchange of prisoners.

[1] See generally as authorities for the rules above given, Bluntschli, sections 580, 585, 590, 593, 594, 605, 608, 609, 612–616; Hall's *International Law*, pp. 362—379. It was the boast of the Romans that they "took vengeance on their enemies by open force, and not by treachery and secret

CHAP. XIII. these various rules, which have for their object the mitigation of the evils of War, may after all be said to rest on the broad maxim of Cæsar's "new way of conquering":—*ut misericordia et liberalitate nos muniamus*: "to protect ourselves with mercy and liberality."[1] The right of killing and wounding armed enemies, of taking and recapturing prisoners, and of punishing those who violate the acknowledged rules of civilized warfare, are rights intended for our protection, but in exercising them we must practise the mercy and liberality which distinguish the humane and civilized man from the uncultured and cruel barbarian. War in short must be made for the sake of Peace.[2]

Law of Neutrality.

Of modern growth.

304. Both in its character and denomination Neutrality belongs especially to the modern system of International Law. It was a notion but little known to ancient times, when a War between two States generally involved a War also with their respective Allies, and when neutral interests were unimportant for the simple reason that, as a rule, there were no Neutrals whose interest needed protection. In modern times the tendency is to localize War and to confine it to the belligerents actually engaged in its prosecution. In antiquity the normal condition of the world was War, in the present century it is that of Peace. And this changed condition of things is due to the large attention which is now given by publicists to the rights and obligations of Neutrals.

Rudimentary principle of Neutrality.

305. The rudimentary principle of strict Neutrality is that of impartiality towards the belligerents, both being treated alike as friends, and no privilege being granted to the one

machinations." Tacit. *Annal.* lib. ii. c. 88. It was also one of their maxims "that war was to be carried on with arms, and not with poison." Valer. Maxim. lib. VI. ch. 5, 1.

[1] *Ad. Attic*, Epist. 8.

[2] As Sallust says:—*Sapientes pacis causa bellum gerunt, et laborem spe otii sustentant*: "Wise men labour with hope of rest, and make war for the sake of peace."

which is withheld from the other. The Neutral State is neither a judge nor a party, and thus, however much it may sympathise with the cause of the one belligerent and disapprove of the action of the other, it must nevertheless maintain an attitude of colourless amity towards both. In times of Peace one Nation may be more favoured than another, for the right of determining the nature and extent of intercourse with foreign Powers is an incident of that Sovereignty which belongs to every Independent State. But in War there is no middle position between a friend and a foe. Hence it is said that Neutrality begins and ends with War.[1]

Rights of Neutrals.

306. Neutrality has its Rights as well as its Obligations, and these may be stated separately. Of the former the following are the most important:—

(*a*) To insist that the neutral territory shall be inviolate and untouched by the operations of War, and its rights of Sovereignty uninvaded;

(*b*) To claim from the belligerents, during War, the same respect for the neutral flag, for the representatives, and for the property of the Neutral and its subjects, to which they have a right during Peace.[2]

Obligations of Neutrals.

307. On the other hand, a Neutral owes certain Obligations or Duties to the belligerents which it must faithfully discharge, if it desires its Rights as a Neutral to be respected by them. But the measure of this responsibility is only co-extensive with its territorial Sovereignty. Beyond its territorial limits its responsibility ceases for the hostile conduct of its subjects, who are then personally liable for their acts to the belligerent against whom they have offended. In like manner, trade between a neutral individual and a belligerent, which is prejudicial to the operations of a country at War, because it supplies the enemy with articles of direct use or

Measure of responsibility.

[1] Bluntschli, sections 742, 744, pp. 413, 414; Rivier, II., p. 381.

[2] Woolsey's *International Law*, sections 162, 164, pp. 270—272.

nullifies the stress put upon a country by Blockade, is a matter which is left to the injured party to hinder or not, as he finds necessary. It is for the belligerent to determine whether the commercial act of the neutral individual is an infringement of his privileges, and if he oversteps the boundary of his rights, he is responsible not only to the individual for his wrongful interference, but in the last degree to the Nation to which the individual belongs, which can demand and exact such reparation as may be needful for the wrong done to one of its subjects. The justification of leaving hostile or commercial acts of a neutral individual to be dealt with by the party injured by such acts lies in its convenience, as being the most beneficial to all parties, and best answering the chief end of the Law of Nations—checking injustice without the necessity of War. As Lord Brougham argued, "If a government were to be made responsible for each act of its subjects" (he is referring to acts on the high seas, or outside the territorial waters of the government), "and a negotiation were to ensue each time that a suspected neutral merchantman entered the enemy's port, either there must be a speedy end put to neutrality, or the affairs of the belligerent and neutral must both stand still."[1] Any other arrangement than the one which existing usage sanctions would thus result in endless hostilities and inconvenience. But the distinction between State Acts and Commercial or Private Acts must not be lost sight of; and it is only by observing this distinction that the clear boundary line of State responsibility can be fixed. Thus, it is a violation of Neutrality for a Neutral State to lend money or supply troops, or open harbours for hostile purposes, or to permit its territory being used as a base of operations by either belligerent. But International Law does not require of the Neutral State that it should keep its citizens or subjects within the same strict lines of Neutrality which it is bound to

Distinction between State Acts and Commercial Acts.

[1] Hall's *International Law*, sections 22—25, pp. 74—77.

draw for itself. Thus, a private person may lend money or sell articles Contraband of War to the enemy of a State at peace with his own country for purposes of War, or can enter into its service as a soldier, without involving the government of his country in guilt. To suppress the callings of private persons because a War exists in foreign and distant countries, in which their nation has no concern, would be hard in principle and impossible in practice. The Law of Nations does not, therefore, require any such internal derangement of the occupations of private persons, and the principle now generally recognized in practice, although occasionally sought to be restricted within narrower limits is, not that trade in articles Contraband of War is a breach of Neutrality, but that the persons engaged in it are exposed to the confiscation of their goods and the other hazards of War.[1] The maxim that "he is an enemy who does what the enemy wishes" (*hostem esse, qui faciat quod hosti placet*) is, in a certain sense, as true now as when Agathias wrote it.[2] But the sense in which it is true does not require that the State shall do more than to abstain from those acts, of which examples have been given above, which may strengthen the side of one belligerent or impede the motions of the other. It is not true when interpreted in the sense of requiring the State to so control the acts of its subjects, as to compel them to cease carrying on their private occupations, which may be as freely utilised by the one belligerent as by the other. But subject to this rule Neutrality must be colourless, and it is when Neutrals faithfully observe this attitude that belligerents realize the truth of Augustine's remark: *It is a greater felicity to have a good neighbour at Peace, than to conquer a bad neighbour in War.*[3]

[1] Woolsey's *International Law*, sections 160, 162, 167, p. 270; Hall's *International Law*, section 25, pp. 78—80. *Cf.* Bluntschli, sections 766—770, pp. 427—431.

[2] Grotius, *De Bell. et Pac.*, lib. III. C. XVII. 2.

[3] *De Civ. Dei*, IV. 15.

INDEX.

A.

B.

C.

F.

G.

H.

I.

K.

L.

T.

U.

V.

W.

Y.

PRINTED BY C. F. ROWORTH, GREAT NEW STREET, FETTER LANE, E.C.